June '11 * missing photos noted *

24 Hour Telephone Renewals 0845 071 4343

Villains' Paradise

Also by Donald Thomas

POETRY

Points of Contact
Welcome to the Grand Hotel

FICTION

Prince Charlie's Bluff
The Flight of the Eagle
The Blindfold Game
Belladonna: A Lewis Carroll Nightmare
The Day the Sun Rose Twice
The Ripper's Apprentice
Jekyll, Alias Hyde
Dancing in the Dark
The Raising of Lizzie Meek
The Arrest of Scotland Yard
The Secret Cases of Sherlock Holmes
Red Flowers for Lady Blue
Sherlock Holmes and the Running Noose

BIOGRAPHY

Cardigan of Balaclava
Cochrane: Britannia's Sea-Wolf
Robert Browning: A Life Within Life
Henry Fielding
The Marquis de Sade
Lewis Carroll: A Portrait with Background

CRIME AND DOCUMENTARY

A Long Time Burning: The History of Literary Censorship in England
State Trials: Treason and Libel
State Trials: The Public Conscience
Honour Among Thieves: Three Classic Robberies
Dead Giveaway
Hanged in Error?
The Victorian Underworld
An Underworld at War: Spivs, Deserters, Racketeers and Civilians in
the Second World War
Everyman Book of Victorian Verse: The Post-Romantics
Everyman Book of Victorian Verse: The Pre-Raphaelites
to the Nineties

Villains' Paradise

Britain's Underworld from the Spivs to the Krays

DONALD THOMAS

JOHN MURRAY

© Donald Thomas 2005

First published in Great Britain in 2005 by John Murray (Publishers)
A division of Hodder Headline

The right of Donald Thomas to be identified as
the Author of the Work has been asserted by him in
accordance with the Copyright, Designs and Patents Act 1988.

I

A CIP catalogue record for this title is available from the British Library

ISBN 0 7195 5734 8

Typeset in Bembo by Palimpsest Book Production Limited,
Polmont, Stirlingshire

Printed and bound by Clays Ltd, St Ives plc

Hodder Headline policy is to use papers that are natural, renewable
and recyclable products and made from wood grown in sustainable forests.
The logging and manufacturing processes are expected to conform to the
environmental regulations of the country of origin.

John Murray (Publishers)
338 Euston Road
London NW1 3BH

To the memory of Peter Helm and John Geary,
without whose teaching this book would not
have been written

Contents

Illustrations

Illustration acknowledgements: plates 1, 2, 5, 6, 21 and 30, Naldrett Press; 7, Alexander Moring; 8 and 11, Neville Spearman; 9, Howard B. Timmins; 12-20, Headline Publications; 22 and 23, Allan Wingate; 25, 26, and 27, Christopher Johnson.

Preface

IF, AS EDWARD Gibbon supposed, history is 'little more than the register of the crimes, follies, and misfortunes of mankind', Britain in the twenty-five years following the Second World War had a generous share of it. If statistics or word of mouth were to be believed, that share increased considerably in the remaining thirty years of the century. By the end of that century, governments who were unable to control crime tilted the scales of justice to ensure that when a suspect was caught, the probability of a conviction should be increased. Finally, the law was changed to remove the presumption of innocence so far as to inform the jurors of a defendant's previous convictions. 'Do you find this crook guilty or not guilty?' as one commentator put it.

In public esteem, the vogue for 'The Great Defender', whether Sir Edward Marshall Hall or Sir Norman Birkett, who won acquittals against the odds and sometimes against the evidence, had passed. Among mass entertainment, programmes like *Crimewatch* put their audiences firmly on the side of the hunters against the, hunted. The observation that it was better for a hundred of the guilty to go free than for one innocent to be convicted was made with some hesitation. In parallel, an unprecedented number of those convicted were later shown to have been not guilty of the crimes alleged, from murder downwards.

Librarians and booksellers had been accustomed to divide 'fiction' from 'crime fiction'. At the end of the century, in life as in literature, crime was no longer a sideshow. People were frightened by it and by the failure of an increasingly unseen and unresponsive police force to curb it. Political parties hastened to put it 'at the top of the agenda'.

It was sometimes argued that there was no more crime than in the past, when it had often not been reported. This might be true of any period but the claim rested on a lack of evidence. An unreported crime might or might not have been committed. The truth would certainly not be tested by judicial process. Of course, statistics alone might be open to question, as some acts were criminalized and others decriminalized. Yet, for example, the rise in crimes of violence in London from 2,500 in 1946 to 25,000 in 1977 hardly suggested that the situation was no worse. Fifty years after the war, governments needed no convincing. Regiments of surveillance cameras and plans for compulsory identity cards were the symptoms of a society which could no longer be taken on trust by its rulers, who seemed less and less its representatives. The roots of this change lay partly in the availability of the apparatus of control, for which the war of 1939–45 had been a proving ground, and partly in the acknowledgement of crime as a main constituent in the history of the years which followed that war.

It is not invariably true that history cannot be written soon after the events which constitute it. Yet the landscape of the period between 1945 and 1970 becomes clearer as it recedes. In England, the dominating feature of the entire century remains the Second World War, which in one sense did not end until the fall of Communism and the Berlin Wall in 1989. Until then, it was unthinkable that the armies of Britain and the United States should withdraw from Germany. Indeed, it was thought impossible to abolish the conscription of young men for military service for almost twenty years after 1945.

The history of the period 1945 to 1970 began with several years of post-war austerity and a wide sense of wartime promises betrayed. Some people even thought the war had not been worth fighting. Why was Britain the land of rationing and shortages, when the United States, France and even Germany had done away with such things? Unhappily for the Labour government this resentment more or less matched its term of office from 1945 until 1951. 'Tell me the old, old story,' sang the crowds to Clement Attlee at public meetings before his election defeat. What was thought and said privately during six post-war years was far more corrosive than any public debate. There followed a decade of comparative affluence balanced by reformist ideas and campaigns, leading to Harold Macmillan's 'never had it so good' speech of 1957 and the first meetings of the Campaign for Nuclear Disarmament.

Thereafter, the first talent of the 1960s appeared to be self-advertisement, which not only purloined the reformism of the previous decade but sought to persuade the exploited that they were actually having the time of their lives. They were 'swinging' years, though as Maurice Baring remarked of the 1890s, neither he nor his friends felt any more 'naughty' or 'gay' than at any other time and often far more downtrodden. In the 1960s, the youthful costumes of Carnaby Street, when run through the fingers, felt like nothing so much as the cheap and threadbare clothes on sale to the imprisoned population of East Germany. In this, as in other areas of commerce, the entrepreneurs of the decade clung to the faith that a fool and his – or, indeed, her – money are soon parted.

It was certainly a time enlivened by the spectacle of the earnest middle-aged striving to keep in step with the music of the young. It was not much enlivened by 'happenings', which seemed so often to be peculiarly uneventful. Despite the promise of nirvana as a narcotic haze or perpetual orgasm, it was an age apt to leave the impression of people standing around waiting for something or someone to turn up. The good time, if that was what it had been, ended in reaction. The Manson murders of 1968 sullied the image of hippiedom and the summer of love in the United States, where an outraged silent majority carried Richard Nixon to power that autumn. Chairman Mao, an icon of Britain's middle-class 'student revolution' of 1968, played host to him. In 1970, the British tired of the Wilson government and turned to Edward Heath. The Conservative party was to rule for all but six of the next twenty-seven years.

If there was a post-war social revolution, so far as it could be matched to a decade, its effects were most evident in the 1950s. The young marched in protest at the execution of Derek Bentley. A Campaign for the Abolition of Capital Punishment was led by Gerald Gardiner QC, a future Lord Chancellor. By 1957, the Conservative government had restricted capital murder to specific categories, in the Homicide Act. The young marched in protest again as Sir Anthony Eden took the nation to war against Egypt in 1956. The invasion was intended to regain the Suez Canal, nationalized by President Nasser through whose country it ran. Eden acted in the face of American opposition and with the desperate assurance that Britain was equal to confronting the Soviet Union unaided. To oppose the government on the streets at a time when its troops were fighting an enemy was a novelty but a good many of the marchers had just completed two years' military service and had no wish to go back.

Though it advertised itself as the decade of the 'Angry Young Man', in the persons and writings of John Wain, Kingsley Amis, Colin Wilson, John Osborne and Kenneth Tynan, these young men appeared to have very little to be angry about and many of them proved to be nature's conservatives. Those of all ages marched again in ex-service duffel coats as the fledgling CND, led by Bertrand Russell, J. B. Priestley and Canon Collins, attracted general attention for the first time. In sexual morality, the Wolfenden Committee considered changes in the law to legalize homosexuality and reform prostitution. A new Obscene Publications Act in 1959 removed a good deal of literary censorship. It often seemed true that while the campaigns and reforms of the 1960s were likely to benefit the campaigners personally, those of the 1950s were more altruistic: the abolition of hanging, nuclear disarmament, even the birth and growth of the Oxford Committee for Famine Relief.

The chapters which follow are an account of the underworlds existing in Britain during twenty-five post-war years. By 1970 many of the problems and solutions of the years ahead were already in place. Though the so-called fall of Scotland Yard in the 1970s is often cited as if it were the beginning of a general corruption of the police force, those who were guilty had little to teach the leaders of the Brighton police scandal of 1957. Drugs were to become the intractable menace of the late century but no more so than they had been when amphetamines eased the path to violence and murder for Teddy Boys and their successors by the late 1950s.

In another sphere, the Moors Murders trial in 1966 and the less celebrated Cannock Chase murder investigation of 1969 were precursors of a fear by parents for their children which was to change profoundly the social life and daily habits of the century's final decades. It was believed by many that children must not be allowed to play outside their homes without supervision and, by governments, that no adult beyond the family could be trusted with a child unless first approved by the authorities. Whether this was a response to a new and unexplained threat to children by predators or to sensationalism and hysteria, the fears were genuinely and tenaciously held. To that extent, such cases as the Moors Murders were the first chapter in a story which belonged to the decades that followed the post-war years.

Crime is no monolith. Governments are apt to encourage a belief in the Mafia or its rivals as tightly organized business conglomerates. The elderly widow must re-identify herself to her bank or investment company to ensure that she is not laundering the proceeds of major crime. Ungrateful though it may seem, such organizations are more than capable of looking after themselves without employing her to launder the trivial sums passing through her account. What use the information may be to sales forces or tax inspectors is another matter.

The evidence of the post-war years reveals a series of underworlds, concerned with robbery, or prostitution, or drugs, or protection, but often overlapping. In this period they converge with the cultural pretensions of Teddy Boys and their kind. A major theme of post-war crime was 'the violent young', whose presence was seen in aggravated robbery, theft with violence, gang fights and murder in 'dance halls', usually no more than the bleak huts of youth clubs with a record player and a stack of discs. As young men in the early 1950s, the Kray twins were no different from thousands of Teddy Boys who went to a Saturday dance for a fight. Despite his later fame as a protection racketeer, whose underling Jack 'The Hat' McVitie peddled drugs on his behalf, Reggie Kray was also a young post-war spiv and 'hammerer' at fake auctions. There was no necessary demarcation between these underworlds or branches of 'the underworld', though demarcation disputes were not uncommon.

Major crime is and always has been disproportionately concentrated in London and its surroundings. Beyond these, there had been gangs before the war in Glasgow, for example, well rooted in religious sectarianism. These had been suppressed, but the post-war gang leader Arthur Thompson was a major figure in the city's crime and worked in loose alliance with the Krays. Elsewhere, as in Liverpool or Cardiff, the nature of crime was less ambitious and often not of a kind to be reported to the police. Routine drug dealing or pimping, rather than well-planned major robberies, were the trades of dockland, where even a brothel was usually no more than the back of a client's car and 'pimps' were sometimes no more than fifteen, supervising girls who were no older and sometimes no more than thirteen. London was the natural terrain of major professional villainy.

Yet it was also true, even before the war, that criminals increasingly operated across the country. This was the method of racecourse protection gangs and led to warfare between them. Subsequently, the underworld leader Jack Spot was active in Leeds as well as London. The Krays, largely occupied with the East End and Soho, also protected clubs in Birmingham and Leicester. Oxford, Southend, Brighton and the South Coast became natural and easy extensions of the capital's drugs trade, as they did of its armed robberies. Criminal mobility and the motor car had been factors in crime at least since the gangsters Frederick Browne and 'Two Gun Pat' Kennedy were hanged in 1928 for shooting PC George Gutteridge. The globalization of criminal activity received a well-publicized boost when members of the Mafia came to London to discuss co-operation with the Kray twins.

As a subject, the post-war underworld may be adjusted to suit individual preferences. In some views, it extended no further than that period of austerity, the heyday of the spiv, which scarcely outlived the end of rationing in 1954. Perhaps in its effects on rising crime and by producing a new and more belligerent generation of criminals at that time, its effects lasted through much of the century. Most forms of crime that were to preoccupy the nation during the last thirty years of the century were evident in some form by 1970. That year was less a frontier than a stretch of highway between two points, receding and approaching. P. J. Helm in *Europe: 1450–1660*

(1973) remarks that history is like the spectrum. The importance of setting a date, as in choosing a colour, is a matter of selection. Orange may be seen equally well as 'the decline and fall of red' or 'the rise and triumph of yellow'. It is in this sense that 1970 suggests the end of a post-war period merging with the birth of a more affluent and self-regarding age, still perhaps too close to be given a definitive title.

As a matter of personal experience, during eighteen months of my military service in the 1950s, one of six members of the billet was a nineteen-year-old professional criminal from the East End of London. He subsequently appeared on the front page of a mass-circulation newspaper, having been arrested and tried on charges of armed robbery. It was a serious matter and yet it was rather like reading of a school contemporary who, by his own lights, had done well in the world. In this case, he remembered the advice which he had passed on to us all at nineteen. When confronted by the law, answer no questions but ask, 'Where's yer bleedin' witnesses?' If they have none, he said, there is no case. So it proved for him. He had arranged his alleged robberies in such a way that he was seen only by the person whom he robbed and so he was acquitted for lack of corroboration. His response failed him at least once as a serviceman, resulting in a three-month absence at Her Majesty's Military Prison, Colchester.

Like the Krays and their competitors, he inhabited more than one world. As a pioneer of the Teddy Boy suit, his invariable invitation on a Saturday evening was, 'Coming down the dance hall for a fight?' Those to be fought were the local civilian youths, no match for his fists or flick knife, and it was proposed that the evening should progress to car theft and criminal damage. No amount of imprisonment or consignment to the guardroom seemed to have the least deterrent effect. A law-abiding youth would fear being caught and would tremble at the consequences. That fear seemed unknown to him. There came a point where he passed through an invisible barrier. Playing poker all night and sleeping all day, regardless of parades and duties, he became a soldier of the Queen whom the authorities abandoned to his own wilful eccentricities.

★

It is a great pleasure to acknowledge those to whose kindness and assistance I have been indebted in writing this book. As in the case of *An Underworld at War*, two institutions have made it possible. The Bodleian Library and particularly the staff of the Map Room have provided a mass of source material and desks large enough to accommodate it. I am grateful to all of them for their patience and helpfulness. For the past two years, my work has been made immeasurably easier by my colleagues at Cardiff University, particularly Professor Martin Kayman and Dr Martin Coyle of the School of English Communications and Philosophy and Professor Richard Whipp of the Cardiff Business School. My thanks go also to Ms Jean Verrier, Mr Dean Burnett, Mr Nathan Heslop and Mr Robert Thomas.

The Cardiff Business School and the Law Library have provided valuable background material. To those of us who live at some distance from copyright libraries and primary sources, work of this kind depends on systematic gathering of material through inter-library loan and other means. Once again, it is a pleasure to acknowledge the Information Services of Cardiff University, especially Ms Sue Anstey, Ms Sue Austin, Ms Sarah Bithell, Ms Helen D'Artillac Brill, Mr Tom Dawkes, Ms Sue Elias, Mrs Chris Hennessy, Mr Peter Keelan, Mrs Ann Lowery, Ms Vicky Stallard and Mrs Ann Thomas. As in the case of its predecessor, this book could not have been written without their help.

I am most grateful to Mr Nigel Griffiths and Ms Kirstie Ayers of Group 4 Securicor for very useful information and for the material included in the firm's company history, *Securicor: The People Business* by Sarah Underwood, published by CPL Books, 1997.

Friends and colleagues who have supplied me with information and material include Mr and Mrs Ben Bass of Greyne House Books, Marshfield, Mrs Marie Elmer of Clifford Elmer Books, Mr Derek Hart, Mr Graeme Holmes and Dr Linda Shakespeare. To all of them I express my thanks, as to those who have supplied information not attributed here.

Among libraries and institutions who have supplied me with material, I should like to acknowledge Bath Central Library; the Bodleian Law Library and Modern Papers Room; Brighton and Hove

Libraries; the British Library Document Supply Centre; the British Library Newspaper Division; Brixton Central Library; Cambridge University Library; Camden Reference Library; Cardiff Central Library; the City of Bristol Reference Library; Hackney Reference Library; Kensington Reference Library; Leeds City Libraries; Manchester City Libraries; the Public Record Office; Romford Reference Library; Tower Hamlets Local History and Archives, and the City of Westminster Library.

I have greatly appreciated the advice of Mr Bill Hamilton of A. M. Heath Ltd, the encouragement of Mrs Caroline Knox of John Murray Publishers, the advice and help of her colleagues, Mrs Catherine Benwell, Mr Howard Davies, Ms Sam Evans, Ms Caroline Westmore and Mr Gordon Wise, and the characteristic enthusiasm of Dr Howard Gotlieb, Director of the Howard Gotlieb Archival Research Center at Boston University. My greatest debt, as always, is to my family.

We may have lost the Ashes, productivity may be lagging, our sportsmen may finish last in many things. But one made-in-Britain skill remains supreme. Our safebreakers are the best in the world.

Peter Ellis, *Weekend*, April 1963

If society does not control criminals, criminals will control society.

Judge John Tudor Rees,
Surrey Quarter Sessions, 14 March 1950

I

After the War

THROUGHOUT THE SECOND World War, the British people
looked forward to the new world which was to follow, rather
than to a resumption of the life they had known before.
Throughout the conflict they called this sunlit future 'after the
war'. To those who had never experienced the war, it would seem
a banal phrase. Yet it summed up the dreams of millions, almost
as if they had spoken of heaven above, where everything would
somehow come right. Crooners and dance bands promised them
that there would be blue skies over the white cliffs of Dover, the
lights would go on again in London, they and their loved ones
would meet again, never more to part. Not least, the good things
withdrawn from the lives of ordinary people 'for the duration'
would be restored. Those who had been too poor to taste the
good things before 1939 would now have their share. Even before
the fighting had ended, there were glimpses of this New Jerusalem,
seen in the visions of those who were now spoken of respectfully
as 'planners'.

By the beginning of 1943, a Ministry of Town and Country
Planning had been set up. In the following year, a fundamental
reform of the school system was undertaken by a new Education
Act. There would be longer and more specialized schooling for all
– and it was to be free, which had not always been the case with
pre-war state education. A free health service would protect all,
'from cradle to grave', as the slogan promised. An end to killer
diseases like smallpox, cholera, diphtheria and polio was in sight.
Nowhere was this wartime dream more seductive than in the promises of the planners. Bright and airy new towns, set among the fields
of the Home Counties, would replace the blitzed slums of London's

East End. The three-headed monster of disease, unemployment and squalid housing was to be slain by new medical provision, skilled trades and modern design.

For those who found such a future hard to envisage, the Ministry of Information adopted the cartoon techniques of Walt Disney to portray in its films a future of round-faced smiling children, babies in prams, aproned mothers and pipe-smoking fathers, in a landscape of fields and trees. Everything from school milk and orange juice to civic amenities or clean public transport had its place in the new settlements.

It was not the role of propaganda to explain how the new world would be paid for by a nation which faced bankruptcy at the war's end. Too often it sounded as if the good things were to be a matter of right, a prize for winning the war, rather than the reward of self-sacrifice and hard work in the future. The plan also left out of account those who did not give a toss for the new order. Its propagandists were usually content with passing references to the selfish rich or the privileged classes of the pre-war years. There was no glimpse of a serpent in the planners' Garden of Eden. Yet the war had shown how easily a section of society might be criminalized when faced by real shortages and tempted by a black market. Millions had been grateful for 'a little extra' or something 'off the ration', for their families or children if not for themselves. The years of post-war austerity would inflict privations which most people found worse than wartime itself.

Rationing was to be an integral part of the new world, for nine years after the war, as opposed to five years during it. Meat was rationed from 1940 until the summer of 1954. One class of 'friendly butcher' made a modest fortune from it. As the housewife reached the counter, he would move his knife along the cut of meat. Then he would smile at his loyal 'regular customer', move the knife a fraction further, and say softly, 'A little bit extra this week!' Gratefully, she would take the addition to her ration and pay 'a little bit extra' as well.

By September 1950, the truth came out. The housewife thought she had been favoured. After the butcher's generosity, it would have seemed absurd to weigh the meat on getting home. Had she done so, she would have found that it was exactly the ration she was entitled to. She had not been given extra, merely charged extra. Even had she discovered this, she was now an accomplice in breaking the Defence Regulations. Some butchers were said to be earning a bonus of £10 or £20 a week in this way, when £5 was still a good average wage, and they had been doing so since meat rationing was introduced in 1940.[1]

No vision of a New Jerusalem was likely to allow for the existence of crime. If people were treated better, would they not behave better? Yet in one view, there were so many post-war regulations and controls waiting to be broken that, as the Chairman of the Conservative Association in Mile End told his members in 1947, 'They have made criminals of us all.' There were proliferating technical and strict liability offences, where innocence of criminal intention was no defence. Far worse, the statistics of armed robbery and violent crime in 1944–5 showed a 40 per cent increase among those whose intention was never in doubt. It seemed a dismal prospect for the peace to come.[2]

The war had two general effects on the attitudes of the majority. First, it radicalized many of them, particularly those who were in the services. They had seen their superiors at close quarters and were not always impressed by the sight. Even the heroes of the war were no longer inviolate. During the election campaign of June 1945, while the war against Japan continued, Winston Churchill as incumbent prime minister made an appearance in Walworth Road. The East End crowds, who had cheered him on the cinema screens a few years before, hissed him and scratched his car. The electoral defeat of the greatest political leader in the nation's history was so decisive that people wondered whether the Conservative party could ever win again.

The Labour party seemed a safe and conscientious custodian of political resentment. Yet one of the most interesting aspects of the 1945 election was seen in seats like Rhondda East. The Labour candidate in this mining constituency might have expected a 20,000 majority against a Conservative opponent. He scraped home by a mere 972 votes. But there was no Conservative candidate. The Labour member had almost lost to Harry Pollitt, General Secretary of the Communist Party. Indeed, the Communists took both West Fyfe and Stepney from Labour. The determination of working people not to go back to pre-war ways, nor to be 'pushed around', and ultimately to have what they believed to be theirs by right had seldom been more evident.

This did not, of course, make criminals of the huge majority of ordinary people, except to the extent to which they were prepared to break irksome regulations, as they had done in the services. Sometimes this revived the custom of service life known euphemistically as scrounging or 'liberating'. Soldiers lived in camp, which was their home, however temporarily. If a hungry man helped himself to food from the stores, it was an offence, yet it seemed hardly worse than helping himself in the larder of his family home. By an easy extension, the argument applied to acquiring clothing or an extra blanket from the bedding store, even to borrowing transport or using petrol, let alone taking anything that was 'lying about', 'spare' or 'gash'. This was not like stealing a widow's silver and leaving her to weep over the loss. The only victim was the Army – or any other arm of the services or government. Such organizations felt no distress and so, the logic ran, there was no victim. 'What they don't know about, they won't miss.'

In time of peace it was criminal to rob a bank or swindle a football pool. Yet, provided that no individual was hurt or distressed, it might be argued by the robber that there was no real victim. The loss would be covered by the insurers and that, as Professor Marcus remarks in *The Ladykillers* (1955), is merely a farthing on everybody's policy. Neither radicalism nor institutional dishonesty became the code of post-war behaviour. Their effect was to chip away at the established morality to which most people had traditionally allied themselves.

A more dramatic challenge followed the end of hostilities. Some men who had learnt the arts of war continued to exercise them in the new peace. This was not done only from greed or the desire for gain. Some robbers who were to spend many years in prison might have made as good a living by honest means. Yet leading a bank raid, blowing a safe, let alone hijacking a mail train brought the high-octane excitement of active service.

Many of these assaults, if carried out against the enemy in war, would have turned such men into heroes. Peta Fordham, attending the trial of the Great Train Robbers in 1964, saw in Gordon Goody the presence and abilities of a natural commando leader. One of the counsel at the trial thought that in wartime Goody would probably have won the VC, rather than a sentence of thirty years in prison. Those who hijacked the mail train and those who sailed an ancient explosive-laden destroyer into the River Loire to ram the gates of the St Nazaire dry dock in 1942 showed a number of qualities in common. Had the Great Train Robbers been parachuted into wartime Germany and come home with £2,500,000 in banknotes from a hijacked train, they would have ranked high on the list of the nation's heroes.[3]

The difference between prisoners of war staging a breakout from camps in Germany and convicts escaping from Wandsworth in 1961 was hardly greater. A leader of the breakout at Wandsworth was Niven Craig, a young armed robber of the 1950s, known as 'The Velvet Kid'. A mock fight was staged in the mailbag shop. When warders moved to break it up, they were overpowered, bound and gagged. Ten prisoners, including Craig and two armed robbers, were handed ropes by other inmates to let themselves down from the windows of the workshop into the yard. They formed up smartly into a double file and marched past the staff married quarters, as though they were a working party. They reached the prison wall, where they had hidden a further set of ropes. They scaled the wall and reached Magdalen Road. A car provided by an ex-prisoner was waiting. By the time the warders were discovered, trussed up in the mailbag room, the escapers had vanished. Mingling bluff and agility, it might have been a classic wartime escape.

There was a further curiosity in the case of Niven Craig. At the age of fourteen, he had been sent to an approved school. It was 1940, the nation's finest hour. He and another boy escaped and broke into a Home Guard store to get weapons. Making their way to the coast, they stole a rowing boat and prepared to set out across the English Channel to fight the Germans in occupied France. The two boys were picked up as they began their crossing and came to no harm. Yet they had behaved with the same patriotic bravado that might inspire a commando raid or an aerial dogfight.

Not long afterwards, Captain W. E. Johns, famous to every schoolboy for his novels featuring 'Biggles of the RAF', and to wartime schoolgirls for 'Worrals of the WAAFs', wrote the first of a new series, *King of the Commandos*, published in 1943. Niven Craig might have been the model for its hero. Nigel Norman Peters, also fourteen, is a public schoolboy at Brendall's School in Essex when the Dunkirk evacuation begins. Every craft of every size from a nearby creek has put to sea to assist the rescue of the Army from the beaches of France. Two masters from the school have set out in a leaky wherry. Three prefects have slipped away in a dinghy. The rising excitement is more than any 'normal healthy boy' can watch without wanting to take part. The child-hero jumps aboard a small pleasure craft and becomes stranded in France while searching for his soldier-father on the beach. He joins a partnership of the resistance movement and commando raiders, led by the formidable 'Gimlet' King. The series of novels ended with the coming of peace, never to reveal whether its frustrated wartime hero was tempted to become one of the post-war public-school cat burglars pursued by Detective Inspector John Capstick and the Ghost Squad in 1946.[4]

Of all the disappointments in the peace which had promised so much, few were more alarming than the increase in serious crimes which might threaten anyone. The published figures were always depressing and sometimes frightening. Many of the young grew restless in a land where what had once been laudable as well as exciting was now forbidden. The adrenalin of battle gave way to a world of free National Health orange juice and counselling by thoughtful probation officers. More disturbing than its mere statistics, the quality of crime appeared to have changed since the last days of peace in 1939. Though the four most famous post-war psychopaths – Heath, Haigh, Hume and Christie – were to have relatively few victims, something of their brutal derangement appeared to affect the criminal class as a whole.

If newspapers were to be believed, it was only necessary to visit the post office in order to be attacked and put in hospital – or worse

– as a cosh gang raided the premises. It was increasingly common to be drawing money at a bank counter when several masked thugs piled out of a car and ransacked the tills, grievously wounding or shooting dead anyone who dared to stop them. Worst of all was the fear of waking at night with a torch in the face and an intruder's voice demanding the key to the safe or the whereabouts of money. True, these threats in the late 1940s were not as savage as they were to become. They did not yet include such persuasion as inflicting injuries on a baby in its high chair, the threatened rape of a daughter or the chopping off of a victim's feet, even the promise to castrate the man of the house, in order to extract the family cash from its concealment.

A natural source of reassurance was the comforting image of law and order. The strength of the Metropolitan Police might be at its lowest since 1885 but cinema screens portrayed a Flying Squad equipped with the latest and most powerful Hillman and Humber Snipe saloon cars. Crime reporters hinted at the secret 'Ghost Squad', and spoke knowingly of such thief-takers as George Hatherill, Ted Greeno, Reginald Spooner, John Capstick, and a score of men to whose surnames was added the sobriquet, 'of the Yard'.

One incident more vividly than any other in the first two post-war years bore the stamp of violent crime as it was and would be. It inspired a film classic, *The Blue Lamp* (1948), and one of the most enduring characters ever to appear on television in *Dixon of Dock Green*. In fiction, it supplied the criminal habitat of such novels as A. J. La Bern's *It Always Rains on Sunday* (1947) and Norman Collins' *London Belongs to Me* (1948), both soon translated to the screen. In reality, it pitted one of the worst London gangs against a Scotland Yard man known to millions. It involved guns and forensic science, as well as the most famous pathologist of the age, Sir Bernard Spilsbury, and the greatest firearms expert, Robert Churchill. Ominously for the future, the oldest of the criminals convicted was twenty-three, the youngest seventeen.

This drama of gangsters and street crime became known rather blandly as the 'D'Antiquis Case', a title lacking the sonority of a 'ripper' or 'brides in the bath'. Yet it had as profound a resonance in the hearts of those who lived through its moment of fame.

There were far worse assaults on law and order in the post-war future, for which reason it faded from public memory within a decade. Yet in the summer of 1947, it seemed a parable of post-war Britain.

2

The Shadow of a Gunman

I

THE EARLY MONTHS of 1947 showed austerity at its worst. In the last few days of January snow showers were forecast. Snow then fell as it had not fallen since 1880. The temperature in London dropped to sixteen degrees below freezing. It was the middle of March before the thaw and the floods came. Meantime the country was icebound, the drifts closing roads and railways. Scotland was cut off, while a single road through Birmingham linked London to the North. Buses ran limited services in the cities and in London it was sometimes necessary to cut off electric power to the tube when, for example, frozen snow was so deep that it short-circuited the system and a length of the rail at Putney glowed red-hot. In all this, a carload of fugitive robbers still managed to outpace the law, having rammed the police at 50 mph after a ten-mile chase through slippery streets on the night of 11 February.

There had been strikes before Christmas, which now resulted in fuel shortages and lay-offs. Even when the stoppage ended, it proved impossible to transport enough coal from the pits. Coal or coke that reached power plants and factories often froze like rock to the metal trucks. Moreover, the best coal had gone for export. After the first great 'shutdown' of electricity supplies on Monday 7 February, two million workers were laid off. Three days later, the government ordered the closing of cinemas during the day, banned greyhound racing to ease the demand on power, and took the BBC's first television service off the air. On 5 March, in the worst conditions on the railways for a quarter of a century, passengers fainted in overcrowded carriages that were iced up and stranded. State-run 'British Restaurants' offered soup-kitchen fare. Never was it plainer that the cost of war had brought Britain to the verge of bankruptcy.

There was a weary reception for slogans urging the people to 'Battle Together For Britain' or 'All Pull Together And We'll Pull the Country Through'. They found little response among black marketeers, who were pulling through very nicely on their own account. The 'spivs' and 'drones' of newspaper cartoons, with their trilby hats, sharp suits and padded shoulders, remained a comically acceptable face of the underworld. The less amiable aspect of that world was the new and universal culture of the gun.

Firearms, rarely seen in pre-war robbery, were everywhere. Luger automatic pistols, capable of firing Sten-gun ammunition, had been taken by the thousand from the defeated Wehrmacht as souvenirs of victory. Small arms from the British or American armies were common, including the Bulldog Special revolver and the Webley .455. Some weapons, like the Eley .455 and its bullets, dated from the war of 1914–18. According to the ballistics expert Robert Churchill, a lot of the ammunition fired by criminals in the streets of London during 1947 was over fifty years old. Some rounds failed to detonate but those that went off were no less lethal because of age.

Older guns could still be bought as 'antiques'. Starting pistols might be modified to fire live bullets. Folding shotguns were readily obtainable. Shotguns were not yet commonly used by criminals because it was so easy to get handguns and more convenient to carry them. In 1952, Christopher Craig as a schoolboy of sixteen had already owned forty such guns. They were swapped like toys in school playgrounds. In 1946, when the Commissioner of Metropolitan Police, Sir Harold Scott, allowed a London amnesty for illegal firearms, 76,000 were handed in with more than 2,000,000 rounds of ammunition. The rest were retained by those who had a purpose for them.

As the press reiterated, it was the finger on the trigger rather than the gun and its bullets that committed murder. A breed of young criminals had been trained in war to be tough and resourceful; a younger generation that had missed the conflict now profited by their example.

If any area of London was regarded as a breeding ground for violent crime, it was south of the river, beyond the wharves and warehouses from London Bridge to Greenwich. Among their honest citizens, the bombed-out streets and temporary housing in Bermondsey and Deptford, Lewisham and New Cross, harboured more delinquents to the square mile than any other district. Or so it was believed by those like Superintendent G. W. Cornish who witnessed the pre-war rise of 'Monkey' Benneyworth and the Elephant Boys. Immigration from Europe into the East End had persuaded many native criminals to move 'over the water'.

By the end of March, the long winter had given way to a fine spring. On 25 April, as a preliminary to the greater crime, three young men with scarves over the lower part of their faces like bandits in an old-fashioned Western film burst into A. B. Davis Ltd, a jeweller's shop in the busy Bayswater shopping thoroughfare of Queensway. A fourth man waited outside as lookout. The three men in the shop held up the staff with handguns, while they looted the firm's plate and jewellery. All four got clear in a stolen car parked outside. A car was usually stolen just before a robbery so that its owner had no chance to report the loss. In this case, it was abandoned a short distance away and the four young criminals completed their escape as passengers on a London bus. The bags they had with them contained plate and jewellery worth £4,517, the price of a pair of modest suburban houses.

Shop assistants and passers-by had been advised not to resist such robbers. The Commissioner of Metropolitan Police warned the public that armed thieves of this type would shoot their way in and out after the manner of a gangster film. Not for the first time, it seemed that the cinema had a lot to answer for in the matter of soaring crime figures. Yet anger as well as fear over these incidents had grown since the war's end. This was not the world for which the nation had fought and its heroes had died. The individual citizen would often take action with a courage that might occasionally have fatal consequences.

2

Four days after the Queensway robbery, at midday on 29 April, the little cafés in the central London thoroughfare of Charlotte Street were busy with shop assistants and office workers during their Tuesday lunch-hour. There was heavy traffic on this route between Oxford Street and the Euston Road. Charlotte Street ran parallel to Tottenham Court Road, just to its west. Tottenham Street, with its plain façades of London brick, greengrocers or newsagents at street level and offices above, ran west from Tottenham Court Road, crossing Charlotte Street and continuing to Cleveland Street.

During the blitz, a number of buildings in the area had been hit. Some were demolished entirely and others reduced to nothing but a patched-up ground-floor relic. A bomb had wiped out the premises on the north-west corner of the Charlotte Street and Tottenham Street crossing. Next to this empty site was a one-storey survival of the original buildings with a distinctly temporary appearance. Above the fire-blackened brick of the front was a signboard, 'Jays the Jewellers'. It looked more like a pawnbroker's premises, which it also was, than the conventional image of a 'West End Jeweller'. A plain wooden sign hanging over a shabby door at one end discreetly announced 'Pledge Entrance'.

By 2.30 p.m. most of the crowds had gone back to work and the sixty-year-old managing director of Jays, Alfred Stock, had returned from lunch. He unlocked the door of the safe to put away several items. Behind him in showcases were rings to the value of £2,000 – about eight years' income for the average worker. With him in the shop was the manager, Bert Keates, ten years older than Mr Stock. Neither had noticed the black pre-war Vauxhall saloon crossing Charlotte Street and pulling up outside. Nor had they seen a passer-by peering through the window at the display of rings.

A moment later the door burst open and a drama of cinematic unreality began. Three young men entered, wearing mackintoshes and with scarves over their mouths and chins. They had revolvers in their hands. One shouted, 'This is a stick-up! Get 'em up and keep quiet!' Another leapt the counter, making for the safe. Mr Stock slammed the door shut, so that it automatically locked. The youth who had leapt the counter shouted at him for the keys. Mr Stock made no movement. The raider grappled with him, knocked him to the ground and began to club the old man's head with a revolver butt.

The manager, Bert Keates, picked up a stool and threw it at one of the masked figures. It missed, but the youth fired back. Passing Mr Keates, the bullet embedded itself in the woodwork of the shop. The explosion of the gun brought assistants from the rear of the premises, five men and a woman. Someone set off the burglar alarm. Mr Stock and the first youth were struggling on the floor by the safe. Another masked raider shouted, 'It's too hot! I'm scramming!'

One of them threw his revolver at the assistants behind the counter. Then, pushing Mr Keates aside, the three masked youths fled through the doorway, into the street and jumped into the Vauxhall saloon. A customer who witnessed the incident in the shop ran out, shouting, 'Police! Police! Stop them!' Other bystanders took up the cry, 'Stop them!'[1]

Outside the shop, the scene was confused. The engine of the car started but, before it could move, a passing lorry driver saw the commotion. He drove his lorry across the path of the car, blocking it in. The car driver then tried to reverse down Tottenham Street. In his agitation, he missed the clutch, sending the car backwards in a jump and jamming the gears. Abandoning their vehicle, the three men scrambled out. They were still wearing scarves across their faces and two of them were waving guns as they began to run down the centre of Tottenham Street in single file, towards the main thoroughfare of Tottenham Court Road. At the first crossing, a motorcyclist was coming down Charlotte Street. Seeing three men waving guns at the crowd and hearing the alarm bell, he turned on to the pavement, angled his bike across it and switched off the engine, one foot on the ground.

Events were now measured in split seconds. The fugitives, about to turn into Charlotte Street, saw their path blocked. Two ran round the motorbike, the third, without hesitation or warning, raised his revolver and shot the motorcyclist in the head at point-blank range. In that second, the bungled jewel raid became capital murder. As the dying man fell, the would-be robbers turned back into Tottenham Street, running between the pavement crowds towards Tottenham Court Road.

Among the bystanders lining the pavement was Charles Grimshaw, an accountant. As the three runners passed him, he stepped out from behind a parked car and managed to trip the second one, who fell full-length, his gun clattering clear. Grimshaw leapt on him and a struggle began. The leader of the three turned back and kicked the accountant in the head. Then the youth with whom the man had grappled scrambled up, snatched the gun, aimed it at Grimshaw and shouted, 'Keep off!' With the scarves on their faces slipping lower, they ran into Charlotte Mews. Finding no way through, they rushed back, and were soon lost to view in Tottenham Court Road.[2]

Alec D'Antiquis, the motorcyclist, lay in Charlotte Street, his body in the roadway, his head pillowed on the edge of the pavement, his lips covered by blood that had dried black. The bullet had entered his head between the left temple and the eyebrow. To those who comforted him, he said, 'I'm all right. Stop them. I did my best.' Then he lost consciousness. He was thirty-four years old, married with six children. With his war-service gratuity, he had started a motorcycle repair business in Colliers Wood, south-west London. He had recently run into the road to stop a bolting horse and had once rescued a child from a burning house. He was the stuff of which the brave post-war world should have been made.[3]

The first policeman at the scene took off his jacket and covered the fallen man for warmth. An ambulance arrived and D'Antiquis was lifted into it. He died about ten minutes after reaching the nearby Middlesex Hospital. Inspector Bob Higgins at Tottenham Court Road police station took divisional charge of the investigation and alerted Scotland Yard.

Chief Inspector Robert Fabian returned to his Whitehall office from lunch. Forty-five years old, a veteran of murder investigations and the Flying Squad, he had a formidable reputation and a gentle manner. He had received the King's Police Medal for single-handedly defusing an IRA bomb in Piccadilly in 1939. In 1956, he was to become more famous than any of his colleagues when his career became the basis for two series of the popular television drama, *Fabian of the Yard*, in which he was portrayed by the actor Bruce Seton. In April 1947, he was deputizing for a senior officer, Superintendent Tom Barratt, then on holiday. The message from Higgins described 'a nasty job in Charlotte Street'. D'Antiquis was in hospital and 'going to die'.[4]

Fabian ordered the Yard's photographic department to Charlotte Street, as well as the divisional surgeon and Superintendent Fred Cherrill, the foremost fingerprint expert. Within a few hours the difficulties were plain. There were no fingerprints on the Vauxhall saloon, stolen from Charlotte Street just before the attempted robbery. There were none in the shop, except a set on the gun that a raider had thrown at the shop assistants. Criminal records found no match for the prints. The Forensic Science Laboratory at Hendon used a micro-camera on the car's upholstery and reported not 'a shred' of a clue.

The raid had the stamp of amateurism, which infinitely multiplied the possible suspects. Fabian thought it might be the work of deserters, on the run from the Military Police. Whoever the young men were, their incompetence as armed robbers was almost more of a threat than their criminality. Though there was little clue to their identity, no reader of the press could doubt what sort of criminals they were. These were young thugs with a history of robbery and violence, careful of their own skins and indifferent to those of others, the new gangsters from whom extreme penalties must be exacted. What they were was as much a matter of public concern as who they might be.

On the evening of the murder, Fabian attended Sir Bernard Spilsbury's post-mortem. The bullet that had killed D'Antiquis was identified as coming from a .320 calibre revolver. The other bullet in the woodwork of the shop had been fired by a revolver of .455 calibre. The third revolver, which one raider had thrown at the assistants, was available for examination. Robert Churchill found it loaded with such a variety of ammunition that it was almost impossible to fire it at all.[5]

If modern science was little use, old-fashioned eyewitnesses at first did no better. Twenty-three gave statements to Inspector Higgins at Tottenham Court Road. They described variously, 'Three enormous men . . . Three dodgy little fellows . . . I think one was lame . . . They all ran like blazes . . . All wearing raincoats . . . They wore battledress jackets . . . Definitely foreigners, swarthy . . . They were blond and wore no hats . . . Caps pulled down over their eyes . . .' The witnesses had only seconds rather than minutes to note the suspects and their conduct.[6]

Fabian set up his headquarters at Tottenham Court Road police station. Three days later he had made little progress, when a young man in a black leather jacket walked up to the sergeant's desk and asked, 'Do you want to know anything about two young fellows I saw disappear into a building off the Tottenham Court Road – just after the murder? They had handkerchiefs knotted round their chins.'

The man was Albert Grubb, a taxi driver. He had been driving a fare along Tottenham Court Road just after 2.30 p.m. on 29 April. Though his flag was down, a man with what he first thought was a bandage round his chin jumped on the running board as the traffic came to a halt at the lights. Afterwards Albert Grubb thought it was not a bandage but a handkerchief. He shouted at the man that he was booked and he pointed at the flag. The man muttered something and jumped off.

Waiting in the stationary traffic, the taxi driver saw the man and a companion go into an office block, Brook House, 191 Tottenham Court Road. He also saw them come out again soon afterwards. One of them had a raincoat when he entered the building but not when he came out. It was late in the day when Fabian heard this story and Brook House was locked up for the night. Next morning he and Higgins, in a Flying Squad car, parked outside at dawn. The first arrival was a porter, Leonard Joel. He knew nothing about two men in the building on Tuesday afternoon but had found a key while sweeping up on Thursday. Fabian told one of his men to try it in the ignition of the stolen Vauxhall. It fitted.

The next arrival was an office boy, Brian Cox, who was standing in the doorway of the building on Tuesday afternoon, shortly before 3 p.m. Two men brushed past him as they came in. The taller was wearing a raincoat. They went upstairs and he saw them looking out of the stairway windows from time to time. They were still on the stairs as he went up soon afterwards, one sitting on a window ledge and the other leaning against a wall. One man asked him if 'a Mr Williams' was in. The boy said he did not know any Mr Williams. He remembered that the taller man no longer wore a raincoat.

As a bonus, a delivery driver, Percy Skinner, was at the door of Brook House when the boy saw the two men go in. Traced by the police, Mr Skinner remembered one man in a raincoat and later without it.[7]

Four witnesses had seen the two suspects without scarves across their faces. In the next few hours, CID officers searched Brook House meticulously. Having worked their way up without success, they reached the top floor and entered a painter's lumber-room among the offices. Behind a dusty counter, someone had stuffed a bundle of clothing: a raincoat, a cap and a scarf folded into a triangle with its ends knotted together. Fabian examined the lining of the coat and cap but in both cases the maker's name had been cut out. While this made identification more difficult, it strengthened the link with the crime.

The Commissioner of Metropolitan Police, Sir Harold Scott, had called a conference of senior officers the day after the murder. He warned them it was now or never that such armed crime as had killed D'Antiquis must be stamped out. Every CID officer in the capital, not on essential duties, was assigned to the case. Scott issued a public statement promising full police protection to anyone prepared to give information about the killers. It was an admission of how little evidence had been gathered but also an invitation to the underworld to hand over its rogue elements for justice. At one point, four thousand officers in the London area were involved in the investigation. Most were maintaining pressure on the routine activities of minor criminals, and watching clubs or pubs. Sooner or later, the underworld might regard the killers as a greater nuisance to its own ranks than to the general public. But no one talked. Fabian and his officers turned again to the evidence.

The raincoat found at Brook House was of the commonest kind worn by millions of men of all ages in the late 1940s, a light fawn mackintosh lined with tartan weave. The grey cap, gloves and scarf offered still less hope. However, the clothes were taken to the Forensic Science Laboratory at Hendon. The laboratory reported that there was no identification in the raincoat, cap, scarf or gloves.

Like many thousands of similar coats, this one had been made in Leeds by Montague Burton for distribution to the firm's retail stores in almost every town and city. Fabian had it unstitched. There was nothing to be found in the lining but inside one of the seams a maker's cloth stock-ticket had been sewn in with a number on it, 7800. Fabian sent this to Montague Burton in Leeds by police car. The firm's records showed that the coat had gone to one of its branches in London, probably to Montague Burton in Bermondsey or to the firm's shop in Deptford High Street.

In 1947 it was still impossible to buy clothes legally without surrendering numbered clothing coupons, issued as a ration card. There was a continuing black market in printed forgeries. Because of this widespread counterfeiting, tailors' and outfitters' shops noted down the name on the ration card from which they cut the coupons. Montague Burton in Deptford High Street had the names of those who had bought raincoats from them in the past year or so.

Fabian scanned the list from all Montague Burton stores in the London area. Some purchasers with criminal records were visited but all had alibis for 29 April. However, there was one name which no one seemed able to identify, though it matched no criminal record. The name was Kemp Thomas. This raincoat had been bought at Montague Burton in Deptford High Street on 30 December 1946. Fabian looked again and realized that in this case the clerk had copied down the names in the wrong order, putting the surname first, as it appeared on the ration card. He checked his own coupon card: Fabian Robert. Put the other way round, he recognized Thomas Kemp. Kemp was not a known criminal but his two brothers-in-law, Thomas 'Tommy' Jenkins and Charles Henry 'Harry Boy' Jenkins, had impressive records. Fabian's identification of these two was not so much a feat of memory as the fruit of twenty-five years' daily experience of the London underworld.

He confirmed Kemp's address, a tenement in Park Buildings, Bermondsey. Mrs Kemp was at home. Fabian showed her the raincoat and asked if it belonged to her husband. Vera Kemp said that it looked like his but he had lost it at a public house five weeks earlier. Fabian appeared satisfied. He went back to the car and drove off. However, before entering Park Buildings he had positioned a CID officer in a second car to watch the woman's movements. As Fabian's car disappeared, Mrs Kemp came out and was trailed to another block of flats. She was there for some time and then went home. Fabian's man checked the flat she had visited. It was let to a family named Jenkins.[8]

3

The elder of two brothers, Tommy Jenkins, was currently serving eight years for manslaughter. This followed a £2,563 lunchtime smash-and-grab raid on a jeweller's shop in Birchin Lane, in the financial district of the City of London, in 1944. A naval officer, Captain Ralph Binney, had stepped out into the middle of the road to block the path of the getaway car. The car drove at him, knocking him down and trapping him underneath the chassis. He was dragged down Lombard Street, over London Bridge, and into Tooley Street where he was thrown clear. He died three hours later from his injuries. The Binney Medal for civilian bravery in assisting the police was instituted in memory of his courage. A passenger in the car was Tommy Jenkins. The driver, Ronald Hedley, was sentenced to death for murder but reprieved. It was suspected but not proved that Tommy Jenkins' younger brother, Charles Henry 'Harry Boy' Jenkins, twenty-one years old, was also in the car.

Tommy Jenkins was still in prison. Harry Jenkins, now twenty-three, also had a criminal record for violence. The brothers had belonged to a well-known but loosely organized group, 'The Elephant Boys', a name derived from a South London racecourse and protection racket of the 1920s and 1930s, the self-styled Elephant Gang of 'Monkey' Benneyworth, 'The Trimmer', and Georgie Sewell. These Elephant and Castle thugs had fought a long war with fist and razor against Darby Sabini's gang from Clerkenwell's 'Little Italy'. That was over and the Elephant Boys now drank in Clerkenwell Road pubs which had once been forbidden territory.

Harry Jenkins had been known to the police from childhood. He had been involved in robbery, had two convictions for assaulting the police and had broken a policeman's jaw. He liked to be known as 'The King of Borstal' and had been released from his latest sentence only a week before the killing of Alec D'Antiquis. He had held his coming-out party at the Griffin, in Clerkenwell Road.

Thomas Kemp was picked up before he reached home that night, driven to Tottenham Court Road and questioned. He said he had been unable to find his raincoat the previous week. He thought he had left it at the cinema. Fabian pointed out that his wife had said the coat had been lost in a public house five weeks earlier. 'Who's making the mistake?' 'We both are,' Kemp conceded. 'She lent it to her brother, Harry Jenkins.'[9]

Fabian and his men drove to Bermondsey next day, Sunday morning 11 May. They sealed off the flat and rang the bell. When Harry Jenkins came to the door, Fabian said simply, 'Come on. We want you inside.' Jenkins came quietly. With the Sunday church bells ringing, he was driven to Tottenham Court Road and shown the raincoat. He told Fabian, 'Except for saying that it looks like Tom's, I am not saying anything more now, as it all looks serious to me.' He would answer no further questions.[10]

He was put in a cell while his known associates were brought in. A boy of seventeen, Terence Rolt, said he had been ill on 29 April and had spent the day in bed. Twenty-year-old Christopher Geraghty came to the station of his own accord and said he had been suffering from boils and was housebound on 29 April. Like the others, these two were released. In 1945, Geraghty had been sent back to Borstal for three years. This followed a £6,000 armed jewel robbery in the West End at Catchpole & Williams, Grafton Street, and another for £1,300 at H. & A. Kimball in the City of London. At Grafton Street, he had beaten the manager unconscious.

The decisive evidence against Jenkins or an accomplice could only come from identification. Twenty-three witnesses had seen the gunmen as they ran from the failed robbery to Tottenham Court Road, four had seen them without masks at Brook House. The office boy and the delivery driver at Brook House had the further advantage of seeing two of them more than once over a period of time.

Fabian arranged an identification parade at Tottenham Court Road for 11 a.m. on 12 May. Jenkins consented to appear but claimed to have an alibi for the time when D'Antiquis was shot. He said, 'I shan't tell you where I was until it comes to the last. I am not a "grass" but I am not having this on my own.'[11]

For a guilty man, the risk of being viewed by twenty-seven witnesses was considerable. But Jenkins was familiar with the routine of such parades. In 1944, when he and his brother Tommy were said to have been in the car which killed Captain Binney, he had faced an identity parade, and a murder charge if picked out. Before the parade began, he had deliberately started a fight in the police station and 'chinned' one of his guards. There was a free-for-all and he got the worst of it. Before the parade went ahead, he demanded sticking plaster for his facial injuries. With Jenkins and every other man masked by plaster the parade was a farce and there was no identification. Injury from the police was better by far than facing a trial for the murder of a public hero.

On the later occasion, Fabian subsequently discovered that Jenkins had asked for a lunchtime edition of a London evening paper to read while he was waiting for the parade. This edition came on to the streets at mid-morning and the suspect's request had seemed innocent enough. It was the trick of a professional. As he was taken to the line-up, Jenkins folded the paper carefully and casually slipped it into his jacket pocket. A witness would think that this could not be the man the police had been holding. He was obviously out on the streets a few minutes earlier, buying a paper.[12]

Jenkins stood in a line of fair-haired men for an hour and ten minutes. He appeared relaxed and confident. Twenty-seven witnesses went past, scrutinizing every face. At the end of the line, each was asked whether a suspect seen in Charlotte Street was standing in the parade. Every one of them said he was not.

Harry Jenkins was released, though Fabian had him tailed day and night. He was followed to his familiar rendezvous, the Griffin in Clerkenwell Road, where he met Geraghty and Rolt. It was reported that they talked quietly and looked worried. Next day, Fabian asked Jenkins and his sister Mrs Kemp to come to Tottenham Court Road police station and make statements about the raincoat. That afternoon, in the interview room, Jenkins said to his sister, as though giving in reluctantly, 'Let's tell Mr Fabian who I lent the coat to.' He paused and lit a cigarette. Fabian noticed that the young man's fingers were steady and the flame of the match did not flicker. The name he gave was 'Bill Walsh'.

Despite boasts of gangland loyalty, it seemed that Harry Jenkins had framed an acquaintance for the murder of D'Antiquis. Why he should have done so was, for the time being, a mystery. William Henry Walsh had a long criminal record and had only recently been released from prison. 'We saw him about a week ago in Southend,' Vera Kemp added. 'He's knocking about with a blonde girl who works in a café on the front.'

Fabian was not entirely surprised by this betrayal. He had, of course, assumed that there was a link between the Queensway jewellers' shop robbery on 25 April and the shooting in Charlotte Street four days later. As if to confirm this, Detective Inspector Fred Hodge, investigating the Queensway case, now produced another informant 'singing his head off' about William Walsh as one of the Bayswater raiders. If he had gone to Southend, it was probably to fence the proceeds of the Queensway robbery. If two men were now betraying him, the fencing very likely involved a double-cross of his accomplices.[13]

With Walsh named as a man who might have shot D'Antiquis, squad cars carrying armed officers reached Southend-on-Sea as the May temperatures climbed into the upper eighties. Fabian read through the local police station Occurrences Book. As a matter of routine at all police stations, each local officer noted occurrences while he was on the beat or on duty, not merely crimes but anything worthy of note. On 25 April at 9.40 p.m., PC Frederick Jauncey had reported the suspicious behaviour of two young men in a Southend telephone kiosk. He had demanded to see their wartime identity cards, which were still in force, and had then let them go. The cards named them as Christopher James Geraghty and Michael Joseph Gillam. It seemed that the underworld was already on the trail of Walsh, presumably hoping to run the stolen jewellery to earth before the police did.

If Geraghty and Gillam were two more of the Queensway robbers, they had still not caught up with the absconder. The murder squad raided the Southend house of a fence with whom Walsh was known to have done business in the past. They found two rings from the Queensway hold-up. Six police cars converged on another house, in South Church Avenue, whose occupant obligingly suggested that

Walsh was living with a woman called Doris Hart. There was no sign of either suspect.

Photographs of William Henry Walsh and Doris Hart were circulated to all police forces, describing them as a couple who were needed to assist inquiries into murder and robbery. The search concentrated on Soho, Bermondsey, the Elephant and Castle, Brighton and Southend.[14]

Walsh had left Southend even before the Scotland Yard officers arrived. While they hunted for him there, he had been living quietly at home with his wife in Plumstead, in a post-war prefab. On 16 May, after so much talk of armed police and shoot-outs, he was arrested by a retired policeman and a bicycling constable, while sheltering from the rain under a tree on Plumstead Common. Instead of drawing a gun, he said plaintively, 'What's all this about?'

As Walsh was arrested, an eight-year-old boy and his friends found a gun on the foreshore of the Thames at Wapping, near low-water mark. They were playing with it when someone noticed them. It was a .320 revolver containing five cartridges and one case. Three cartridges had misfired. Soon afterwards a .455 Bulldog Special was found nearby, loaded with .450 ammunition which was too small for proper use. It contained bullets more than fifty years old. Robert Churchill test-fired the guns and compared the bullets with those found at the scene of the Charlotte Street crime. He identified the .320 revolver as the murder weapon and the .455 as the gun that fired a shot into the woodwork of Jays the Jewellers.[15]

Fabian questioned Walsh at Woolwich police station. When he warned the suspect that the charges would certainly include armed robbery but might easily extend to murder, Walsh, a thirty-seven-year-old labourer, paused. He was an opportunist thief now frighteningly out of his depth. He asked for a glass of water. When the water came, he gave in. 'I can see it's serious. I'll tell you about my part in the Queensway job, but I've nothing to do with the Charlotte Street business.'[16]

Walsh admitted being at the Queensway robbery, which he claimed was carried out by Harry Jenkins, Christopher Geraghty and a man he would only call 'Joe'. His own part was merely to stand outside the shop as a lookout. 'Joe' was Michael Joseph Gillam, the ex-Borstal Boy seen with Geraghty in the Southend phone kiosk. Because Walsh had double-crossed Jenkins over the proceeds, Jenkins had implicated Walsh in murder. Walsh also admitted reconnoitring Jays on behalf of Geraghty, Rolt and Jenkins, but insisted he took no part in the raid. Indeed, he had an alibi for that afternoon.

In the small hours of the next morning, the final arrests began. Geraghty was first. When told at his home in Islington that he was to be questioned by Fabian again, he said, 'I hope he doesn't think I'm going to open up and get a revolver in my back.' At 2.30 a.m., seventeen-year-old Terence Rolt was badly shaken by the experience of being dragged from sleep and taken away by armed police. As he arrived at the police station, he saw Geraghty in custody and said, 'I'll tell you what happened. Chris never meant to kill that man.' Jenkins, bundled from sleep into a Black Maria by six armed policemen, seemed unconcerned. 'Don't you guys ever sleep? Do you work night and day?' he asked wearily. As the van drove through the dark South London streets, he burst into song, 'Night and day, you are the one . . . You, only you, under the sun . . .' He did not behave like a man who expected to be charged with murder.[17]

Christopher Geraghty made a confession of his part in the Charlotte Street killing. He implicated himself, Rolt and another man he would not name, apart from insisting that it was not Jenkins. Rolt had driven the getaway car. Geraghty admitted that he himself had fired the shot in the jewellers' shop as well as the bullet that killed D'Antiquis. He had only meant to frighten D'Antiquis. There was no advantage in killing a man if it was possible to scare him off. He evidently hoped that this explanation would reduce the charge to manslaughter. He soon found that his excuse was not a valid defence to a charge of murder. In any case, as the judge at his trial pointed out to the jury, Geraghty had not fired high or wide. He had shot his victim in the head at close range. The intention to kill could hardly have been plainer.

Geraghty's story involved himself, Rolt, and the man he would not name. On the night of Saturday 26 April, they had broken into a gunsmith's in Union Street, near Borough tube station. They spent the night choosing guns and ammunition. At noon on Sunday, they sauntered out with their haul, unnoticed. On Tuesday 29 April, they met outside Whitechapel tube station at 11 a.m. and caught the underground train to Goodge Street. They 'took sight' of jewellers' shops in the area of Tottenham Court Road. Rolt went to Jays but came back saying he thought there was only jewellery to the value of £2,000. Geraghty went to look. He thought it was more like £5,000 but there were too many people in the lunchtime crowds. They went to a café and had a meal to pass the time.

Afterwards, Rolt and 'that other fellow' stole a car in Charlotte Street. With Geraghty, they drove to Tottenham Street and parked outside Jays. It seemed that Rolt misunderstood the plan and thought the raid was to begin at once. Being next to the pavement, he got out and dashed into the shop waving his gun. The others had no choice but to follow. From that moment everything had gone wrong.[18]

Rolt was told that Geraghty had made a statement implicating him. He made a statement of his own, admitting that he, Jenkins and Geraghty had been present at the crime. Rolt was the only person, among witnesses or accused, who placed Jenkins in Charlotte Street. On the evening of Monday 19 May, almost three weeks after the death of Alec D'Antiquis, the three youths were charged with his murder. Geraghty and Jenkins, as well as Walsh and Gillam, were also charged with the robbery of A. B. Davis in Queensway, though the charges against Jenkins and Geraghty were not proceeded with.

4

The murder trial opened at the Old Bailey on 21 July. Forensic evidence was given by Sir Bernard Spilsbury and Robert Churchill, police evidence by Bob Higgins, Fred Hodge and Robert Fabian. Geraghty's defence was that he had not intended to harm Alec D'Antiquis. On his behalf it was argued that he lacked the necessary intent to kill and was guilty only of manslaughter. Rolt, at seventeen, was too young to face the death penalty. Harry Jenkins, the only one of the three to give evidence, offered an alibi. He described being at work with his sister on 29 April from 10 a.m. to

4 p.m. This was not Vera Kemp but another sister, Mrs Burns. Seven people had seen him there that day. These alibi witnesses duly gave their evidence.[19]

The judge reminded the jury that where three men committed a crime in the course of which a man was killed, in the manner that D'Antiquis had been, it mattered not whose finger pulled the trigger. All were equally guilty. As for the plea of manslaughter, where an escaping felon prevents a private person from stopping him, 'the felon does so at his own risk and is guilty of murder if that violent measure results even unintentionally in the death of the victim.'[20]

The jury were out for less than an hour. They had not believed Jenkins' alibi witnesses and returned verdicts of guilty against all three defendants. Jenkins and Geraghty were sentenced to death. Rolt, because of his youth, was sentenced to be detained during His Majesty's pleasure. He was released from prison in 1955. After their appeals in the murder case had been dismissed, a reprieve was refused. Harry Jenkins and Christopher Geraghty were hanged at Pentonville prison on 19 September 1947. At the Central Criminal Court on 6 October, William Walsh and Michael Gillam, the surviving members of the Queensway raid, pleaded guilty to the robbery, and were sent to prison for five years each.

Robert Fabian and his admirers saw the case as a check to the use of guns by the post-war young. After Jenkins and Geraghty had been hanged, discarded firearms were found in parks, under bushes, in dustbins, dropped through the floors of bombed houses, fished up by Thames River patrolmen in nets from the low-tide mud. Yet a great many more remained in the hands of their owners. The deterrent effect of the executions did not save George Black, manager of Lloyds Bank sub-branch in Wells Road, Bristol, from being shot dead on 7 January 1949 by a gunman who escaped with £1,444. Nor did it prevent a similar murder in the same city on 13 March in the following year, when a witness was shot dead as he and others chased two gunmen who had robbed the Northview branch of Lloyds. The two murderers, twenty-three-year-old Poles living in Bristol, were caught and hanged. The proceeds of the robbery amounted to £28.

Neither the Bristol bank murders nor the shooting dead of cinema managers at the Bristol Odeon in 1946 and the Liverpool Cameo in 1950 rivalled the earlier crime. As surely as Jack the Ripper evoked the Whitechapel slums of the 1880s, the D'Antiquis case formed cinematic images of British crime in the years of post-war austerity. The bomb-shattered ruins of central London and the close-packed housing of Plumstead or Bermondsey, the dog tracks, fly-spotted cafés, drab and rationed clothing, evoked its world. In *The Blue Lamp*, the fallen hero was to be a uniformed policeman rather than a public-spirited citizen. Yet the film used such elements of the original case as the identification of the killer by a mackintosh and the discovery of the weapons by children playing at the waterside. It also portrayed two of the youthful gangsters. The leader, a sharp-suited, Brylcreemed young gunman, was played by Dirk Bogarde as a bully in his actions and a coward in his heart, a cliché of post-war screen drama, as Bernard Lee's performance was an early person-ification of the patience and determination of Fabian.

The film showed justice being done in the end. This was not quite the cliché it might seem. Though detection rates varied between about a quarter and a third of crimes committed, the propor-tion of persistent criminals caught was much higher. It only needed a professional thief or gangster to make one mistake in several crimes to bring him to justice. Billy Hill, who boasted of being 'Boss of Britain's Underworld' from the 1930s to the 1950s, spent some sixteen years of his life in prison. Such gang leaders as the Krays and the Richardsons were to spend much of their adult lives behind bars. The incompetence of young men like Harry Jenkins, Christopher Geraghty and Terence Rolt was equally self-evident.

5

The characteristics of such crimes dovetailed with the apprehensions of many ordinary people. Guns seemed as common as penknives among the criminal young and were used as weapons with little more compunction. Crime had taken on the characteristics of war itself. It was a game for the young and the ruthless, in which no quarter need be shown to the enemy. The ease with which Geraghty had taken the life of Alec D'Antiquis, or Thomas Jenkins and Ronald Hedley had butchered Captain Binney, was indicative of that.

It was easy enough to show that there had been violent crime of the most lurid kind during the relatively peaceful years of the 1930s. The gang fight at Lewes racecourse in 1936 with its blatant intimidation of witnesses became part of sporting folklore. The Wandsworth Greyhound Stadium murder of the same year was followed by a collective loss of memory among underworld witnesses. Robberies far more brutal than that attempted at Jays the Jewellers were carried out by such gangs as The Mayfair Men in 1937. Six young robbers who were residents of Mayfair, two from titled families and all from public schools, lured a director of Cartiers to the Hyde Park Hotel. He had brought samples of jewellery for their inspection and approval. In robbing him, they beat his head with a mallet until his skull was fractured in six places, not as a last resort but as part of their plan. It was no thanks to them that he did not die of his injuries.

Of course, it was not much consolation to victims and their families in 1947 or 1950 to be told that their ordeals or bereavements were no worse than some in cases before the war. On the other hand, the best that could be said for statistics was that they had yet to demonstrate whether crime was out of control or whether the post-war world was still 'getting back to normal'. Offences like housebreaking and smash-and-grab had dropped between 1932 and 1939. They then increased by a third until 1943 but fell back to 1936 levels in the following year. There then followed a formidable upsurge in almost all types of crime, particularly those involving violence, in 1944–5. Only in Scotland was this delayed until after the war.

Most people's first concern was at the escalating violence against the person. The annual murder rate in England and Wales had risen only from 135 to 141 in the course of the war. In the first three wartime years grievous wounding had risen by 78 per cent overall. It then rose by 44 per cent in 1944 alone and by 65 per cent in 1945. At this rate, such offences would double again in less than eighteen months. It would not have reassured the frightened householder in

London to know that in the next thirty years, from 1946 to 1977, crimes against the person would increase in the metropolis more than tenfold, from 2,155 victims annually to 25,793.

During the war, 1943 was a turning point. In January 1942, the first American troops had arrived, reaching a total of more than a million in the next two years. With their arrival, the danger of a German victory vanished. The mood in the nation grew more relaxed as Britain's Finest Hour gave way to the Grand Alliance. At the same time, the entire country became a cosmopolitan and over-crowded military camp, a fertile breeding-ground for crime. As for the post-war figures, the first years of any peace brought more crimes as the soldiers returned. This had been as true in 1750, in the aftermath of the War of Austrian Succession, as it was to prove in 1950.

Future statistics were to show that the first post-war years formed a plateau of high crime figures which declined somewhat in the 1950s. Thereafter, they would go very much higher and stay there. Yet in the months after the trial of D'Antiquis' killers, the nation's view of itself and the spectacle it presented to the world were of more immediate concern. On 12 June 1948 a brief but significant announcement was made by the British Board of Film Censors, which still controlled film censorship in the British-occupied zone of Germany. The board had banned the showing in Germany of *Brighton Rock* (1947), based on Graham Greene's novel, with Richard Attenborough as the teenage gangster Pinkie. The board was not prepared to have the British seen yet again by foreigners as 'a nation of razor-slashers and racecourse thugs'. The language of the statement made the Finest Hour of 1940 seem as remote as the Battle of Agincourt.

3

Welcome Home

I

T HE SOCIAL AND economic reconstruction of Britain, at which
the post-war Labour government aimed, would have seemed
an heroic project even in a time of unusual prosperity. In 1945 the
commitment to a welfare state and a programme of mass national-
ization was dwarfed by the immediate challenge of demobilizing
five million servicemen and women. At home, there were scarcely
rations for them all. There were certainly no 1918 promises of homes
fit for heroes.

Financial aid from America, essential to the conduct of the war,
was the means of financing post-war renewal. However, within a
few days of the war's end, the United States terminated the Lend-
Lease agreement. The government dispatched a mission to
Washington to negotiate a massive 'American loan'. The left wing
of the Labour party was dismayed. During the Washington negotiations, Aneurin Bevan would ask from time to time if there was
'any danger of an agreement tonight'. A prominent backbencher,
Sydney Silverman, was to denounce America in the House of
Commons as behaving like a 'shabby moneylender'. Unfortunately,
John Maynard Keynes spoke the truth in a famous memorandum
from the Treasury to the Cabinet when he described the country
as facing a 'financial Dunkirk'.[1]

Such was the economic reality of the post-war world for those
who had returned to it. Only unemployment, the pre-war economic
scourge, was no longer a threat. The shortage of skilled labour was
so acute that within two years the government was begging women
to return to industrial work and trying to outlaw unproductive
labour. The shortage of workers was to have a bizarre effect on attitudes to honesty. In November 1949 two employees of Levers

Optical Company were convicted of stealing lenses from the firm. One of the partners begged the magistrate not to send the thieves to prison. The company proposed to take them back immediately. Dishonest they might have been but without them Levers could not meet their commitments to the new and struggling National Health Service.[2]

Reconstruction and the command to 'export or die' in pursuit of dollars meant good money for most workers. Yet direct taxation and purchase tax at punitive levels might take an unusually large portion of this. There was also less and less to spend the money on legitimately. 'For export only' was a standard prohibition, principally on luxury goods. A good many were diverted illegally to the home market.

It was hoped demobilization would be complete in eighteen months, priority being given to age and length of service. Most troops waited philosophically. Sometimes there was disorder, with riots at Aldershot and Fort Darland in 1945 and a general refusal by men to board the troopship *Orion* for further duty. These were followed in 1946 by a general mutiny of the 13th Parachute Regiment in Malaya and 'strikes' by RAF men at Manipur and several other bases. Closer to home, thousands who were weary of military life after six years deserted without fuss. In 1947 there were still 18,000 of them at large. In the first year of peace they were augmented by several thousand absentees from the US and Canadian forces. Such men had reason to be grateful to thieves and counterfeiters who sold them forged or stolen ration books and identity cards, and whose accomplices they sometimes became. Official embarrassment at having so many deserters on the loose was relieved at last by a general amnesty in 1953, on the pretext of celebrating the Coronation of Elizabeth II.

Minor incidents showed how attitudes had changed in the course of the war. Servicemen returning from overseas were not pleased to find themselves treated by Customs and Excise as rogue holidaymakers. The waterguard on duty at points of entry took a confiscatory approach to many returning heroes. Troops waiting in the long dockside queues saw those ahead of them having bottles of wine or spirits confiscated and took immediate action. Assuming that some dishonest Customs officer would drink their prize, they decided it was not to be enjoyed by a man who had spent the war, as one of them put it, 'sitting on his fanny in a reserved occupation', while others did the fighting. The bottles were opened at once and passed round the queues in an atmosphere of general revelry and incapacity, which required intervention by military and civilian police.

Trivial though such incidents might seem, they indicated a more widespread threat to the nation's revenues. As the liberation of Europe progressed in late 1944, a drive against wholesale smuggling had begun. In the last weeks of war and the first months of peace, RAF aircrews ferried home watches and brandy; crews of Royal Navy supply lorries brought back well-tailored black market clothing from Germany. One US air transport squadron produced a thousand bottles of duty-free champagne for sale in Chelmsford after a single trip.[3]

Rank was no guarantee of honesty. A British smuggling ring broken up in April 1945 included a squadron leader, two flight lieutenants and an army officer. They were fined £1,500 each with an alternative of a year in prison after being caught with 771 watches, on which import duty would have been prohibitive. The watches had been bought for £4 each from a café owner in Gibraltar, flown back in a Spitfire to a military airfield, and were being sold at £10 each to RAF personnel, as well as in pubs and to cinema queues. The smugglers' profit in modern terms was £36,000 in a single flight. In September 1944 an investigation had already begun into what was called 'organized smuggling' at RAF Halton, involving officers and men. Six members of Bomber Command at the station were convicted in January 1946. Their cargoes had included champagne, whisky and perfume.[4]

Even more serious, in the view of the Treasury, was currency smuggling. When an RAF flight lieutenant was sent to prison in December 1944, he had flown to Paris with £1,450. The franc was cheap in France but more expensive in London, where the government tried to discourage speculation. As a result, the flight lieutenant came back with an amount of French currency which he turned into £3,210, more than doubling his money in a matter of hours. His profit in modern terms was some £65,000.[5]

Despite the work of the RAF Special Investigation Branch, there was little surveillance at many of its airfields and none at all by the Americans, who were outside British jurisdiction anyway. Group Captain Nicholas of the Special Investigation Branch warned Customs and Excise that smuggling was 'rife'. Rare stamps and even dentures were among items recently brought back for illegal sale. The Americans continued to fly in large quantities of wine and perfume for their own purposes. As MI5 pointed out, there was little to stop them ferrying uncustomed goods on behalf of British servicemen or civilians, as a business arrangement, or even at the behest of the British underworld.[6]

Some of those who were now demobbed had spent the war relatively close to home. Millions of others came back with little but the uniforms they wore. Demobilization for all included a visit to the Civilian Clothing Store, where tailors measured each man. Every new civilian was equipped with a 'demob suit' in light grey chalk-stripe, a sports jacket and flannels, a hat, tie, mackintosh, shirts, underwear, shoes, and the minor items of his wardrobe. Before leaving camp, he was issued with a ration of clothing coupons, needed for the next four years, and a travel warrant to take him home. Within a few hours, many had sold the demob suit to a spiv for the going rate of £10 and parted with their clothing coupons for sixpence or a shilling each. The spiv would get as much as three shillings or three shillings and sixpence by reselling the coupons in a more affluent area. A similar coupon racket had been worked for some time outside factories, when women workers sold their coupons during a lunch-hour visit to the pub or after clocking off.

2

Those who turned from the duties and sacrifices of war to the rights, entitlements and privileges of peace were no less honourable and decent than their predecessors. Yet the 1942 Beveridge Report and any number of political speeches from all parties had promised them the rewards of victory which in too many cases were nowhere to be seen. Welfare, health care, better housing, improved educational opportunities, and what was now called 'leisure' were supposed to be theirs as of right. If they fell ill, National Health Service nurses would come and look after them in their own homes. When they grew old, there would be 'state hotels' for the elderly.

Such promises were swiftly undermined by the conditions of the post-war world. Even those who made them did not foresee that food would have to be rationed, in total, for nine years after the war, as opposed to five years during it, until July 1954. Rationing had been ended long before in countries like France who were supposed to have 'lost' the war. The more generous American system had been abolished within a few weeks of the war's end. 'Who won the war, anyway?' was the frequent British complaint. To boost the vital export drive the government sponsored a 'Britain Can Make It' exhibition of 1947, ungratefully known as 'Britain Can't Get It'.

Even the vanquished, whose aggression was held to have started the conflict, seemed to be doing better than the victors. In May 1946, headlines protested that the Germans were eating white bread, unlike the grey rationed loaves of the British diet: 'The Germans Are Not Starving' and 'Has Germany Hidden Food?' Petrol in Britain was strictly rationed for five years after the war. In 1945, a modest allowance of about ninety miles a month had been allowed for private motoring, as if to celebrate peace. Then during 1946–7 private motoring was banned. There were no dollars to buy petrol.[7]

The diaries of ordinary people, kept under the Mass Observation project, exude a cloud of resentments during the years 1945–8, leading in some cases to the conclusion that the war had not been worth winning. The government was resented for shipping food to Germany at the expense of its own people; the Americans were resented for doing themselves very nicely, as it seemed from the cinema screen, while Britain struggled for survival; the BBC was resented for its solemn celebrations as the people of India were given their independence in 1947, while ordinary people were 'glad to be shot of them'. Some entries were both anti-Nazi and anti-Semitic, as underground gangs in Palestine began to murder British soldiers, culminating with the hanging of two sergeants in an orchard. Jewish leaders in Britain who deplored the atrocities were dismissed as insincere. It was also observed that crime and criminals had become glamorous.[8]

As the Army came home, its men heard a far more widespread lament that food was now 'worse than it was during the war'. In the autumn of 1947, the butter and meat rations were further cut and the bacon ration was halved. It was true that bananas and exotic fruits not seen since 1939 had appeared in small quantities and at irregular intervals but the meat ration soon included such unpalatable items as Antarctic whalemeat, which tasted of cod liver oil, South African snoek, an unappealing relative of the barracuda, and Russian 'rock salmon', otherwise known as dog-fish. There was also 'chicken' which was actually rabbit, and horsemeat, which on principle most British people felt revolted by and normally used as pet food.

Even in a time of shortages snoek proved unsaleable, despite an official 'snoek-tasting' party at the Ministry of Food, presided over by the minister, Dr Edith Summerskill, and a government recipe for 'snoek piquante'. Two years later, the unsold tins were quietly relabelled as cat food. Four thousand unwanted tons of whalemeat sailed the seas in a refrigerated cargo vessel, looking for a buyer.

Bread, never restricted during the war, went 'on the ration' in July 1946, at nine ounces a day. On 7 June, during the Whitsun weekend, six-hour queues for bread had been reported in London, the first customers taking their places at 4.30 a.m. The Minister of Food warned the country that it had supplies for only eight weeks. Women wondered aloud how they were supposed to feed their families, despite radio assurances from officials and experts that the national diet was wholesome and nourishing. To make matters worse in 1946, the government diverted several more food ships from Britain to needier parts of the world. Lord Woolton, as chairman of the Conservative party, accused it of being 'too internationally-minded'.[9]

In 1946, Mrs Eleanora Tennant launched a Face The Facts Committee on behalf of housewives and attacked the introduction of bread rationing. When she published a poster listing all the MPs who had voted in favour of the measure, the House of Commons held her guilty of a breach of privilege, while admitting that it was 'on a petty and insignificant scale'. Next year, a vicar's wife in Kent started a Housewives' League to hold government ministers accountable for mismanagement of the food supply. She attracted thousands of supporters. The government reminded the protesters that there had been two bad harvests and a world shortage of wheat.

Critics pointed out that other countries managed food supplies far better. Unfortunately, few people could go to other countries to see for themselves. The government had imposed a £25 limit on the holiday allowance to protect the nation's shrinking dollar reserves. To buy more than the limit of foreign currency was a criminal offence, punishable with fines and imprisonment. In the spring of 1947, the victims of a splendidly named currency racketeer on the French Riviera, Max Intrator, were to discover these penalties for themselves. Convictions for currency offences rose from 322 in 1946 to 4,583 two years later.

With the overseas world closed to them, seven million visitors headed for Blackpool during 1947 and many thousands more filled to capacity the new 'holiday camps' of Billy Butlin. Most of these were former military camps which had been renovated, though at Skegness the blankets still bore the insignia 'H. M. S. Royal Arthur'. To lighten the austerity gloom, Butlin hired the San Carlo Opera Company for the season and, subsequently, the London Symphony Orchestra, conducted by the comedian Vic Oliver.

The 'good time' which most people for the past six years had equated with 'after the war' remained ever more elusive. Particular figures in government became targets of resentment. The terse and tenacious Prime Minister showed traits of the 'Major Attlee' he had been before the war. Among others, Ernest Bevin as Foreign Secretary was spoken of as 'a soak', while little popularity attached to the austere and lofty presence of Sir Stafford Cripps, Chancellor of the Exchequer, whose unfortunate duty it was to tax and restrict. The pound had traditionally traded at about five dollars and it was Cripps in 1949 who announced a dramatic devaluation, pegged at

$2.80. Few people could now afford to travel outside the sterling area, even had they been permitted to do so.

There were more immediate objects of dislike. Not all food was rationed and when it was coupon-free a queue formed. A principle of post-war life was, 'If you see a queue, join it.' Some shopkeepers exploited the desperation of housewives and would not open their doors until they felt the queue was long enough, even if it was so long that those at the end got nothing. Unsurprisingly, one fishmonger was attacked by an exasperated customer with a wet haddock.

3

In a time of severe shortages, it was not hard to make criminals of those who had never thought of themselves as such. By 1947 the Chief Constable of Birmingham attributed rising crime to the ease with which stolen goods found a ready market among those who would not normally buy them. George 'Jack' Frost, retiring from the Flying Squad at the end of the war, identified the cause more precisely. Service life had conditioned men and women to crime. They had learnt for years to get away with what the services called scrounging, 'but which in Civvy Street is theft'.[10]

The moral attitude to official property was certainly more relaxed than it had been before 1939. Yet the change went deeper. Before the end of the war, Sir Richard Acland, a former Liberal MP, had formed a new political party and had given away his estate to the nation. The Common Wealth party meant exactly what its title implied. It advocated the common ownership of everything that could reasonably be owned in common. This was far more revolutionary than anything in the Labour manifesto. During the war, by convention, political parties did not contest by-elections but allowed the party of the former MP a clear run. The Common Wealth party ignored this.

Its policies might sound like an eccentric splinter group of Cromwellian politics three centuries earlier but its candidates did well in by-elections. They were not, on the whole, working-class socialists but a new middle class. At the Chelmsford by-election in April 1945, Wing Commander Millington, twenty-eight years old, commander of an operational bomber squadron, was the Common Wealth candidate. He seemed an improbable revolutionary but he overturned a government majority of 16,624 and was comfortably elected by 6,431. His party was not to survive the general election of 1945 but its successes were a pertinent comment on attitudes to wealth, privilege and common property.

The boundaries of law and criminality in this area were dramatically put to the test in the summer of 1946, almost a year to the day after the last shots of the war were fired. The greatest post-war problem, it seemed, was not food. However unappealing the diet, no one starved. Nor was it to be clothing. At the worst, one could 'make-do-and-mend'. It was certainly not employment. The worst damage that the war had done, and the most difficult to repair in the short term, was in what the economists called vaguely 'the housing stock'. More simply, many of those returning from the services were virtually homeless.

As demobilization continued and men rejoined their families or created new ones, the extent of the deficiency was clear. Houses which had been condemned before the war were still standing, fit for nothing but demolition. They would have to be occupied in the emergency. Towns and cities were scarred by thousands of rubble-strewn bomb-sites, some not cleared until well into the 1950s. About 250,000 houses had been destroyed by enemy action but about fifteen times that number had been more or less severely damaged. Many thousands would never be habitable again. Even where the damage to buildings was less, there had been neither the materials nor the manpower during the war to do more than patch them up. By 16 November 1945, the situation had deteriorated so far that Aneurin Bevan, as minister responsible for housing, invited the more fortunate to join a 'share-your-home' plan. If a voluntary scheme failed, he threatened to use a Defence Regulation to impose wartime billeting again.

The government had initiated a building programme to produce council houses of a high standard. By 1950, it claimed to have built a million homes since the war but its opponents pointed out that more than a third of these represented temporary accommodation. Some were estates of 'prefabs', metal bungalows whose sections were made in factories and then bolted together on site. Though intended to last only ten or twenty years, a few were still occupied by satisfied tenants sixty years later. 'One hundred thousand houses a year' remained an electoral slogan for a decade after the war.

In the summer of 1946 the shortage was at its worst. Two million servicemen and women had been demobbed in twelve months with more joining them every day. There were also 160,000 Polish servicemen who chose to stay in Britain rather than return to Communist-ruled Poland. Against this flood the government had done its best. It had built 60,420 houses, two-thirds of them as estates of prefabs. It had repaired 100,000 damaged houses and, in all, had housed 210,000 people. There had been 400,000 people in need of rehousing in London alone. Families throughout the country, a large proportion of them with small children, found temporary refuge with their relatives or else in sub-standard accommodation. In the summer of 1946, one woman described to a newsreel reporter how she and her husband shared a single room with another married couple. Such conditions were little better than the London slums of the 1880s.

In August 1946, a movement began which in the 1930s might have been denounced as robbery and even now had an air of political revolution. With 40 per cent of its troops demobbed, the Army had declared 800 sites redundant, the Royal Air Force added forty-five camps and the Royal Navy another five. They varied from those big enough to become holiday camps to others which were individual anti-aircraft batteries or Royal Artillery coastal batteries with living quarters and facilities for the gun crews. Once the services had withdrawn, the property became the responsibility of the Ministry of Works.

For some weeks a number of 'squatters', as they were now called, had been living on a former army site near Sheffield and another at Beighton in Derbyshire. No one in authority had apparently noticed them or, at least, no one had cared. Then, on the weekend of Saturday 10 August, thirty families moved into army huts near Middlesbrough and were installed there before the local authority or anyone else knew what had happened. The invaders were not families of the work-shy but those who had come to take jobs and were without accommodation. There had been no guard on the sites because it had not been thought necessary.

On the same weekend, other families occupied thirty-two army huts at Harnham, near Salisbury, which had stood empty for six months. Eight miners with their wives and children, who had nowhere to live and were staying with relatives, moved into Royal Artillery huts at Seaham Harbour. The arrivals were orderly. Men and women chalked their names on the doors of the huts, elected camp committees to see that no damage was done, and put seven shillings a week into a 'rent pool' to show that they were willing to pay the owners of the accommodation.

In most camps vacated by the services there was no water supply, sanitation or electricity. Doncaster Rural District Council was the first to turn on water for its new tenants. As news broke of the weekend occupations, the movement drew followers from all parts of the country. On Monday 12 August, a hundred squatters took over Vache Camp at Chalfont St Giles, Buckinghamshire. This had been prepared by the Ministry of Works for Italian women whom Polish soldiers had met and married in the Mediterranean campaign. Army officers with Military Police escorts visited the camp but made no attempt to intervene. These squatters also showed their good-will by forming a camp committee and putting seven shillings a week into the rent pool. However, the chairman of the committee told the press, 'We must resist any effort to turn us out and by sticking together we can do it. If the local authorities try to move us, they will have a bit of a job now.'[11]

The public soon learnt of the conditions from which some squatters had escaped. A Liverpool man had moved with others on 12 August to Nissen huts at a disused anti-aircraft camp near West Derby, even though there was no water supply nor was there likely to be, since Liverpool corporation had passed responsibility for that to the War Office. For three years, this man, with his wife and daughter, had been living in one room of a Liverpool house, long ago condemned by the sanitary authorities. He saw no other escape and a Nissen hut could be no worse.

Their actions showed that these were decent and honourable people, desperate at the conditions in which they and their children were living. On the other side, the government protested that such camps were only temporarily vacant. They had been intended to house Polish soldiers, as well as their wives, who had nowhere else to live. Some sites had been intended as centres for emergency teacher training and others for training badly needed skilled labour. The word 'anarchy' was heard, as was the argument that the families who got such accommodation were those who pushed themselves forward most vigorously and not necessarily those who might be in greater need but who obeyed the law.

To impose law in this situation would have been difficult. The movement had gathered speed within hours. Before Monday was over, perhaps because news was breaking throughout the country in radio bulletins, fifty families arrived at White City Camp, near Bristol. They stood patiently in the rain while a police inspector, through a loud hailer, instructed them in the law of trespass. Then they bypassed the guard on the gate and moved in. By evening, more miners had joined those on the seafront at Seaham, others had occupied a disused miners' hostel near Doncaster, and a further group had taken over a camp near Jarrow.

The Ministry of Health was still the government department responsible for housing. As the occupations gathered pace, it warned the squatters and local authorities that some camps were not fit to be lived in and must be cleared out before a slum developed. It insisted that the proper course for those wishing to occupy unused sites was to discuss this with the local authority and the area office of the ministry. Unfortunately for the ministry, most local authorities quickly decided that restoring supplies of water and electricity was preferable to having an epidemic on their hands. Any attempt to evict the squatters would also have had to take into account a very large number of children. The occupants at Chalfont St Giles had now increased to seventy families, including 130 children. In the event of evictions, what was the local authority to do with these?

Next day, twenty families occupied an anti-aircraft battery near Newport and thirty more took over condemned tenements in

Edinburgh. Three more camps were occupied round Bristol. While the city council's Housing Committee warned the squatters again about the law of trespass, Alderman W. H. Hennessey went out to the camps and addressed the occupiers.

> Sit tight. Carry on. Take no notice of rumours. The police cannot touch you. They cannot drive you out of your huts unless they are given sanction by the Ministry of Works in London and I am satisfied the minister will not give the police power to enter this estate and turn the people out.[12]

By this time, within two days of its first occupations, Vache Camp, near Chalfont St Giles, was an organized community. Some of its billets resembled prefabs, though many were metal Nissen huts. Each family had a single room divided by a curtain into bedroom and living room. There were old-fashioned army stoves which allowed a primitive means of cooking, fuelled by dead timber nearby. Each door had the chalked message 'Taken by ——' followed by the name of the family.

On 14 August there were further legal warnings and announcements that some evictions might be necessary either where the huts had been occupied before they had been declared redundant or where the accommodation was insanitary. Yet no move was made to evict the squatters. Instead, Grimsby council handed over the keys of twenty-two RAF huts, turning on water and electricity. Overnight, nine more camps were occupied in the Bristol area. For its size, Bristol had been one of the worst damaged cities during the war. Its squatter population was now so large that the police and the city council could do nothing but leave them where they were. Further occupations on the same day occurred in Warwickshire, Chesterfield, Durham, Ellistown in Leicestershire, Worthing, Coventry and Carlisle.

It was just four days since the first occupation. On the fifth day, the nine camps occupied round Bristol increased to twenty. Seven were taken over in Birmingham and others in Cowley, Chester, Barking, Gloucester, Salisbury, Eccles, Basingstoke and a United States Air Force camp at Watford. The RAF police started an armed patrol at the WAAF camp at Driffield and squatters at Kingsway, Derbyshire, were given notice to leave. They sent a telegram to the Minister of Health, Aneurin Bevan. 'Occupants Army huts Derby being turned out, all homeless, require your immediate assistance.'

Bevan, the standard-bearer of post-war socialism, who denounced the Conservative party and capitalism as 'organized spivery', and confessed that he had regarded its members as 'lower than vermin', was not in an easy position. His sympathies were entirely with the squatters but a minister of the Crown, as his civil servants reminded him, must not incite people to break the law. In another three months five squatters' leaders would stand in the dock of the Old Bailey on precisely that charge. Bevan said wryly that he understood the squatters' action but could not give it his official support, otherwise the families would complain to him about the conditions in the camps they had occupied. Ironically, his support was echoed by Mrs Churchill, whose husband was now leader of the opposition. Opening the first two council houses to be completed in his Woodford constituency since the war, she remarked:

> These people are referred to by the very ungraceful term 'squatters', and I wish the press would not use this word about respectable citizens whose only desire is to have a home and to keep their families together, and who are perfectly willing to pay rent, rates and taxes.[13]

As Mrs Churchill was speaking, a deputation from Vache Camp went to Downing Street to ask for the Prime Minister's assurance that other vacant camps in the area would be handed over to the homeless. Occupations continued elsewhere. Near Taunton, War Department police ejected squatters from Burnshill Camp, whereupon they went away and occupied two other sites.

By now the movement had turned its eyes to other properties which were not vacant. Prestwick aerodrome, the most important in Scotland, had been handed over to the RAF by the Royal Canadian Air Force as it left for home. On the Saturday night of Mrs Churchill's speech, messages flashed on cinema screens or were telephoned to dance halls in the area, summoning RAF personnel back to camp. They were needed to guard the aerodrome from an invasion of squatters who were already in possession of fifteen huts.

A week after the beginning of the occupations, it seemed that the squatters had won the battle. Local councils negotiated the transfer of service personnel so that more camps could be used to house the homeless. The RAF Regiment was moved from Belton Park, Grantham, and other units from Braunstone Park, Leicester. The Ministry of Health gave in and instructed all local authorities to secure supplies of water and electricity to the camps. At Milton Park, near Peterborough, Captain W. T. Wentworth-Fitzwilliam welcomed squatters to the huts on his estate. As he was walking round the grounds, a man chalking his name on the door of a hut turned to the captain and asked amiably, 'Have you picked yours yet, chum?'

There had hardly been time to discuss whether the conduct of the squatters amounted to a crime, as opposed to civil trespass, or whether such vacant property should be available to anyone who needed it. However, before the end of August, there were signs that expropriation would spread from government to private property. So far, the action was characteristic of the wartime years; it had been on a par with 'scrounging' or 'liberating' in the services, where no one was hurt because the property belonged to the government, which meant that it belonged either to no one or to everyone. Moreover, the squatters' action had relieved the government of a major embarrassment over its housing policy, if only in the short term.

To cross the line by occupying private property appeared a step towards criminality. On 16 August, Oxford squatters, who had previously occupied a rocket battery at Cowley Marsh, took over temporary Admiralty huts on Balliol College playing fields, in Jowett Walk. Elsewhere, members of a sports club at Gravesend went to a meeting at their headquarters and found a family in residence. The father told them, 'You can't hold a meeting. I am living here now.' The police were informed but the family remained in possession.

August 1946 had seen occupations accompanied by good sense, tolerance and humanity. The same was not true of September. On 8 September came London's 'Great Sunday Squat', organized by the

Communist Party or, at least, by those who happened to be officials of that party. At 2 p.m., about a thousand people representing
four hundred families began to converge on Kensington High Street
underground station, most of them carrying bedding and quite a
number having come from Stepney. They were marshalled and
escorted to a large block of luxury flats in Duchess of Bedford's
Walk, between Campden Hill and Holland Park. The flats had been
requisitioned for refugees during the war and had just been refur-
bished by the Ministry of Works before being handed back to their
owners. Within ten minutes of arrival, the families were inside the
block and were being directed to individual flats. They were mostly
young, carrying suitcases and bedding for the night, some of the
women with babies in their arms. Taxis arrived with those who
were more heavily laden, followed by furniture vans carrying the
first of the household possessions.

It was evident that even a block of this size could not accommodate so many. New arrivals increased the total number to some
500 families. The vestibule was full of those who waited patiently
to be told where to go, while others stood outside in pouring rain.
The police summoned the Women's Voluntary Service to provide
cups of hot tea. Two organizers of the occupation, Councillor
Rosen of Stepney, who had led the Stepney Rent Strike before
the war, and Denis Goodwin, sent out scouts to see what other
property in the area might be available. By 5 p.m. squatters had
taken possession of a number of vacant houses nearby and had
marched three abreast to occupy a block of sixty flats at Melcombe
Regis Court in Weymouth Street, Marylebone. They also took
over Moray House, the home of Lord Ilchester, and five other
buildings.

Families who existed in a single room suddenly found themselves
in possession of flats with four or five rooms, tiled bathrooms and
kitchens, whose weekly rent of ten guineas was three times their
weekly wage. Other squatters, who were installed in Abbey Lodge,
Regent's Park, occupied flats with a rental of £24 a week, which
might take two months to earn. There could be no question of
compensating the owners.

Whatever its ethics or legality, the Sunday Squat had been a model of protest in action. Its organizers were jubilant. 'We have been waiting long enough for places such as this to be taken over for housing the homeless,' said Denis Goodwin. 'We hope the action taken today by 1,500 Londoners will call attention to the existence of places such as these.'

It certainly called the attention of the government to problems of housing and public order. Ten days later, Aneurin Bevan received a deputation from the London Trades Council and assured them that 120,000 London families numbering 400,000 people had been housed in the past sixteen months. The deputation, representing 600,000 workers, demanded that all empty buildings should be requisitioned immediately and all materials controlled at source to prevent their use for inessential purposes.

By this time, the Ivanhoe Hotel in Bloomsbury had also been occupied, as had Abbey Lodge and Fountain Court, Victoria. Police subsequently tried to seal off some of the buildings with the result that crowds of sympathizers threw food to the squatters and staged protest marches with banners demanding that water supplies should be restored. But the tide of sympathy had begun to turn. Some regarded the Sunday Squat as Communist agitation and it was pointed out yet again that it might give homes to the most vociferous and unscrupulous, rather than to those most in need. In some cases, it also deprived people of accommodation which was lawfully and rightfully theirs, merely passing on the problem of homelessness.

An injunction was granted to the owners of Fountain Court, obliging the squatters to leave. Withdrawals began at the other premises. The London County Council was left to provide for the families. They were promised accommodation at Bromley House in Bow but the building workers who had been billeted there refused to move. Some were housed at Alexandra House in Hampstead, a home for elderly women. Most returned to their original addresses.

The repercussions, such as they were, followed in October and November. Trespass was a civil wrong rather than a crime, though a court retained an ancient right to punish a trespasser as well as award compensation to the plaintiff. In the autumn of 1946, injunctions were readily granted to evict the remaining squatters from private property. Addressing one defendant, Mr Justice Wynn-Parry made trespass sound like a crime. 'You have broken into a flat. That is a trespass, and you have no right to stay there. Whatever grievance you may have it cannot justify breaking into premises.'[14]

The five Communist organizers of the Sunday Squat faced criminal charges of 'conspiring together and with other persons unknown to incite people to trespass upon real property in London'. Apart from Morris Israel Rosen, the young Stepney councillor, they included two Westminster city councillors, a London county councillor who was also London district secretary of the party, and a bookshop manager who was secretary of the Hammersmith branch.

At their Old Bailey trial, the five pleaded not guilty but were convicted. They were fortunate in their judge, Mr Justice Stable, who showed wisdom enough not to make martyrs of them. They were bound over for two years. The judge told them that he accepted their motive was to find homes for these 'unfortunate people' and that they had been moved by 'a very genuine sense of distress'. For that reason alone he would not send them to prison. 'This case has made it clear that activities of this kind can only lead the actors to a criminal court. If people persist in this sort of thing they will come here, and the next time they will not go away for some time.'[15]

The homeless waited. In the immediate future, a shortage of building labour was a greater impediment than the scarcity of materials. A partial solution was to let those without proper homes move into the estates of prefabs before work was entirely complete, allowing tenants to finish the job for themselves. Those who accepted the offer often interpreted it as an invitation to help themselves to whatever was available at other council building sites. Raiding these at night, because no nightwatchman was thought necessary, the home builders stole bath taps, refrigerators, even asbestos panels, and whatever else was needed and light enough to carry away. A fence was put up by the builders to protect their property but by the next night it had gone. As one of the new tenants confessed cheerfully, 'Everyone was on the nick.'

Sometimes the losses from prefab sites had all the signs of professional robbery. Fifty refrigerators were stolen in a raid on a building site at Harlesden during the last weekend of May 1946. Refrigerators, as well as gas and electric cookers worth thousands of pounds, had been stolen from other sites in recent weeks but there had been a surge over this May weekend with twelve raids, all bearing the marks of a single gang. They had occurred across the South-East of England at Harlesden, London, Margate and Brighton, as well as at Bournemouth. Some prefab tenants already in residence were quick to see what could be made from the fittings of their own houses by selling the council's refrigerators and cookers to black market-eers who called at their doors.

The National Assistance Act 1948 required local authorities to provide accommodation for the homeless. Neither this nor an increase in the number of houses available ended the occupation of camps by squatters. Four years after the summer invasion of 1946, some families were still in residence. The worst that the authorities had predicted had come true. For example, a colony of 1,200 people was housed among picturesque surroundings at Theale in Berkshire, in wartime army huts. These tenants consisted principally of those who had worked in a nearby munitions factory during the war and had stayed on in the district.

Many of the huts at Theale were now sub-standard by any descrip-tion, a single space divided by a curtain into living room and bedroom but with no window in the 'bedroom' itself. There was green mould on the furniture, rotting linoleum on the floor, flooding in winter, and an infestation of rats. Sickness among the children was well above the average for the area. The government allocation of new houses to the district was sixty a year and there were 720 applicants on the waiting list. It would be a long time before anything was done for the 1,200 squatters, unless they could do it for themselves. The air of a makeshift holiday camp, which had kept spirits high four years earlier, had long ago dissipated.

Conditions were as bad at Blackbushe airfield, on the road between Camberley and Basingstoke, when the local council met to discuss the fate of the squatters in August 1950. 'Can we give no hope to the people living in huts at Blackbushe?' asked one member anxiously. Strict financial controls on building dictated the reply, 'We should not give them hope, because there is no hope.'[16]

4

Squatters were increasingly regarded in the post-war world as people who were otherwise instinctively law-abiding but who had been driven to escape intolerable conditions for themselves and their children. Whatever the courts might think, they had only done what a million more fortunate families might have done in their circumstances. For others, post-war scarcity evoked thoughts of plunder. No area of opportunity offered a more tempting prospect than so-called 'war surplus'. There were already successful entrepreneurs like George Dawson who signed contracts with the government for removing scrap and the wreckage of conflict from the battlefields of the war. The trick elsewhere was to contract for wreckage, while helping oneself to brand-new equipment.

The aftermath of war was also the heyday of the arms trader. An armoured car could be bought for £45 and even a bomber for a few hundred pounds. Bren guns were sold wholesale. In Palestine, arrangements had been made for the withdrawal of the British Army in 1948, leaving the Jews and the Arabs free to decide the future of the territory in the war that was to follow. Colonel Thomas Gerard Gore, DSO, OBE, was a former Deputy Director of Ordnance at the War Office. He had been taken prisoner after a valiant last stand at the siege of Tobruk in June 1942. Having escaped from his captors, he reached Corsica in a small boat, and became a hero of the Normandy beaches at D-Day. In February 1948, five months before the British withdrawal from Palestine, Colonel Gore was sent out to command No. 614 Ammunition Depot, about twelve miles from Haifa. His second-in-command was Major Ralph Newman and the senior NCO was Staff Sergeant Grieves. The depot contained large quantities of small arms and ammunition, principally Bren guns and Browning machine-guns. The orders from the War Office were to dump the entire stock of arms and ammunition in the sea.

It seems that Major Newman was the first to suggest that they might just as easily sell all the guns to the highest bidder. At this time, according to the major, Colonel Gore had become 'infatuated' with an Egyptian woman and had agreed to sell the guns to the Arabs. To cover the sale, there was a surreal plan in which it would be made to seem as if the weapons had been stolen while being transported near the Syrian frontier and that both officers had been killed. They would both make their escape through Syria. 'A bogus ambush was to be staged . . . A burned out car and two unrecognizable bodies were to be found. On reflection I realized this plan was not practicable. When Gore and I arrived in Syria we would be liquidated. This fate was in fact planned for us.'

If the guns could not be sold to untrustworthy Arabs, the Jews would be ready customers. Major Newman contacted the Jewish underground organization Hagana. With the agreement of Colonel Gore, it was arranged that the weapons should be transferred to Hagana for an approximate sum of £20,000, or £600,000 in modern terms. Staff Sergeant Grieves supervised the transit of six truckloads of machine-guns and ammunition, a task for which he received £1,000. Staff Sergeant Dennis Ivers acted as escort, standing in the back of the truck with a Sten gun. The arms were taken to a Jewish camp five or six miles away.

Major Newman's contact at the camp was Bob Silver, a Jewish civilian. However, the payment of the money for the weapons was to take place in England. Silver tore a £1 note in half. One half remained with him and the other was given to the major. The money and Bob Silver's half of the note would be sent to England. When Major Newman or Colonel Gore produced their half of the note, the cash would be handed over. This had been arranged through Bob Silver's brother, Bernard Silver of Dewsbury. In the following year, the major met Bernard Silver in Dewsbury and handed over his half of the banknote. They met again a few days later in London and, at Euston Station, Mr Silver handed Major Newman a suitcase containing £18,000 in British banknotes.

Major Newman celebrated this windfall by purchasing four bungalows at Deepcut, a café at Didcot and a yacht. He drew attention to himself and, subsequently, suspicion. At his court martial, where the evidence at once implicated Colonel Gore, he was sentenced to be cashiered and imprisoned for six months.

Though Colonel Gore pleaded not guilty, he was convicted on three of the five charges against him, cashiered and sent to prison for two years. He had not been the moving spirit in the fraud but he received the heavier sentence as being the senior officer. How truly he was in command of the situation might be doubted. The officer who acted as his escort at the trial revealed that the colonel seemed happiest when left to himself to read his favourite magazines, the *Gem* and the *Magnet*, with their adventure stories for schoolboys.[17]

Many of the civilian war surplus swindles seemed foolproof and some were so devised that any attempt by the police or the authorities to find out who had perpetrated them went round in a complete circle. One of the neatest in 1945–6 consisted of buying new military cars, lorries, jeeps and smaller items, invoiced as though they were scrap, and selling them quickly at full price. The racket flourished in England but was endemic in Europe and particularly in the British zone of occupation in Germany. Operations were conducted by limited companies, set up and liquidated in short order, taking with them any proceeds of the black market currency deals by which the whole process was often funded.

At the war's end, the vehicles left behind by the departing American forces, as well as those no longer needed by the British services, were gathered into dumps and vehicle parks. In 1945–6, one of the largest parks of American vehicles was at Nottingham. They were offered for sale and bought almost at once. Soon afterwards, an anonymous letter was received at Scotland Yard alleging that the sale was a fraud. These were brand-new cars, lorries and jeeps, which had been invoiced and sold at scrap metal prices.

Chief Inspector Harry Fluendy of Scotland Yard undertook the investigation. He was handicapped from the start by a doubt as to whether the British could claim jurisdiction over American property. If not, it was unlikely that the American authorities would any longer concern themselves with vehicles of which they simply wanted to be rid. As the investigation progressed, no one disputed that the vehicles had been brand new. It was not even difficult to trace the agents for the buyers. They had paid the prices asked and they had receipts for the transaction. There was no apparent crime.

The first question was how someone at the Ministry of Supply had put an absurdly low value on the vehicles. The second was the identity of the true 'buyers' behind the agents. The brains were operating from Europe. If it was possible to bring them to account, Scotland Yard could surely locate the official in the Ministry of Supply who had presumably been bribed to value the vehicles so cheaply. Short of that, this would appear like a legitimate sale, though at prices which were little short of robbery.

The Continental market in war surplus was scarcely controlled at all. Indeed, in the first two years after the war the modern equivalent of £40,000,000 in vehicles and wireless equipment did not come up for sale because it had vanished before anyone could put it on the market. In general, it was possible for currency racketeers to launder their profits and to buy war surplus at knock-down prices simultaneously. This was done by a simple standard-form contract with the Allied Control Commission. The form which the pseudonymous purchasers filled in entitled them to buy a stated number of vehicles of a particular type from the lorry parks at set prices. The proceeds of currency fraud were thereby invested in vehicles, but also in gun carriers, rifles, food and even medical supplies from army dumps.

Detective Superintendent Charles Vanstone and Detective Sergeant Ronald Vivian set out for the British Zone of Germany. Their visit and their recommendations prevented the worst abuses from 1947 onwards. However, two years after the end of the war, those who had laundered black market money through that system had vanished. They disappeared, as if in the receding images of magic mirrors, into a mist of limited companies who, one after another, had gone into liquidation and thin air. The explanations given to the investigating officers were far from satisfactory but the worst discovery was to be made when they returned to London.

The Ministry of Supply was a wartime creation rather than a permanent department of government. Sooner rather than later it would be wound up, and its present condition resembled a 'closing down' sale. It had lost a lot of the information which should have been at its fingertips. It was also overrun by bureaucratic demands of post-war disposal and dispersal. Some of its records were misplaced among thousands of others and a good many had disappeared. In the light of such conditions, it seemed quite possible that the transport at the vehicle park in Nottingham had been innocently valued by an official in London who had never seen the vehicles but acted on information from a third party, now unknown.[18]

A further problem was that the Ministry of Supply remained an easy target at dumps it could not properly guard. On 1 October 1947, Flying Squad officers raided barns in the village of Cuddesdon, near Oxford, after a long Scotland Yard investigation. They discovered twelve lorryloads of furniture, cooking utensils and typewriters, all stolen in recent weeks from the ministry's dumps across the country. Even within the same area, they found another twenty-five lorryloads of the ministry's property soon afterwards.

The ministry was also the victim of a widespread racket which surfaced at a supply dump on Newbury racecourse in 1947. A purchaser would bribe a foreman and his assistants to load his vehicle with goods for which he had not paid, as well as with a few which he had bought legitimately. Six men went to prison for the Newbury thefts but, short of catching the swindlers in the act, the authorities might have to accept that the missing stock had become yet another haul for thieves who had broken in from outside.[19]

Some swindles were merely a matter of paperwork. One of the simplest, running in January 1948, was to buy a consignment of war surplus for export, which automatically exempted it from purchase tax, and then to divert it to the home market, pocketing the substantial amount that should have been paid in tax. It was an offence, in any event, to divert to the home market products licensed only for export, but it was far harder to catch those who did not export goods when they should have done than those who had exported them when they should not. When six men went to prison in October 1953 for periods ranging from five years to eighteen months for diverting goods from the export to the home market contrary to government regulations, Mr Justice Sellers in the Court of Criminal Appeal described the whole area of post-war export controls as 'a free field for the dishonest trader'. To track the goods and make sure that they, rather than their packaging or invoices alone, had been sent abroad was well beyond the current resources of the Ministry of Supply or the Board of Trade.[20]

But by no means all the agencies of enforcement were as ineffective as the Ministry of Supply had proved to be. The Special Investigation Branch of the Royal Corps of Military Police, created early in 1940 as an equivalent to the civilian CID, was extremely active in the immediate post-war years. Among other information which came its way in 1947 was the story of wholesale fraud at the Royal Ordnance Depot at Honeybourne in Worcestershire, apparently involving almost everyone at the camp. No one at Honeybourne was complaining, but there was enough evidence to warrant an investigation. Because the conspiracy appeared to be so widespread and there was no certainty that anyone already there could be trusted, SIB sent in an undercover soldier as a first step. This was done unobtrusively by waiting for the first vacancy at the camp and posting in a replacement who was their own man.

Honeybourne had been a US Army camp. When the Americans left a year earlier the establishment was handed over to British military personnel who held it on behalf of the Ministry of Supply. The depot was extensive enough to be called 'a small town of huts'. A large amount of equipment left behind by the Americans was described airily by the ministry as being worth 'hundreds of thousands of pounds', which would equate to many millions in modern terms. The stores housed medical supplies, refrigerators, washing machines and transformers, as well as considerable quantities of bedding, towels and dressing gowns. The last three items were all rationed in England for another two years and the rest were unobtainable anyway. Indeed, washing machines were almost unknown in England except insofar as they were depicted in Hollywood films. Most of the items in the stores were the stuff of which the black market was made but soldiers alone were not well placed to handle them, certainly not in the case of refrigerators and washing machines.

The first information reaching SIB suggested that the racket involved the lieutenant colonel, who was the commanding officer, his major, a captain, a lieutenant and two civilian contractors. It was actually far more widespread than that, though the lieutenant colonel and the major were ultimately to be acquitted on charges of conspiracy. There had been no sense of alarm among civil servants because everything appeared to be in order at Honeybourne. Sometime before this the Ministry of Supply had sent one of its officials, James Hampson, to make a careful inventory of the good things which the Americans had left behind.

Unfortunately, Mr Hampson had been deeply implicated from the start in the ransacking of the depot and was to go to prison three months later for the theft of a large quantity of bedding from the stores and sixteen refrigerators. These were not small domestic refrigerators of the kind that prefab tenants were stealing to complete their homes, but large commercial machines. One of those at Honeybourne was sold to a hotel in Hereford for £200. Refrigerators were uncommon and expensive in 1947 but the modern equivalent price in this case would be about £6,000 each. Sixteen of them would have helped to buy Mr Hampson a very substantial house, had he not already had one in London with a sitting tenant. The tenant complained that there was very little bedlinen there. By carrier from Honeybourne came twelve fine quality brand-new sheets containing enough material to wipe out most of an annual clothing coupon allowance, followed by a further delivery of blankets.

The next stage in the conspiracy involved two South Wales contractors. These were a factory manager from Whitchurch in Cardiff and a motor engineer or garage owner from Tylorstown. Between them they had enough transport and drivers to take the stolen goods wherever they were needed. These entrepreneurs were far too careful to drive goods direct from the depot to the customers or to their own premises. So far as the ministry was concerned, it was better that the loads should get 'lost' somewhere along the way. The route between the thieves and their clients ran first through another Ordnance Supply Depot on the South Wales coast at Barry. Goods would be loaded up at Honeybourne, consigned to the depot at Barry and then driven away from Barry, which would not miss them because it had not been expecting them in the first place.

Another of the conspirators, Lieutenant Herbert, was stationed at

Barry and able to supervise the arrival and departure of the loads. In the event of trouble at Honeybourne, it could be shown that the goods had gone to Barry and that any problem must lie there. By that time, the trail at Barry would have gone cold. It would look like yet another act of bureaucratic mismanagement. In a few more months, as interest in war surplus declined and the ministry was wound up, no one would bother to investigate its past history.

The goods taken from Barry were stored at warehouses in Cardiff. Lorry drivers who knew nothing of the plot were hired by the factory manager or the motor engineer to drive down from London to a rendezvous in Westgate Street, Cardiff. On the return, they were not given the address of their destination. Instead, they would follow a Humber car back to London where their load was to be delivered. Some of these loads were substantial and one driver recalled taking sixteen of the American refrigerators in a single journey.

Though they had been careful, the downfall of the conspirators was their failure to keep their mouths shut. Everyone at Honeybourne seemed to know what was going on. Since the lieutenant colonel commanding the depot and his major were subsequently acquitted, it must be presumed that they knew nothing, but they must have been almost the only two people who remained unaware of what was happening. Some of those who heard of the swindle decided to make the most of it on their own accounts.

Private soldiers now began to deal with the motor engineer from Tylorstown on his visits to Honeybourne. As one of them described it, they were already being paid by him for loading up his lorries with stolen supplies. Seeing how easy it was to rob the depot, Private Shaw and Private Ingham decided to 'do the same thing'. According to Private Shaw:

> We arranged over the phone for Mr Seal to send a wagon to the depot and we would supply him with things. I arranged to meet Mr Seal in Evesham at the roundabout at nine o'clock at night. With my assistance Mr Seal collected four loads and each time Ingham and myself were paid £100 between us. The loads consisted of dressing gowns, towels and transformers.

Not only did everyone else at the depot seem to know of the looting but now, said Private Shaw, 'everyone else was doing it'. This line was to become a familiar refrain at Worcester Assizes. The two South Wales entrepreneurs assured the privates that 'all the officers were in the swim as well.' Since those who were in the racket could not very well punish them, Shaw and his friend decided to stage a robbery at the depot, making it look like an outside job. Why they should have gone to such lengths was not explained. Perhaps they could not quite believe the motor engineer's assurance that everyone else was stealing from the stores.

The two soldiers pretended to go on leave and, with this as their alibi, crawled back through the barbed wire. Unfortunately, they were caught by the sentries, held in the guardroom, and brought before the major next day. They asked to see him in private and warned him, 'If you say anything about this, you will all be involved.' That, at least, was true.

The undercover soldier from SIB could hardly have failed to find out what was amiss. However, the investigators now faced a difficulty. If everyone in the conspiracy was to be prosecuted, there would be virtually no one left to give evidence for the Crown. In any case, civilians were involved. For this reason, Special Investigation Branch now handed over the inquiry to Worcester CID and the Director of Public Prosecutions. The director decided that the only way forward was to give immunity to everyone at the camp except for the ringleaders. Immunity, of course, would mean giving evidence for the prosecution. Those who eventually appeared in the dock included five army officers, the two South Wales contractors, and Mr Hampson from the Ministry of Supply. Though the commanding officer and his major were acquitted at Worcester Assizes, Lieutenant Herbert, who re-routed the stolen goods at Barry, went to penal servitude for five years, the motor engineer and the Cardiff factory manager for four years, Mr Hampson went to prison for eighteen months and a lieutenant at Honeybourne for six months.[21]

There was a litany of such cases in the immediate post-war years. In 1946, for example, RAF Halton became an outlet for stolen goods sold without coupons, 'a black market case from start to finish', as the Board of Trade prosecutor described it. In South Wales, during December 1949, it was the RAF Police who robbed their own camp. In 1951 it was discovered that five culprits at Moreton-in-Marsh had for some time been running an RAF equivalent of 'dead men's wages', by drawing pay for a unit of 'ghosts' or non-existent airmen. The Honeybourne case in 1947 was like many of its kind, though writ large. War surplus seldom made quite so much news again.[22]

The downfall of the conspirators seemed assured by their total lack of discretion and their decision to dispose of the stolen goods with the assistance of men who were less than dependable. Other men saw that they might create major enterprises in the post-war world by simply acquiring equipment which was war surplus and making use of it themselves.

London Aero Motor Services, which began life in 1946, yielded rather easily to temptation. At the end of the war, ex-RAF aircraft could be bought cheaply and adapted quite easily for carrying cargo or passengers, at a time when travellers by air expected little in the way of luxury. The firm purchased eighteen RAF Halifax bombers and the use of the wartime airfield at Stansted, taking over from the Ministry of Civil Aviation a year after the end of the war. For some time, the RAF remained in possession of the hangars, which were used to store equipment, but the newly arrived firm had begun civilian flights within a year. It also involved itself in what Mr Justice Humphreys at Chelmsford Assizes was to describe as 'bare-faced, wholesale conspiracy'.

The running costs of an airline were high, and equipment for maintaining aircraft or running an airfield was expensive. A good deal of what was needed sat in the RAF hangars which lined the runway. Four members of the firm discussed how best to rob the poorly guarded hangars of useful apparatus. They were assisted by the technical expertise of a wartime squadron leader from RAF West Kirby.

There was nothing subtle in their methods. The RAF guard on the hangars was so slack that when darkness fell the conspirators had only 'to help themselves to whatever they required'. All the same, one of them kept watch with a red torch and flashed a danger signal if anyone approached while the rest were in the buildings. The RAF commanding officer at Stansted noticed that a good deal of his equipment had gone and doubled the guard. This caused amusement at London Aero Motor Services. The man with the red torch remarked that the double guard provided 'double the number of men to carry away the stuff'.

The downfall of this scheme was over-ambition and a false sense of security. The removal – or theft – of enough radio equipment to operate the central tower at the airport seems to have been the last straw. The police were called by the station commander and six months later the four conspirators went to prison. It was hard to see how they had expected to get away indefinitely with blatant theft of this kind and on this scale. The most probable explanation was that they had an assumption in common with the squatters of 1946, though without such moral justification. They were helping themselves to property which no one else was using – or perhaps would ever use – and which really belonged to no one. Whether or not the RAF guards helped them to carry the goods away, it seems that they thought such assistance was quite likely. What was this theft, after all, but the serviceman's code of wartime 'scrounging' enhanced and applied during peacetime austerity?[23]

The fraudulent purchase of military vehicles as a means of laundering black market currency in the British Zone of Germany, investigated by Detective Superintendent Charles Vanstone and his team, had been the work of professionals. Honeybourne and Stansted bore the stamp of amateurism. The men from London Aero Motor Services were applying the maxims of active service to civilian life; the officers and men of Honeybourne committed a crime of opportunism, as Aladdin's cave opened before them. Both crimes, not least their participants, had a touch of Ealing comedy about them. There was nothing of the brutality rapidly being associated with professional post-war villainy. It was not hard to imagine Alec Guinness or Stanley Holloway, translated from the Lavender Hill Mob to Stansted runway, realizing as they stood there that the RAF hangars contained everything they needed to run an airline.

It had been a truism of war that the professional criminal was a poor match for the civilian opportunist. Frederick Porter of

Liverpool, who cheated the government of a modern equivalent of £20,000,000 while repairing ships for convoys in 1940–41, could have bought up Billy Hill and most other self-proclaimed 'kings' of the underworld several times over. 'Civilian' crime of this sort outlasted the war and dwindled in the 1950s. Long before then, the face of the professional post-war criminal was plain to see.

4

The Land of the Well-Greased Palm

WAR SURPLUS CRIME was the unfinished business of the world conflict. At some point, however, goods of questionable origin must be passed to the public and this required a man with a particular expertise. His was the face, the voice, the vocabulary, and the dress that people knew. He had sometimes masqueraded to the Victorians as a costermonger and to the pre-war world as a barrow boy or a tout. When he appeared in court, he preferred to describe himself as a 'general trader', which too frequently meant a receiver of stolen goods. For five or ten years after the war, he was universally known as the 'spiv' and by government ministers in 1947–8 as a 'drone', though this name never caught on.

The spiv talked with the speed of Max Miller deploying the music hall repartee of Frankie Howerd, Sid Field or Arthur English. He was the child of the racecourse, the wartime black market and the years of austerity. As a rule he was identified by his loud suit, padded shoulders and narrow waist, his soft trilby hat perched on Brylcreemed hair and feet encased in 'brothel-creeper' suede shoes. Side whiskers were a trademark, though not all spivs wore them. He might be young or middle-aged.

He was characteristically seen at the kerbside selling smuggled or stolen nylons from a cardboard suitcase, moving on when his lookout signalled the approach of the police. He had a great ability to supply the needs of the moment and to offer the very goods or services currently unobtainable. At the Wimbledon tennis tournament in July 1947 he rented stools to those who stood for hours in the queue or offered to keep their places by sitting there himself. A pavement spiv had bigger spivs on his back, who kept him supplied. 'No questions asked,' was the catchphrase. He was the man who could not only sell you what had fallen off the back of a lorry – if necessary, he could sell you the lorry itself.

Until the war was over, few people thought much about the spiv or where he came from. Now he was immediately recognized from newspaper cartoons or films like *Passport to Pimlico* (1949), where he wheeled his barrow with a cry of 'Nylons! Genuine stolen nylons!' To many, he was the 'cheapjack' with a stack of cut-price clothes or household goods, standing by his stall, chanting, 'Two quid in the shops – fifteen bob to you.' For more than a hundred years he had haunted the racetrack or obscure street corners, inviting passers-by to join him in a game of 'Find the Lady', as he dealt three cards face down on an upturned barrel. The few punters who won, and who were his accomplices, were rewarded with a lavish counting-out of banknotes to entice the dupes. The Queen of Spades was never quite where she ought to be, because that card was in his pocket all the time. Only his 'gees' or 'ricks' in the crowd were allowed to win. John Nevill Maskelyne had warned his readers against this 'sharp' and his frauds as far back as 1894. But the spiv defied warnings and even exported the Queen of Spades trick to the United States as 'Three-Card Monte'.[1]

Holidaymakers saw the spiv as a 'hammerer' in post-war Blackpool or Clacton, Margate or Southend. His pitch was usually a lock-up shop, temporarily untenanted and known as his 'run-out'. He became an auctioneer of bankrupt stock or cancelled orders, on behalf of a 'respectable jeweller'. An introductory canteen of cheap cutlery, 'Twenty quid in the shops', might be offered to an opening bid of five pounds. Without pausing, the spiv rattled on. 'Did I say five quid? Call it three. Three quid for what was selling last week in the shops down the road for twenty. Three quid. All right, then, two quid.'

By now purchasers were jostling one another, bidding fingers raised. The offers might have gone higher but the item was swiftly knocked down for two pounds. The dupes looked on and wondered how it was possible for this open-handed philanthropist to part with the goods at such prices. Not all his gifts were as bountiful but some were undoubtedly sold for less than they seemed to be worth. Most bargains were sold to his accomplices and the punters found that they had paid as much as in the 'shops down the road' for rejects. Genuine reductions were likely to be stolen merchandise to be passed on quickly. It was the spiv's role to receive goods 'knowing them to be stolen', as the charge sheet read.

Whatever his business, the spiv required an undeviating eye for human weakness. He could raise a sham auction to an art form, trading on greed and gullibility. The 'luxury' goods on offer in an age of austerity included fashion jewellery, canteens of cutlery, plated goods, cheaply produced and temptingly wrapped. A stock of more expensive items, not included in the auction, was displayed round the shop to attract the crowd. The auctioneer or 'hammerer' had his clerk, his doorman, and several ricks or gees in the crowd to help the bidding. He would soon identify a 'sarker' or two in the crowd, likely dupes in holiday mood whose avarice would get the better of their purse. The sarker was allowed to make a winning £5 bid for a 'solid silver' cigarette case. The hammerer avoided showing the case too closely during the sale but let him assume that it would be the specimen displayed on the wall.

Once the bait was taken, the hammerer went on to 'gazoomph' the sarker before the first purchase had been wrapped up by the 'clerk'. The second item was something like a canteen of cutlery, the hammerer letting the ricks and gees run the price up, then urging the sarker to make a winning bid of, say, £15. When he hesitated, the hammerer promised, if he made a winning bid, he should have the £5 silver case and the return of the money he had paid for it. The case was placed before him with his £5 on top. If the spiv was right, he had picked a mug, unable to see how he could lose. As a rule he agreed, buying the canteen for £15. But the 'gazoomph' had not yet matured.

Having bought the cigarette case and cutlery, the dupe might be persuaded to bid for a 'fine' carriage clock, with a promise of more favours to come. The ricks and the gees pushed the bidding to about £45. The sarker was again invited to make a winning bid. If he did so, he would have the silver cigarette case and his £5, as well as the canteen of cutlery and his £15. The goods and money were piled in front of him. It was increasingly difficult to draw back. When he agreed, he would find he had paid £50 for goods which, closely examined, had a total value of about £15 and were nothing like those displayed round the walls.

His prizes would be wrapped and ready for him at the end of the sale. If he saw that he had been cheated, he might not complain for fear of appearing a fool. If he confronted the hammerer he would also face the clerk, the doorman and, if necessary, the ricks and gees. He might well face a beating as a last resort. One successful hammerer was youthful boxer Reggie Kray, whose technique in a quarrel was to wait until his antagonist had his mouth open, talking, and then to deliver an uppercut which would shatter an open jaw. A complainant at a dishonest racecourse game might be confronting Jack Spot or Billy Hill, who ran gaming swindles for many years. The spiv came in far more guises than the cartoons allowed for.

Most people in the years of austerity were not concerned with carriage clocks or canteens of cutlery, however willing they might be to buy them when the price seemed right. The spiv's immediate attractions were butter and bacon, sugar or dried egg powder and the more exotic kinds of tinned food. To supply this demand, he did not always need the housewife to come to him, he would find his way to her, selling his goods door to door. Other hawkers might advise him where to call.

He dealt more flexibly and moved faster than any provision merchant. Sometimes he was a black marketeer and sometimes he practised simple fraud, though not as a rule in his own area. There was, for example, 'The Bottle of Whisky Trick', which ensured that the victim would never be in a position to complain. At a time when post-war whisky was scarce and heavily taxed, he would present himself at the doors of the unwary with several bottles in his hands. His story was plausible, suggesting an innate kindliness. He was the mate of a lorry driver whose vehicle had shed its load half a mile down the road. Most of the bottles were broken but a few had survived the accident. Of course, the entire cargo would be written off for insurance purposes. He was passing the house on his way back from the phone box and wondered whether the occupier would like to buy a few bottles for a pound or two.

The householder's honesty was usually laid to rest during these negotiations. What possible harm could the deal do to anyone?

Money and whisky changed hands. The kindly driver's mate went on his way. Only when the purchaser opened the first neatly repackaged bottle did the contents prove to be coloured water. A well-organized spiv with his car parked out of sight might visit twenty or thirty houses and be on his way before any alarm was raised. But what alarm could there be, unless the victim confessed an intention to receive stolen goods?

On other occasions, the spiv benefited everyone. He might call at a door and invite the housewife to buy tinned salmon – not a tin or two but an entire case. No coupons were needed, though the price was high. He was seldom refused because a housewife would feed her own family on some of the tins, selling the rest to envious friends at a little more than she paid the spiv.

Neither the Board of Trade nor the police had the manpower to pursue every individual citizen involved at this level of the trade but sometimes, thanks to a malicious tongue or information received, an arrest was made, especially where the woman seemed to go into business for herself. In September 1946, for example, a housewife's larder in Bloomsbury yielded, among other strictly rationed goods, 322 packets of dried egg powder, 63 tins of evaporated milk, 100 pounds of sugar, 107 tins of sardines, 250 bars of chocolate, 500 sheets, 250 pillowcases, 25 blankets and 70 towels, which the police not unreasonably suspected must have been 'stolen or unlawfully obtained'.[2]

Such food stocks were often staging posts in a chain of supply, when the goods were not perishable. Tinned produce, dried egg powder or sugar were the stuff of lorry hijacks or warehouse thefts. Perishable goods had to be moved quickly and perhaps injudiciously. They were more often the cause of a trader's downfall, as when Israel Fox, clothes manufacturer of Great Portland Street, was sent to prison for six months and fined £200 on 4 April 1947 for dealing illegally in rationed eggs, or Leslie Docking, provision merchant of Bermondsey, went down for three months in February 1950 for acquiring twenty sides of bacon 'without Food Ministry approval', in other words from the black market. Convictions for illegal trading in rationed food reached their height in 1947, when according to a statement of the Minister of Food in the House of Commons on 8 March 1948, 24,265 convictions were recorded.[3]

2

A spiv was only as good as his sources of supply, which usually constituted a steady trail of day-to-day dishonesty. Poorer people could not often afford to buy expensive rationed foods like bacon and butter. Unscrupulous retailers sold their 'leftovers' now described as pet food to the small-time black marketeer. As late as August 1951, the President of the National Meat Traders Association warned his members, 'I will tell the Minister [of Food] that within twenty miles of his own headquarters of the Meat and Livestock Division at Guildford cows are being slaughtered under the guise of dog-meat supplies and all the prime cuts are being openly collected for use in cafés, restaurants and hotels.'[4]

A greater danger was posed by spivs literally getting their hands on black market food. Nameless men began a 'coupon-free' sale of unhygienic ice cream from London barrows in the first peacetime summer of 1946. There were no serious incidents until the unauthorized trade reached Glasgow two weeks later, where thirty-six people were soon in hospital because the hands that served their cones and wafers belonged to a typhoid carrier.

The increasing traffic in stolen goods was evident in every new set of crime statistics. Thefts from road transport in Britain had soared from £2,500,000 in 1938, the last full year of peace, to £13,000,000 in 1947. In 1948, thefts from the railways reached £3,000,000. Road and rail combined were being robbed of the modern equivalent of almost half a billion pounds annually. It hardly needed the newly formed 'Ghost Squad' of Scotland Yard to fathom where the spiv's supplies were coming from.

Worse than the losses alone, there was a culture of dishonesty in these areas of freight transport. Industrial relations on the railways were deplorable and when two porters at Liverpool Street were caught filching tomatoes for their lunch in July 1946, and were prosecuted, the entire London area of British Railways Eastern Region came out on strike, as if a perk of the job were under threat. The matter was resolved by the magistrates, who calmed tempers by giving the men a conditional discharge. Systematic thefts continued in other industries, as if they were a supplement to wages. As late as 1965, a London dock strike followed a six-month prison sentence imposed on a worker who was caught stealing lamb carcasses. The Lord Chief Justice, dismissing his application for leave to appeal, remarked, 'I feel his real grievance is that he was the one who got caught.' Indeed, it was part of the defence at the original trial that similar thefts happened at the docks 'every day of the week'.[5]

Elsewhere on the railways, a dozen men manning the cloakroom at King's Cross were found to have been running a swindle for seven years, in which used cloakroom tickets were reissued to the public and the payments pocketed. Not until 1959 was a similar 'luggage fiddle' at Charing Cross brought to an end, when three men were sent to prison. Once again, it seemed like a perk of the job. The least guilty of the three told the police, 'You are not wanted if you don't fiddle. There are only two who don't. I have only been here since Christmas. I wish I had never seen the place.'[6]

The railways were scarcely an area of life where the spiv had much to fear. The chaotic state of the goods network enabled customers to combine with workers in supplying the black market. A Clapham High Street tailor was in the habit of sending parcels by way of Clapham Junction goods depot. The parcels clerk would agree to label them incorrectly, re-routing them to the tailor's shop. The tailor would then claim for the loss against the railways, in whose labyrinthine processes the clothes had been allegedly mislaid or stolen. The claim was paid. The tailor meantime had sold the clothes to the black market, coupon-free, at a considerably higher figure than he would have got legally. He was richer, his accomplice in the parcels office was rewarded, and the spiv who retailed the clothes could boast of contented customers.

The situation in the newly nationalized British Road Services depots was even worse than on the railways. Some of the recently recruited drivers were drawn from the ranks of the 18,000 military deserters still at large, men who were often trained service drivers, now equipped with false identity cards and ration books. As a rule they were in the pay of the men who had provided the forged or stolen documents. As late as March 1950, after five years of peace, forged ration books were changing hands at £10 to £20 each. No one any longer knew how many deserters were still on the run but the government assumed that 10,000 had made their way home to Ireland and 1,000 more to the Continent.

In the summer of 1945 a modest conspiracy involving a driver, an antique dealer and a Shoreditch tobacconist showed how easy thefts from a lorry might be. Arthur Hurndall was driving a load of 280,000 cigarettes in twenty-six packing cases to the London docks for shipment to troops in the Middle East. Hurndall stopped his lorry near Gray's Inn Road and went into a café. By the time he came out the vehicle had been stripped of its packing cases. It was one crime like many others and Hurndall's story was hard to disprove.

The insurers were inclined to cover the loss. The matter might have ended there had not the CID, as a precaution, shadowed the driver. He was seen with an antique dealer, Charles Smith. The name was common enough but this Charles Smith, though he had earned no convictions for twelve years, had a file at Scotland Yard. He was not so much an antique dealer as a junk merchant and twenty-five of the packing cases of cigarettes were found in his shop. Simon Hyatt, retail tobacconist of Shoreditch, was the outlet for the stolen goods. Smith went to prison for twelve months and Hurndall for six, Hyatt being bound over in recognition of a previously good character.[7]

Twenty years later, Superintendent Ian Forbes claimed that employees' complicity in major thefts from road transport had been endemic and was not checked until the introduction of Regional Crime Squads in 1964, which formed a nationwide network of intelligence and surveillance. By then, thefts from goods vehicles were at three times the alarming figure for 1947. In Forbes' view, a significant minority of drivers had been prepared to be 'overpowered' by a hijack gang, tied up and dumped, in exchange for a cut of the proceeds. In other cases, a driver like Hurndall would 'accidentally' leave his van unlocked, returning to find its load gone but an envelope of banknotes on the seat.[8]

Thousands of deserters joined an annual migration to the seaside in search of casual labour. Army drivers found work all the year round. If they lacked the wit for any more sophisticated crime, they had only to stay in the job for a few weeks, then drive off with a

load of goods and never come back. Anyone who wo
a spiv got his ration-free food had only to listen to the
stole a lorryload of sugar for his underworld mentor in
and who was promised grievous bodily harm if there
cross. The market for lorryloads of sugar, butter, e
powder remained active until rationing ended.[9]

Though the items might sound mundane, these w
consignments, nor were the quantities small. An eight
stolen near Stafford in March 1946 and abandoned
had lost 400 cases of butter, representing the rations
of people. Though such rations were increased as ti
lorry with sugar for 6,700 people had been stolen in
a time when guards were being mounted on Lond(
to prevent deserters breaking in and stealing the
coupons. A record for the value of food stolen seem
set by a robbery on Mitcham Common on the night
1951. A man in police uniform signalled a lorry to s
was seized, bundled into the back of a van, bound a
eventually dumped in Epping Forest. Two of the
the van away. It contained tobacco, cigarettes, packii
extract, tea and sugar, with a modern value of som

Major thefts were not always of goods on the r
when these were of luxury quality. In 1947 police
of thieves who dealt in 'fully fashioned' silk stockii
to nylons and manufactured for export. Hinckley i
had prided itself on being the home of the silk stoc
and now had almost seventy firms involved in the 1
80 per cent of all the machinery in the country
severely plagued by losses but could not see how tl
ring. The manufacture of silk stockings went thr(
processes. Each stocking came from the machine a
undyed silk. It was then seamed but was as yet 1
trimmed. The stockings were then bundled into b
dozen and sent for finishing. Security at the dyeii
stage seemed foolproof and no one could sell a stc
crude piece of silk.

In January 1947, Leicester CID received an anon

all which assured them that employees were stealing the stockings and 'flogging them at Derby and Nottingham'. They began a surveillance operation and discovered that a worker on the night shift was entering the 'white hose' room through a window with a faulty latch and stealing bags of five dozen unfinished stockings at a time. These were then taken to a man in a public house who worked as dyer and trimmer for another firm. He simply put the stockings through their final stages in his own firm. Because they were extra to the production quota there, no one noticed their departure as 'pure silk, fully fashioned'. Within a day or two they were in shops and on barrows across the Midlands and in London.[10]

The infrastructure of theft which supported the spiv and his black market was a buttress of the post-war crime wave. Some robberies involved the entire contents of warehouses of stockings or cosmetics, including Helena Rubinstein and Colgate Palmolive in 1946 and 1947, and millions of cigarettes. The Colgate Palmolive robbery was carried out with duplicate keys, which once again indicated inside help. Even razor blades became scarce as the dollar crisis and the shortage of steel took effect. Two deserters teamed up with a trio of civilian thieves to burgle Blades Industries Ltd of Slough. They were able to offer 262,000 blades at twopence each, equivalent to about £85,000 for their night's work.[11]

For several years after the war, cigarettes were in short supply. This was in part a recognition that as late as 1947 they still constituted an unofficial currency in Europe. One market in the spring of that year was financed by an Allied official who bartered an allocation of cigarettes sent to a Displaced Persons camp at Bergedorf in Germany. A consignment of 100,000 cigarettes had been diverted and sold for German marks, the money used to buy furs, cameras and jewellery from German civilians for shipment and black market sale in England. Captain E. P. Bellamy of the Special Investigation Branch of the Royal Military Police headed the inquiry. One consignment of cigarettes from Bergedorf had been sold on the illegal market for enough money to buy two fur coats, unobtainable in London. The furrier gave evidence that she had been paid a total of 78,000 marks, almost £2,000, for coats. Captain Bellamy searched the British suspect's home and found identifying

labels, which had been removed from the coats. The anonymous furs had then been illegally exported to England for sale on the black market.

In the tobacco market at home, the spiv and his associates were cared for by such robberies as the theft of 4,000,000 cigarettes from the Redhill NAAFI warehouse on the night of 31 March 1947. In that week, 8,000,000 cigarettes were stolen in the London area alone. In August 1948 the Board of Trade cut the supply of tobacco in order to conserve dollars. In the resultant shortage, there was a period when some West End tobacconists had no cigarettes to sell. Those who stared forlornly into empty windows were approached by street loiterers and offered packets of twenty at five shillings and sixpence or six shillings, almost twice the retail price. The supply remained precarious enough to make cigarettes a worthwhile target for several years.

Few robberies would match the Redhill NAAFI raid or the emptying of Wolsey's warehouse in King Street, Leicester, of the entire consignments of nylon stockings destined for London and Manchester. The thieves had entered the Leicester warehouse silently on the night of 1 December 1946 and, just as silently, tossed down the featherweight packets of stockings to their accomplices below. These might only be English 'utility' nylons but to the spiv's customers they were the soul of Hollywood glamour. At Hinckley in October 1951, thieves hacked their way through a factory wall to steal 4,000 pairs, while in London on the same night another gang drove away a van loaded with 'export only' nylons and vanished into the fog.

Nylons had been an unobtainable feminine luxury at the war's end, when most women made do with leg make-up on formal occasions and the assistance of a friend with a straight eye and a cosmetic pencil to draw a 'seam' up the back of each calf. Thereafter, they had been taxed as luxuries and while they could be sold for export at five shillings a pair, the price at home was three times as much. To the spiv, they also had the advantage of being light and easily portable, a cargo for a suitcase rather than a barrow.

A further source of supply was from those like the 'Atlantic Gang' who managed to smuggle the precious hosiery from the United

States. The 'gang' seemed to consist of individual crew members from the two great Cunarders, *Queen Mary* and *Queen Elizabeth*, who ran the gauntlet of Customs and Excise and were then met by spivs at the quayside. In November 1946, the West End price among those who marketed these contraband nylons was said to have reached the astonishing figure of £4 a pair, about 80 per cent of a weekly wage.

Nylons retained their air of American glamour and illicit possession long after clothes rationing was abolished in February 1949, but while import duty was still levied on them as luxury goods. As late as December 1951, when a Bethnal Green street trader was fined for harbouring stockings on which import duty had not been paid, the Old Street magistrate described the scale of the continuing illegal trade, whose less successful entrepreneurs appeared before him, as 'terrific'.

Police and Customs intensified the hunt for those who dealt in such goods. Two men were jailed and a woman fined in March 1952, after Scotland Yard broke up a gang whose method was simply to bring export nylons by train from Derby to London, then divert them by van to the East End black market, pocketing the ten shillings a pair which should have been paid in purchase tax. Yet the main target remained the Cunard smugglers. Customs launches patrolled the arrival of the great liners at Southampton and on one occasion found three green paper parcels of nylons, pushed through a porthole when a ship's greaser lost his nerve.[12]

In October 1951, Customs and Excise finally broke the 'Atlantic Gang' which they had been hunting for two years. They seized 10,000 pairs of smuggled nylons in raids on houses throughout the Southampton area. In the following July, the leaders of the conspiracy were sentenced at Winchester Assizes. They were not crew members of the ships, who were now spoken of as having been corrupted by these men, but a gown-shop owner from Marylebone, a bookmaker from Hammersmith, and his clerk, who were sent to prison for terms of twelve months to two years. Their system had been ingeniously simple. Trunks and suitcases loaded with nylons were sent from New York to Southampton with the names of bona fide travellers on them but with the wrong initials. Because the luggage belonged at a glance to genuine travellers, it passed through Customs and was then collected by other members of the gang. The genuine travellers would know when they saw it that it could not be theirs because the initials were wrong. However, if the luggage was opened for inspection they and not the smugglers would be held answerable.[13]

Once again, it was a tribute to the lure of the nylon stocking that, even after this, a weekend gang in February 1953 was still prepared to tunnel its way into a warehouse in Mansell Street, Stepney, to steal 20,000 pairs.

3

The only cure for spivery in the end was the abolition of shortages, particularly in the areas of clothing and petrol, where rationing continued until 1949 and 1950 respectively. Up to then, the government insisted that the dollar debt made the import of more petrol for private use impossible, while clothing, particularly luxury items, was still needed for export. In the meantime, the spiv did his best to supply the nation's needs. Though he could hardly transport stolen fuel, the currency of petrol or clothing might be supplied as forged or stolen coupons. It was not impossible to steal fuel, of course, and in Stratford East, during the last week of 1947, thieves made off with two tankers parked there containing eight tons, but theft was not common.

There were better methods of dishonest dealing in petrol on a far larger scale. On 22 December 1949, the Birmingham stipendiary magistrate sent twelve men to jail – petrol depot workers, tanker drivers and garage proprietors – for terms ranging from three to twelve months. Their scheme had a classic simplicity. The private motorist's meagre petrol ration consisted of white undyed petrol. Supplementary petrol was allowed for official and business use only and it was dyed red. It was therefore easy to catch and punish the private motorist who obtained supplementary petrol by bribery or persuasion and who was found with red fuel in the tank. The answer for these garage owners was to pay the workers at Shell Mex BP

Co., as it then was, to leave the red dye out of some of the supplementary petrol – or to let their supervisors see them putting the
dye into the tankers but to let it out through the discharge pipe
before the petrol went in.

With depot workers and tanker drivers in the scheme, the garage
proprietors had white petrol, in one case 7,259 gallons, which could
be sold coupon-free far above the regulation price. Petrol remained
strictly rationed, even though the war had been over for four years,
and it did not improve matters for the culprits when the defence
pleaded in mitigation that 'It is a thing going on practically wholesale throughout the whole of the trade.'

Yet dealing in petrol was not something for the average spiv.
Coupons remained the natural currency of the underworld. As early
as 11 January 1946, the Ministry of Fuel and Power admitted that
the thousands of counterfeit coupons in circulation were under-
mining the post-war petrol rationing system as a whole. Coupon
robberies of all kinds were also proliferating. Three nights later, a
well-organized gang stole 280,000 clothing coupons in a raid on the
Ministry of Labour offices at Hendon and ransacked the office at
Chiswick, taking 30,000 more, two nights after that. The major
petrol coupon robbery of the year, enough to supply 750,000 gallons,
took place at the Petroleum Board offices in Cardiff during the
weekend of 9–10 November.

By 3 February 1947, it was estimated that there were at least a
million stolen petrol coupons in circulation, at a time when private
motoring was still limited to about a hundred miles a month. To
the spiv, the systems of rationing were almost a licence to print
money. Sometimes, however, there were casualties in his ranks. On
7 August, two men were convicted of dealing in 12,000 forged
clothing coupons and were sent to prison for nine months and three
months respectively by the Old Street magistrate. The magistrate
looked at Alfred Goldfine's 'appalling record' and asked why he had
not been sent to the Old Bailey where, if found guilty, 'he could
have gone to penal servitude for fourteen years'. The prosecutor
said there was 'a reason'. Goldfine had saved himself by volunteering
useful information. Even in the culture of the spiv, 'grassing' played
its part. As a result of information given in this case, in January 1948

the major printers of counterfeit clothing coupons in Britain were brought to justice, having been discovered with their press at a house in Notting Hill.

Coupons were useful commodities to the spiv so long as petrol rationing lasted. Despite clothes rationing, his stock-in-trade had always been clothes themselves, nylons if he was fortunate and furs if he was extremely lucky. The articles themselves were preferred to any number of coupons. At this point, the spiv or his suppliers turned to professional gangs of thieves and the gangs, beyond his control, ultimately turned to armed robbery even for frocks and blouses.

For the time being, it was perhaps as well for both sides that in the state of post-war Britain an amateur could undertake major robberies with nothing more sophisticated than a penknife. On 9 January 1946, Scotland Yard warned shopkeepers of the danger to their stock. In cities all over the country, shops stood with their bomb damage on display. The most common result of bombing had been the blowing out of plate-glass windows, which almost every shop in the centre of a major city had suffered. There had not been the materials nor the labour to repair these fully. Nor had it been desirable to reinstall windows which burst into lethal fragments if a bomb dropped nearby. The remedy had been to insert a small window at the centre of a display frame which was otherwise filled by a form of hardboard. The material was supplied in the government's scheme for emergency repair of bomb damage.

Not until the war had been over for several months did the Ministry of Works admit that 'windows' made of this substance could be cut out by using any sharp but simple knife. The replacement material was not so much hardboard as cardboard. Half the robberies of shops in London were committed by cutting through it or, in some cases, simply by tearing it. As the manager of a clothes shop in Hammersmith explained, after suffering his fourth burglary, there was no point in removing goods from the small display panel at night if the thieves had only to cut the board and have the entire shop at their disposal.

The ministry, while admitting how easy it was to cut through the emergency boarding, protested that there was no timber to spare for repairing such premises, 'It is wanted for other things.' Glass, cement and asbestos were also in short supply. A possible precaution, the officials suggested, might be to put wire netting over the entire shopfront.

As if in response to this news, thieves descended on the nation's shops by night in the first days of 1946. Indeed, the night before the meeting between Scotland Yard and the retailers, a gang had emptied one of the most famous Bond Street gown shops, Netta, of £1,200 of its creations. By the simple method of a frontal assault on cardboard, on the single night of 22 January, they also emptied Joyce Lingerie of Shoreditch, Dorothy Perkins and Jean Jay of Harrow, and Bronhills of Fulham. It was just as easy to get into carpet shops and wireless stores, so they turned to these, as well as stripping carpets from hotels, country houses, and from the liner *Queen Mary*.

There were few better times to be a thief or a receiver than in the immediate post-war years. Goods were in short supply and yet, as the receipts for holidaymaking, cinema-going and all forms of betting soon showed, most people felt they had never had so much money. Wages were good and many servicemen had been demobbed with war gratuities of about £250 or a year's wages for a working man. The nation had won the war and believed it had earned a good time. It was in the mood to spend and the spiv ensured that it should have the opportunity to do so.

Frankie Fraser was not a spiv at the end of the war, rather a young man who controlled or supplied spivs. He recalled that robbing tailors' shops or clothing warehouses was more immediately rewarding than attacking a jeweller's shop or a bank vault, far less complicated and with a lower risk in disposing of the goods. His contemporary Ronald Hedley, the driver of the car which killed Captain Binney, had been known to his friends as Silver simply because he had burgled Silvers, the tailors at the Bermondsey end of Tower Bridge, time and again. At most clothes shops and warehouses it was easy to rob and come back, while the proprietor claimed forlornly on the insurance. Not only were suit lengths easier to steal and less trouble to dispose of, so long as material was rationed, another tailor who guessed where the cloth had come from would 'bite your arm off' to get rolls of cloth stolen from his competitors.[14]

The attack on the retail clothes trade was so extensive during rationing that even items sent to the laundry were not safe. Advance Linen Services, which catered for better quality items of soiled linen from the United States and Canadian armed forces, was described by the judge sentencing those who had looted it systematically for six months as 'the heart of the linen black market'. Certainly the stolen contents of a dry-cleaning shop in an affluent area would supply 'brand new' and expensive clothes for the spiv. A woman in a coupon-free 'new frock' was quite possibly wearing the soiled garment which a fortnight before had been sent in for cleaning and pressing.[15]

New and used clothing was stolen indiscriminately. On the night of 27 September 1946, a gang emptied Jean Lowis, cleaners, in South Moulton Street, Mayfair, while a rival group removed the stock from Gertrude Carol of Knightsbridge, whose window filling of 'thick cardboard' had been torn open without even the use of a knife. Elsewhere, quantity rather than quality was the aim and on 23 December a gang emptied the factory of Diana Dresses in Tottenham Court Road of six hundred dresses in a single visit. The 'cleaning ramp' reached its climax on 21 November 1947. A lorry belonging to AVS Cleaners had been left parked in Rampayne Street, Victoria, while the driver was briefly away from it, delivering laundry parcels. By the time he returned, his vehicle had gone. On board were clothes to be returned to 2,000 customers in the West End of London. The total value of the suits, costumes, overcoats and frocks was £15,000, or £300,000 in modern terms. By the time these clothes became 'coupon-free' bargains, the proceeds were probably enough to keep a score of spivs in comfort for the next year.

Rivalling the clothes robberies were nightly attacks on furriers' premises, whose proceeds supplied the luxury trade of the black market. While there were major robberies at firms like Worths of Grosvenor Street in January 1946 and Dickins & Jones in 1947, there was also a trade in burgling less-protected premises where furs had been sent for repair or alteration. In May 1947, Scotland Yard

revealed that fur thieves were employing those with some knowledge of the trade to alter the stolen coats and destroy their identity. This was important because fur coats were expensive and had
a special form of identification. Sewn inside was a tab pricked through
with letters or numbers giving the date and origin of the garment.
It was the first thing to be altered.

4

Where clothes shops or warehouses could not be entered simply by
cutting out a cardboard window, post-war thieves were still prepared
to give the same kind of attention to premises that they might have
devoted to a jeweller's safe before 1939, as when they tunnelled on
a June night in 1946 from one building to another to reach a hundred
rolls of silk at Lupin & Crook of Poplar with a modern value of
£140,000. Given the value put upon such goods, it was not long
before some of the clothes robbers began to carry firearms.

As the nightly attacks on tailors and furriers increased, confronta-
tions between police and criminals were inevitable. There were few
effective defences against robbery and a good many vulnerable
features in shops and warehouses. Superintendent Leonard 'Nipper'
Read recalled a post-war tailor in Camden Town who installed one
of the first alarm systems, which he described as a gramophone
record and a telephone, both contained in a tin box. If the system
suspected the presence of thieves, the telephone automatically dialled
'999' and the gramophone record complained of intruders on the
premises. Even a device of this sort was rare and was regarded at
first as an eccentricity rather than a necessary precaution.[16]

More sophisticated systems were in use by some West End fashion
houses, including the Mayfair firm of Honore in South Audley
Street, where a 'Burgot' alarm had been installed. On the night of
15 January 1946, it was set off either by one of the thin 'trip wires'
being touched or possibly by an electronic beam being broken. The
message went out, 'There are burglars at 45 South Audley Street.'
The response was too slow. A pair of policemen on the beat were
alerted and ran to the shop, in time to see two men outside. Though

a police car caught sight of the fugitives' black saloon car, it soon lost them in the streets of Kentish Town.

A week after the robbery at Honore, there was a more serious incident. A black Humber saloon, stolen from a US Army depot, was seen parked in Harrow just before 4 a.m., its back filled with women's dresses. As several men appeared and walked towards it, a night porter went across and was knocked down when he tried to speak to one of them. A few minutes later, a police car was overtaken by the stolen Humber in Seven Sisters Road, Holloway. As the chase began, the fugitives zigzagged through side streets towards Crouch Hill at about 50 mph. The police driver pulled out to overtake and tried to force the thieves off the road. A single shot was fired from the back of the saloon, followed by three more, while the police driver swerved to avoid the bullets. At that point all the lights of the Humber saloon were turned off and it drove at speed into thick fog. Scotland Yard radioed the patrol car to break off the chase for fear of an accident in the murk or a bullet finding its mark. The Humber was found abandoned at 6 a.m. in Hornsey. There was a splintered hole through its rear window, where the occupants had fired at their pursuers.

Two weeks later, on 6 February, there was another night raid in Mayfair which had all the signs of being by the same gang. Soon after 3 a.m. a dark saloon car drew up at Arline Blundell in Mount Street. Four men got out and one of them smashed a side window with a jemmy. A woman put her head out of a window of the Connaught Hotel, overlooking the scene, and one of the men shouted at her, threatening to shoot her. By now the shop alarm was ringing. A stolen army truck appeared in Mount Street to carry away the booty, which amounted to fur coats worth £3,000, twelve years' income for the average worker. Another man came out through the broken window and the two vehicles drove off towards Piccadilly. The next sighting was by a policeman on the beat who noticed the truck near St Pancras at 4 a.m. An hour later he saw it coming back down Rosebery Avenue. When he shone his torch to wave it down, a revolver shot was fired by one of the occupants and the driver accelerated towards City Road.

Criminals who fired on the police were still unpopular with much of the underworld. Next day, acting on information received, the Flying Squad arrested John Papworth, a soldier in the Norfolk

Regiment, and George Albert King, 'Ginger' King, who described himself as an undertaker's assistant of Clerkenwell. Two days later they also detained William Vigors, a young coalman from Kentish Town. The three men were charged with the theft of fifty-two dresses and other clothes from a shop in Tufnell Park on the night of 2 January and the robbery of Arline Blundell. A woman and her daughter were charged with receiving. Fourteen of the Arline Blundell furs had been found in their rooms at Barclay Street, St Pancras, as well as a revolver and ammunition. There was also a Mauser automatic in the pocket of a jacket at King's rooms at Farringdon Buildings, Clerkenwell, and a Luger under his bed. Detective Inspector Judge reported that 'In a drawer were a jemmy, a knuckleduster and a dagger, and some rounds of ammunition, and inside a glove was a collection of keys to fit various cars.'

King admitted his part in the crimes, saying that he had bought the guns from a Canadian soldier. In Mount Street, he had waited outside with his Luger pistol strapped to his waist during the fur robbery, while the Mauser on the front passenger seat was fully loaded. He was sent to penal servitude for seven years. The shallow amiability of Jack the Lad faded from the face of the black market to be replaced by the scowling gunman with a record of violence who fought his accomplices in the dock when the verdicts were pronounced.[17]

Many citizens who had lived on their rations and done their duty read of such things and thought that if it were not for the spiv and his customers, violent crimes of this nature would not occur. Why did the government not do something to eradicate the pest? The government made one patriotic effort to exterminate the species and seemed to have chosen its time well. Two years after the end of the war, almost to the day, the 'financial Dunkirk' of which John Maynard Keynes had warned came upon leaders and people alike. The spiv was now the prime target of official fury.

5

Despite its shortages, the fine summer of 1947 had seemed, deceptively, the best time since the war. After a bitter winter, the nation went on holiday in weeks of almost unbroken sunshine. More than 30,000 people filled Lords cricket ground for the test match and Neville Cardus the cricket commentator described the crowds, pale-faced from living on rations, as they watched the grace of Denis Compton 'in full flow'. Yet, as 120,000 holidaymakers left Paddington in a day, with 45,000 more from Waterloo, a reckoning was at hand.

With the parliamentary session approaching its end, the Prime Minister, Clement Attlee, came to the dispatch box on the afternoon of 6 August. His message was plain and there was a tone of anger in it. In 1945, with Britain virtually bankrupt, the new Labour government had negotiated the loan of £987,000,000 from the United States. It was intended to 'buy time' and see the country through its period of reconstruction. It was assumed by economic planners that the funding would last until 1949 and possibly into 1950. But less than half that time had passed and three-quarters of the loan had gone.

Immediate measures would include further duties on imported goods, a cut in the meagre petrol ration, a further tax on luxuries, and a reduction in the travel allowance. 'This is your battle,' Attlee told the nation. The British people must work as never before in order to export their way out of the crisis, though the labour shortage was worse than ever. Five months earlier, the government had agreed to import 4,000 workers a week from the Displaced Persons camps in Germany, where refugees of war were still housed. Some 3,900 Polish ex-servicemen in Britain were now employed in the mines and in industry.

'I am reminded', Attlee continued, 'that there is a section of the public which renders no useful purpose. Its members continue to make money in all kinds of dubious ways. We shall take all action open to us against these – I think they call themselves "spivs" – and other drones.'

Within days of this speech, the government committed itself to direction of labour in peacetime, a measure so extraordinary that Winston Churchill and the Conservative opposition accused ministers of introducing 'serfdom'. A wiser opposition comment came from Quintin Hogg, when he remarked that the measure might penalize the law-abiding but 'spivs and drones will not pay the slightest attention'. None the less, the law proposed to enforce their attention and their compliance.[18]

In August, the Supplies and Services (Extended Provisions) Bill was hurried through both houses of Parliament before the session ended, giving the Minister of Labour powers to deal with spivs and idlers. They were, as he told his National Joint Advisory Council on 23 August, 'men and women who are making no contribution to national well-being, including employees of football pools, gambling undertakings, amusement arcades and nightclubs, and certain classes of street traders'.

Few people before had seen the spiv so largely in terms of gaming. Perhaps the nonconformist conscience of socialism found it a natural redefinition. Indeed, it was not difficult to understand Attlee's exasperation, when £200,000,000, equal to a quarter of the American loan, was gambled every year on the dog tracks of Great Britain – four times the pre-war sum. Gambling at dog tracks or racecourses was legal but there was also a Byzantine network of illegal street betting, staffed by bookies' runners who were rarely, if ever, caught.

Gambling, directly or indirectly, employed an estimated third of a million people, more than either cotton or chemicals. The figure might be outrageous to the government but was scarcely astonishing when most families in the land filled in their forecast coupons for the pools every week. Half the nation had bet on horses, a third on football pools, and a fifth on dog races. Ten million people attended horse races every year, thirty million went to dog tracks and forty million to football matches.

Under the impetus of the government's attack, the spiv leapt from the pages of parliamentary reports to the cinema screen, the music hall stage and the advertising hoardings. Sanforized Shrunk Fabrics issued 'Spivs A La Mode', in which it pointed out that its own shirts, however 'loud', were pre-shrunk and would not contract after washing like those sold by a spiv. In any case, the spiv could easily be identified because he wore his hair long, 'like a perriwigg'. Soon his title became a clue in the crossword puzzles of *The Times*, while racehorses with names like Morborne Spiv and Spiv III appeared on courses throughout the land.

The Regulation of Employment Order 1947 – better known as the 'Spivs and Drones Order' – became law at the beginning of December and required such unproductive people to sign on within days for 'essential work'. It authorized officials, including under-cover staff of the Ministry of Labour, to search gambling under-takings and other likely venues in pursuit of defaulters. This proved to be little more than an exercise in moral indignation. The press visited nightclubs and amusement arcades but found no change in personnel. What use, after all, was an amusement arcade lout in Harringay to a textile mill in Lancashire? What Rhondda miner would want to entrust his safety and his life to a resentful and work-shy nightclub minder from Soho? 'Lice on the locks of victory' were, perhaps, one of the prices to be paid for the winning of a war.

The spiv had been shifted centre-stage and revelled in it. There were now 'spiv cafés', in Soho's Old Compton Street and Kentish Town Road. There was a real Spivs' Union with its own green membership card and a joke which rattled round the music halls for the next few months. One spiv was asking another about the union. 'Well,' said the other, 'it's like this, see? You pays your subs. Then, if you're down the Labour Exchange and they offers you a job, the union fights your case for you.' It seemed like the final comment on an autumn of outrage and threatened compulsion.

It was never likely from the start that the 'Spivs and Drones Order' would be effective, for one reason if for no other. The spivs included a good proportion of the thousands of deserters still at large, who had no intention of giving themselves up. They could not have registered for 'essential work', even had they wanted to, unless they were volunteering for a court martial and a military prison. As for the others, George Isaacs as Minister of Labour was able to announce with pride in the House of Commons on 16 March 1948 that 70,780 of those targeted had signed on. Of these, 13,174 were street traders, 23,289 were not gainfully employed, and 34,317 had been employed in 'non-essential' undertakings. Unfortunately, he then had to add that of the 70,780 the number who had been found suitable for 'work of national importance' amounted to just 1,692, or 3.5 per cent. When asked how many officials of the Ministry of Labour it had taken to get 1,692 idlers into work, he replied uneasily that he could not say, because 'I would have to get a mathematician to work that out.'

Most spivs, including deserters, were still in business in 1951. As if in a final insult to authority, they fastened on the Festival of Britain, a celebration on the south bank of the Thames intended to commemorate the new forward-looking nation that had arisen from the ashes of war. As a public entertainment the festival seemed rather earnest with its educational Dome of Discovery and its high-minded Festival Hall. This was the summer of Noël Coward singing, 'Don't Make Fun of the Festival'. However, there was also a funfair in Battersea Park. Spivery set up its stalls and barrows, selling rationed sweets and sticks of rock illegally. Others, who were temporarily employed as 'civil servants', began working a fiddle in which tickets collected from those just leaving the exhibition were resold to others who were just entering. This derived from the railway station cloak-room ticket fraud which had worked for years. In court, the rock-sellers pleaded that their sales had been poor because throughout the English summer rain had fallen steadily on this season of national self-congratulation. The London County Council, ignoring the order to be festive, brought seventy-five prosecutions against them.[19]

As for the exhibition tickets, this was what one of the perpetrators called 'a terrific racket'. However impressive the Dome of Discovery may have been, the turnstiles through which the public entered and left the Festival grounds were hardly an advertisement for British manufacture. One of the significant defects was in the pedal, which counted the number of people passing through. Even when operated honestly, it produced considerable discrepancies between the number of tickets sold at the entrance and the total of those leaving at the exit. On one day the difference was said to have been 10,000, often it was shown to be 200 or 300.

Three men, including a turnstile operator and a supervisor, decided to try their luck. Unfortunately, there were two spot-checkers working on the site. The conspirators approached one of them, who immediately agreed to join the swindle. The other was told that he should concern himself with the further turnstiles but need not bother with this one. The woman at the entrance kiosk recalled how the used tickets were brought back to her wrapped in news-paper because the tricksters learnt that security staff were keeping the site under observation through telescopes from the exhibition offices. She did not join the swindle but, up to this point, if the money was a little short at the end of the day, she had made it up from her own purse. Now she no longer needed to do this.

There was nothing novel about the methods for adjusting turn-stiles. In the following January the operator at Hackney Wick dog track was caught while using a system based on a duplicate key. This would halt the mechanism which checked the number of punters passing into the stadium, allowing their ticket money to be pocketed. The downfall of the Festival of Britain swindlers came when they decided to expand their operation by trying to draw the second spot-checker into their scheme. They took him to a pub near the Elephant and Castle one evening and explained the whole thing, adding that they were making enough to double a man's weekly wages without incurring any liability to income tax. The second spot-checker agreed. Next day, however, he went to the Festival authorities and thereafter acted 'under police instructions'. At the Old Bailey on 31 October, one of the men in the scheme went to prison for fifteen months, two others for twelve months each. The first spot-checker who had joined the scheme whole-heartedly to begin with was subsequently helpful to the police and escaped with a fine of £25.[20]

The turnstile racket was not at all the image of the nation which the Festival of Britain had been intended to promote. Yet, in many ways, the greater offence had been the sight of the illegal traders spoiling the scene of the festivities with the spivs' cheerful cry of 'Festival rock! Never mind the coupons!'

5

'My Victim's Body Had Followed Me Home'

PERHAPS THE GOVERNMENT had been ill-advised to engage in direct conflict with those they denounced as spivs and drones, a brawl from which it might emerge as bespattered as they. Even while legislation and warnings dominated the new parliamentary session, spivery on a far grander scale was twining itself round ministers and officials in an embrace which brought resignations and recriminations in the following year.

The spiv was not only a barrow-boy receiver of stolen property or an amusement arcade idler, though he might share their moral suppleness. He sometimes moved in what became known as 'the corridors of power', and sometimes he resorted to murder. Sidney Stanley, a stateless Pole and undischarged bankrupt, was a spiv who moved easily among the élite of the post-war government and its placemen. He convinced other clients of his influence with individual government ministers and of his power to win favours from the highest in the land. Naturally there was a price for using such influence, since all great men in government must have a price.

Those to whom he offered favours were ready to believe him. Despite the country's desperate need of dollars and the shortage of materials essential to industry and exports, he promised that Jacob Harris should have a special £150,000 allocation of US steel to manufacture his gaming and amusement machinery, an amount worth several million pounds in modern terms. Harry Sherman, of Sherman's Football Pools, was to be permitted by the President of the Board of Trade to ignore the controls set up by the Paper Order 1942 and to issue as many forecast coupons as he liked. A current criminal prosecution against him for evading the order was also to be dropped. All this was to be accomplished thanks to Stanley's ability to insinuate himself among those in power. Of course, it was all a pack of lies. Mr Harris and Mr Sherman would have done well to heed the comment of their associate Francis Price that Stanley was 'the biggest villain unhung'.[1]

Perhaps it was as well for Jacob Harris that he merely lost money to Sidney Stanley. In December 1952, Wetzel Ltd of Acton were convicted on seventy-nine charges of infringing the Iron and Steel Order and of having deliberately 'engaged in black market transactions', despite being previously convicted. They remained liable to penalties of £330,000, more than £10,000,000 by modern values, and meantime were fined £31,700, the equivalent of almost a further £1,000,000, for having disregarded regulations 'passed to safeguard the vital needs of the country'.[2]

The gullibility of the hard-faced men of business in the presence of Stanley's ebullience was astonishing. Whatever his promises, it was hard to think of two enterprises more distasteful to the government in its mood of moral resolve in 1947 than gaming machinery and football pools. They were precisely the social evils denounced by Attlee and his colleagues. Perhaps Stanley's greatest accomplishment was to persuade his dupes that men of apparent political integrity were no more honest in reality than he or they. There was never the least chance that the favours would be granted but Stanley's supplicants were not to find that out until long after they had parted with their money and self-respect. On the other hand, a director of the Bank of England and the Parliamentary Secretary to the Board of Trade were to come to grief in consequence of a plot whose existence they realized far too late. Both were to resign in disgrace. 'This is all Jack and the Beanstalk!' the Secretary to the Board of Trade cried as the trap closed upon him. 'Stanley is a dirty lying little bastard!'[3]

This was spivery writ as large as it would ever be. For several weeks in November and December 1948, before the Lynskey tribunal, mud flew and attached itself without distinction to innocent and guilty in the Labour administration. When cornered by the Attorney-General in cross-examination, Sidney Stanley replied simply, 'Do not try to trap me with the truth.'[4]

Such men were far abler and more unpleasant spivs than any that had appeared in Attlee's repertoire of idlers. They controlled the heights as well as the depths of a black market economy. On the heights, there were such episodes as wholesale racketeering in cases like the 'Oil Scandal' of 1945–6, involving men who might otherwise have seemed to be captains of industry.

In this case, it was discovered that 'a most enterprising gentleman' named Rumseyer had rented two 500-gallon oil tanks at Unicorn Wharf, Bow. The tanks were empty but not for long. On 29 January 1945, fourteen defendants were charged with offences concerning 56,000 gallons of linseed and castor oil, vital in the chemical industry and the manufacture of paint, valued at £14,000 – or £280,000 sixty years later. The oil was brought from the North of England to London for refining. The wharf foreman measured the tank on each lorry by a dipstick and checked it as correct against the driver's note. However, when the lorries were pumped out a quantity was left in the tank for delivery to Ernest and Charles Rumseyer of Bow.

Rumseyer went to penal servitude but during the case seven other men, including a broker and four company directors, were found to have bought the stolen oil and shipped it across the country to Glasgow and Derby, Wollaston and Halifax. Not only had they received stolen property, they had also broken the Defence Regulations controlling the use of this essential commodity. At the Old Bailey in October 1945, two of them went to prison and five others were heavily fined. In March 1946, seven more defendants, including six company directors, were fined £2,825 for illegal dealing in oil.[5]

The Rumseyer fraud had begun while the war was still two years from its end. Other wartime frauds carried on into the 1950s. In 1951–3, for example, the trick known as the 'bomb lark' during the London blitz of 1940–41 was still being practised by such men as Arthur Bertram Waters, estate agent and barrister, a former Chairman of West Yorkshire Quarter Sessions and Recorder of Doncaster. The wartime 'lark' had consisted of claiming under a false name against the government for bomb damage that had never been suffered. Even by 1950 so much property remained to be repaired or rebuilt that the claims were not difficult to make.

During the war this fraud had been the prerogative of certain East Enders with financially agile brains. Now it had been adopted by men such as Waters whose speciality was to buy up slum property in London and elsewhere, then to apply to the War Damage Commission for compensation to repair it. The money was paid but either his property had never been damaged in the first place or the repairs were never carried out. By 1953, it was estimated that he had made the modern equivalent of more than £3,500,000 from his scheme. In order that the sums claimed should not seem immodest, he had been careful to apply under a series of fictitious names. At his first trial, he had been found guilty and sent to prison. Unfortunately, as the Court of Criminal Appeal pointed out, the judge had failed to sum up the defence case adequately to the jury. Lord Goddard reluctantly quashed the conviction on these grounds, while remarking that 'the word fraud is written across the case in the largest possible letters.' Two months later Waters was brought back from Dublin and indicted on eleven further charges relating to compensation fraudulently obtained in the name of 'H. G. Gray'. He was acquitted on these for lack of evidence.[6]

Elsewhere there were men who masterminded car rackets, involving the use of 'ringers' which had been sent for scrap but whose registration numbers now adorned stolen vehicles. There were cars for export only, which found their way to the home market while the sellers pocketed the purchase tax paid by the buyers. Others smoothly evaded the manufacturers' covenant which prevented a customer who bought a new car from profiteering by selling it until six months or a year had passed. It was in this shadow world of the second-hand and stolen car trades, that a case occurred in 1950 which was to kill stone-dead the image of the post-war spiv as a loveable rogue.

2

Few thriller-writers could have contrived a better title than that of the murderer's confession: 'My Victim's Body Had Followed Me Home.' The drama itself raised spivery from the Gilbert and Sullivan banter of the barrow boy to crime of a kind that seemed almost Wagnerian in scale. On 4 October 1949, a forty-six-year-old car dealer and black marketeer, Stanley Setty, went missing from a flat in Maitland Court, Bayswater, where he lived in some luxury with his sister and brother-in-law, Ali Ouri. His own brother, Max Setty, owned a smart London nightclub, the Orchid Room, and occupied a fashionable apartment in Grosvenor Square. The disappearance of Stanley Setty was not a matter of much importance for most newspaper readers, compared with a small increase in the meat ration, a rise in petrol prices, and the alarming discovery that the National Health Service was now having to fund 7,000,000 prescriptions a year and 5,200,000 pairs of spectacles. Few people, beyond the Euston Road and Warren Street trade in black market cars, had ever heard of the missing dealer.

Stanley Setty had been born in Baghdad as Sulman Seti. He was a self-made man who had first gone wrong for obvious and dishonourable reasons. Since the beginning of the war, it seemed that he had prospered for reasons that were obscure but perhaps equally dishonourable. He had come to England at four years old and was put to work in a Manchester cotton mill at fourteen. By the time he was sixteen, he and his brother had borrowed £3,000 and gone into business as 'shipping agents'. Two years later, the business foundered with debts of £15,000 and assets of £5. Aged only eighteen, Setty could not be made bankrupt as the law then stood. In no time at all, he was a 'shipping agent' again. The second venture failed and this time he fled to his father in Italy. When he returned in 1928, he was sent to prison for eighteen months by Manchester County Court for offences under the Debtors and Bankruptcy Acts. He remained an undischarged bankrupt for the rest of his life.

As a bankrupt at the end of the war, Setty was debarred from having a bank account and owning a chequebook. Yet he was said to have £50,000 behind him and his wallet was always well stocked. He was a 'pavement dealer' in the second-hand car markets round the Euston Road, with his garage in a mews behind the Regent's Park terraces, and he acted as a 'kerbside banker' outside the Goat and Compasses public house on the corner of Warren Street. Though he had no bank account, he combined with those who possessed one in order to cash cheques on commission for large sums of money. He was also a financier for gun-running to the Middle East and for the forgery of petrol coupons.

How far his activities stretched into the underworld market for illegal petrol or stolen cars, or cars for 'export only' sold on the home market, was not known to the police and Setty was soon in no position to assist them. His world was one of shabby pubs about the Euston Road, cafés and milk bars round Warren Street, the Hollywood Club near Marble Arch, and the affluent home he shared with Ali Ouri. Those grimy thoroughfares of salesmen and pavement dealers between the Tottenham Court Road and Euston were superbly evoked before the war in Patrick Hamilton's London trilogy *Twenty Thousand Streets Under the Sky*. Setty, with his oddities and enigmas, might almost have materialized from Hamilton's pages. He liked to be comfortable. His photographs show him as a large, expensively suited man of thirteen or fourteen stone, with a taste for florid ties, silk shirts, and a heavy and balding appearance suggestive of his origins in Iraq. The only woman in his life was Miss Connie Palfreyman to whom, she later revealed, he was engaged to be married.

When Setty went missing, Scotland Yard appealed for information. The police thought that he might have been abducted and murdered by an underworld gang who knew of the large quantity of cash which this 'banker' was carrying in his wallet. On the morning of 4 October, he had arranged the sale of a Wolseley saloon car and had received £1,000 in £5 notes for this. To a woman in a Warren Street café he had spoken of going that evening to make a 'profitable deal' on a car at Watford, which was to be the purchase of a Jaguar. His last message was a phone call to Connie Palfreyman, explaining that he could not meet her because of this appointment. It seemed that he never reached Watford. His cream-coloured Citroën was found abandoned near a garage which he rented in Chester Place, St Pancras. There were fingerprints on the wing mirror, as if someone had altered its position, but they led nowhere.

For some years after 1949, £5 notes had such value that banks which issued them would make a note of their numbers and of the person drawing them. By 8 October, it was known that £1,000 of the notes in Setty's wallet had been paid out to him by Laurie Lewis who bought the Wolseley and that they were numbered M41 139001 to M41 140000. Scotland Yard instructed bookmakers to look out for these numbers, particularly at Ascot where there was racing that day. It was now said that Setty had seemed nervous for some months about underworld warfare in the illegal car market and feared that he might be its victim.

By mid-October there was no evidence that he had come to harm and speculation suggested that his disappearance was a means of evading the Inland Revenue or some other investigation into his financial affairs. On the afternoon of 7 October, however, Ali Ouri and his wife went out. On returning they found their front door wide open. They found no sign of a forced entry and it seemed that the two mortice locks on the front door must have been opened by Stanley Setty's keys. The couple offered a reward of £3,000 for news of their brother's whereabouts. The police, it was said, were content to wait 'for something to turn up'. This was to prove an unfortunate choice of phrase.

After two weeks of silence, on 21 October, Sidney Tiffin, a farm worker, set out in his punt to hunt wildfowl on the Essex marshes at Dengie Flats, about fifteen miles from Southend. The incoming tide was filtering among the mudflats and grass near the sea wall, bearing with it a large bundle. Mr Tiffin thought at first it might be an RAF drogue dropped by one of the pilot-trainers that flew over the area. As the tide ebbed, he went to investigate the 'drogue'. It proved to be a large package wrapped in felt and bound with cord, lying about a hundred yards beyond the wall. He pulled away the felt and saw a torso and the arms of a body, the head and legs cut off. The mutilated corpse was dressed in a silk shirt and shorts. He tied the package to a stake and went for the police.

There was strong evidence to suppose that the torso and arms belonged to Stanley Setty. The proof of this was established by Superintendent Fred Cherrill of Scotland Yard's fingerprint department. Despite the body's fortnight of immersion in the sea, he was able to remove the wrinkled skin from the fingers and, after treatment, stretched it as 'stalls' on his own fingers, which he covered with rubber gloves. By this means he took prints and found them a match for those of Setty, whose conviction for fraud in 1928 meant that he had a file in the Criminal Record Office.

It was still thought that Setty had either fallen foul of a black market gang who knew about the money that he carried or that he had double-crossed a Jewish underground organization in Palestine, which he was supplying with illegal arms. Neither was the case. On 24 October, Scotland Yard announced that it was looking for an unnamed man and woman in connection with the murder. On the following day, some of the missing banknotes were said to have changed hands at a club in Southend. Next day a 'Setty Fiver' was found at Romford Greyhound Stadium and five more were traced to the dog track at Southend. On 28 October a man was arrested and taken to Albany Street police station, near Regent's Park, while a flat was searched in Finchley Road close to Golders Green tube station.

The man detained was Brian Donald Hume, who had first been introduced to Setty at the Hollywood Club in 1947. Their dealings had included black market nylons, forged petrol coupons, and cars which Hume stole for his partner to sell. Born in 1919, Donald Hume had endured a chaotic childhood. The illegitimate son of a schoolmistress, he was sent to an orphanage as a baby, retrieved and brought up by his 'Aunt Doodie', whom he discovered later to be his natural mother, and for whom he felt an abiding hatred. He was proud, he said, to be born with a chip on his shoulder. Despite a grammar school scholarship, he was an academic failure and ran away from home, sleeping rough on Barnes Common. After a period as a teenage car thief, he joined the Communist Party, 'because I thought I could get something for nothing', and tried unsuccessfully to enlist in the International Brigade during the Spanish Civil War.

In 1939 he joined the Royal Air Force Volunteer Reserve as a pilot, a career cut short by a serious injury in 1940 and an attack of cerebro-spinal meningitis. A medical report at the time of his discharge described him as suffering from 'a degree of organically determined psychopathy'. Though now a civilian, he exploited his knowledge of the RAF by turning to fraud, still wearing his uniform, decorated with medal ribbons to which he was not entitled, visiting

RAF messes to enjoy a free meal and pass a dud cheque. When caught in 1942, he was bound over for two years.

Having escaped a prison sentence, Hume opened a shop as the Hume Electrical Company of Golders Green. He designed and manufactured the 'Little Atom Toaster', selling 50,000 of these, and went on to devise an electric towel-rail. He also married a beautiful and accomplished divorcee. After the failure of his electrical business, he drifted into the kerbside trade of Warren Street. A gross of black market nylons brought him into contact with Stanley Setty. By this time, Hume had qualified for a civilian pilot's licence and had begun a post-war career as what he liked to call 'The Flying Smuggler'.

On 1 October 1949, there had been an argument between Hume and Setty in Hume's flat at Golders Green. If Hume was to be believed, he thought that Setty was paying too much attention to Cynthia Hume. In the course of the quarrel, Setty aimed a kick at the dog. Hume snatched an SS dagger from the wall and in the struggle Setty was stabbed to death. It seemed more like demented rage than an accident, since Setty was stabbed five times. Hume later cut up the body, wrapped the pieces in felt, and dropped them from an Auster light aircraft, near the Channel Islands. Though the felt-wrapped fragments were not weighted, he must have thought the world had seen the last of Stanley Setty. Unfortunately for him, the sea gave up its dead by means of a prevailing current, which carried the torso and the arms all the way to the Essex marshes.

3

When Hume was charged with the murder, he admitted disposing of the body but denied killing the rival spiv. He described how three members of a black market gang, Max, Greenie and The Boy, used to hang around Setty's garage and had met him there. He was frightened of them and they had persuaded him, against his better judgement, to get rid of three packages by dropping them far out at sea. These packages were said to contain printing plates for forged petrol coupons. The coupons were in circulation and the police were hunting for the plates. He now realized the packages contained

Setty's dismembered body and that Setty must have been murdered by these criminal associates.

Without the story of Max, Greenie and The Boy, there was little doubt that Hume would have been convicted and hanged for Setty's murder. After the fatal quarrel he had briefly hidden Setty's body in a cupboard and had then cut it up on the floor of his flat, when neither his wife nor the cleaner was on the premises. He had even gone down the Finchley Road to get his carving knife sharpened. Not only did the police find blood of Setty's group on the floor-boards of the flat, there had evidently been so much blood that it had dripped through the boards to the plaster below and the carpet had been sent for cleaning. Hume had paid his rent a few days later with a £5 note and his landlord saw that the wallet was uncharacteristically full of these. As it happened, Hume had had to discard much of Setty's cash because of the bloodstains on the notes.

According to his version of events, Hume had agreed to cooperate with the gang of racketeers associated with Setty's garage. They knew of his pilot's licence and that he was well known at certain aero clubs. Their first demand was that he should drop two packages in the English Channel, in return for £50 and the cost of hiring the plane. On 5 October, they brought the packages to his flat. Hume had then driven by rented car to Elstree and hired an Auster light aircraft, stowing the packages by the pilot's seat. There was no reason to suppose that they contained anything but the printing plates described by the gang. He had flown out over the Thames estuary and dropped the parcels four or five miles beyond Southend pier. Because it was getting dark, he had not returned to Elstree but had put the little plane down at Southend airport. A hire car returned him to London, where Max, Greenie and The Boy were waiting for him with the third and final parcel.

This time it was larger and the payment was £90. After the three men left his flat, Hume moved the parcel and heard it gurgle. He noticed there was blood on the floor, seeping through the felt wrapping. Not surprisingly, he was extremely frightened at what the parcel contained, though the men had assured him it was only another set of printing plates. He was terrified by these gangsters and what they might do if he failed them. He went to Elstree, hired another Auster and dropped the last parcel in the sea. This was the one which had come ashore.

Was it possible that he could be telling the truth? Almost everyone who met him agreed that Hume was a thoroughly unpleasant man with a fierce temper and a capacity for violence. The story of the three gangsters was implausible. Yet evidence of the police interrogation showed that when Detective Superintendent Colin MacDougall and two Scotland Yard colleagues interviewed Hume they had questioned him rigorously. They asked him a question which would have caught most liars. Could he describe the three gangsters he claimed to have dealt with? He did so with phenomenal accuracy and detail, repeating the descriptions without error or contradiction. Briefly, even the Scotland Yard team began to think his story might be true. Only when they had left the interview room did the three detectives realize, collectively, that what Hume had done was to describe them, as they faced him across the table. When his statement was read out in the course of the trial, its apparent accuracy impressed the jury.

He could hardly have hoped for corroboration of his gangster story and yet, at his trial in January 1950, he was given it. The defence was able to call a former army officer, Cyril Lee, who was a stranger to Hume but who had lived within earshot of Setty's garage for three years. Mr Lee was not pleased by his neighbour. The garage was not patronized by 'the sort of people I would like to see round my doorstep'. They included two whom he heard called 'Max' and 'The Boy'. He also saw a man corresponding to Hume's description of Greenie.

Such uncorroborated evidence might not have saved Hume. Towards the end of the trial, however, the defence asked permission to call a further witness, Douglas Clay, who said that he had formerly served with MI5. The name under which he had previously appeared in court was not revealed. Under both names, he was a writer who had been working on a story in Paris. 'I encountered a number of people there who were part of a gang: they were engaged in the smuggling of arms to Palestine and cars to this country . . . There were two members of that gang who were employed on general duties, but generally strong-arm work, who were known as The Boy and Maxie.' Mr Clay passed the information to the International Sûreté and the British Embassy. He also contacted Scotland Yard and was interviewed there. Since then he had been approached by Hume's defence lawyers. He encountered the gang while cashing traveller's cheques and had been present at the arrest of one of its members.

This evidence was enough to sway some members of the jury. To send a man to the gallows, if the witness had spoken the truth, would be a terrible thing. Mr Clay was not known to Hume and there seemed no reason why he should not be telling the truth. At the end of the case, the jurors could not agree upon a verdict. There was nothing for it but to discharge them. The Director of Public Prosecutions decided that it would not be 'in the interests of justice' for there to be a retrial of the case. Hume was permitted to plead guilty to being an accessory after the fact to a murder committed by others, presumably Max, Greenie and The Boy. He was sent to prison for twelve years.[7]

A month later, under his real name, Mr Clay was committed to the Old Bailey on charges of bigamy and jailed for two years. Unknown to Hume's jury, he had been fined in 1940 for unlawfully wearing military decorations; bound over in 1941 for forging cheques and obtaining money by false pretences; bound over for bigamy in 1946; cashiered and sent to prison for larceny by a court martial in the same year, and sent to prison for twelve months for fraudulent conversion in 1947. The Hume murder trial had been his latest frolic.[8]

Soon after his trial, Hume made a statement to the Governor of Wormwood Scrubs, where he served the first weeks of his sentence. As a result, the existence of a gang which might have murdered Setty was further investigated by Superintendent MacDougall and Chief Superintendent Hatherill. Dossiers were supplied by the Sûreté on American deserters in France during 1945–8 and the nicknames by which they were known. This inquiry got nowhere. On his release in 1958 Hume sold to the Sunday Pictorial his story of how he alone had murdered Setty and how the little gang of Max, Greenie and The Boy had evolved in his own well-nourished imagination.

Yet Hume was no ordinary spiv and, indeed, no ordinary murderer if there was such a type. On Saturday 2 August 1958, a man in a blue suit and carrying a brown overcoat visited the Midland Bank in Boston Manor Road, Brentford, just before 11 a.m., to inquire about opening an account. He was given information and promised to return shortly. Just as the bank was closing, an hour later, he reappeared. The cashier who was closing the main door recognized him, let him in, then shut and locked the door. Once inside, Hume drew a .22 automatic pistol and shouted, 'This is a stick-up!' Thinking the clerk was about to attack him, he thereupon shot the man in the stomach. He demanded money from a tin box, which amounted to about £1,200 in notes, tore the telephone wires from their socket, ordered the staff to tie one another up, grabbed whatever banknotes he saw, and fled. He had arrived in London from Zurich and stayed at a hotel using the name 'Donald Brown'. His flight back was already booked and his luggage was waiting at the Cromwell Road airport terminal. He was out of the country before the hunt for the bank robber had properly begun.

When he learnt that the bank staff had concealed £40,000 from him, he decided to return and punish them by raiding the same bank again. That branch had meantime moved to the Great West Road but on 12 November he tracked it down. Again he waited until just before closing time, then rushed in waving two guns. This time the plan went wrong. Some of the staff escaped to the basement, others went to the windows and shouted for help. They had recognized him and one of the girls shouted, 'It's the Irishman! It's the Irishman again! Get downstairs and lock yourselves in!' Hume was not Irish but might have disguised his voice on the first occasion. Edward Aires, the manager, appeared and grappled with the raider. Hume also shot him in the stomach with his .22 automatic pistol, severing an artery. Though he got away, he had found only £300. He hurried to Kew Bridge station and then by train and bus to Hammersmith and London airport. Though he got safely to Zurich, he left on the train a raincoat with the name 'Donald Brown' inside it, which identified him to Scotland Yard as Hume.

How long he would have evaded capture for the robbery was never to be known. He was named by Scotland Yard as the man responsible for the two attacks at Brentford and was hunted across

Europe for almost three months, during which time he contrived to get to Canada and back. On 30 January 1959, knowing that another attack in London was too dangerous, he walked into the Gewerbe Bank of Zurich and pushed a note in German across the counter. It informed the clerks that this was a hold-up. There were only two cashiers in the bank. One of them tried to ring the alarm bell, at which Hume shot him in the stomach, seriously wounding him. He hit the other cashier over the head with his gun, tried unsuccessfully to open the safe, and ran off empty-handed.

At some distance down the road, a taxi driver, Arthur Maag, attempted to stop him. Hume shot him in the stomach, fatally wounding him, and ran on. A restaurant cook, Hans Angstmann, joined the chase and brought down the fugitive in a rugby tackle. Hume threatened him with the gun but in the struggle Angstmann disarmed him. When the police arrived it was not so much to arrest the killer as to save him from a crowd which threatened to lynch him.

When questioned, Hume entered wholeheartedly into another fantasy almost as intricate as Max, Greenie and The Boy. He was John Stanislav, American citizen, working at the United States Air Force base at Wiesbaden. The son of Polish immigrants who had settled in America, he had come from Germany to Switzerland lured by the promise, as he put it, that the streets were paved with gold. Within hours his fingerprints were sent to Zurich from Scotland Yard and the deception was at an end. In reality, he was homeless and had slept the last few nights in a lakeside park. He had less than £2 when he reached Zurich. Once this was spent, he decided on an impulse to rob the Gewerbe Bank.

On 30 September 1959, a Swiss court sentenced him to life imprisonment, the maximum sentence for murder. He was sent to Regensdorf prison and from there many years later was transferred to Broadmoor. He was released shortly before his death, almost forty years after his Zurich trial.

Stanley Setty was a successful spiv, hungry for any cargo from machine-guns to nylons. He lived like another equally notorious undischarged bankrupt, Sidney Stanley, in a rustle of banknotes and West End luxury, far removed from the stained pavements outside the Goat and Compasses. Donald Hume was a spiv of another order. With the suppleness of the well-greased palm he combined the ruthlessness of the post-war gangster, the robber who shot first without bothering to ask questions of his victims. Masquerades were his peculiar talent. He was Pilot Officer Hume, Battle of Britain ace in uniform and bogus medal ribbons, bought for £5. His was a service career of air force imposture and fraud. He was the inventor and entrepreneur of the Little Atom Toaster and the Hume Electrical Company. He was the master of beautiful women, not least the model girl whom he had married. He was the gangland associate of Max, Greenie and The Boy, living a lie in which he seemed truly to believe. In all these, as in his final impersonation of John Stanislav, he was the player of parts. He only played himself, as one psychiatrist at his Swiss trial thought, when acting the criminal.

With his rage, plausibility and lack of scruple, Donald Hume was an outstanding figure in whom three of the most resonant post-war criminal types combined. He was easily recognizable as a profes-sional spiv, far above the level of the barrow boy or racecourse tout. He was an armed robber of the kind with which the peace was becoming resentfully familiar. Last, he was a psychopathic fantasist of a type which seemed peculiar to the years immediately after the war, notably in the criminal personalities of Neville Heath, John George Haigh and John Reginald Halliday Christie.

6

'Real Butter on the Scones'
The Post-War Psychopaths

IN RETROSPECT, IT was not always easy to see why the psychopath appeared to be such a novelty in the public's perception of post-war crime. It was, of course, true that such individuals gained notoriety and popular interest by being denizens of both the underworld and the asylum. The men who committed the most lurid murders of the time were not otherwise law-abiding individuals suddenly besieged by uncontrollable sexual or homicidal impulses. The most famous of them, Heath, Haigh and Christie, had previous criminal convictions of a more common kind, all involving imprisonment for theft, impersonation and dishonesty. Nor were they a passing legacy of war. So far as there can be a tradition in such things, they seemed to set a pattern for many who came after, whether in murder or lesser crimes. They illuminated a dark corner of human desire and the means to its fulfilment. Their conduct also seemed to parallel a callous and even jocular criminality in the post-war underworld as a whole. In a classic analysis of their mid-century type, by Anthony Storr in *Human Aggression* (1970), they became almost a subject for popular science.

Though legal rulings on insanity classified them as bad rather than mad, the appellation 'psychopath' became common. A few decades hence, criminal gangs and political terror, especially when inspired by religious or nationalist fanaticism, would make use of such deviants. Among individuals, few crimes in the second half of the century would endure more powerfully in the collective memory than the 'Moors Murders' of 1967. The fate of the children was not the extreme of horror. It was followed by an infamous recording of the events and a gloating over their crimes by the perpetrators, which seemed entirely of a new age.

Similarly the mid-century apprehension of a sex maniac hiding behind every bush blossomed into the discovery of the 'paedophile' in the 1980s, sometimes from evidence and sometimes from hysteria. A network or underworld of monsters appeared to exist everywhere, growing in numbers and confidence. By the century's end, so many parents feared for the safety of themselves and their children that 'the school run' in the family car had become a twice-daily middle-class obligation. The children of the 1940s could only stare and wonder.

Glimpses into this subterranean society showed how many oddities nourished murderous longings which might never mature in reality. In 1950, for example, a labourer was sent to prison for eighteen months after writing a number of letters to a family to whom he had sold a horse. 'Tell your wife and daughter to enjoy the life God gave them. Remember the time is ticking towards tragedy in your home. Any evening from now on I will strangle you both and tie you up by your feet.' The letter was signed 'The Avenger' and was followed by one addressed to 'Brainless Inspector' at Maldon police station. 'Mr Everitt, wife, and daughter will be slowly strangled by me . . . I always get my victims clean and clever.' It might almost have been the work of 'Reg' Christie who was still alive and not yet suspected of strangling women for pleasure in his Notting Hill slum.

When the man was traced and tried at the assizes, he was known to the authorities only as a public-spirited citizen who a few weeks previously had applied to the Home Office for the job of assistant hangman. Not only was he acquainted with the family but he had given some of his paintings and a poem to the daughter, whom he now included in his homicidal ambitions. He was sent to prison for eighteen months with no apparent provision for treating his grotesque compulsion. It was not unknown in medical experience. Havelock Ellis devoted a section of *Studies in the Psychology of Sex* to the grisly phenomenon. In the new world of information technology, during the trial of Graham Coutts for the murder of Jane Longhurst in 2004, it was said to have its websites on the internet.[1]

The family in this case had been badly frightened but not physically harmed. This was not always so, when post-war criminality and insanity ran parallel. In January 1957, a young woman who was a shop assistant in South London was woken in the small hours of the morning by a stranger in her bedroom. She was evidently no stranger to him, though the reason he had chosen her was never explained, since he pleaded guilty at his trial and offered no evidence. He ordered her to come with him on the pillion of his motorcycle to a house where he lived alone.

His prisoner spent almost four months in a cavity under the kitchen, which he ordered her to excavate and turn into a room. She was to wear only her underwear, presumably to prevent her from escaping, since he made no sexual advances to her. He went out to work each day, leaving her secured under the kitchen and with orders to continue digging. She was rescued after a note was seen on a stick, which she had pushed up through the earth of a flower bed, giving her name and saying that she was 'down the big hole at the bottom of the garden'. This curious drama might have been a model for John Fowles' novel *The Collector*. If the man was secretly obsessed with his victim before her abduction, it was with someone to whom he had never spoken and about whom he could have known very little, unless he had patiently acquired information in the preceding months.

He was sent to prison for three years by Mr Justice Finnemore, who remarked only that 'This astonishing affair is something quite outside normal human experience.' It was increasingly within human experience in the post-war world to fear lurkers in the shadows who contentedly dreamed dreams of abduction, grievous bodily harm and murder.[2]

Psychiatric analyses were the province of the few. Nowhere was the psychopath whose time had come displayed in finer detail than in Patrick Hamilton's story of Ernest Ralph Gorse in *The West Pier* (1951), *Mr Stimpson and Mr Gorse* (1953) and *Unknown Assailant* (1955), a series later to be televised as *The Charmer*. The acclaim which Hamilton received was, in part, confirmation of the public's enduring fascination with such types. Gorse, described as a mixture of Bertie Wooster and Satan, was based on Neville Heath and 'George Smith, the bath-murderer'. A final volume, unwritten when

Hamilton died, was to describe his hero as destined to die pain-lessly, quickly, and not in bed.

Within the underworld, professional criminals were to nail victims' feet to the floor, connect electric current to their genitals, threaten to burn petrol-soaked security guards or rape the women-folk of a family unless cash was produced. Nor did they seem to think that they were doing anything exceptional. It was this tone of indifference or self-justification that rang a note of insanity and made Heath, Haigh or Christie seem like pioneers of a new crim-inal morality.

Psychopathy in the 1940s was still a relatively new science, the word and the diagnosis dating from the 1880s, much of it from the work of Richard von Krafft-Ebing. Its presence was detected in those whose actions exhibited a total disregard for others and an entire lack of remorse. This was reflected in robberies and crimes of violence as surely as in the murders of Heath and his rivals. The psychopath was an emotional pygmy, constitutionally incapable of forming affectional ties. Yet as a trickster he might be affable and considerate when it suited him. Psychopaths acted without fore-sight even in respect of their own safety, which was often why they were caught. Neville Heath, with all the country alerted for him, paraded in Bournemouth as 'Group Captain Rupert Brooke DFC'. Famous murderers and youthful gangsters alike courted detection and must have known it if they gave the danger a moment's thought.

Psychopaths were perceived as instinctively deceitful, truthful only when it served their purposes. This was true of criminals in general, yet men like Heath and Haigh had to perfection a power to charm and persuade. Men and women who had known the culprit and heard of his passage from the criminal courts to the condemned cell were astonished and even felt this could not be the same man or that he had been overtaken by schizophrenia. The pianist Albert Ferber had met Haigh, of the nine acid bath murders, after Wigmore Hall recitals. He was convinced Haigh must be morally if not legally innocent. 'Can this be the same man?' he asked. It was. Ferber visited him shortly before his execution and wrote to him, wishing that he had been allowed to have a grand piano brought to Wandsworth prison to play for the condemned killer.

The character of the psychopath seemed to converge with what became known later as the sociopath. Psychopaths cared nothing for society; indeed, most instinctively despised it and were indifferent to its approval, disapproval or hostility. Allied to this, the psychopath knew himself superior to the human 'trash' surrounding him and to be clever enough to conceal this contempt. He shared the contempt of Billy Hill and his kind for law-abiding 'mugs'. 'Never give a sucker an even break,' said Neville Heath confidentially.[3]

In the classical diagnosis of the day, the psychopath's route lay through paranoia or paranoid schizophrenia, and a grievance over persecution or humiliation. As Dr Anthony Storr pointed out, such people had an affinity to the Miller of Dee: 'I care for nobody, no not I, since nobody cares for me.' The victims of Heath or Haigh often provoked irritation or dislike in their destroyers. Heath with his film-star looks claimed that to attract women, 'I only have to press buttons.' After his conviction, he added that he actually hated women and that they were all 'crooks'. John George Haigh escorted Mrs Durand-Deacon to his 'factory', shot her dead and forced her body into a drum of acid. The dead woman then became what he described peevishly to Detective Inspector Albert Webb as 'a confounded nuisance – far more trouble than any of the others. She simply would not dissolve and next day, when I expected her body to be entirely dissolved, I found a large piece of buttock floating on top of the sludge and grease that was the rest of her.' His irritation and Heath's anger were part of a culture in which armed robbers or housebreakers, as well as murderers, would soon blame their victims for inviting the harm they suffered. Had they submitted and obeyed, had Mrs Durand-Deacon dissolved, had Heath's girlfriends kept their mouths shut, the world would have turned more smoothly on its axis.[4]

A macabre humour often went with such crimes, though it was not a novelty. Apart from the 'Jack the Ripper' notes which taunted the police in 1888, Dr Neill Cream, poisoner of Lambeth prostitutes in 1891–2, had contacted Scotland Yard as a private detective, offering to solve his own murder of Ellen Donworth for £1,000, and then closed down the Metropole Hotel by a circular to guests warning them that the poisoner was working in the kitchens. Major Armstrong of Hay-on-Wye attempted to poison a rival solicitor at tea in 1921 by arsenic introduced into a piece of sliced cake. To ensure his victim ate the fatal slice, he lifted it and handed it across the table, saying happily, ''Scuse fingers.' Neville Heath, immaculate in his cocktail-bar chalk-stripe suit, was offered a sustaining glass of whisky just before the hangman entered the condemned cell. In the last words he was to utter, he seemed to salute his two victims. As the whisky was poured, he called to the officiating warder, 'While you're about it, you might make that a double.'[5]

It would be wrong to suggest that the post-war public took such men to its heart, but its ambivalent attitude was well illustrated by the alacrity with which the *Sunday Pictorial* paid a large sum for the rights to the stories of both Heath and Christie, undertaking the costs of their defences and caring for their families, while the *News of the World* did the same for Haigh. The editors knew their market. The public also responded with macabre pleasantries of its own. '"You need a bath," said Haigh acidly,' went the round of pubs and clubs. When the skeletons of six women murdered by Christie had been exhumed from 10 Rillington Place, such notoriety attached to the dingy cul-de-sac that the London County Council was obliged to change its name. The winning suggestion was to bury Rillington Place as 'Rushton Close', but the wags of Notting Hill preferred 'Filleted Place'.

The psychopath's detachment from the horror of reality was reflected in these asides. Haigh was cornered in a Kensington tea shop by the journalist Conrad Phillips, shortly before his arrest and when both men knew the game was up. As they sat at a table, and the police prepared to move in, Phillips questioned Haigh about Mrs Durand-Deacon's disappearance and got nowhere. A waitress brought plates under aluminium covers. Haigh at last leaned forward confidentially, his nine corpses and the acid bath forgotten in the pleasure of the moment. Why had he chosen this tea shop to make his last stand against the press and the law? Nodding at the plates, the multiple murderer explained approvingly, 'They put real butter on the scones.'[6]

2

On 15 February 1946, in the Socialist weekly *Tribune*, George Orwell had published his essay on 'The Decline of English Murder'. He described the father of the English family, fortified by a Sunday lunch of roast pork, apple sauce and suet pudding, settling into his armchair and opening the *News of the World* to read the details of a satisfying murder trial. Orwell lamented the banalities of modern murder compared with the great cases of the past, many of which formed part of the folklore of the Sunday readers: Dr Palmer, the Rugeley Poisoner; Jack the Ripper; Neill Cream, his Lambeth rival; Mrs Maybrick; Dr Crippen; George Seddon; George Joseph Smith and his Brides in the Bath; Major Armstrong of Hay-on-Wye, and the partnership of Edith Thompson and her lover Frederick Bywaters. All but three of the nine cases involved the poisoning of a spouse, a near relation or a dupe. An unhappy marriage was also the cause in the case of Thompson and Bywaters.

Orwell thought such crimes, with their intense loves and hatreds, almost worthy of major fiction. Murder victims in the 1940s were increasingly strangers, the crimes were committed by gangsters or typecast figures from the shadows of wartime society. The occasion of his essay was a book describing the so-called 'Cleft Chin' murder of 1944, in which an American deserter and a waitress-cum-striptease dancer had shot dead a London taxi driver during a rampage of armed robbery. To Orwell, this wasteland drama of dance halls, milk bars, movie palaces, cheap perfume and stolen cars was 'meaningless'.[7]

In the most famous cases – Heath, Haigh and Christie – the facts were not in dispute. All three pleaded insanity to escape the gallows, Heath with reluctance, his rivals with alacrity. This defence failed. Heath was hanged in 1946 and Haigh in 1949. Though Christie was not caught and hanged until 1953, his murders had begun at least ten years earlier and his crimes of violence long before that.

Sex was the compulsion for Heath and Christie, money was the motive in Haigh's case, as in Hume's. It also seemed that something in the moral ether of the new peace had nourished their well-concealed ambitions. Orwell in his essay notes the brutalizing effects of the war itself.

In his previous career, Neville Heath had held a commission in three armed services and had been dismissed or cashiered in each case for theft or dishonesty. He had military and civilian convictions for wearing uniforms and medals to which he was not entitled. He had civilian convictions for fraud, theft, dishonesty and housebreaking, as well as a three-year Borstal sentence. Haigh had been sent to prison for crimes of dishonesty in 1934 and 1937, a total of five and a half years, and for stealing in 1941. When 'Reg' Christie volunteered as a War Reserve policeman in the crisis of 1939, no one checked whether this meticulous clerk, living with his wife and 'medical' books in the grimy cul-de-sac of Rillington Place, might have a criminal record. In 1920, as a temporary postman, he had served three months for stealing. Bound over for false pretences and put on probation for violence in 1923, he later served nine months for theft, six months for malicious wounding, and three months for stealing a motor car. The wounding, called by the magistrate a 'murderous attack', was on the woman with whom he was living and whom he beat over the head with her son's cricket bat in the course of a quarrel about money. He was one of many unsuspected criminals in responsible wartime employment.

3

By 1946, the last year of his life, Neville Heath had mastered the techniques of the trickster as an officer and gentleman. There was no element in his youth to explain his ultimate cruelty, no strictness or religious rigour such as Haigh and Christie had experienced. His childhood lay in the comforts of middle-class Wimbledon and Rutlish School, where he was an athlete, got his School Certificate, and developed the looks of a 'matinée idol'. His adolescence was passed among parties and parlour games, the palais de danse and the golf club.

A Cranwell cadet commissioned in 1936 and a natural pilot, he was posted to Duxford, and Mildenhall a year later. As Duxford sports officer, he at once pilfered mess funds, a theft he knew would be discovered as soon as he left. He deserted from Mildenhall, writing to his commander to resign as 'the easiest way to save dragging the name of a decent squadron in the mud'. Arrested in Wimbledon on 22 June 1937, he faced a court martial at RAF Debden. On his honour not to escape, he stole an RAF sergeant's car and disappeared.

Brought back again, he was court-martialled. Because he had tried to resign, the sentence was lenient. He admitted theft and being absent without leave, and was cashiered. The Air Ministry reduced this to dismissal. Heath did not deny his dismissal to those he met, substituting a story of hazarding his aircraft, which he maintained he had flown under the span of a river bridge for a bet. He told the lie with such conviction that it was still thought true at his murder trial nine years later. His counsel, J. D. Casswell, never doubted it.

From Mildenhall, he descended on East Anglia as 'Lord Dudley', in reality a friend of the Duke of Windsor, 'Bruce Lockhart, the Cambridge Blue', and 'Lord Nevill'. He lived at the Lion Hotel, Cambridge, under the modest title of 'Jimmy Dudley', but gave his addresses as 'Trinity College, Cambridge', and 'c/o The House of Lords'. The charade ended at the Sherwood Inn, Nottingham, late in 1937. His bill was unpaid and he had tried to buy the landlord's car with a forged cheque. A stranger approached him in the bar and asked, 'Excuse me, sir. Are you Lord Dudley?' 'As a matter of fact, old man, I am.' 'Then I must tell you that I am Inspector Hickman of Nottingham CID.' 'In that case, old man, I am not Lord Dudley.'[8]

On 11 November 1937, Heath appeared before Nottingham magistrates. Contritely, he spoke of his crimes as escapades which had got out of hand. So far as this court knew, he had no previous convictions. He was put on probation. Eight months later at the Old Bailey he faced charges of car stealing, theft and fraudulent use of cheques, false pretences, stealing his fiancée's golf clubs, and housebreaking. He had burgled a friend's house in Edgware and then gone to stay with the man in Brighton. He had only worked for a fortnight since his last conviction – at John Lewis's department store in Oxford Street, on the basis of forged references. The Recorder, Sir Gerald Dodson, spoke sadly of youthful promise betrayed and Heath's undoubted 'instincts to do right'. 'I cannot believe you have lost all of them at your age.' He sent the twenty-one-year-old 'ex-public school boy and former RAF officer', as the press called him, to Borstal training for three years.[9]

In September 1939, Heath was released for war service. Charm and plausibility never faced a greater test. In eighteen months he was an officer and gentleman once more, acting captain in the Royal Army Service Corps, promoted from the ranks, guarding the Haifa to Baghdad oil pipeline. Within a few months he had stolen a second paybook and was drawing double pay. He had also been absent from duty, in the fleshpots of Cairo, and had bought his commanding officer's car with a worthless cheque, selling it for cash. The Army cashiered him and put him on the troopship *Mooltan* for England.

This might have ended a career of polished dishonesty but Heath jumped ship at Durban. After a period as 'Captain Selway of the Argyll and Sutherland Highlanders', with a Military Cross and a limp, he joined the South African Air Force as 'James Robert Cadogan Armstrong', Trinity College, Cambridge, a double Blue in rugby and boxing. Not surprisingly, he seemed to have a natural gift for flying SAAF Hurricane and Tomahawk fighters.

Before his squadron was seconded to the RAF for the aerial attack on Germany, Heath married a daughter of the Pitt-Rivers family, a son was born, and his trail of debts was honoured. From RAF Finmere he flew American-built B-25 Mitchell bombers over the Ruhr. For the benefit of girlfriends, he forged entries in his logbook and countersigned them to make his exploits more impressive. On 29 October 1944, his plane was hit and caught fire. Heath ordered the crew to bale out and found his way back to Allied lines.

With the approaching end of war in Europe, 'Jimmy Armstrong' was repatriated to South Africa. There had been another side to the psychopath. For a year, he had worked to raise money for Merchant Navy charities through the Alexandra Rams, who knew him only as genial and generous 'Diamond Jim from Jo'burg'. 'We shall miss you,' they wrote as he left for Cape Town, 'your breezy manner, with your popsies and "git aht of its".' In July, the Durban magistrates fined him £25 on fraud charges. He abandoned 'Lieutenant Colonel Graham', 'Captain Blyth' and 'Major Danvers', but not 'Lieutenant Colonel James Robert Cadogan Armstrong, DFC, OBE'. The magistrates case ended his marriage. He was courtmartialled for fraud and was again dismissed the service. On 5 February 1946, he arrived back at Southampton.[10]

Within a few months he was under observation by Inspector Capstick and the 'Ghost Squad' as a potential cat burglar. His good looks and charm also continued to attract women, with some of whom he went to bed. Only with a few did he share bedroom dramas of a sado-masochistic kind. There were subsequent allegations that this was nothing new to him but the stories were not matched by evidence. Paull Hill, his adjutant in the Middle East, wrote of Heath's boast of a sadistic encounter with two sisters in a Cairo brothel. It might have been true but Heath, an inveterate liar in any case, could equally well have been 'shooting a line', to use his favourite expression. He told psychiatrists who examined him at the time of his trial that the sadistic phase began only after the end of his marriage. Whether he could be believed remained an open question.

Heath and a young woman were thrown out of the Strand Palace Hotel on 22 February 1946, a fortnight after his arrival from South Africa, when he was found caning her in their room. The house detective, who thought he had rescued her, saw the couple leave the hotel 'arm in arm'. Yet Heath's public notoriety still owed far more to a continuing career of dishonesty. As 'Squadron Leader Walker of the South African Rugby Union', he duped Prime Minister Attlee and Foreign Secretary Ernest Bevin into sharing with him and his friends an official box at Twickenham for a rugby international in 1946. A photograph of the group hung for some time on the wall of a Fleet Street pub. Less appealingly, he was fined

£10 at Wimbledon magistrates court on 5 April for wearing a military uniform and decorations to which he was not entitled.

For two months, he cadged money and drinks from journalists in Fleet Street pubs, offering to fly them abroad at a price. He never bothered to qualify as a civilian pilot. He haunted the Nag's Head in Knightsbridge and the Panama Club near South Kensington tube station. For a while, he lived at the Normandie Hotel near Hyde Park Corner and may have helped to empty the wall-safes of the unwary. Yet it seemed that, at twenty-nine, his course was run.

In April 1946, he was introduced to Margery Gardner, two years his senior. She had left a husband and child in Sheffield for Chelsea's bohemia. A competent artist, she had written part of an autobiographical novel, and worked as a film extra. It seems she was, in her erotic life, a masochist. Such was the view of the pathologist Keith Simpson, Chief Inspector Reginald Spooner who led the investigation into her death, Heath's defence counsel, and reporters on the case. She had no criminal record, but was known to the police from an incident in September 1945, when a car was driven at 50 mph round Hyde Park on the wrong side of the road and stopped only after being rammed. The driver was charged but Margery Gardner was not.

On 16 June Heath moved to the Pembridge Court Hotel in Notting Hill, a family-run establishment of nineteen rooms, three of them close to his. He signed the register, 'Lt. Col. and Mrs N. G. C. Heath, Black Hill Cottage, Romsey'. The previous night, he had met another young woman at a dance and begun what seemed a lightning romance. They passed 16 June together and he asked her to spend the night with him. She refused. On 17 June, they became engaged and she went back to the hotel with him. She agreed at his trial that he treated her with kindness and she was never afraid of him. On 18 June she returned to Worthing to tell her parents of the engagement.[11]

Heath passed Thursday 20 June drinking in Fleet Street, taking cash from a *Daily Mail* journalist for a promised flight to Copenhagen. He met Margery Gardner in Knightsbridge, taking her to dinner and a party at the Panama Club. They left at midnight by taxi, drunk enough to require each other's assistance on the hotel steps.

No disturbance was heard that night, though three rooms within ten or twelve feet of them were occupied.

Next day, Margery Gardner's body was found face down on the bed, marked by a diamond-weave whip. Her ankles were tied by a handkerchief and flushing indicated that her wrists had been tied behind her back. Keith Simpson diagnosed suffocation, probably by her face being pushed into a pillow. The scene suggested an assault on an unsuspecting victim by a maniac, one of the most lurid murders of the age. If not, surely the man would have sought assistance or explained how a sexual drama had ended in tragedy. Yet of the 'Lieutenant Colonel' and his luggage there was no sign. If psychopaths lived by impulse and cared little for consequences, his disappearance confirmed him as one. Far from covering his tracks, Heath had signed the register in his own name, already filed in the Criminal Record Office with his photograph and description.

By then he was in Worthing, where he dined and danced that night with his fiancée, before posting a set of implausible lies to Superintendent Barratt of Scotland Yard. He had lent his room to Mrs Gardner and a man with whom she was to sleep for reasons that were 'mainly financial'. He had returned at 3 a.m. as arranged and found her 'in the condition of which you are aware'.

On 23 June, 'Group Captain Rupert Brooke' booked into the Tollard Royal Hotel, Bournemouth. He had just returned from South Africa, was not even in England at the time of the murder, and was preparing for the King's Cup Air Race. Though the police were hunting Neville Heath, they had decided not to issue his photo to the press, for fear of contaminating evidence of identification at a trial. Only the *Police Gazette* carried his picture. In any case, to Sir Ronald Howe, Assistant Commissioner, the murder seemed an aberration. Heath was a con man and thief but not a potential killer.

His freedom in Bournemouth lasted thirteen days, during which he breathed new life into the Tollard Royal Hotel by arranging dances and entertainments. On 3 July, his second Wednesday, he was introduced to a girl on the undercliff promenade. She was a nineteen-year-old Wren on demob leave, Doreen Marshall.

Friendship ripened in hours. They had tea and she dined with him at the Tollard Royal. At midnight, they set out on foot for her hotel, the Norfolk, at the resort's centre. Heath told the porter he would be back in half an hour. Doreen Marshall said, 'He'll be back in a quarter of an hour.' Being tired, she wanted to go straight to bed. She was never seen alive again.

When her body was found in Branksome Dene Chine, Heath was already in custody. Yet this crime, in which the victim was repeatedly stabbed and mutilated, had the stamp of Jack the Ripper rather than a bedroom sadist. Because he was tried for the murder of Mrs Gardner, Doreen Marshall's fate was cited merely to show his insane violence. Who but a madman would do it? Had he done it in order to prove his insanity, if caught? But, as he said repeatedly, he would rather be hanged than sent to Broadmoor.

His escape to Bournemouth had gone better than he dared hope. The police still feared he would get his hands on a light aircraft and escape abroad. Yet by Doreen Marshall's disappearance, he drew the hunt to him as the last person seen with her. Oddly, her hotel was half a mile east of the Tollard Royal and she had insisted on going there. Yet her body was found a mile to the west. At the height of the season there were people on the promenade, too many for Heath to force her westwards, let alone move a body. No doubt he used the full battery of his charm to take her on that walk.

Was there a motive for his destructive rage? Heath was a psychopath but cunning rather than simple-minded. The risks involved in a second murder would surely have to be outweighed by a more important development. His photograph had been withheld but his description, his service connections and the details of Margery Gardner's murder were in every newspaper. It is not impossible that something about him alerted Doreen Marshall's suspicions or that Heath thought they had been alerted. If anything of that sort passed between them, he may have decided that he dared not let Doreen Marshall live to tell others.

At Bournemouth police station three days later, 'Group Captain Rupert Brooke' explained the missing Wren to PC Souter. Doreen Marshall had told him she was going off with a GI boyfriend. That was where she was. The drama was over. He was leaving the police station, within sight of freedom, when he saw her ghost walking towards him. Souter watched him go pale. The 'ghost' was Doreen Marshall's sister, walking with her father, the girls being as like as twins. Heath recovered and was introduced. Yet in his panic he had loosened his pilot's silk 'escape' scarf with its map of Germany. Scratches were revealed on his neck. Souter consulted the *Police Gazette* and detained him as Neville Heath.

Heath told his counsel, J. D. Casswell QC, that he intended to plead guilty to the murder of Margery Gardner and get the matter over with. Casswell urged him to fight, for the sake of his family. 'All right,' Heath said indifferently. 'Put me down as not guilty, old boy.' Insanity, under the M'Naghten Rules, was his only possible defence. He would be deemed sane unless his counsel could convince the jury of the contrary. The M'Naghten Rules of 1843 required proof that he suffered from 'such a defect of reason due to disease of the mind' that either he did not appreciate the nature and quality of his act or that, if he did appreciate it, he did not know it to be legally wrong. The defence did not have to prove this beyond reasonable doubt but on the civil law 'balance of probabilities'.[12]

Defendants did not easily navigate this judicial maze. Neither sadism nor psychopathy was accepted by the law as a disease of the mind, merely as a moral failing. Uncontrollable impulse had also been dismissed by Lord Hewart in 1925 as 'merely subversive' of the criminal law. It was not part of that law, 'and it is to be hoped that the time is far distant when it will be made so'. Heath did not give evidence but Dr William Hubert, an eminent psychiatrist, was called on his behalf. Casswell did not know that Hubert was also an eminent morphine addict. Because his taxi was involved in a collision, he arrived at court late and needing an injection.[13]

Casswell was dismayed at his condition but Hubert injected morphine before giving evidence. He made euphoric statements during his evidence-in-chief, which were cut to pieces by Anthony Hawke in cross-examination. Dr Hubert agreed that Heath knew what he was doing. Hawke put a series of further questions. Did Heath know he was doing wrong when he tied the young woman on a bed, beat her with a thong, suffocated her by keeping her head pressed down? Hubert insisted that Heath did not, indeed he thought he was doing right. The scepticism on the faces of the jurors bordered on incredulity. Hubert then appeared to say that a man who forged a cheque on an impulse could also claim an acquittal. The expert witness thought he had triumphed but Casswell described his performance as 'absolutely appalling'. The expert witness died of a drug overdose in the following year.[14]

Had Heath's sadism been described in relation to Margery Gardner's masochism and the couple's drunkenness, her death might have appeared as a misadventure. But the only witness of that was the deceased. Any juror who read a newspaper in the previous two months would know of Doreen Marshall's death. Heath's conviction and the death sentence were a foregone conclusion.

He refused to appeal. During three weeks in the condemned cell at Pentonville he was the gallant pilot on a last mission – a 'one-way op', as he called it – from which he would not return. 'I have done many things of which I am ashamed but never in the air.' He made light of his execution. In case there was 'anything in this reincarnation business', he advised a friend, on the day before he was hanged, 'Please break your morning egg very gently for the next couple of months because it may be me.' He read *The Thirty-Nine Steps* twice. The authorities had refused him two American crime novels, D. B. Olsen's *Bring the Bride a Shroud* and Paul Whelton's *Call the Lady Indiscreet*. He wrote to his mother on his last night that he wanted to see the dawn again because it evoked 'early morning patrols and coming back from nightclubs'. He was the young war-hero facing execution by the enemy.[15]

4

Despite the luridness of his two murders, there is no evidence that Neville Heath planned either. His behaviour was callous and self-serving but distinguished from Haigh and Christie who contrived the deaths of their victims with care.

Like Heath, John Haigh was a vain man who believed that a moustache not unlike Adolf Hitler's gave him a resemblance to the film star Ronald Colman. Unlike Heath, he saw his childhood reflected in his crimes. Born at Stamford, Lincolnshire, of parents who were austere Plymouth Brethren, he won a choral scholarship to Wakefield Grammar School. This seems to have given him a place as a choirboy and later assistant organist at Wakefield Cathedral, a centre of ritualistic High Anglicanism. He attributed his 'vampirism' to the taste of blood on his hand after his mother punished him with the bristles of a hairbrush and to the images of Christ's wounds on the Cross.

In 1934, at twenty-five, he first went to prison with a conviction for dishonesty. His fraud showed some ingenuity but it was soon detected. He took an option on a garage that was for sale. Using its notepaper and his skill in forging handwriting, he wrote to hire-purchase firms, falsely certifying that people of substance in the area had bought cars from him. He was applying on their behalf for hire-purchase loans. The finance company advanced the money to the garage and Haigh pocketed it. Had he seen that as the moment to abscond, he might have escaped. Instead he was caught and went to prison for fifteen months at Leeds Assizes on 22 November.

Members of the Plymouth Brethren tried to rehabilitate the young man by setting him up in a dry-cleaning business. The business failed and he made his way to London, operating a bogus branch of an established firm of solicitors. On the pretext of winding up an estate, he offered shares at a discount in exchange for a 25 per cent deposit. He absconded with the money and set up the fraud in another area. He was eventually caught at Guildford and sent to penal servitude for four years at Surrey Assizes in November 1937.

By the time of his release in 1940, the bombs were falling on London and he became a firewatcher. He recalled that wartime fires fascinated him and it seemed a pity to put them out. His most poignant memory was of talking to a nurse during an air raid and of a bomb falling just after they had parted. He sheltered in a doorway and, a moment later, the nurse's head rolled past his foot.

He was free for less than a year before receiving twenty-one months at London Sessions for stealing furnishings and kitchen goods. While working in the tinsmith's shop in prison, he also practised dissolving the bodies of mice in sulphuric acid. Released in 1943, he was required to register for military service. He did so, but never attended a medical board. Though the authorities searched for him, there were too many of his kind and they never found him. In 1945 his file, like thousands of others, was marked 'No further action'.

So far, it seemed, Haigh's life had led from one act of dishonesty to another. In September 1944, at thirty-five, he found a new sense of purpose and an ideal victim. In the bar of the Goat public house in Kensington he met a young man whom he had known eight years earlier, William Donald McSwan. The McSwan family had owned an amusement arcade, managed by Haigh in 1936 between spells of imprisonment. He had impressed them. In 1944 the young McSwan was facing call-up for military service. He was most anxious to avoid it. Haigh agreed to help.

By this time, Haigh was working for Hurstlea Products Ltd at Crawley in Sussex. He had his own London workshop in the Gloucester Road where, he told McSwan, he repaired pin-tables for amusement arcades. It was arranged for the young man to bring a table for repair. On 9 September 1944, in the basement workshop, Haigh battered him to death with the leg of a pin-table. By his own account, Haigh the vampire made an incision in the dead man's neck and drank the blood from a tea mug. He retrieved a water butt from a bomb-site, brought it back on a handcart, forced the body into it and covered the corpse with concentrated sulphuric acid. The acid darkened and grew warm but McSwan did not entirely dissolve. Haigh was obliged to assist the process with a cleaver and a mincer, bought from the kitchen department of Gamages. He greased the floor first of all so that there should be no bloodstaining. Finally, he poured what remained of McSwan down the basement drain.

The McSwan parents knew of their son's intention to avoid military service. Haigh went to see them and explained that the young man was now on the run. He then forged a letter in McSwan's handwriting, asking the parents to forward money through his trusted friend John George Haigh. Further letters were written in McSwan's name until, in July 1945, the parents were invited to visit Haigh's workshop. They were never seen again. In the aftermath of this, by forgery and impersonation, Haigh contrived a power of attorney under which McSwan junior gave him management of four substantial freehold properties.

By 1948, Haigh was in need of more money. He boasted of having his own factory at Crawley and of being a director of Hurstlea Products Ltd. The truth was that he rented a two-storey brick shed from the firm. It was here, in February 1948, that he shot Dr Archie Henderson and his wife Rose, taking a glass of blood from each, and dissolving the bodies. By means of forged letters and forged deeds of transfer, he acquired the Hendersons' house and sold it. However, he looked after their red setter until the dog's night-blindness obliged him to send it to kennels in the country. .

To most who knew him at this time, Haigh was charming, courteous and cultivated, eloquent and dapper with his Ronald Colman moustache. Since his days as chorister and organist at Wakefield Cathedral, music had been his passion. He knew several celebrated musicians from visits to the Albert Hall and recitals at the Wigmore Hall. His companion was a platonic girlfriend, much younger than he, whom he met when she was fifteen. He attended Foyle's literary lunches and had, as if by nature, a courtly manner with women. There was a boyish jollity in his speech when, for example, he brought out such Wodehousean exclamations as 'Good egg!' He was the last man thought likely to have murdered nine people, his boasted total.

By the beginning of 1949, he was again in reduced circumstances, living at the Onslow Court Hotel, South Kensington, and a favourite with its elderly female residents. On 18 February, the wealthy Mrs Durand-Deacon did not return for dinner. She did not return on the following day. No one was more concerned than Haigh who went with Mrs Durand-Deacon's friend, Mrs Lane, to Chelsea police station to report the disappearance. Mrs Durand-Deacon had been to various functions as his guest and he had invited her to his factory in Sussex. She was nowhere to be found when the time had come to set off for Crawley. The police questioned the hotel guests, including Haigh. Because he had not bothered to use a different name, it was discovered that he had a criminal record. There was no crime of violence in this but he had already described himself, untruthfully, as a director of Hurstlea Products. It seemed sensible to ask the West Sussex Constabulary to take a look at his 'factory'.

The search revealed various papers and, surprisingly, a revolver. The police also found a receipt for a Persian lamb coat from a firm of cleaners in Reigate. It proved to belong to Mrs Durand-Deacon. On the afternoon following her disappearance, her jewellery had been brought to a jeweller in Horsham for valuation and sale.

Haigh meanwhile was sitting in an armchair at Chelsea police station. 'I will do anything to help you,' he told Inspector Webb, unaware of the search in Sussex. As the conversation continued and he was accused of murder, he asked what the chances were of anyone sent to Broadmoor ever being released. Webb refused to comment but Haigh began an elaborate account of murders he had committed. It was not money that he wanted but blood. His life since his schooldays at Wakefield Cathedral and the beatings with the hairbrush had been a pursuit of vampirism. The foundation for his defence of insanity was laid even before he was charged. In case it did not work, he had a more prosaic response. 'How can you prove murder, if there is no body?' In this he was mistaken. Murder might well be proved in the absence of a corpse.[16]

He was also wrong to suppose that there was no 'body'. Haigh had tipped the sludge from the drum on to waste ground outside. A careful search identified fragments of bone and gallstones belonging to Mrs Durand-Deacon, as well as dentures made for her.

Haigh's trial at Lewes Assizes in July 1949 provoked intense public curiosity. He described more than once in letters to his elderly parents how he 'hooted with mirth' at newspaper reports of the case, hooting again when a fat policeman to whom he was hand-cuffed tripped over the sill of the car door. Proceedings would begin, he assured his parents, with arguments over his mental fitness to face trial. This would be 'fun'. Again, he reported the 'fun' of the trial. At the magistrates court, when counsel for the Crown was awkwardly demonstrating a stirrup pump used to fill the vat with acid, the gowned figure splashed his hand with a few drops still in the barrel. Onlookers in court were anxious or nervous, except Haigh in the dock who was rocking gently, eyes sparkling, cheeks and mouth compressed in a pantomime of silenced mirth. Nor did his bizarre conduct end at the trial. While in the condemned cell at Wandsworth, he tried vainly to persuade the governor to stage a dress rehearsal of his execution, so that each man involved would know the part he must play and the performance would go smoothly on the all-important morning.

A further curiosity of proceedings against Heath and Haigh was the fascination which the murderers seemed to exercise upon female spectators. A young woman had announced to the press that she was adopting Heath in Brixton prison as her correspondent. A redhead who seldom took her eyes from him during the trial combed her long hair slowly for his benefit, like a siren of the Lorelei. When Haigh was charged before a special court in the town hall of Horsham on 2 March 1949, women in the crowd were reported to have torn headscarves from each other and knocked policemen's helmets off, attempting to storm the town hall doorway to get near him, as if to touch the hem of his garment. During the hearing, they stood on barrows and climbed on to ladders to peer through the windows. A crowd of several hundred surged round the police car as it edged forwards, leaving Horsham for Lewes prison. These scenes had much in common with the funeral of the musical idol Ivor Novello in 1951, when they were imitated at Golders Green crematorium.

At a second hearing, police tried to smuggle Haigh out through a back door but he was seen and mobbed by the leaders of the crowd in fur coats and their proletarian sisters carrying babies. Some barred the path of the car and others tried to open its doors. To feel the Austin Reed suit of the acid bath killer with his Ronald Colman looks might have been to draw strength from the vampire. It seemed that such men radiated, in a debased and corrupt form, the most prized quality of wartime and the austerity which followed. Tarnished and tawdry, there hung about them an air of glamour. Perhaps the tarnish and tawdriness, even the nature of the crimes, gave such glamour a secret and illicit appeal.

The outcome of Haigh's trial was scarcely in doubt. His vampirism was judged to be fabricated as a 'proof' of insanity. A cupful of blood would almost certainly act as an emetic and he evidently did not know this. This man who 'hooted with mirth' at the 'fun' of being tried for his life and wanted a dress rehearsal of his own hanging was not insane within the M'Naghten Rules. Dr Yellowlees for the defence lost his battle in two final exchanges with Sir Hartley Shawcross, cross-examining as Attorney-General.

SHAWCROSS: I am asking you to look at the facts and tell the jury whether there is any doubt that he must have known that according to English law he was preparing to do and subsequently did do something which was wrong.

YELLOWLEES: I will say 'Yes' to that if you say 'punishable by law' instead of 'wrong'.

SHAWCROSS: Punishable by law and, therefore, wrong by the law of this country?

YELLOWLEES: Yes, I think he knew that.[17]

Despite their different compulsions and a marked difference in their origins, Heath and Haigh exhibited what seemed to be classic symptoms of psychopathy. They were ruthless and undeviating in their dishonesty, apparently devoid of remorse, indifferent to the judicial process and to the society it represented. They took no thought for consequences, relying on spry wits to remain ahead of the game. Haigh, in every sense prepared to do his own dirty work, had a longer run of luck than Heath. Yet both seemed doomed to detection and the gallows; even Haigh's luck would fail him at the first hint of a victim's mysterious disappearance. Their rival, John Reginald Halliday Christie, was not their social equal nor as adept in dishonesty. Yet he enjoyed a far longer career of homicide than either.

5

On 30 November 1949, in what at first seemed an unrelated matter, a young van driver named Timothy Evans walked into a South Wales police station to admit that he had 'disposed of' his wife Beryl in London by putting her body down a drain. Four months pregnant with a second child, she had wanted to get rid of it. Evans got a 'little bottle' from a man in a transport café. Beryl Evans took the contents and was dead the next day.

Following a telephone call from the Central Police Station at

Merthyr Tydfil, the Metropolitan Police lifted a manhole cover outside 10 Rillington Place, Notting Hill. It was too small for a body to pass through, there were no human remains under it, and Evans could not have lifted it alone. This information came back to South Wales CID. Evans made a second statement, implicating Reg Christie and his wife Ethel, ground-floor tenants in the house. Reg Christie, 'training for a doctor before the war', had shown Evans medical books and promised to aid the abortion. Evans was illiterate and unaware that the 'medical' books were first-aid manuals of the St John's Ambulance Brigade. In this version of events he came home from work and heard Christie's 'bad news'. Beryl Evans had died during the attempted abortion. Her body was still on the bed but Christie promised to put it down the outside drain.

Next day, police from 'F' Division, Notting Hill, interviewed the Christies, who understood from Evans that his wife and the baby were in Brighton. Evans was brought to London from Wales on 2 December as officers searched 10 Rillington Place. Behind wood stacked in an outside wash-house, they found the bodies of Mrs Evans and Geraldine, her daughter of fourteen months. Both had been strangled. Evans arrived under escort at Notting Hill police station at 9.45 p.m. Told he would be charged with the murders, he said, 'Yes.' He made two statements, first admitting the murder of his wife, then of both his wife and daughter. The Evans marriage had not been one for the faint-hearted. On 8 November they quarrelled over the debts Beryl was running up. Blows were exchanged and, Evans said, he strangled his wife and hid her body. Two days later he strangled Geraldine. Christie was not involved.

When charged next morning with his wife's murder, Evans said, 'Yes, that's right.' He made no reply when charged with murdering Geraldine. Almost at once, he withdrew his confessions. At the magistrates' hearing, he told his mother, 'I never done it, Mum.' 'Christie done it,' became his defence. He had confessed because news of his daughter's death left him nothing to live for and he feared the police would beat an admission from him. His intelligence became an issue. Dr J. C. M Matheson, Principal Medical Officer of Brixton prison, put his IQ at 65 and his mental age at eleven. Medical officers advising the Home Secretary termed his education 'faulty' but found him of 'average intelligence'. He could only be tried for one murder at a time and the Crown chose the case of his baby daughter, where the defence could scarcely plead provocation. Christie became a key witness for the prosecution.

The police in Notting Hill and at Harrow Road knew something of Reg Christie. Inspector Jennings thought him 'a decent type of man', though apt to complain over trivial antisocial conduct. In 1939, at forty-one and too old for military service, he had volunteered as a War Reserve constable and proved a 'capable officer'. His father was a latter-day north country patriarch, founder of the Halifax Conservative Society. Christie was a scholarship boy at Halifax Secondary School. At twenty, he was blinded for five months by the blast of a mustard gas shell on the Western Front. Thereafter he lived on middle-class aspirations and working-class wages, as a cinema projectionist and a clerk.

To his superiors in 1949, Christie was an efficient white-collar worker, perhaps born for something better. In private life, he seemed a prig, particularly towards the conduct of women. He frequented the fly-spotted little cafés and snack bars of Notting Hill or Hammersmith, avoiding the public houses of Ladbroke Grove or Praed Street, patronized by prostitutes from 'short-time' hotels in the avenues and squares round Paddington railway terminus.

In his neighbourhood, his horn-rimmed glasses and balding head gave him a studious air. He liked to hear himself called 'The Doc' by patrons of the little cafés. During his war service he was seen reading the *British Medical Journal* and the *Lancet*. It was thought by some that he had been a 'medico' who abandoned his studies after an accident. In 1934 he had been knocked off his bicycle, suffering concussion, and underwent operations to repair his knee and collar-bone. In truth, he had never been a student of any kind. He was sometimes said to have been a pre-war doctor, struck off for performing an abortion. This rumour brought him into contact with women 'of a certain class'. Fastidious, pedantic, censorious, 'The Doc' was a man from a better-educated class than his neighbours. Spoken of as a medical student and certainly a policeman, he became their adviser on medical and legal problems.

Reputation was all to him. Dr Hobson, for his defence, found

Christie more upset by the revelation that he had picked up a victim in a public house than by the charge of murdering her. 'He feels that going into public houses is something very disgusting, and very morally wrong, and he strongly denies that he has been in public houses.' Christie insisted he did not drink alcohol. He frequented public houses in Praed Street and Ladbroke Grove as a sexual predator. Their impoverished prostitutes scarcely required enticement.[18]

As 'The Doc', Christie would sympathize in the cafés with sufferers from headaches, 'sinus trouble' and the like. He may have promised to aid abortions but it seems he never attempted to carry one out. Mrs Margaret Forrest, who was saved from his attentions by his arrest, complained of migraines. 'The Doc' had just the remedy: a new gas inhaled for ten minutes would in most cases clear up the problem. What came through the tube in the patient's mouth was a mixture of friar's balsam and a gradually increased quantity of town gas from the fireplace, controlled by Christie, a mixture he first used to prepare Ruth Fuerst in 1943.

No one, in the crisis of 1939, checked whether the industrious clerk, living with wife and 'medical' books in the grimy cul-de-sac, had a criminal record. By then he had had a clean record for six years. He served in the police until 1943 and the scandal of a divorce action, when a serviceman had beaten him up after returning home and finding Christie with his wife. Yet his time at Harrow Road earned him two commendations and duty as a plain-clothes officer. Efficient and officious over blackout regulations, the residents dubbed him 'The Persecuting Counsel'.

Before Evans' trial, the Crown discovered Christie's criminal past but presented him as a man who had redeemed errors of distant misconduct. In any case, Evans had at first confessed to the crimes and implicated Christie only as an abortionist. The autopsy on Mrs Evans showed no evidence of attempted abortion. Again, if Evans knew nothing of the murder, why did he sell his wife's wedding-ring to a Merthyr Tydfil jeweller shortly after her death? He insisted Christie was the killer, but could not persuade Christmas Humphreys or the jury. 'Can you suggest why he should have strangled your wife?' 'No, I can't.' 'Can you suggest why he should have strangled your daughter?' 'No.' At a time when Christie was supposed

by Evans to be carrying a body about the house, he was incapaci-
tated by fibrositis. The jurors found the young van driver guilty and
the legal process passed him briskly to the hangman. He was executed
on 9 March 1950, maintaining to the last that 'Christie done it.'[19]

In 1966, Roy Jenkins as Home Secretary ordered a judicial inquiry
into the Evans case by Mr Justice Brabin. After sixteen years, Lord
Brabin could not test new evidence 'beyond reasonable doubt'. On
a balance of probabilities, he judged it 'more likely than not' that
Evans did not murder his baby, for which he was hanged, but that
he did kill his wife, for which he was not tried.[20]

6

This 'decent type of man', as Chief Inspector Jennings had called
Christie, went on his way. Until 1950, he was a ledger clerk at the
Post Office Savings Bank at Kew. His conviction for stealing postal
orders in 1920 came to light and he was dismissed. He found a
job in the accounts department of British Road Services in
Hampstead. In the New Year of 1953, he spoke of being 'transferred'
to Birmingham. After sixteen years, the Christies would leave
Rillington Place. He had taken a lease on a flat in Birmingham and
Mrs Christie had gone on ahead. No one had seen her in Rillington
Place since mid-December 1952. In March 1953, he let the flat to
a Mr and Mrs Reilly for three months for £8 13s. 0d. in advance.
On 20 March he left the district.

Notting Hill was changing with the first West Indian immigrants.
Christie was distressed and sure that the top floor contained black
men with white women who were prostitutes. Charles Brown, the
landlord, let the ground floor to a family, Mr Beresford Brown with
his wife and newborn baby. The Reillys were told that Christie had
no right to let the premises and that they must leave. On 24 March,
Mr Beresford Brown decided to install a radio set on a bracket in
the kitchen. Behind one wall was a space, variously termed an alcove
and a cupboard, papered over. Mr Brown tore a little of the wall-
paper to examine the surface. He found himself looking at a bare
human back.

The police were followed by Professor Francis Camps, Home Office pathologist. He found three bodies in the alcove. One stood on its head, wrapped in a blanket secured with plastic-covered wire. A second also stood on its head, in a blanket. A third sat on the head of the second, leaning forward but held in position by a corner of the second body's blanket tied to the back of its brassiere. The wrists of the third body were bound together.

All three women had suffered carbon monoxide poisoning and at least two had been strangled. Sexual intercourse had occurred at about the time of death. They were identified as Rita Nelson, Kathleen Maloney and Hectorina MacLennan, prostitutes 'among the most forlorn of their company', as Lord Brabin termed them. Rita Nelson went missing on 19 January. Kathleen Maloney and a female friend had gone to a studio with Christie in December, when Christie took nude photographs of the other young woman. In January, Kathleen Maloney had stayed with Christie, whose wife had 'just died'. She received a gift of Mrs Christie's clothes. She was with Christie about a fortnight after Christmas, in a Praed Street public house, and was not seen alive again. Hectorina MacLennan visited Rillington Place later. On 6 March she vanished.

On 24 March, the floorboards were lifted. Under the sitting room lay Mrs Christie, last seen in mid-December. Unlike the others, she showed no sign of carbon monoxide poisoning and no evidence of sexual intercourse. The Christies had lived together during most of their thirty-year marriage but there had been separations. Christie explained that he strangled his wife as an act of mercy, during a choking fit which followed an overdose of phenobarbitone. There was no sign of phenobarbitone. In the light of the other murders, it seemed that he had got rid of Mrs Christie to free the flat for his macabre purposes.

Three days later, the police dug the garden and found two skeletons which proved to be Ruth Fuerst, an Austrian émigrée, and Muriel Eady, who had worked for Ultra Radio manufacturers in Acton, where Christie found employment after leaving the police. He had strangled Ruth Fuerst in 1943, during a separation from his wife. Muriel Eady was gassed to unconsciousness in October 1944, then suffered the same fate.

Christie evaded capture for only a few days, arrested by a constable who found him staring at the river near Putney Bridge. The culprit did not deny his crimes, indeed he embellished them. His defence was insanity and his only evidence was psychiatric. If he was believed – and perhaps in this matter it was safe to do so – he was a necrophiliac whose satisfaction came from strangling women before, after, or during intercourse.

With so many murders to choose from, he was tried for killing his wife. He had admitted this and the other five homicides, pleading not guilty by reason of insanity. While awaiting trial, he finally confessed to murdering Beryl Evans. 'The more the merrier,' he told the prison chaplain. Yet there was no evidence of the intercourse with Mrs Evans, which he claimed had taken place. A second post-mortem in 1953 showed no trace of carbon monoxide gas either. He retracted his confession.

If there was a single motive for his conduct, it might have lain far in the past. On a Sunday evening in his teens, following the evening service which his family attended, he went with a girl to a local 'lover's lane'. She complained to friends afterwards that he had been a sexual failure. 'Can't-make-it-Christie' was, according to the writer and criminologist Fryn Tennyson Jesse, shouted after him in the streets.[21]

What some young men might have regarded as a temporary embarrassment, born of inexperience, may well have lived on as anger and humiliation in Christie, fuelling a lingering fear and hatred of women. Perhaps he felt safe in his sexual relations with them only when they were unconscious or bound, or dead. Shortly before his execution, he was reported as saying, 'They dress and paint up and give you the come-on, and you can't help thinking they wouldn't look nearly so cheeky or so saucy if they were helpless or dead.' He also thought pregnancy was a humiliation for women and made them look ridiculous, a view shared by the anti-heroes of Sade's *Justine*.

Chilling though these private outbursts were, they were echoed at his trial. Christie presented himself, or acted a part, as a man whose mental state prevented any clear recollection of the murders. However, he recalled that Rita Nelson and later Hectorina

MacLennan followed him home and forced their attentions on him. He was affronted and disgusted by this, especially as Rita Nelson began to strip in front of him. There had been a struggle with each girl, as he tried to march her out. He could not remember exactly what followed but the next thing he knew was when the girl was lying dead on the floor. He could not remember putting their bodies in the alcove but accepted that he must have done so if that was what the evidence indicated. He could not remember killing them but, again, accepted that he must have done so if that was what the evidence showed. They had been the aggressors. Of Rita Nelson he said, with a vague helplessness, that she threatened him with the 'boys' at Notting Hill. 'Well, I strangled her. That is when, I think, the intercourse must have happened.' He spoke like a detached observer talking of another man's actions. Presently he added reassuringly to the court, 'I did not want to hurt her. I have never hurt anybody.'[22]

As he said this, it was necessary to remember that he had killed at least six women, perhaps many more. But if there was no hurt, why should there be self-restraint, moral inhibition, respect for truth, or remorse? This new and comfortable philosophy had taken root in other areas of post-war life. Who was hurt by thefts where the insurance company would pay? What harm was done by printing counterfeit clothing coupons when the industry itself complained of a glut of supplies? How much did it matter if an entrance ticket to the Festival of Britain travelled two or three times past the turnstiles?

'I have never hurt anybody.' With these words Christie was united with two of literature's memorable psychopaths. Another earnest strangler, 'Porphyria's Lover', spoke them in one of the young Robert Browning's *Madhouse Cells* in 1836, explaining that he had to strangle his young mistress because otherwise she would not have stayed with him. Now she was his for ever. 'No pain felt she/I am quite sure she felt no pain.' Browning's famous 'morbid anatomy' showed him as a man far in advance of his time. A century later, George Harvey Bone, the schizophrenic hero of Patrick Hamilton's *Hangover Square* (1940), killed his faithless mistress in the bath, telling himself that he must not hurt her. He then dispatched her lover with a blow to the head from a number seven golf iron, inquiring as the man fell, 'Are you all right, old boy? I'm sorry. I didn't hurt you, did I?' How did Christie persuade himself he had done no harm?[23]

'Mad as a hatter, but not within the M'Naghten Rules,' was a psychiatrist's verdict on Neville Heath. 'Mad as a March hare,' was a professional view of Christie. Yet in the world beyond the gas-filled kitchen of the cul-de-sac, Christie's transparent lunacy was another aberration which the M'Naghten Rules could not accommodate. He went to the gallows on 15 July 1953 but in the days prior to his execution he was the central figure in a public inquiry, ordered by the Home Secretary into the Evans case. Christie's evidence was to be given in Pentonville prison.

On 9 July, John Scott-Henderson QC and his colleagues, including the Assistant Chief Constable of the West Riding and an official of the Treasury Solicitor's office, assembled to take Christie's evidence. It was the last and most prestigious appearance of 'The Doc'. Those who surrounded him were no longer the humble patrons of cafés in Notting Hill and Hammersmith but representatives of the highest in the land. They brought him from the condemned cell, sought his advice with respect and listened attentively to his opinions, addressing him as 'Mr Christie' and thanking him for his help. When the hearing was over, the highest in the land sent him back to the death cell and hanged him six days later. Lord Brabin's report was still thirteen years in the future. This first inquiry concluded that Timothy Evans had murdered not only his daughter but his wife as well. He was rightly hanged.[24]

7

The eight years that followed Hitler's war might take their choice of such freaks of nature as the famous psychopaths. Their immediate popularity was confined to the entertainment of the Sunday afternoon newspaper or the clockwork models on seaside piers, where garishly painted toy figures in glass cases re-enacted in miniature the executions of the best-known homicides of the recent past, performed for the price of a penny in the slot. Fewer than twenty victims had the misfortune to encounter any of these three men in reality. Other cold-hearted crimes that reflected the post-war world to itself were not theirs.

The journalist Conrad Phillips, who had met Heath, Haigh and Christie before their arrests, concluded that all criminals of whatever kind were sadists. They were callous, vicious and cared nothing for the suffering they inflicted. If they showed no remorse, it was because they felt no identity with the society around them, which they despised as consisting of 'mugs' or weaklings. To that extent Billy Hill and his kind were psychopaths. In Phillips' view, Raffles, Robin Hood and the loveable rogue were merely sentimental creations of the novelist.[25]

So long as the squatters of 1946 had confined their seizures to government property, they had been admired for their courage and initiative. The starving Victorian beggar, or indeed the pre-war unemployed worker, who stole from a richer victim to feed a family in the slums might be sympathetically regarded. A century earlier, in Pierre-Joseph Proudhon's definition, to possess property was itself an act of theft, an obstacle to justice and liberty. Raffles the Gentleman Cracksman echoed this when he sought to justify his activities on the grounds that the distribution of property is 'all wrong'.

Post-war criminals certainly displayed a moral indifference and a truculence which prompted such reactions as those of Conrad Phillips. Nor did they necessarily harm themselves by this. Some who set out on their careers in those years would live long enough to sell publishing rights to their life stories or appear at length on television, talking of their accomplishments as professional men and posing for admiration. They would speak with satisfaction of their achievements, usually without a shred of remorse. A bank that was raided felt no more pain than a government whose military surplus supplies were 'liberated'.

This overlooked the uncomfortable truth that a wage-carrier who had ammonia squirted into the eyes might be blinded or that men and women who had the misfortune to be in the way of a robber were likely to be injured and sometimes killed. A man who shot dead two policemen in 1967 told the *Guardian* twenty-six years later, 'The police aren't like real people to us. They're strangers. They're the enemy. And you don't feel remorse for killing a stranger. I do feel sorry for what we did to their families. I do. But it's like the people I killed in Malaya when I was in the Army. You don't feel remorse.'[26]

By this time, of course, the police were no longer 'Old Bill' or 'the bogies' but 'the filth'. Those who got in the way, let alone resisted a criminal, had only themselves to blame. Some, like the injured driver of the train which was the subject of the 1963 Great Train Robbery, were dismissed by the underworld as 'shamming' their disability for personal gain. Similarly, Christie maintained that Rita Nelson and Hectorina MacLennan had precipitated their own murders by their disgusting conduct towards him. Haigh was irritated with Mrs Durand-Deacon because one of her buttocks failed to dissolve. Heath told the police that women were attracted to 'rascals like me' because they were weak and stupid, and basically crooked, with the morals of alley cats.

Though the cosh boy or the bank raider might not have been flattered by the association with Heath, Haigh or Christie, he and the psychopaths seemed jointly to confirm the truth of a comment by Tacitus almost two thousand years earlier, in his biographical memoir of his father-in-law Agricola, 'It is human nature to hate those one has injured'; also, perhaps, those whom one was about to injure.

George Orwell, who saw the new shabbiness in English murder in 1946, also observed the triumph of the psychopath in the influential culture of the common reader. Though he was writing in the review columns of *Horizon* in 1944, the new amorality of crime was not something he attributed solely to the effects of the war. The book under review was by James Hadley Chase, *No Orchids for Miss Blandish*, and it had been published in 1939. In their advertisements, Jarrolds the publishers confessed that they, as well as the printers and the readers, were still convalescing from shock. 'They thought they could take it until they ran into Slim Grisson', the novel's professional killer, as the jacket blurb put it. In the early stages of the war, sales had been huge, not least among members of the RAF in which its author was a serving pilot. Its title became a byword for the sensational, the violent and the pornographic. When Jarrolds were convicted of obscenity in 1942 over another of Chase's novels, *Miss Callaghan Comes to Grief*, the earlier title was temporarily withdrawn.

The story describes Miss Blandish, kidnapped for ransom, flogged with rubber tubing by Ma Grisson to force her to submit to the old woman's slobbering idiot of a son, Slim the killer, known generally for his sadism and his taste for little girls. The ensuing rape, the victim's obsessive love for her rapist in the aftermath of the crime, her suicide when he is killed and she released, is matched by gang warfare in which brutal murder is the small change of life. Though Chase was a British author, the book is written as if the author and the action were American. It contains a good deal of 'soft round thighs smooth under the silk dress', yet the tone, as Orwell suggests, is too violent to be pornographic. Slim Grisson ties a captive to a tree and skewers the man to it with a knife through his navel. Sitting down to await his victim's death, Slim tips his hat forward, lights a cigarette and says, 'Take your time, pal.' In the bleakness of the story, the police are as unscrupulous, sadistic and corrupt as the criminals.[27]

Chase's world of sardonic cruelty is tuned to a higher pitch than that of Heath, Haigh or Christie. Yet its ultimate contempt for the victim and the constant triumph of the strong over the weak has much in common with them. The appeal of this mixture at the outbreak of the war was strong enough for the novel to sell half a million copies at its first appearance. It had a long run as a stage play and was adapted as a film in 1948. Perhaps the whimsies of the post-war psychopaths were not such rarities after all.

During the war, 'Yank mags' circulated freely and widely, not least among children. Brutality was justified in cartoon dramas because it was carried out in the name of the Allies upon brutal Germans and subhuman Japanese. Yet the American best-seller of 1947, Mickey Spillane's *I, the Jury*, marked a return to the world of James Hadley Chase. The 'buddy' of its private-eye hero, Mike Hammer, is shot in the stomach and left to die. Hammer vows to find the killer, to be 'judge, jury, and executioner', and to kill the murderer in the same manner. The culprit proves to be the book's heroine, who performs a detailed striptease on the last page in an attempt to lure the hero to his death. When she is naked, Hammer shoots her through the navel. As she falls to her knees, she asks stammeringly how he could do such a thing. His riposte is ready, in the last line of the book. '"It was easy," I said.' Eroticism and sadism are supercharged with the hero's self-righteousness. This combination was not unknown to the psychopaths, certainly not to Christie as the prostitutes of Paddington forced themselves upon him. In fact and fantasy, such figures as he opened the way to the dehumanization of criminality.[28]

7

Professionals and Amateurs

THE PROFESSIONALISM OF the underworld in the immediate
post-war years took many forms. There were spectacular fail-
ures, including the Kentish Town bank raid, in which the kidnapped
'bank manager' proved to be a Flying Squad officer who had volunteered to take the real manager's place. The success stories included
the Catford Stadium safe-blowing of 1950, the Eastcastle Street mail
robbery of 1952 and the climber who made a clean sweep of the
Duchess of Windsor's jewels in 1946.

In parallel with such dramas, there were the journeymen of crime
who worked, year in and year out, with quiet purpose and for
modest rewards. One man whose career and criminal convictions
stretched back not only beyond the Second World War but beyond
the First World War and the Boer War was not arrested for the last
time until 1963, when a policewoman in plain clothes trailed a little
gang of six pickpockets to the platform of Paddington underground
station. Once there, the men never exchanged glances or made any
sign of recognition. They signalled to one another by whistling a
variety of pre-arranged tunes. Perhaps they sensed the policewoman's
presence but, for whatever reason, they became uneasy. A final tune
was the signal for these 'dippers' to make their way up, individually, from the station to a café in Praed Street. Having got them
bottled up, PCW Patricia Willey phoned for assistance and all six
were arrested.

Three men were sent to prison for three months each and two
were fined for loitering with intent to pick pockets. The real
problem, as the magistrate described him, was Louis Simons from
Stepney. He was the 'front man' behind the gang and the brains of
the organization. Louis Simons was eighty-three and his thirty-nine

previous convictions stretched back to 1897. Though not as nimble as he had been then, this octogenarian thief was the guarantee of escape for his younger accomplices in their twenties and thirties. If the alarm was raised during the purloining of a wallet or the palming of a watch, he would assume the role of an aged but gallant 'have-a-go' hero in the vanguard of the pursuit. His technique was to bumble about in the path of other concerned citizens, keeping them back. If that failed, he had a knack of dropping his walking stick to trip up the swiftest and most agile. The magistrate confessed he did not know what to do with the old man. He gave him a conditional discharge, saying helplessly, 'It is time you gave up this sort of thing. You are too old for it.' The evidence, however, pointed the other way.[1]

Louis Simons was a professional, though he had never been part of the big time. On the other hand, there were amateurs in the two post-war decades who sometimes put professionals to shame. As the post-war years passed, government and law enforcement became increasingly fearful of the spectre of organized crime, whether the threat came from the North American Mafia with covetous eyes on England or from professionals at home. While this danger certainly existed, an entire landscape of the post-war world was dominated by what could only be called disorganized crime.

In 1961, at a time when carefully planned bank raids, safe-blowings or the hijacking of a security van would rarely produce more than £50,000, there was a diamond theft involving £250,000 at Heathrow Airport. The robber and his accomplices were eventually caught and sent to prison. The principal was not a Raffles of modern crime but a BOAC loader. When caught, he showed a sporting realism. 'I have had a good run,' he told Detective Inspector Robert Field of the area CID. 'It has been a good wicket.' Inspector Field asked him to describe the plan by which he had contrived to steal a major consignment of diamonds and carry it through airport security. 'Guv'nor,' said the thief candidly, 'I just shoved it up my jumper and walked off.' He went to prison for six years.[2]

The loader and almost all his accomplices were described as good workers. Only two of the ten had previous convictions. Such circumstances always made a case more difficult to investigate. As the airport thieves were awaiting trial, national headlines announced on 22 August 1961 the most spectacular art theft in British criminal history. Goya's portrait of the Duke of Wellington, painted in 1812 and valued at £140,000 or some £2,000,000 in modern terms, had vanished from the National Gallery. It had been standing on an easel at the top of the main staircase, in full view of the public and its guardians.

Ports and airports were watched. Interpol and FBI were alerted. Special Branch officers, equipped with descriptions of international art thieves, mingled with holidaymakers leaving the Channel ports. Cars and luggage were searched. Nine days after the theft, the news agency Reuters received a ransom demand for £140,000, written on plain paper in block capitals and posted in the NW1 postal district of London. The money was to be sent to charity. Two days later a telephone call demanded that the ransom should be donated to the Campaign for Nuclear Disarmament. Next day, another call named the CND as such a worthy cause that the ransom would be reduced to £50,000. On 6 October, a nineteen-year-old typist who pleaded guilty to stealing a portrait tablet valued at £10 from the National Portrait Gallery confessed that she was also the leader of the gang who had stolen the Goya. She was nothing of the kind.[3]

Two days afterwards, the *Evening Standard* received a call from a man who said that unless the ransom were paid, the picture would be destroyed. There was then silence until the following July when a letter demanded that some 'non-conformist person', like Field Marshal Montgomery or Sir Billy Butlin, should start raising the £140,000. Four days later, a letter offered to return the painting in exchange for a £1,000 donation to a cancer charity. Caught between international art thieves and opportunist hoaxers at home, Scotland Yard and Special Branch got nowhere.

The rest of the year passed and the year after that, until 31 December 1962, when a letter from another crank offered the return of the painting so long as the thief should be allowed to do this wearing a hood and with a guaranteed amnesty. 'The Yard are looking for a needle in a haystack,' the message added, 'but they haven't a clue where the haystack is.' That seemed only too true. To make matters worse, the first James Bond film had been released in that autumn as *Dr No*. When the camera panned round the walls of Dr No's Caribbean lair, it came to rest on an image of the stolen portrait. It was an unwelcome joke.

The years passed until 22 May 1965, when it was announced that the picture had been found unharmed in a left luggage locker at New Street station, Birmingham, protected by hardboard and wrapped in sacking. On 19 July, the culprit surrendered at Scotland Yard. This 'international art thief' proved to be a sixty-one-year-old unemployed lorry driver from Newcastle, named Kempton Bunton. At Scotland Yard, he said, 'I am turning myself in for the Goya.'

Detective Chief Inspector John Welsner interviewed him and asked, 'Are you saying you stole it?' 'Of course,' said Bunton. 'That is why I am here.' He wanted to know if there was still a reward for the discovery of the thief because he believed someone was about to betray him and hoped to make sure they did not benefit by this. 'If there is still a reward, I want to give myself up to stop them getting the reward. If there is no reward, then we can forget it, as the job is as dead as a dodo. Now make up your mind. Are you going to charge me or not?' He was charged. Ironically, it was thought best not to charge him with theft, since it seemed he had not intended to deprive its owners permanently of the picture. Instead, he was charged with stealing the frame and went to prison for three months. He admitted 'honest-to-goodness skulduggery'.

According to Bunton, he had been visiting the sights of London and had taken a fancy to the portrait. The warders had gone for tea, so he lifted it from its easel and walked away. The frame made it cumbersome but he had gone down to the Embankment and stripped that off, breaking it in the process. Realizing the gravity of the crime, he had tried to get rid of the picture by writing eight of the ransom letters. Those who had hunted the wraith of the expert art thief might have recalled that the theft of the Mona Lisa from the Louvre in 1911 proved to be the work of Vincenzo Perugia, an Italian house-painter and decorator. It took place fifty years to the day before the disappearance of the Iron Duke from the National Gallery.[4]

Expert international thieves were also credited with 'the biggest art theft ever' on 30 December 1966 at Dulwich Gallery. Three Rembrandts and three Rubens were among the haul, whose value was put at £1,500,000. The 'gang', it was reported, had been led by a brace-and-bit expert who drilled out a panel in a rear door, enough for a very thin man to get through. Within a week, the paintings were found and the 'gang' identified as a thirty-two-year-old unemployed man making a protest about the neglect of contemporary art. Short of stealing to order for another 'Dr No', any professional knew from the outset that Rembrandt, Rubens, Goya and other artists far less well-known would be completely unsaleable.[5]

Less dazzling than jewel robberies and less mesmerizing than Old Masters were persistent forms of dishonesty among amateurs who were otherwise regarded as law-abiding. In some professions the routine thefts amounted only to minor pilfering. By 1964, however, the amount of meat being stolen from the London docks and ships berthed there was valued at £100,000 in four months. A good many of these thefts were carried out almost casually with the aid of local butchers. The current total was equivalent to half a dozen major bank robberies a year.[6]

Even this gave too favourable a view of the nationwide situation. There had been a thriving trade in stolen meat, before and after the end of rationing in 1954. Meat worth £3,500 or £100,000 in modern terms disappeared between June and August 1955 in the Home Counties and several provincial towns alone. Most of the carcasses were stolen from lorries and a significant amount was taken while the driver stopped at a café for a meal. According to an assessor for the carriers, the driver was told to 'take your time over your meal' and money changed hands. 'Often the meat bears identification marks, but one flick of the knife and the mark has disappeared.' There was no shortage of 'shady butchers' content not to question where the supplies came from.

While amateurs accomplished major crimes, professionalism was no guarantee of success. At Fulham in 1957, a three-man gang decided to tackle a half-ton safe in a large butcher's shop when its crop of cash was at its fullest. They arrived during the night with all the equipment necessary to cut it open. Before they could begin work, they heard sounds of other footsteps in the building and guessed that the police must have been shadowing them. Trapped on the premises they waited gloomily for the worst. However, the new arrivals were not the police but another gang which, by co-incidence, had decided to rob the same shop on the same night.

There followed a spirited argument as to who had the right to burgle the safe. Neither side was prepared to give way and they agreed to share the job. They were all Fulham men, except for one leader who came from Battersea, and all had previous convictions. With so many extra hands, it was possible to take the safe where it could be dealt with at leisure and without interruption from the police. It needed two men from each gang to carry it. Outside the shop, it was loaded into a van and driven to a lock-up garage to be cut open.

By this time, the two break-ins at the premises and the distur-bance caused in the middle of the night by four men stumbling out with a half-ton weight had made both gangs conspicuous. The police had little difficulty in tracking them down. Their receiver, who scarcely had the opportunity to receive anything at all, was also caught. With the rest, he appeared at London Sessions in July. Despite their expectations, the shop's takings had already gone to a bank night-deposit and the safe contained only £100.

There was a good deal of mutual animosity in the dock. Yet after their conviction the Common Serjeant, attempting to quieten the courtroom squabble, addressed them kindly and tried to offer some comfort by assuring them that 'I don't propose to pass heavy sentences on you.' He sent them down for terms ranging from twelve to eighteen months, urging them to find some other form of livelihood.[7]

Some robberies of this kind might have been scripted as film com-edies. It was not unusual for prisoners to contemplate ways of getting out of prison but rare for those outside to make plans for getting in. On the night of 19 December 1963, a Liverpool gang turned from banks and jewellers to burgle Walton Gaol, of which they presum-ably had inside knowledge. During the night, they climbed an eleven-foot wall, crossed the main yard and entered the administration block through a ventilator window. They gathered carpets from several rooms to deaden the sound and packed explosive into the keyhole of the main office safe. Their safe-blower was successful in muffling the blast, since no one in the building heard anything. Unfortunately, he was completely incompetent in his use of gelignite and rammed too much into the keyhole. The explosion was so powerful that it jammed the mechanism of the lock and the robbers could do nothing but make a quiet exit by the way they had come. As it happened, this safe contained only prison documents. With so many criminals in the building, the prison authorities kept their cash in a strong-room.

2

In cricketing terms, there was no doubt that a number of criminals thought of themselves as gentlemen rather than players. A Chelsea group of safe-breakers and cat burglars, well educated and well spoken, prided themselves on living with what Chief Superintendent John Capstick of the Ghost Squad called their glamorous women in 'swagger apartments'. These premises were frequently searched by the squad without their tenants' knowledge but to little effect.

The Chelsea thieves in 1945–6 were said to include Neville Heath and the public schoolboys who were his friends. They affected an air of effortless accomplishment, as if in imitation of Leslie Charteris' fictional creation 'The Saint' facing the stolid authority of Inspector Teal. During the summer of 1946, Capstick returned from an evening's surveillance of a group of them in a Chelsea restaurant and sat down wearily in the driving seat of his car. He felt that something was wrong and found the well-spread lid of a treacle tin sticking to the seat of his trousers. Also in the car was the tin, on which one of the gang's women had traced a large kiss in lipstick. This branch of the profession was far removed from the scar-faced animosities of Billy Hill. Its post-war élite survived until the mid-1950s, when a former 'public schoolboy, amateur jockey, and actor', with a fashionable address and a bespoke Allard car, was caught driving away from Chester Street, Belgravia, with £5,000 of jewellery purloined from a dressing-room table.[8]

In contrast, protection rackets in Soho or the Krays' domination of the East End were to shape the gangland of the 1960s. In the commission of major post-war crimes, these gangs were also a recruiting ground from which a team might be formed to carry out a major robbery. Team members would do their jobs and then disperse as soon as the proceeds had been shared out. Both Jack Spot and Billy Hill were to be the organizers behind such thefts.

A gangster's vision of robbery conjured up bullion, or banknotes, or jewellery, possibly all three. Bullion raids had the greatest glamour but they had not been a feature of wartime crime, if only because there was not much bullion to steal. In 1939 the British government had begun to send the nation's gold abroad for safe-keeping during the war and shipments increased as the threat of a German invasion grew in mid-1940. This operation was one of the better-kept secrets, though most nations under threat had taken similar precautions. At Glasgow, in order to conceal the shipments from the eyes of the underworld and Nazi agents alike, gold bullion was delivered direct from the banks to the Atlantic convoys in ordinary removal vans, though each pantechnicon was accompanied by police officers carrying revolvers.

A total of more than £1,000,000,000 in gold was shipped abroad. These shipments of reserves went first to Canada and the United States, a good many of them on the liners *Queen Mary* and *Queen Elizabeth*, which were faster than any U-boat. The bullion was taken to Ottawa or New York and then stored at naval bases. After the war, when the treasure had been safely returned in the summer of 1945, it was revealed that as much as £150,000,000 had been on the water at any one time and not an ounce was lost. This was true only of the transatlantic crossing. An alternative route had been used in 1940–41 to reach the West Coast of the United States via the Cape. On one voyage the steamer *Niagara* had sunk with £2,000,000 of gold bars on board. All but £80,000 of this was salvaged by the Australians. The remainder, if not 'lost', was certainly beyond imme-diate reach. This route round the Cape and across the Pacific was not only much longer but too hazardous once the Japanese entered the war in 1941.

By 1948, a peacetime bullion trade had resumed, though exchange controls deprived it of the freedom which it had enjoyed before the war. Those whose trade was to stage major robberies naturally turned their attention to the vulnerability of gold in transit. Such raids were nothing new. In one of the most accomplished thefts in criminal history, the Victorian train robbers of 1855 had removed almost a quarter of a ton of gold, carried on the overnight express from London to Paris in conditions of maximum security, and had done it with such skill that the police knew neither who they were nor what had become of the gold. Indeed, they did not even know in which country the robbery had occurred or who should pay the insurance claim.

The years before the Second World War, when bullion was first carried by air, had seen both street and airport robberies. On 15 July 1936, in the second Clerkenwell Bullion Robbery, an LNER railway van was carrying a packing case from King's Cross station to the Sheffield Smelting Company's London branch in Clerkenwell. It contained gold ingots, coins and gold dust. In the narrow thoroughfare of Aylesbury Street, the way was blocked by a coster's barrow across the road. A stolen car followed the van. The van driver, with no idea what the packing case contained, thought someone was playing a joke. He got out and confronted three men. One threatened him and the van boy with an iron bar, while the rest broke open the doors and loaded the case into the stolen car. Having let the car through, they swung the barrow across the road again to impede any pursuit.

Within a week, there were three arrests. James Francis, who planned and led the hold-up, had a criminal record stretching back to 1902. A sports car with false number plates was parked at a Euston garage where the robbery was planned. These were noticed and as soon as the robbery took place, the garage was raided. Francis accepted arrest philosophically. 'If you win, good luck to you,' he said to the detective inspector who charged him, 'I am going to have a go for it.' He went to prison for two years.[9]

In March 1936, Croydon Airport was still the main London terminal for international flights. Three boxes of gold were stolen from its strongroom during the night, in the short time that it took the duty officer to walk out to the runway and back to meet an incoming flight. Three men were eventually arrested. Two were acquitted and the third, found in possession of the boxes but not the gold, was sent to penal servitude for seven years. The gold was not recovered.

By the summer of 1948, Croydon Airport scarcely existed, having been overtaken by London Airport, only half-finished and soon to be known as 'Heathrow'. Already it was a repository for bullion entering or leaving the country. There were rumours of a thriving, though illegal, trade carried on by some employees of the British Overseas Airways Corporation, BOAC. This involved buying gold in Britain and smuggling it out to countries like Pakistan, where it could be sold for a good deal more. Customs surveillance was increased and an airport hangar became a temporary bonded warehouse. Its safe would normally contain some £250,000 in gold and diamonds, often a good deal more. If a raid occurred late at night, after a South American flight had landed, the safe might yield a further £1,000,000 in gold making the total almost £20,000,000 in modern terms.

Jack Spot was credited with being the 'Guv'nor' in the planned robbery of this building, though he was never arrested. He was the man who gathered information, laid the plan and financed it but would not be present at the crime. If there were leaders of the raid, they were Alfred Roome, forty-two years old and known as 'The Ilford Kid', and Teddy Hughes, who at forty-eight was the oldest man there. About fifteen men would be needed. There had been delays in the construction of the airport and many of the buildings were little more than the huts of a wartime aerodrome. Breaking into the hangar which contained the safe would be far easier than when building work was complete.

The aim was to raid the bonded warehouse at night, when it was occupied only by two BOAC loaders and a security guard, preferably after the evening delivery of bullion from a South American flight. The time of the raid was set for 1 a.m.

For some weeks in the summer of 1948 the robbers took turns in a discreet twenty-four-hour watch on the makeshift Customs warehouse from a café opposite the airport gates. They timed the movements of staff and arranged to have parcels sent from Ireland so that they could collect them there and see the internal layout of the hangar.

The plan was to dope the coffee as it was brought from the canteen to the two loaders and the security guard during the night. This would involve 'straightening' a member of the airport staff. When the pheno-barbitone had taken effect, the raiders would force their way in, take the keys from the unconscious guard and open the safe. A good deal was left to improvisation but in refining the plan the robbers had a stroke of luck which was almost too good to be true.

Alfred Roome and another gang member went for a drink in a pub near Epsom. In the bar, Roome met Anthony Walsh, whom he had last seen when they were prisoners of war in Germany, good friends in adversity. Now the former friend worked at the airport as a loader and had occasion to visit the Customs warehouse. He had previously held a better-paid job as a security guard but had been demoted, as he saw it. His resentment against BOAC seemed promising. The routines of the Customs warehouse were discussed.

At the end of the evening, the friends agreed to meet again and the loader was then introduced to other members of the gang. It was suggested that he might like to earn £500, more than two years' wages, for inside information. He agreed. Among the information was the question of whether it would be possible to drug the coffee of those on duty overnight in the Customs warehouse, the two loaders and the guard. He thought it would be. 'They told me they meant to take the gold, and that they were the biggest gang in London. If I squeaked, they would carve me up, but if I kept my mouth shut they would look after me and give me a share.' More specifically, they warned him that if he 'grassed them up', he would not leave hospital until after Christmas and on his release even his own mother would not recognize him.[10]

Walsh was apparently not the only BOAC employee involved in the plan. One became an informer. The police, for obvious reasons, refused to reveal his identity but two members of the gang subsequently told their counsel that he was a loader named Gillan. Certainly, he was an insider – possibly Walsh himself who, having second thoughts, made contact with Donald Fish, the Chief Security Officer of BOAC, in early July. Fish, a former Scotland Yard detective inspector who had served in the Flying Squad, passed the information to area CID and Detective Chief

Superintendent Bill Chapman, the present commander of the squad.

At a further meeting in the pub near Epsom, Walsh received final details of the plan. As he left, he memorized the number of a Vauxhall parked outside, perhaps to have something to trade with the police if everything went wrong. When the registration was checked, it proved to be a car owned by Jack Spot. Almost at the last moment, he was told the raid would take place on the night of 28–29 July. The gang's inside contact was given the phenobarbitone tablets, a dose so large that it was afterwards said they might have killed the three intended recipients rather than knocked them out.

Scotland Yard launched 'Operation Nora' for the night of 28 July. The informant went on duty at 8 p.m. with the phenobarbitone tablets in his pockets. From the café by the gates, the robbers were able to see the BOAC van deliver its load to the Customs warehouse. Their view was imperfect. They could see that it had backed up to the hangar and that something had been taken in, presumably bullion. There was no bullion but under cover of the delivery two more Flying Squad officers joined their colleagues. By 11 p.m. there were fourteen officers in place, under the immediate command of Superintendent Bob Lee. They wore the uniforms of BOAC workers. Two of them dressed as loaders and one as a security guard were in a small office near the safe, where the robbers would find them sitting slumped over the table, as if the tablets had taken effect. Others were hidden behind packing cases. Reinforcements were in a BOAC van, parked with its lights out close to the doors of the warehouse, waiting to cut off the robbers' retreat. The van was also to block the path of any escape vehicle or, if necessary, ram it. Further police officers from the local division were positioned round the perimeter of the airport.

Just before 1 a.m., a covered lorry driven by Sydney Cook drew up at the hangar door and a dozen men got out of the back. They carried iron bars, leaded coshes and shears. All but one wore gloves or socks on their hands and stocking masks with eye-slits. Cook, dressed in a BOAC uniform, stood guard at the door with a starting-handle while the others began to break their way in. Inside the hangar, the scene was what they had expected.

Charles Hewitt, George Draper and John Matthews, the three detective sergeants who had volunteered to be 'drugged', were slumped across the table in the little office. The intruders advanced on them, each face grotesque in a stocking mask whose leg, according to Charles Hewitt, hung down in front, swaying like an elephant's trunk. The apparent victims of the drug were examined by three of the gang and then tied up with adhesive gags across their mouths. One was hit on the back of the head with an iron bar as a final precaution and another was kicked. Neither gave any sign of consciousness. Those who had examined them then took a bunch of keys from the security guard's belt, came out of the little room and handed the keys to another man. As he inserted the first key in the lock of the safe, there was a sudden movement. Detective Divisional Inspector Roberts of 'T' Division emerged from behind a packing case and shouted, 'We are police officers of the Flying Squad! Stand where you are!'

There followed 'The Battle of Heathrow'. The cornered robbers shouted, 'Kill the bastards!' and 'Get the guns!' Fortunately there were no guns. Inside the hangar, the Flying Squad was outnumbered and the raiders had no compunction in using their coshes, iron bars and shears. Superintendent Lee had his scalp lacerated by a blow from an iron bar, one of his detective sergeants had his thigh laid open by a pair of shears, another had his nose broken, another his arm, and one was brought down by blows from wire-cutters and a cosh. When the raiders saw that they were holding their own, their first instinct was to take advantage of this and run. As they emerged from the hangar, the Flying Squad men outside and CID officers from the local division closed in on them.

It was the most dramatic battle in the history of the Flying Squad and was widely seen as a major victory at last in the struggle against post-war crime. There was no doubting the satisfaction with which the press reported that eight robbers appeared before the Uxbridge magistrates later that morning, weary, bloodstained and some with arms in slings. One had his hand bandaged, another had a cut under a closed eye and several had blood on their shirts. A ninth man was still in hospital. Walsh the loader had been picked up and was 'singing' to the police.

Four robbers were said to have escaped in the confusion of the fight outside the hangar. One had fallen into a ditch while being chased. Knocked unconscious, he had furtively got clear once he came round. Franny Daniels, the friend of Billy Hill, claimed that he had clung to the underside of a police van and been carried to the yard of the police station at Harlesden. Once the police officers and suspects had gone inside, he crawled out from under the van and disappeared. During the drive, his shoulder touched the ground and he carried the scar of the burn for the rest of his life.

The failure of the raid did little for the reputation of Jack Spot in the eyes of his gangland rivals. Even his robbers had shown more ingenuity than he. Not wanting the police to discover the drugging of the 'BOAC men', as they intended to use the trick again, they had taken among their weapons fresh tea to replace the doctored liquid in the cups and teapot on the hangar table. None the less, eight of them were convicted at London Sessions on 17 September and went to prison for terms ranging from five to twelve years. Walsh, if not the informer, had been lavish with information in his statement. He was bound over for two years at a separate trial. All of the eight sent to prison had changed their pleas to guilty. 'You went prepared for violence and you got it,' said Sir Gerald Dodson, voicing public satisfaction as he passed sentence. 'You got the worst of it and you can hardly complain.'[11]

The helpful BOAC loader whom the thieves had trusted too readily was said to have been flown to Australia by Scotland Yard with a new identity, beyond the reach of underworld vengeance. Worst of all for those who now began their long prison sentences, they learnt that the aircraft which was to have brought a million pounds in bullion to them that night had been delayed by fog.

3

Billy Hill was in prison at the time of the London Airport robbery. Jack Spot had been given the first chance to show what he could do as an architect of crime and had failed. By 1952 Hill was out of prison and ready to take up the challenge. Yet he faced a greater risk. He had served a number of years of preventive detention. If he were to be caught for a crime as serious as the attempted airport robbery, he could expect to have ten years added to any other sentence that might be passed.

Hill remained the best-known British gang leader of the 1940s. In his trenchcoat and trilby hat, he was said to pride himself on a resemblance to Humphrey Bogart. The truth was that he had a greater sullenness than Bogart and a razor scar across his face but little of the actor's humour and charm. He did not lack physical courage or the intelligence of the strategist. Of all the gangs, his was the closest to the organized American model. In 1953, with these advantages, he was to pull off the nearest thing to the perfect post-war robbery. It would bring him almost £6,000,000 by modern values.

Just as there were dishonest drivers in the haulage industry, so there were men in the postal service with a criminal past. One of these, with no recent criminal record, was a post office driver known to Hill. They met in a pub at the Angel, Islington, and Hill questioned him about post office shipments of cash. According to Hill's account, he arranged for a few men known to him to get jobs as drivers and sorters. Despite their minor role, these men may have preferred to forget that when the post office was the target, the penalty for getting caught might be fourteen years in prison.

Registered post was now used for regular consignments of banknotes from the West of England being returned to London. Some were being sent back to the Bank of England for pulping, most were going to head offices of banks in the City. They were brought by train to Paddington, where they arrived after midnight, and were then driven by post office van to the East Central Post Office at St Martin's-le-Grand. A single van was used with a driver, a postman and an unarmed guard. There was a button to activate a siren, which once started could not be stopped. The back of the van was bolted and barred. The value of the notes inside was usually between £40,000 and £50,000.

Hill's plan was not particularly original, indeed it resembled the Clerkenwell Bullion Robbery of 1936, in which his later accomplice Harry Bryan had been involved. Yet the 1952 plan required the hijack of the van, rather than a robbery on the spot. This would have to take place in central London but it would be at the quietest time of night when many side streets on the route through shopping and office areas of the capital were deserted. Even so, to transfer thousands of banknotes, while the van was in the middle of a street, would take too long. Difficulties dictated the method. The van must be stolen with the mailbags of banknotes still inside it.

Unlike Jack Spot, Billy Hill ordered the robbery to be rehearsed repeatedly. He took his men and vehicles out of London at night to stage the action on little-used country roads, even when the landscape was covered in snow. It suggested the making of a crime film. Indeed, when a policeman on a bicycle rode by during the third rehearsal, one of the men called out to him, explaining that the team was a film company getting everything into place for the next take.

Like the hijackers in the 1936 Clerkenwell robbery, Hill and his team drove over the route and timed individual distances between street corners. The post office van was also followed discreetly and timed throughout its journey. Hill told his drivers to check quiet residential streets for cars suited to the crime and then chose those which could be stolen when the time came. He decided which robbers would be in which cars and what their jobs would be. The place for the robbery was Eastcastle Street, a minor thoroughfare north of Oxford Street and parallel to it. There were several sets of traffic lights in the smaller street, which the robbers could control. The post office van would be halted between two sets with one car blocking the way in front and another at the rear. As a bonus, the road was being repaired, which would slow down the van. It must not get too close to Oxford Street, busy at any hour of day or night.

At 4.17 a.m. on 21 May 1952, the van from Paddington carrying £287,000 in thirteen mailbags halted as Hill's men turned the traffic lights from green to red. As usual there were three men inside: the driver, postman and guard. A black Riley saloon pulled out from the kerb at an angle and blocked the road in front. A green Vauxhall saloon drew up behind and prevented the post officer driver reversing. Eight men, gloved and masked, scrambled out of the two cars. They wrenched open the driver's and passenger's doors of the van. The driver had time to press the button of his siren but there was only silence from the device. As the Postmaster General, Earl De La Warr, admitted elegantly in the House of Lords on the following day, 'The siren had been interfered with and the fact not ascertained by the chauffeur. He was not in a position to test it on normal days because if he set it off there is no way of stopping it.' The money Hill had passed to post office employees now paid dividends.

Back in the darkness of Eastcastle Street, the 'chauffeur' was fighting for his life against a couple of thugs with coshes. He and his companions were beaten, left semi-conscious and dazed, as the post office van and the two cars drove off.

The attack had taken eight minutes and there had been several witnesses. A maid at Berners Hotel, overlooking Eastcastle Street, woke to hear shouts and screams. From her window she saw the van wedged between two cars and three men attacking two postmen. When one postman shouted for help, he was hit over the head with what looked like a length of piping. A hotel guest saw the scene from his window, dialled 999, and went back to the window to see the two cars and the mail van driving off. By the time the police came, there was nothing in the street but three injured men, a raincoat, a wooden truncheon and a pair of blue bolt-cutters. None of these offered any clue to solving the crime.

The stolen cars were driven to Covent Garden market, already busy with deliveries of fruit, vegetables and flowers. They were parked and left in the knowledge that it would be some time before anybody noticed them in the bustle of the new day. Seven minutes after leaving Eastcastle Street, the post office van drove into a yard two miles off, in Augustus Street, Camden Town. The yard did not belong to Hill. One of his men climbed the wooden gate and opened it from inside. Another van was waiting, dilapidated and second-hand, with false number plates and a new coat of brown paint. Partitions had been built inside so that notes from the mailbags were stowed within the structure of the vehicle itself. An inquisitive policeman at a roadblock would see nothing.

Billy Hill, if he had not been present at the hijack, was certainly in the yard at Augustus Street. The post office bags were ripped open and the banknotes pushed into the concealed spaces. The mail van was left to be discovered by the police at 8.30 a.m. By that time, Hill and one companion had driven the brown van away. For a while they left it parked in Spitalfields market with £287,000 inside while they went to have a cup of tea in a café. Then it was driven away towards Essex. Strict discipline was imposed on the robbers. They were allowed £3,000 each for the time being and only six months later did they get the rest of their shares. A good many thieves for centuries past had been betrayed by one of their number spending money like a drunken sailor as soon as he got his hands on it. Hill was not prepared to give his subordinates that chance.

Six of the mailbags were found by schoolgirls on the evening of 10 June, in a flooded sandpit at Dagenham. Of the notes there was no sign. Theories abounded. It was suggested that US deserters had carried out the raid. Scotland Yard detectives were said to be shadowing a mysterious woman connected with the robbery but, if they did, she led them nowhere. A reward of £14,500 was offered for information which brought the criminals to justice. It was never claimed. Suspects were arrested, questioned and released. As the inquiry petered out in the autumn, it was admitted that the van driver had not the least idea what he was carrying. The Postmaster General replied querulously to his critics that the methods employed to protect such consignments had served well enough for thirty years and there had been no reason to change them.

Billy Hill was arrested and taken to Scotland Yard for questioning. There was no direct evidence against him and he was released. Edward Noble and Robert King were found in possession of some of the stolen notes and were tried but acquitted as receivers. According to Frankie Fraser, Billy Hill 'got into' the jury. Whatever the reason, the money had to be returned to the defendants.[12]

Because the crime involved a vicious attack on post office employees, it never aroused the sympathy which was felt for the bloodless ingenuity of the Victorian bullion robbers in 1855. Yet it was the best organized major robbery in the ten years following the war. It had a temporary fame, soon overtaken by grander schemes. In 1955, in the film comedy *The Ladykillers*, when the innocent and elderly Mrs Wilberforce feels it her duty to report a bank van hijack to the police, the robbers threaten her with incrimination in something far worse. 'We'll tell them she planned the Eastcastle Street job.'

4

The Eastcastle Street robbery had cost a good deal to prepare. It was also discovered that some notes had been initialled by the cashiers who counted them at the start of their journey. Hill and an assistant had to weed these out and destroy them. The numbers of some £5 notes had been recorded by the banks. These also had to go. It was unlikely that many of those involved would come away with more than £5,000–£10,000.

By contrast, three masked men carried out a safe-blowing at Catford Greyhound Stadium on the night of 12 February 1950 with precision and comparative gentility. They chose a time when the strongroom would contain the Saturday takings from one of London's best-known dog tracks. Breaking into the offices was not difficult. Two elderly watchmen were overpowered and tied into chairs in the managing director's office but not injured.

The way into the strongroom was guarded by an outer steel door, a steel grille, and a five-inch-thick steel door with a filling of asbestos cement. Working meticulously, the intruders spent two hours setting up and detonating three charges of gelignite. The last and most powerful blew open the steel door, revealing tin containers of banknotes worth some £15,000. Despite the popular belief in gelignite as a sure means to blow open any safe or vault, it was seldom used with this precision. At the worst, the explosion might cause the collapse of the building and very frequently the only outcome of filling a lock and detonating it was to jam the mechanism so that neither the burglars nor the owners were able to open it.

At Catford Stadium, the cracksmen got away with as much money for a few hours' work as many of the Eastcastle Street robbers had received individually. Their descriptions detailed little more than clothing and approximate height. Though Chief Superintendent Ted

Greeno led a Scotland Yard investigation into sales of 'plastic gelig-nite' and men were interviewed by track security officials, no one was charged.

Many of the most successful post-war professionals worked in small groups or alone, their criminality sometimes not suspected. Despite the gang culture of Hill and Spot there was room for a self-effacing but talented wraith like Barry Fieldsen, *alias* Barry Redvers Holliday, *alias* 'Johnny the Gent'.

A youthful thief, born in South London, he had apparently reformed many years before. Fieldsen was fifty-one in 1949 and with no record of a criminal past since a conviction for a minor offence at twenty-five, when the present senior officers of Scotland Yard were still very junior in rank. No one in the police seemed to know what had become of him after the misdemeanours of his youth. They knew him only as Barry Fieldsen. As Barry Redvers Holliday, he owned a five-storey house in Chelsea; a flat with mirrored cock-tail bar and expensive carpets; a green and cream turreted villa, Jour de Fête, on Friary Island at Old Windsor. He drove a Bentley, a Mercedes and a motor boat. In Windsor, he was known as 'The Squire', in Kensington he was said to be a property owner or a retired Hatton Garden diamond merchant. He was an amusing talker, an excellent dancer, immaculate in Savile Row suits, handmade shirts and shoes. In one morning, he spent £400 on new suits, more than a year's wages for most workers, and had backed a horse in a single race for £1,000. The police had no reason to think this could be the man seen twenty-six years earlier, asleep in a doss-house.

As Barry Redvers Holliday, he entered society as a guest at house parties, balls and hunts. He rode with several packs and in return organized his own hunting parties in Dorset. No one suspected his honesty or his wealth, except older residents who later told the *Daily Telegraph* that they had regarded him as a 'spiv type'. Though he was married, few people seemed to know him intimately. It would have been preposterous to suggest that he was a thief, let alone the most successful jewel thief of his generation, or that after his death he would be remembered as 'Raffles in Real Life'. Yet in 1946 alone the jewel robberies subsequently credited to him included £52,000 from Sir Bernard and Lady Docker at their Mayfair home, two robberies of precious stones totalling £40,000 from the Sunningdale mansion of Mrs Marjorie Cunliffe-Owen and £20,000 in jewellery from the London home of Lord Bearsted, a total worth about £3,000,000 sixty years later.

These thefts would have made headlines but there was one other that year which went into criminal history rather than into ephemeral press reports. On 16 October 1946, the Duke and Duchess of Windsor were staying with their friend Lord Dudley at Ednam Lodge, Sunningdale. The Duchess went up to her room to dress for dinner. She looked for her large leather jewel case but it was not there. Neither it nor its contents, 'The Windsor Jewels', were ever seen again, except in whatever form they were re-cut for the market in stolen gems. The leather case had contained complete matching sets of sapphires, emeralds, diamonds, rubies, turquoise, topaz and onyx, as well as a diamond tiara, a collection almost beyond price.

New Scotland Yard, in the person of Superintendent Bob Lee, was given charge of the case. There were no fingerprints and no signs of entry. It had all the marks of Raffles. Barry Fieldsen was a faded memory. The man the police knew twenty-six years earlier had been a failure, not least as a thief. Even now, very few people in the stolen gems trade knew what he looked like. He would sometimes describe the jewellery to one man and agree a sale even before he stole it. Sometimes he would keep it for several years before he offered it. His receivers could not betray him because they seldom saw him. He was only a voice on the telephone. The jewellery was delivered by a messenger who took the payment back to the man generally known as 'Johnny the Gent'.

As Johnny the Gent he had come under suspicion. It was said that the newly formed Ghost Squad sought him for five years without success. This cannot have been true since the squad was not set up until January 1946 and Barry Fieldsen's career came to an end in December 1949. However, a number of jewel robberies in 1946 had occurred in the Sunningdale area and Bob Lee ordered a check on those living in the vicinity. This produced no immediate results. Ironically, after the successful plundering of a fortune in jewellery, the downfall of the Gent was caused by the theft of a cheese.

This occurred in the bar of the Dumb Bell Hotel, Taplow, where 'Holliday' was a regular customer. Just before closing time, the barman saw him in the mirror slipping a small unpurchased cheese into his coat. It would have been absurd to make a scene and lose a valued customer but the barman mentioned it as a joke to the landlord, who also thought it a joke. 'Mr Holliday' was a friend. Yet the joke was so good that the landlord mentioned it to a local policeman, attributing it to 'The Squire's' absent-mindedness. The story reached Chief Inspector Tomlin of the Buckinghamshire Constabulary. A policeman went to the house on the island, where he confronted the owner. But the Squire also laughed at the story and denied it. It reached Superintendent Lee. The local policeman found himself studying photos at Scotland Yard. Despite changes of appearance in twenty-five years, he identified the man as an older Barry Fieldsen.

Bob Lee took a pair of binoculars on his next visit to Sunningdale and went to the bank of the Thames. When he saw the Squire, he too recognized the man who had been a petty thief a quarter of a century before. By a further irony, as a young policeman he had had dealings with Barry Fieldsen. Within hours, the addresses and movements of 'Barry Redvers Holliday' were under observation.

It seemed that Fieldsen knew by instinct when he was being followed. For months it appeared that those who tailed him were wasting their time. He was adept at losing his shadows on the underground system, stepping in and out of trains at the last moment, as the doors were closing. Yet sooner or later he must surely make an error of judgement. Banks and safe deposits in London were checked but nothing could be linked to him. He had taken care that they should be in his wife's name.

In December 1949, on an afternoon when he thought he had shaken off his followers, he was seen entering a bank near Sloane Square with a parcel and leaving without it. There was enough evidence by this time for a warrant to search a suspect safe-deposit box at a bank. It contained jewellery to the value of £10,000, some of the jewels belonging to items stolen in recent robberies.

He was arrested as Barry Fieldsen. Questioned by Detective Sergeant Easterbrook at Chelsea police station as to where the jewellery came from, he would only say, 'Well, you know the onus is on you to prove where it came from.' That was as far as questioning went, though he did inquire what further charge might be brought. Easterbrook said, 'Receiving.' It was common for the police to bring this charge to hold a prisoner until theft could be proved.

On 14 December 1949, Barry Fieldsen appeared before the West London magistrate charged with being in possession of jewellery, 'thought to have been stolen or unlawfully obtained'. He applied for bail and was allowed it in the sum of £2,500 by the magistrate, who confessed he did so with 'misgiving'. Perhaps he felt sympathy for the genteel figure who must otherwise spend Christmas in prison.

Eight days later, Scotland Yard detectives were called to the well-appointed comfort of the Wheatsheaf Hotel at Virginia Water, Surrey. In Room 23, Barry Fieldsen was sitting up in bed. He had shot himself dead with a walking-stick gun which lay by his side. He had left a note. 'Hope I am not causing any trouble.'

After Christmas, there were exhibitions of jewellery at Scotland Yard, all of it retrieved from safe deposits hired by Fieldsen across London. The total value at the time was £100,000. Owners were invited to come and claim their gems. Some diamonds had been re-cut but there was a good deal of silverware bearing the crests of the families to whom it had belonged. Of the most famous haul, the jewels of the Duchess of Windsor, there was no sign.

5

Barry Fieldsen was a refreshing instance of the post-war individualist, working outside the shifting fraternities of gangland. His case was also one of the first to have the name of the 'Ghost Squad' attached to it. By the end of 1945, some patterns of post-war crime were clear and in certain areas it appeared out of control. Under the aegis of the Assistant Commissioner, Sir Ronald Howe, and under the command of Detective Inspector John Capstick, known throughout the underworld as 'Charley Artful', Scotland Yard set up this Special Duties Squad on 1 January 1946. It was a novel and dangerous undertaking.

Consorting with criminals was an offence under police regulations. At the same time, most CID officers were dependent on information from those who were, as a rule, criminals themselves. The
creation of a Ghost Squad institutionalized the practice. Apart from
Capstick, its first four officers included John Gosling, then a detective sergeant and a future chief superintendent, the only officer to
remain in the squad throughout its existence.

The squad acted like plain-clothes officers, infiltrating the underworld and gathering information. The difference was that its
members remained undercover after identifying a criminal, passing
their information to the Flying Squad or divisional CID but not
revealing themselves by arresting suspects. Their transport was
nondescript, their clothes sometimes so shabby that two of them
sitting on a park bench were once given a few coins by a kindly
lady to get themselves a cup of tea.

There was no doubt of the squad's success. Its members penetrated the underworld and, largely thanks to informers, brought to
justice in 1946–7 those whose thefts included consignments of typewriters, lipsticks, carpets, shoes and leather goods, razor blades, cigarettes and tobacco, suit-lengths, cloth and clothing, amounting to
more than £60,000. By the time it was disbanded in September
1949, it had been responsible for the arrest of 789 suspects, the
clearing up of 1,506 crimes, and the recovery of over £250,000 in
property, now equivalent to some £5,000,000.

The impact of the squad was well illustrated by such cases as the
Cricklewood Whisky Robbery of September 1948. On 19
September, in the early darkness, several lorries arrived and parked
near sidings, which ran along the top of a railway embankment. Six
men left the first lorry, climbed the embankment and disappeared
among railway trucks. The target was whisky to the value of £15,000
(£300,000) for an hour's work. Three more men from a second
lorry disappeared among the trucks. Presently the men reappeared
and for half an hour slid cases of whisky down the slope of the
embankment to be loaded into the lorries. One man nervously told
the others not to make so much noise but the plan was simple and
ingenious.

As the men came down, there was a shout, lights in an adjoining builder's yard went on and Flying Squad officers, briefed by the 'Ghosts', appeared from the shadows. The robbers fought a desperate fight, in the course of which one managed to start a lorry and drive off with four others inside. The rest were pursued on foot and brought back, battered and bloodstained. The whisky had been saved and the shock of finding the police waiting had knocked the fight from the captives. 'All right. I admit it. We were caught,' said the first. 'Somebody must have split on us,' said the second. 'Where did you all come from?' The third could only add, 'We're caught. What is there to say?' The last man used a phrase seldom encountered except on the screen: 'There is nothing to say – you got us bang to rights.'[13]

Quite apart from such routine victories, the Ghost Squad indicated a change of philosophy in dealing with the underworld. CID officers were to operate incognito in a way that would have seemed scarcely credible before the war. In the snowbound February of 1947 an informant heard of a North London raid that was being planned on the Midland Bank in Kentish Town Road by a group of men from Walthamstow. The aim was to ambush the bank manager on his way home, steal his keys, leave him tied up, return to the bank and rob it. The men were a team rather than a gang.

Sergeant William 'Dixie' Deans, later to be praised and decorated for his 'cold courage', bore a resemblance to the bank manager and volunteered to act as a decoy. It was arranged that on four nights in February Deans should leave the bank after it had closed, taking the place of the manager, walk the short distance to Kentish Town underground station, travel to Woodside Park, then follow a footpath to Holden Road and the manager's house in North Finchley. On 7 and 14 February, he was aware that he was being followed but no one approached him. On 21 February, he saw two of the men later convicted, standing on the underground platform at Kentish Town. They boarded the same train, got off at the same stop and followed him to the footpath. Two of them walked ahead of him, a third came up behind and he was knocked to the ground with a blow to the head from a sock packed with three and a half pounds of wet sand. As he lay on the ground, he was beaten into unconsciousness with four blows of the weighted sock.

Sergeant Deans was one of the few victims of post-war crime able to give a precise account of a violent robbery. He described how he came round in the back of a green van, his scarf tied over his eyes and adhesive plaster fastened over his mouth. When he groaned, something hard was pressed into his side and one of the men said, 'This is a stick-up. Keep your fucking mouth shut or it's your lot.' One of the others asked anxiously, 'Are you sure it's the right bloke?' 'He's the geezer all right. He's got the keys in his pocket.'

They robbed William Deans of his wallet, watch, fountain pen, and four banknotes from his fob pocket. One man asked, 'Are you sure he's all right?' Someone felt his heart and pulse, then put an ear to his nose to make sure that he was still breathing. One of his eyes was forced open and a torch was shone into it. 'He looks bad,' the first man said. 'You hit him too hard, Jim.' The only 'Jim' in the group was James Cunningham, a young motor fitter from Walthamstow. 'It doesn't matter. No one saw us do it. We'll make our way to the bank by cab and bus. You doodle around for an hour and then dump him.' It seemed that two men went to the bank and the rest remained in the van. After a long time, one of those in the van said, 'We'll dump the bastard here. No one will find him for a while.'

Sergeant Deans was lifted over a man's shoulder, carried for some distance, and thrown face down in a pile of frozen snow. He managed to get up and stagger to a house, suffering the effects of concussion and exposure to the bitter night. His assailants were wrong in thinking no one had seen the attack. Detective Inspector Crawford had watched the whole thing. He was back at Kentish Town Road with Chief Inspector Bob Lee in order to arrest Leslie Beck as he attempted to open the rear door of the Midland Bank with a stolen key.

'Me?' said the astonished suspect, when told that he was being arrested for robbing Sergeant Deans with violence. 'Not me. I was passing along here when two men stopped me and told me they would give me a hundred nicker to open the bank door for them. They gave me the keys.'

As for James Cunningham, he and his green van had been seen

by police at the scene of the attack. When it was found and searched, in his yard at Walthamstow later that evening, the van still contained an elastoplast tin and adhesive tape. At first it seemed that he thought the police were talking to him about a fight at a local pub. 'I thought you meant some trouble around the Gardeners. I don't know about anything else.'

In March 1947 the six robbers, five of whom had pleaded guilty, were sent to penal servitude at the Old Bailey for terms ranging from three to seven years. For his courage, William Deans was awarded the King's Police Medal for Gallantry, later incorporated with the George Cross.[14]

6

An increasing number of professional robberies seemed to be committed with the aid of those who were entrusted with keys. By September 1953, when there was a £38,000 robbery at Maples the furnishers in Tottenham Court Road, the steel doors to the strong-room had been blown open as a 'blind'. The robbers already had keys but carried out the explosion to protect those employees who had supplied the duplicates. A series of robberies in the seven preceding years had been carried out with copies of keys, including in 1946 the Regent Street jewel robbery at Leopold Levinson, the Dickins & Jones fur robbery and the cosmetics raid on the factory of Helena Rubinstein.

These were major robberies but many routine thefts were also carried out by the use of duplicate keys because they were extremely simple to obtain. Donald McKenzie, as a professional thief, recalled that almost all British cars were supplied with keys for doors, ignition and boot originating from one firm, MRN. A thief had only to have paper printed with the billhead of a non-existent firm at his own address in order to buy a complete set of such keys. Not only did this make vehicle theft easy but it gave access to all the locked cases of valuables which might be in the car's boot.[15]

Far worse was the discovery, in the attempted robbery of Barclays

Bank, Waterlooville, Hampshire, in December 1950, that the use of duplicate keys was linked with a leak of information from Scotland Yard. Still more alarming, the information that was being leaked related to the Flying Squad.

Information about the intended robbery had reached Scotland Yard. The target was named and the robbers identified as men suspected of being involved in the stolen key syndicate. Scotland Yard was not limited territorially in its operations and its officers were in position at the time of the planned robbery. They had been chosen from the Flying Squad and Detective Inspector Periam was watching the bank from an overlooking flat. As soon as he saw the three suspects, he surreptitiously joined the rest of his team who were hidden in the bank.

The ambushers could hear the voices of the three men outside the rear door of the bank. John Saxton was trying various keys and saying, 'I can't find the twirl, Curly.' James Howells said, 'Keep on trying, Jack.' Then the door opened and the intruders found themselves confronting the Flying Squad men. The would-be bank robbers dashed out on to the forecourt, where Periam jumped on to Saxton's back to stop him escaping. 'Let me get at you, you bastard!' Saxton shouted, and then, 'Curly, we're done!'

The failed robbery was less important than its sequel. Seven men and two women were arrested. Keys in their possession were duplicates for safes in the manager's office of the Odeon Cinema, Newton Abbott; Crosse & Blackwell's offices, Soho Square, London; the Borough Treasurer's Department, Mitcham Town Hall; the South East Electricity Board accounts office, Surbiton; Rayleigh Stadium, Southend; Forte's Restaurant, Tottenham Court Road; The Jewel Box, Oxford Street; the Deputy Borough Treasurer's Office, West Ham Council; the manager's office, Odeon Cinema, Hounslow, and the Borough Treasurer's Office at Lewes, Sussex. A search also revealed keys to a number of post office safes. So far as there was a leader of the organization it was Billy Hill's friend Harry Bryan, bookmaker of Clerkenwell, who had already made history in the 1936 Clerkenwell bullion robbery and with Hill in the Hemmings & Co. jewellery smash-and-grab of 26 June 1940. At the end of the case, according to Superintendent

Bob Lee, Scotland Yard had 'only touched the fringe' of the organization behind the conspiracy.

Seven of the nine defendants, including a locksmith who pleaded guilty, were convicted in April 1951, five of them on charges of conspiracy to break into premises and steal from safes. Harry Bryan, who went to prison for ten years, drew the heaviest sentence. 'This was a widespread conspiracy, highly organized, and of a most dangerous character,' Mr Justice Byrne told him. 'I am convinced that you were the brains behind it.'

Since 1941, there had been 200 robberies committed by opening safes with duplicate keys, an alarming commentary on those in positions of trust and the ingenuity of others who set out to corrupt them. Far worse was the admission that information was reaching criminals from Scotland Yard. Periam spoke of 'a traitor in the police'. The source of the information appeared to be the Yard's so-called Duty Book. Detective Chief Inspector Wilfred 'Flaps' Daws revealed that a secret plan was implemented to put false information in the book with the hope of misleading those to whom it was passed.

The betrayal was suspected after Flying Squad observation on four post offices at nine weekends, as a result of which raids said to have been planned did not take place. They occurred when there was no watch. According to Chief Inspector Daws, 'Our information was – to use our own phrase – that we had been shopped, and we could not understand why we had been shopped. From that date it was decided that only a small number of officers should know about this book.' As a further precaution when, for example, it was necessary for Periam to mount observation on a post office at Axminster, Devon, even the confidential Duty Book listed him instead as being transferred to duties in 'P' Division, Metropolitan Police.[16]

After the successes of the Ghost Squad, the duplicate keys trial was chastening. Despite the risk of individual low-level corruption in an organization as large as Scotland Yard, such crimes had been rare. Criminals like Billy Hill claimed they knew some senior officers to be corrupt. But Hill and his kind were not the best witnesses. The true problem was that crime from the 1940s onwards could only be effectively curbed with the aid of informers. Police regulations had forbidden fraternization with criminals for the most high-minded of reasons. In the new post-war world, as amateurs gave way to professionals, high-mindedness of that kind seemed incompatible with effective intelligence.

8

Young Thugs

I

IT WAS A cliché of the war, particularly in its later years, that the nation would pay a high price for the absence of so many fathers on active service. A generation of sons was growing up without the paternal authority and example which were society's safeguards of decency and responsibility. This warning was usually applied to sons rather than daughters, who might exercise a maternal influence. Given the call for munition workers and auxiliary services staff, there were bound to be mothers who were committed to war work in their own right. Though allowances were paid to the wives of servicemen, earning a proper wage was both a necessity and a patriotic duty. In these circumstances, it would not be surprising if the teenagers of the war years became the difficult young men of the 1950s, while the infants of the war became the teenage rebels of the immediate post-war period. Once peace was established, the social priorities changed. By June 1951, the London County Council's report on juvenile delinquency was urging working wives to 'put the family first'.

Juvenile crime in wartime included a range of antisocial conduct: the rifling of gas meters during air raids while the occupants of the houses were in the communal shelter; the looting of toys from damaged premises by pupils who had not been to school for a twelvemonth; adolescents who disguised themselves as adults in ARP helmets in order to ransack unoccupied buildings without being challenged; nine-year-olds who staged a smash-and-grab on a sweet-shop, or the five-child gang, aged between eleven and thirteen, who carried out systematic raids on railway wagons for such treasures as toffee and fish paste. When junior criminals were caught, their response often showed a new self-confidence. As one pair confronted the police, the eight-year-old, in the tones of James Cagney, announced that he would 'take the rap'. In another case, the infant robber told his accomplice to keep his 'trap' shut. 'I'll do the talking.'[1]

Some youthful crimes had shown a martial spirit. These included the robbery of Home Guard stores for weapons and equipment, as children strove to mimic the defiance of Hitler shown by their elders. In the summer of 1943, two adolescents sat in one of Brighton's largest cinemas with their stolen hand grenades, periodically releasing and closing the pins, testing how long it was safe to take their thumbs off the mechanism before the device blew up. Another raid on an arms store by children yielded a tommy gun, 400 rounds of ammunition, a bayonet and a cash box. Inquisitive ten-year-olds tried to detonate stolen ammunition by hitting it with a chopper. Two others acquired sixty live shells from US servicemen and kept them in their bedroom toy cupboards. Each round was capable of demolishing a building and wiping out all those in the vicinity.[2]

Most such offences were an exercise in bravado, though a few were criminal by any description. These included an assault by youngsters who demolished the ICI boardroom in Blytheswood Square, Glasgow, in January 1944 with the aid of thirty-two stolen hand grenades and two boxes of detonators. Older children were more likely to put crime before patriotism, as when three seventeen-year-olds and an eighteen-year-old raided an armaments store at Hayes in March 1943 and then held up the cash desk of the Ambassador Cinema with three Sten guns and a rifle.[3]

It remained to be seen whether the family or, if necessary, the police and the courts could exert authority over the young when peace came. In the last days of war, the omens were not encouraging. The chairman of an East London court, trying twenty-six cases of larceny by four defendants in July 1945, described them as the 'worst gang' ever to appear before him. The robbers, who pleaded guilty, were aged between twelve and fourteen. A good many children owned up to what they had done or proposed to do, some of them shrewdly aware that they were too young to incur much punishment. When two boys, aged fourteen and seventeen, were found at Finsbury Park with an automatic pistol in January

1946, they claimed that they were going to use it 'to stick-up people'. 'Ridiculous!' said Daniel Hopkin, the magistrate. 'A kid like you talking of sticking people up!'[4]

It was ridiculous no longer. As this case was being heard, another 'gang' led by a blue-eyed girl, aged about eighteen and about five feet tall, was holding up housewives in North London, targeted because they appeared to be alone during the day. A week later, after a breaking and entering at Edgware, a boy of sixteen turned an automatic pistol on the police who had cornered him in a Paddington street. When he was disarmed, he fought on even after being hit over the head with a truncheon. Twenty-four rounds of ammunition were found in his pocket.[5]

The problem of these apprentice criminals was not exclusive to London nor was it always at its worst there. It was a curiosity that the peak age for juvenile crime in the capital was sixteen by 1946 but thirteen in the country as a whole. Early delinquency was a particular problem in such areas as Liverpool, where crime and disrespect ran high. In June 1946 a gang of five decided to loot the Liverpool Exchange Building, part of which was in the process of being rebuilt. The time chosen was after the exchange had closed and its workers had gone home, leaving it in the care of a watchman.

Four of the gang were aged between eleven and thirteen, while the lookout was a nine-year-old. The four intruders were found on the thirteenth-floor premises of the local Food Office by the watchman, who promptly locked them in and went to phone the police. Undaunted by this, the four infant burglars climbed out of the window, thirteen floors up and adjoining the rebuilding project. They slid down the girders of the unfinished structure to the level of the fifth floor. At this point, one of them shouted down to the watchman, 'You won't catch me!' They then walked in file, balancing on a horizontal girder of the fifth floor, to a point where they could slide down a vertical to ground level. When the police arrived, the gang had vanished, 'much damage' had been done to the offices, and an uncertain amount of property had been stolen.[6]

By no means all child criminals were as old as the Liverpool Exchange gang. The record for post-war infant bank robbery appears to have been held by an eight-year-old from Glasgow, who was caught during a break-in at the British Linen Bank, Gorbals Road, in December 1949. Had he been any younger he would have been under the current age of criminal responsibility. However, when he was brought to court, the boy was so small that his chin barely cleared the top of the magistrate's table. The court decided to admonish him and let him go.[7]

Inevitably, there was an early attempt to identify the causes of this increasing criminality. The most plausible reason appeared to be the deficiencies of home life and particularly the lack of parental care. Children who played truant from school formed a natural pool of criminal labour. When the figure for truancy in London reached 10,000 a month in 1950, the fact that both parents were often out at work all day was cited as a probable cause of this. Broken homes, which were certainly a significant reality by 1947 when the divorce rate reached four times its pre-war peak, might also encourage children to attach themselves to gangs, as if to a substitute family.

Most groups who came to the attention of the authorities were small scale. Juveniles who imitated the territorial hostility of the Sabinis, the Elephant Boys, the Hoxton Mob, the Whites or Billy Hill were not at first a post-war problem. By 1948, however, the territorial gang was in evidence. In April that year the situation in Croydon, where 'rowdy' gangs of teenagers were said to be making women and children afraid to go out at night, appeared alarming enough for the police to institute 'anti-hooligan' squads, patrolling the streets after dark. This was a long way from the street gangs of the 1950s but in the autumn of 1949 their violence took on a new form.

On a Sunday night, 11 September, a running fight between two groups of adolescents broke out in the streets of Islington. It was apparently started by twenty-five or thirty youths armed with knuckle-dusters and truncheons. The ages of those involved were almost all between fifteen and seventeen. This first outbreak was in Canonbury Road, where the fighting spilled across the roadway and the pavement, regardless of traffic or pedestrians. Women caught up in the brawl were terrorized and children knocked to the ground.

Inquiries indicated that this was pure gang warfare. It had been provoked when two youths had had their noses broken a few days earlier in an attack by 'The Diamond Gang'. On 11 September the police were entirely unprepared but they arrived in time to arrest four youths taking part. The court was also unprepared for such an affray and, not wanting to make matters worse, fined two of the culprits and discharged the others.[8]

For several months, there was a pause in public disorder, though juvenile misbehaviour remained disturbing. There were reports of children aged ten to thirteen who shot a rabbit with a bow and arrow and then, for fun, cut it up while it was still alive, while a similar group poured petrol into trees in order to burn squirrels alive. Two boys, aged eleven and fourteen, burgled their school in East Ham, as well as robbing a nearby shop, then set fire to the school, destroying the headmaster's study, the laboratory and three other rooms. It was not until five months later, in February 1950, that crime on the streets became a significant problem again.[9]

On 15 February there was trouble in South London when a gang of fifty youths, aged sixteen and seventeen, attempted to wreck a fair after dark at Rotherhithe, pelting the employees with bricks and milk bottles. The idea that fairs and circuses were easy targets to attack for fun soon caught on. In July, eleven members of a gang who had raided another fair in Southwark Park were sent to prison by the Tower Bridge magistrate who told them, 'The public must be protected, and I propose to do it.' In the following month, as if in revenge, gangs of about twenty from other areas gathered at Friern Barnet to attack Lord George Sanger's Circus. Their aim was to terrorize the circus employees who slept on the site by deflating the tyres of trailers, releasing the brakes to put vehicles in motion, while smashing the circus lights, defacing the trailers, and using the knives they had brought with them to cut their initials in the wood. The sole agent of law enforcement at the site was a woman park attendant, though the police promised to send a uniformed constable to guard the circus ground after dark.[10]

It was not quite true to say that such things had never happened in the past. Ironically, it was Lord George Sanger's Circus which was wrecked by a mob of 'roughs' from Bath, at Lansdown Fair on 10 August 1841. The showmen caught and flogged the leaders of the riot, while another wrecker who crippled a policeman was hanged. In 1950, this was scarcely the point. By the outbreak of war in 1939, the nation prided itself on having moved on from such things, as it no longer hanged culprits for grievous bodily harm.

What united two incidents more than a century apart was the vandalism of spite. In 1950 this was not confined to attacks on open-air entertainments but extended to all those who were vulnerable. When Christmas came, some squatters of 1946 who were still home-less remained in huts at Hothfield Camp, near Ashford. During the holiday many of them visited more fortunate families or friends. There had been trouble with local youths who were collectively identified with what now followed. The returning hut-dwellers found windows and doors smashed, drawers emptied on the floor, sheets, clothing and linen covered with ink, jam and flour. The primary motive had been vandalism rather than theft, though gas and electricity meters had been forced and their contents taken. China and ornaments were broken, and furniture hacked with knives. As at Sanger's Circus in Friern Barnet, knives were part of the attackers' dress.

The damage at Hothfield was inflicted on those probably far poorer than the families of the attackers. This was also true in the new decade, when gangs of youths greeted Caribbean immigrants with what was called 'nigger-hunting' as a nocturnal sport. Hollywood meantime glamorized the vulnerable, misunderstood, self-destructive teenager, casting James Dean in *Rebel Without a Cause* (1955).

In the streets adjoining the war-battered length of the Caledonian Road, just north of King's Cross, the new year of 1950 also began badly. A group, called variously 'The Angel Gang' and 'The Diamond Gang', numbered about fifty youths and a dozen of their girls. It was a further cause for dismay that crimes of violence were now sometimes committed by girls. Most of the gang were already on probation and came from homes in streets near the Angel. In February 1950, they targeted a youth club adjacent to the Caledonian Road, which offered dances and games. It was housed in the Winton London County Council School. In a first attack the youths smashed almost every window, and assaulted Miss Bastable, head of this

The lights go on again in Piccadilly clubland after six years of blackout. The blackout had been reduced to a 'dim-out' in the autumn of 1944. During the war – and in the peace that followed – clubland became the primary source of revenue for protection rackets

Problems of wartime crime persisted for several years afterwards, with almost 20,000 deserters from the British forces easy recruits to the underworld. The American military jeep in the shadow of Scotland Yard is a reminder that many US deserters were also still on the run

Guns used by young robbers in the D'Antiquis murder of May 1947 illustrate the story of the case

Top: A .455 Bulldog revolver, misloaded with .450 ammunition, fired during a struggle at the West End jeweller's shop

Middle: A rusty Bulldog thrown at the shop assistants before the three youths fled, loaded with out-of-date ammunition of varying calibres and almost impossible to fire

Bottom: The .320 revolver used by Christopher Geraghty to shoot dead Alec D'Antiquis, who barred the way to the escaping robbers. Later found on the foreshore at Wapping, it had been fired once and contained five live rounds: three had misfired

Below: Patrick Carraher, a small-time but violent Glasgow criminal, who was twice sentenced to death for street murders – first in 1941, when he was reprieved, and then in 1946, when he was hanged. In the post-war world, a suit and tie, as well as a trilby hat outdoors, went with a cosh or a cut-throat razor

Billy Hill (*centre front*), the self-styled 'Boss' of Britain's post-war underworld, at the age of nineteen with his pre-war adult gang. Hill was credited with planning the £287,000 Eastcastle Street mail van robbery in 1952. Though he was detained for questioning and subsequently wrote a detailed account of the hijack, he was never charged

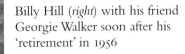

Billy Hill (*right*) with his friend Georgie Walker soon after his 'retirement' in 1956

PUBLISHED BY AUTHORITY.

Special Notice

MURDER

M.P. FH. It is desired to trace the after-described for interview respecting the death of MARGERY GARDNER, during the night of 20th–21st inst. NEVILLE GEORGE CLEVELY HEATH, alias ARMSTRONG, BLYTH, DENVERS and GRAHAM, C.R.O. No. 28142–37, b. 1917, 5ft. 11½in., c. fresh, e. blue, believed small fair moustache, h. and eyebrows fair, square face, broad forehead and nose, firm chin, good teeth, military gait ; dress, lt. grey d.b. suit with pin stripe, dk. brown trilby, brown suede shoes, cream shirt with collar attached or fawn and white check sports jacket and grey flannel trousers. Nat. Reg. No. CNP 2147191.

Has recent conviction for posing as Lt.-Col. of South African Air Force. A pilot and believed to possess an " A " licence, has stated his intention of going abroad and may endeavour to secure passage on ship or plane as passenger or pilot. May stay at hotels accompanied by woman.

Enquiries are also requested to trace the owner of gent's white handkerchief with brown check border, bearing " L. Kearns " in black ink on hem and stitched with large " K " in blue cotton in centre.

Above left: Neville George Clevely Heath, hanged in 1946 after committing two of the most lurid sexual murders since Jack the Ripper. His previous career of dishonesty included dismissal as an officer of three different armed services

Above right: Neville Heath on the run. After the discovery of Margery Gardner's body in the bedroom of the Pembridge Court Hotel in June 1946, Scotland Yard alerted all police forces via a special notice in the *Police Gazette*. The photograph was not published in the press because this might have prejudiced evidence of identification at trial

Below left: Margery Gardner, 31, the first of Heath's victims. A member of Chelsea's 'bohemia', she was an accomplished artist and novice writer

Below right: Margery Gardner, as seen in a film strip in 1946. She was apparently recruited as a film extra for the Gainsborough romance *Caravan* (1946), starring Jean Kent and Stewart Granger

Going out in style: Neville Heath refused to appeal against his death sentence, preferring execution to a life in Broadmoor. Using his alias 'Jimmy Armstrong', he sent a friend this breezy farewell just hours before he was hanged at Pentonville

My dear […],

Just a line to say cheerio.

I don't know what licensing hours they have where I'm off to, but I'll be there at opening time. Order one for me in the 'Falstaff' and remember me to the boys.

To my mind, this is just a one-way 'op', but if there is anything in this reincarnation business please break your morning egg very gently for the next couple of months because it may be me.

Many thanks for what you've done for me in the past and the very best of luck be yours always.

Ever yours,

Jimmy

Left: John George Haigh, the 'Acid Bath Murderer' and 'vampire', at the time of his 1940s killings. He believed the moustache gave him a resemblance to the Hollywood idol Ronald Colman. To support his defence of insanity, he confessed to more murders than the six known or suspected

Below: Haigh's forged letterhead, used in 1937 to defraud the clients of a respectable solicitor. He went to prison for four years. Also a forged power of attorney from 1945, giving Haigh access to his dead victim's money

WM. CATO ADAMSON
SOLICITOR
—
TELEPHONE GUILFORD 3078

11. HIGH STREET

GUILFORD

B ...OWER OF ATTORNEY I William Donald McSwan of
Claverton Street, London, S.W.1 APPOINT
e Haigh of Thirty eight Queens Gate Terrace,
7. and of the Onslow Court Hotel, Queens
don, S.W.7. my attorney for me and in my name
to execute all or any of the following acts deeds

A letter written by Haigh in March 1945 to 'keep alive' the Amusement Caterers' Association membership of Donald McSwan, whom he had dissolved in acid on 9 September of the previous year

ONSLOW COURT HOTEL

QUEEN'S GATE,
SOUTH KENSINGTON,
S.W.7

Telephone :
KENsington 6300 (8 lines)
Telegrams:
Onslowotel Southkens London

6 March 1946.

The A.C.A.
19 Charing Cross Road,
London W.C.2.
Dear Sirs.

        With reference to the enclosed circular I notice that the amount of the subscription is not indicated. I find that the amount for last year was £3/13/6. Is it still so?

        Mr MacSwan is not in business at all at present and I am merely keeping his membership alive in his absence . Does this affect the position in any way?

                Yours faithfully,

                J.G.Haigh

                ATTORNEY FOR
                W. D. McSWAN.

Haigh's macabre working clothes and equipment. The stirrup pump is a relic of his wartime service as a firewatcher during the London Blitz. The pump was later used to transfer sulphuric acid from a bucket to the vat before Haigh disposed of his victims' bodies

Left: Haigh's first-known victim, Donald McSwan, in 1944. Haigh promised the young man and his parents to arrange for his disappearance to avoid military service. Having battered McSwan to death and dissolved him, he defrauded the victim's parents using forged letters and documents until July 1945, when he murdered them too

Right: Dr Archibald Henderson and Mrs Rosalie Henderson, murdered and dissolved by Haigh at his 'factory' in Crawley, Sussex, in February 1948. He used forged documents to empty their bank accounts, as well as to sell their car, jewellery and London home

Left: Mrs Olive Durand-Deacon, murdered and dissolved in Crawley on 18 February 1949. She was Haigh's final victim. Though he believed that he had disposed of her remains, a gallstone and dentures in the sludge identified this missing guest from the Onslow Court Hotel in Kensington, where she and Haigh had been guests 'recreational institute'. The assailants also 'attacked my boys with hammers, razors, and with knives like daggers'.

The leader, who was arrested while brandishing the leg of a broken chair, complained that he had been defending himself and that the police had treated him roughly. 'I am not going to hear any complaint about the police arresting a man who was brandishing a weapon like this,' said the magistrate, indicating the exhibit. The assailants had gone on to tear the keys off the piano, smash the radio, throw chairs and benches into the street, and wrench off the old-fashioned lamp brackets so that the building was filled with escaping gas. No one in the club could stop them nor was this mere youthful high spirits. The Diamond Gang carried knuckledusters or bicycle chains, and fought with feet as well as fists. Some had razor blades fitted in the toes of their shoes and the peaks of their caps. In the wake of the attack the building stood forlornly with steel sheets replacing its window glass.

The same gang twice turned its attention to the nearby Copenhagen School Youth Club but the organizer was a police warrant officer who 'dispersed' them robustly and called his colleagues to clear them from the street outside. There was also a vigorous response from the Claremont Youth Club, near the Angel. Yet, once again, the superintendent remarked, 'The dead-end girls are as bad as the boys. I know of one gang led by a girl of eight.'

On the night of 22 February, police were called four times to the Winton School Youth Club, where the premises were under attack by a gang of fifty to seventy youths who had formed up in the Caledonian Road. 'We have been called there hundreds of times for cases of assault,' said Inspector Gorner, 'but people won't take any action for fear of reprisals in the future.' Intimidation and shouts of 'We know where you live!' ensured that. The situation was no better in Stepney, where a jocularly named 'Spivs Club' for young people had been forced to close by the end of the month, after visits from the local 'Eagle Gang', whose members were somewhat older, between seventeen and twenty-five.[11]

Many of the attacks were not made directly against the clubs but on their individual members. In Holborn, in the area round Theobalds Road, there were groups of about eight youths, aged sixteen or seventeen, whose victims were boys in their early teens. According to the Chairman of the local Youth Committee, five cases were outstanding in which these younger children had been beaten up with bicycle chains. 'The motive was not robbery but sheer sadism and brutality.' There was no need after that for the vandals to attack the clubs, since members kept away because they were too frightened of being beaten on their way home.

By 1950, adults seemed no more immune to attacks by gangs of youths than children had been. On 5 December when fourteen youths from Clapham, armed with bicycle chains, attacked a school in West Dulwich, where evening classes were held, they beat up the headmaster who was still at work and wrecked his room for good measure.

Alarm at the growing frequency of attacks was reinforced by crime figures for 1948, published in February 1949. The more serious or indictable crimes by offenders under twenty-one were accelerating at 28 per cent a year, a rate at which they would double every three years. Among those aged seventeen to twenty, such crimes had risen by 40 per cent since the beginning of the war but it was the latest increase which caused most concern. Sir Harold Scott, Commissioner of Metropolitan Police, deplored the repeated probation or binding-over by the courts, releasing the offender to commit further offences. He demanded a crusade against the crimes of the young. The irresolute response by magistrates and chairmen of juvenile courts was widely denounced. Mr Justice Humphreys, by now over eighty but still on the bench, described juvenile courts forthrightly as 'laughing stocks'.

It was rare for the very young to be manipulated by adult criminals, as they had been in the Victorian period, on the grounds that they could carry out serious crimes but receive only a light sentence. Yet a fifteen-year-old remanded in June 1950 at East London Juvenile Court refused to give evidence, being 'in terror' of a gang of more than fifty boys to which he belonged. 'He has been threatened and it is almost impossible to break away. Several older men are known to be guiding the gang and planning raids.'[12]

Children of ten or eleven were now appearing in court as members, and even leaders, of gangs. At Birmingham in June 1950, in the stabbing of a nine-year-old boy, the accused were gang members aged seven and eight. At these ages they were more likely to be victims. By March, members of teenage gangs accused of inflicting violence on their juniors were frequently appearing at the Old Bailey. Three members of Bermondsey's so-called 'Brick Gang', described as 'corner lingerers', two of them sixteen and one seventeen, had attacked a schoolboy, slashing him with a knife. One of his wounds had required seventeen stitches. Eight others from Walworth, aged fourteen to seventeen, had allegedly beaten up a fourteen-year-old with an iron cosh because of his attentions to a girl. In such cases as these, the higher courts heeded the suggestions of Sir Harold Scott. In the slashing case, the principal offender was a sixteen-year-old who, despite any question of inhumane punishment at such an age, was sent to an adult prison for two and a half years. The judge's only comment was to regret that he could not order the offenders to be birched.[13]

A child under sixteen could not be sent to prison and yet some of the most vicious conduct came from children in that group. In March 1948 a fourteen-year-old 'gang boss' from East London, who shrieked 'I'll murder you' at his accuser in court, had been in command of ten-year-olds. They had made another fourteen-year-old boy bring them his Post Office savings book, which contained only thirty shillings. The 'gang leader' accused the child of having misled them by saying it contained £6. The victim was then offered the choice of 'taking his punishment' in the ruins of a blitzed house or having his pet dog strangled. In order to save his dog, the boy allowed himself to be beaten up with a wooden knuckleduster, so savagely that one of his eyes was permanently damaged. It became increasingly difficult for the liberal-minded to show why the hope that delinquents might respond to kindness should take precedence over a commonsense urge to exact retribution.[14]

Elsewhere, gangs aged ten to fourteen staged 'armed hold-ups' using air pistols and catapults to steal pocket money and sweets. The rewards were trivial but, once again, the violence was not. One such gang, at Reading, confessed to 128 thefts when they were caught. Its local rival was led by a girl of eleven, assisted by four girls of twelve.[15]

2

The youthful crime wave of 1949–50 and the gang warfare which accompanied it were variously described as 'appalling', 'sensational', 'an alarming increase' and 'a grave menace'. What would happen when a generation containing so many criminals became parents and voters? As it happened, many post-war youngsters were to grow up as reactionaries, deploring the lack of respect shown by the next generation and exalting the benefits of 'a good hiding', which they were no longer allowed to confer. In the meantime, this was little consolation to those who were robbed, beaten, slashed, stabbed and even shot.

Lord Lloyd, in a parliamentary debate on 21 March 1950, reminded the government of its duty to protect the people. 'The problem cannot be laid aside in the hope that one day better social conditions may make such a duty unnecessary.' The post-war dawn had illuminated the moral and social disintegration of a generation. Judge Tudor Rees put it more cogently at Surrey Quarter Sessions on 14 March, when he said simply, 'Unless the community control criminals, criminals are going to control the community.'

For some, the cause of youthful violence had nothing to do with the war but everything to do with the policies which followed it. At the Old Bailey on 1 March 1950 two cases came before the Lord Chief Justice, Baron Rayner Goddard. Appointed in 1946, Goddard was destined to become the most controversial of post-war jurists for the severity of his sentences and his reactionary views. The first trial was of a man of twenty-five who had violently robbed an elderly woman. In the second, two youths of fifteen and seventeen had attacked a thirty-one-year-old woman on a train between Lewisham and Blackheath, knocking her unconscious and pushing her body under the seat. The guard found her with what were described as appalling injuries. At the time of the trial, her life remained in danger. A Webley air pistol, a length of rubber and the lead which had filled it as a cosh were also found. 'I only hit her across the head once,' said the seventeen-year-old, as if too much fuss was being made. 'You may still be tried for murder if she dies,' Goddard told him with some satisfaction.

In the first trial, Goddard sent the defendant to prison for ten years. In the second, he sentenced the two youths to seven years each. This second trial had been 'the most shocking and disturbing case to come to my notice in my seventeen years as a judge'. He had told the earlier defendant that the new level of violence throughout the country was outrageous. 'I believe that is largely due to the fact that you men now know that you can no longer be whipped for it. The only alternative is longer sentences.' In the case of the two youths, he remarked that eighteen months earlier, 'I could have had you whipped. Now I can no longer take that course, but I am going to pass a longer sentence.'

There was one other remedy which Goddard and his brother judges could employ to reassure the public and strike fear into the criminal class. It had usually been the case that a man convicted of a crime had nothing to lose by appealing against sentence or conviction, or both. His appeal might be refused but he would be no worse off. When Frederick William White appeared optimistically in the Court of Criminal Appeal in February 1946, he was appealing against a two-year sentence for shopbreaking. Lord Goddard agreed with him that the sentence was incommensurate with the crime – and doubled it. Longer sentences were necessary.[16]

Frank Gordon Clarke, who held up a cashier with a toy pistol, also had his sentence increased by Goddard from four and a half to six years on appeal. Stanley Simpson, who had been sent to prison for attacking and robbing an elderly man in the Whitechapel fog, challenged the harshness of his six-year sentence. 'In our opinion,' said Goddard, 'the sentence passed on this man is quite inadequate and is increased to ten years.' Old lags began to think twice before appealing to the new Lord Chief Justice.[17]

Public unease at increasing violence in 1950 was coupled with resentment that Parliament had made an irrevocable and unpopular decision in the Criminal Justice Act of 1948. One of the Act's provisions abolished all forms of corporal punishment, except in the case of mutiny or serious assault by convicts. In a new and idealistic world, it had seemed to the Labour government and to enlightened opinion that the barbarism of the cat-o'-nine-tails, which scarred a man's back for life, or even the birch, was repugnant.

Such punishments had been progressively abolished since 1809, when the public flogging of women was ended. It seemed only a question of time before even the remaining provisions for punishing prisoners were done away with.

Public opinion favoured the flogging of violent criminals – and did so by very large majorities. Even in the late 1960s, support ran at about two-thirds of the electorate. Yet despite the criminality of the post-war young, Parliament was in no mood to reverse its decision. To calls for a repeal of that section of the Criminal Justice Act, Chuter Ede, a schoolmaster who had become Labour's Home Secretary, insisted in the House of Commons on 9 March 1950 that there could be no going back.

This might be government policy but it had not prevented the magistrate, when two boys of eleven and fourteen set fire to Napier Road School, East Ham, from saying wistfully, 'Had these offences been before the passing of the Criminal Justice Act there is not much doubt that we should have had both these boys birched.' Parents in this and other cases were, inevitably, criticized for not dealing harshly enough with their delinquent children. Yet by now their position was something of a lottery. They might be congratulated or convicted, depending often on the mood of the magistrate. At Bedford Quarter Sessions on 28 August 1952, a boy of fourteen was put on probation for garage breaking. The implication was that his father should put a stop to his criminal career. The father asked: 'If I give my boy a good hiding, what will happen to me? I'll get six months.' 'Not in this court,' said the chairman reassuringly.[18]

The House of Commons, with a large anti-hanging majority of Labour MPs, had also voted in 1948 to abolish capital punishment. On 16 April, the Home Secretary promised that all murderers condemned to death, as they were bound to be since the sentence was mandatory, would be reprieved until Parliament had reached a decision on the proposed abolition. In the event, abolition was defeated in the House of Lords and the death penalty then continued to be carried out. Throughout his tenure of office, Chuter Ede strictly followed Home Office advice in the matter and allowed such men as Jenkins, Geraghty, Heath and Haigh to go to the gallows without intervening.

Goddard's views at the Old Bailey were echoed on 20 March 1950 by the Recorder of Southend Quarter Sessions. He had been told that a violent youth appearing before him would respond to kindness. 'I hear that over and over again,' he said, 'and every time I come here the calendar is just as heavy.' When two young shop-breakers of sixteen and seventeen followed the youth into the dock, he added, 'These boys ought to be whipped but I have not the power.' Such sentences would stop 'the spate of shop and house-breaking in this borough'.

On the following day, the issue was debated in the House of Lords, as newspaper headlines demanded 'Cat or Cosh?' The Lord Chancellor, Lord Jowitt, again insisted that the law had been changed and 'it would be politically quite impossible to go back on that now'. A majority of the house, led by Lord Goddard and Lord Lloyd, opposed him. Without the sanction of the Commons, however, the upper house was little more than a debating chamber. Government supporters argued that there was no evidence of the cat-o'-nine-tails or the birch deterring violent young criminals. Their opponents insisted that delinquents were manifest cowards whose first concern was for their own skin. It was common sense that the threat of physical punishment would be effective.

There was another theme in this debate, heard often in the years that followed. Lord Lloyd questioned 'the effect of the cinema on the adolescent mind and whether a rather stricter censorship of the worst type of gangster film is not necessary'. By the 1950s this extended to the output of television and the import of 'horror comics'. Books were sometimes included, though the case of the youth who led the attack on a club in the Caledonian Road was not uncommon. It ran into procedural difficulties when he proved to be illiterate. A further difficulty had been defined by Virginia Graham, when reviewing the new James Cagney film *White Heat* in the *Evening Standard* the previous November, under the heading, 'This Film Glorifies Violence'. In the course of the review she added that 'The terrible thing is its excellence.' Defining 'the worst type of gangster film' would not have proved easy and was never attempted.

There was a move shortly after the House of Lords debate to ban the BBC radio series *Dick Barton – Special Agent*, which was transmitted from Monday to Friday on the Home Service from 6.45 to 7 p.m. The programme's preoccupation with crime and criminals was regarded by magistrates and schoolmasters as one cause of juvenile delinquency. So, for example, at Horsham Juvenile Court on 1 April 1948, a father whose ten-year-old son was charged with stealing a wristwatch complained that it was all the result of the child listening to *Dick Barton*. 'Children are too fond of playing at Dick Barton. He is the curse of this country.' The court put the child on probation for a year on condition that he should not be allowed to listen to the programme during that time. It was still running when the year's probation ended.

An audience of seven million adults and eight million children continued to follow the adventures of this celibate and teetotal radio hero who, with his assistants Snowy and Jock, ensured that crime never paid and virtue was triumphant. An eleven-year-old wrote to the press to protest that Dick Barton set a good example to the young as a crime fighter who always got his man. The BBC cautiously appointed John Burke, a probation officer in a London court, as script editor and 'watchdog' of the series, to prevent undesirable influences creeping in. Unfortunately, there had been an agreement that his name should not be associated with the programme and when this was ignored, Mr Burke resigned.

The effect of films and entertainment on the young was already a matter of concern to the government. On 5 May, a Home Office committee under Professor K. C. Weare, an eminent constitutional lawyer, recommended that films with 'sequences that are brutal, antisocial or licentious' should be banned to children. The report added reassuringly that 'There is little evidence of the serious imitation of gangster characters by children in real life and no evidence of imitation that is anything more than pantomime.'

3

So far, most of the damage had been done by the young to one another with makeshift weapons. Those who were grateful that the street fighting in the Caledonian Road during November 1949 did not involve firearms had not much longer to wait. On the night of 16 April 1950, shots were fired when rival teenage gangs met outside a Baptist chapel in Canterbury Road, Kilburn. An eighteen-year-old known as 'Mongy' drew away from the scrimmage, took a revolver from his pocket and fired five or six shots into the crowd. He was charged with the attempted murder of Patrick Twomey. It might have been a murder charge but, 'Fortunately, Twomey carried in his breast pocket his ration book and cigarette case, and the bullet seems to have gone through the ration book and lodged in the case. He was hit in the thigh and ankle.'[19]

Their elders might wonder what would happen if such violence extended to crime between the generations. If vandalism became robbery and the automatic pistol replaced the cosh, the line between assault and murder would easily be crossed. If that should happen, courts would have no option but to sentence those who had reached the age of eighteen 'to be hanged by the neck till you be dead'. While it was true in 1952 that no murderer as young as eighteen had been hanged in the past thirty years, only an act of mercy by the Home Secretary of the day had prevented it. To many who felt that youthful hooligans had got away with too much for too long, the prospect of an exemplary hanging was not entirely unwelcome. Before the year was over, there were calls for the age at which murderers could be hanged to be reduced to sixteen. It was time that the 'little fuckers', as Frank Cassels QC described his clients, should be taught a lesson.

Yet such post-war delinquents as these did not belong to the type of East End and South London criminals who killed Captain Binney in the Birchin Lane jewel robbery of 1944 or Alec D'Antiquis in the bungled jewel robbery of 1947. Tommy Jenkins, who was charged with the murder of Captain Binney, went on to become a career criminal and was to be jailed for five years for conspiracy to rob in 1953, when his accomplice was jailed for life for the attempted murder of a policeman. Harry Jenkins and Christopher Geraghty, hanged for the murder of Alec D'Antiquis, already had impressive records as armed robbers.

Sir Harold Scott, as Metropolitan Commissioner of Police,

upholding the value of the ultimate penalty as a deterrent before a Royal Commission on Capital Punishment in October 1949, attributed the rise of armed gangs in 1944–7 to the failure to execute Tommy Jenkins and Ronald Hedley for the death of Captain Binney in 1944. He further attributed the breaking up of many professional armed gangs after 1947 to the execution of Harry Jenkins and Christopher Geraghty in that year. The arguments over the effectiveness of hanging as a deterrent still had many years to run.

The danger after 1948 came from those who were not professional criminals but delinquent teenagers. Their ages were likely to be between fifteen and eighteen, and their first aim a victory in the street warfare of rival gangs or a successful career of petty theft. Vandalism seemed to attract them more than either. They usually possessed guns or knives as if wearing fashion accessories to impress their girlfriends. Yet these fashion accessories were no less lethal, and in the hands of an amateur frequently more dangerous, than when carried by a professional. It seemed a sign of the times that while those who had attacked showmen in 1950 used milk bottles or bricks, a group of boys between eleven and fifteen who attacked and robbed campers in May 1951 promised that 'This gun will kill you at 300 yards.'[20]

The most serious crimes of youth were often as striking for their aimlessness and ineptness as for their viciousness. A fortnight after the Diamond Gang had announced its presence on the streets of Islington, for example, the centre of Leeds was sealed off on the morning of 16 November 1949, after a killing that was typical of its kind. That morning, shortly after 10 a.m., Abraham Levine, a fifty-three-year-old ex-serviceman, was alone in his Albion Watch Depot in Albion Street. Two youths came in, one fair and one dark, both wearing the familiar fawn raincoats of the 1940s male but without hats or any form of disguise. They told him they had 'old watches' for sale. Mr Levine said that he had 'no use' for old watches. He suspected they were trying to sell him stolen property. One youth then produced a gun and hit him in the face with the butt, drawing blood from his mouth.

The shop was overlooked by first-floor premises in the street, including a solicitor's office where five clients were waiting and the

Outlook Club. There was a shout and Mr Levine was seen struggling with a youth in the shop doorway. Though he had been hit on the head with the gun butt, he was trying to hang on to his assailant, as if to detain him until someone came to his aid. There was a shot at point-blank range into his stomach and he fell. The youths ran across the street, though a man who was passing by tried to close with them and more shots were fired. The solicitor on the floor above and his five clients ran down to the street door, where a bullet shattered the plastic nameplate beside them.

It was as if civil war had broken out on this morning in the centre of Leeds. A bullet smashed through the window of a gown shop, almost adding to the number of casualties and sending its occupants running for cover. A woman from the Outlook Club ran out with towels and a basin of water, joining a man who was kneeling beside Mr Levine, bathing his head. The wounded jeweller was moaning, 'Oh, my stomach,' as the two teenage gunmen took to their heels. Someone had already dialled 999 and carloads of armed CID officers began to arrive from police headquarters about half a mile away.

Within the improvised cordon, armed police entered the Civic Hall and stood guard on the Gaumont Cinema in Cookridge Street while it was searched. Disused buildings in the area were inspected but no suspect was found. Then a car driver saw the two youths nearby, in Vernon Street. He followed in his vehicle until one of them turned, saw what he was doing and fired back at him. The pair then dashed across the street, into the entrance of the Leeds College of Technology and out through the back of the building. Though the police cordoned off the college, it was in the hope of finding a discarded coat, a weapon or some other clue. The youthful gunmen had long gone.

Mr Levine lived until the following afternoon. He had been shot with a .310 bullet used by slaughterers to kill cattle. It was impossible for surgeons to remove it without killing the patient. Next day, a gun was found abandoned in the doorway of a jeweller's shop in Hunslet, about a mile and a half from the shooting. When Nathan Cohen went to open his shop he found that someone had climbed the six-foot metal gate, which protected the entrance area, and had almost cut through the padlock on the door. It seemed that the intruder had then been frightened off, dropping the gun and a hacksaw as he fled.

From what they already knew, the city CID were able to identify their suspects as Walter Sharpe, a nineteen-year-old, and George Lannen, seventeen, both from Leeds. Descriptions were issued and the two youths were arrested the following morning on the Lancashire coast at the holiday resort of Southport.

At Leeds Assizes on 10 March 1950, it took the jury only twenty minutes to find both defendants guilty of murder. Walter Sharpe, who had passed his birthday in prison and was now twenty, was sentenced to be hanged. Gordon Lannen at seventeen was too young to be hanged and was to be detained 'during His Majesty's pleasure', in practice for ten to fifteen years. There was little sympathy for either youth. 'Law Saves Killer (17)' said the headlines grudgingly, though adding for consolation, 'But Gunman Of 20 Is To Die'. Mr Justice Streatfeild, addressing the two murderers after their conviction, directed his words to the world beyond them.

> It is a dreadful thing that in 1950 in England we should have had instances of what is nothing less than gangsterism. It is shocking, indeed, that when large sums are spent on education they should not have instilled into them the difference between right and wrong.

Nor was it merely a matter of progressive educational theories, increasingly despised by the populists. Large sums had been spent on the health, housing and general comfort of this generation. Youth clubs were provided to answer the complaint of there being 'nothing for young people to do' and in return young people wrecked them. These delinquents were now protected against chastisement either by the law or even in the home. Survivors of the recession-bound 1930s, as well as veterans of the blitz or active service, when so many had laid down their lives for the world the young now enjoyed, saw the thanks they were to receive. The two youthful gunmen had left Abraham Levine to die in agony over a day and a half. They had killed him with a gun from a slaughterhouse. As an afterthought, critics usually concluded with the assertion that hanging was 'too good' for young thugs who turned to murder.

By no means all intended victims allowed themselves to suffer the fate of Mr Levine. William Beth, a Southend taxi driver, was hailed at night by two boys of fifteen and sixteen who told him to take them to Shoeburyness. On the way they ordered him to stop. He felt a blow on the head and turning round saw the sixteen-year-old pointing a gun at him. Mr Beth was having none of this. He climbed into the back of the taxi and struggled with the boys, taking the gun from the elder while the younger continued to punch him. Then the younger boy ran off in panic only to be caught soon afterwards. Mr Beth detained the sixteen-year-old, as Mr Levine had sought to do his attackers. When the pair were charged, the sixteen-year-old pleaded with the station inspector: 'I did not mean to hit him. He won't die, will he? I don't want his money. Tell me he won't die, mister. I am no killer. This will kill my mother.' The outburst illuminated the alter ego of the juvenile gangster who scornfully informed his victims that 'This is a raid!' or shouted 'Stick 'em up!' in imitation of screen drama. The disclaimer of violent intent failed when it was discovered that the youth of sixteen was carrying a holster for his revolver, a jackknife and sheath, two cloth masks and a knotted cord.[21]

4

The gun had become commonplace among juveniles. Even among professional criminals the long-held aversion to carrying firearms was outmoded. A greater taboo had been to use a firearm or, indeed, any kind of weapon against a policeman. Not only would it substantially increase a man's sentence but, in the worst case, the murder of a policeman by a known criminal and the hunt that followed it would cause the rest of the underworld a great deal of disruption. Those who prided themselves that they had never informed against a fellow thief would betray a police killer out of self-interest.

The young amateurs had fewer scruples because, it seemed, these had not been bred into them. Yet the public was disproportionately alarmed by police murders because if the police were not safe, who was? The humdrum bobby-on-the-beat was transformed into a front-line hero of a fight against an enemy as loathsome to many as Adolf Hitler's street bullies. Yet those who demanded that the breakers of this ultimate taboo should face the ultimate penalty were to endure several years of frustration.

The most famous case of its kind in the post-war years was one in which, if any defendant merited the death sentence, it was surely this culprit. Just before 8 p.m. on Friday 13 February 1948, Police Constable Nathaniel Edgar, a married man of thirty-three with two children, was on plain-clothes 'burglar patrol'. There had been a sudden rise in burglaries in the Winchmore Hill area of North London. Nat Edgar and his colleague, PC John McPartland, had been walking along Winchmore Hill Road, following a hatless man in a dark overcoat whom they believed to be acting suspiciously. They lost sight of the man after ten or fifteen minutes and decided to split up, taking the minor roads to either side. Edgar saw the man again at 112 Wades Hill, where it seemed he was about to climb a garage drainpipe in the front garden of an unoccupied house. Noticing someone else in the road, however, the man came out of the garden gate and Edgar stopped him. When questioned, the man said that he had just been to visit a friend who was not in and offered to take Edgar back to prove it.

At that moment a light went on in the house and the suspect's bluff was called. Edgar asked him for his identity card and was able to read his number and his name, 'Donald George Thomas'. As the policeman turned away, possibly to look up the road for his colleague, the suspect produced a Luger automatic pistol and shot him three times from behind. The shots were heard by witnesses in the area who saw a young man running from Wades Hill through the darkness. They went to investigate. Dr Edward Samuels arrived to find PC Edgar lying in the gateway of the house. He examined the injured man and gave him morphia. Another constable, William Crow, arrived and Edgar gave him the suspect's name and number from the identity card. 'I do not know if it is right. He shot me in the leg with three shots. The pocket book is in my inside pocket.' Edgar then lost consciousness and died soon after being taken to hospital.

Donald George Thomas was twenty-three, an army deserter previously absent for two years who, after serving 160 days' detention, had deserted again, four months before the present shooting. His civilian criminal record was slight. As a child he had been put on probation and, at sixteen, was sent to an approved school. He was of good intelligence and gave an articulate, if unconvincing, account of the death of Nathaniel Edgar. He wanted to get away and meant to frighten the policeman with his gun. He was standing behind Edgar when he drew it, while the policeman looked up the road. There had been a struggle as Edgar reached back for the gun and tried to wrest it from the suspect's grip. Thomas lost control of the angle at which it was held and it went off accidentally three times. The jury heard the witnesses who had been in the neighbourhood describe three measured shots, which did not sound like an accident. Each would require the trigger to be squeezed. The jurors chose to believe that Thomas had deliberately shot Edgar three times from behind, in order to escape. Medical evidence showed the gun had been angled downwards but the wounds had been mortal.

The manhunt was intensive but it was over in less than four days. On Saturday, the day after the murder, armed CID officers raided fifty houses in North London and mingled with crowds at football matches, dog tracks, public houses and on tube trains, all to no effect. Thomas was still at a South London boarding house in Stockwell. He had been living there for several weeks with a young married woman, Noreen Winkless, who worked as a cinema usherette. On the day of the murder, which was her day off, they had spent the morning at the ABC cinema in Brixton, then after a cup of coffee had gone into central London to the New Victoria Cinema, where she worked. They went home to Stockwell by tram and at 6.30 Thomas had gone out again to Winchmore Hill, presumably in search of a house to burgle.

He came home next morning, saying he had been out with a friend called 'Vic' but they had not had 'any luck' in finding somewhere to burgle. Later he asked if she had seen the papers and admitted that he was the man who shot the policeman, merely intending to 'maim' him. Noreen Winkless promised to stand by him.

By Tuesday morning the police knew from Noreen Winkless' husband that she had gone off with the wanted man. Her photograph was given to the press. Unlike the Heath case, this would not compromise identification at a trial since no one need identify her. The Stockwell landlady's husband recognized her in the paper next morning as one of the 'ideal couple' who lodged with them, 'Don and Noreen Winkless'. The landlady, Mrs Connie Smeed, went out into the street and stopped a uniformed policeman. When she took the couple's breakfast tray upstairs at 8.30, she was followed silently by Inspector William Moody, sixteen stone and six feet tall, leading three armed officers in their plain clothes of trilby hats and mackintoshes.

As the landlady opened the door a little, Thomas glimpsed the men outside and slammed it in their faces. Moody and one of the armed officers, PC Wheeler, burst it open at once. Thomas, who had been standing in his underwear, ran to the bed where Noreen Winkless was still lying. Wheeler dived for his legs and brought him down. Thomas had grabbed for something under the pillow and had drawn out the Luger pistol as Inspector Moody with his sixteen stone landed on him. 'As he turned the gun towards me,' said Moody, 'I jumped at him, caught his right wrist with both my hands, fell across his head and right arm, bent his right arm over my left arm as I fell and pulled the gun from his hand. He, myself and PC Wheeler lay on the bed when I heard a voice from underneath me saying, "What is going on? Let me get up!" and I saw that it was Mrs Winkless.'

Moody asked him if the blue-black Luger pistol was loaded. 'Yes, full up,' said Thomas, 'and they were all for you.' As he was driven away to Brixton police station in handcuffs, he added, 'You were lucky. I might just as well have been hung for a sheep as a lamb.' On the other hand, he alleged that he was told by Divisional Inspector Stinton, 'You bastard! You are just the right build to string up, and I am going to make sure you go.'[22]

There was little doubt about the likely verdict in the case or about public reaction. When Thomas was driven from Brixton to Wood Lane police station in North London, a cordon of policemen with linked arms was needed to keep back a jeering crowd of several hundred. A few broke through, spitting at the slowly moving car and hammering on its windows. The moral of this public mood was not lost on Tower Bridge Juvenile Court. On the last day of Thomas's Old Bailey trial, its chairman told two boys of twelve and fourteen – 'beastly little gangsters' – who had robbed a nine-year-old, 'You are the type who shoot unarmed policemen when you grow older and think you are doing something very brave.'[23]

At the Old Bailey, the killer of PC Edgar was found guilty on 20 April and sentenced to death by Mr Justice Hilbery, who wore the traditional black cap and recited the familiar formula. The world knew the murderer would not be hanged. Four days earlier the Home Secretary had promised the House of Commons an automatic reprieve for all murderers until the result of the debate on the abolition of hanging was known. In such circumstances, public anger was not mollified by reports of the convicted man asking his warders anxiously, 'What do you think? They won't hang me, will they?' and exercising his right as a temporary occupant of the condemned cell to ten free cigarettes and a pint of beer a day.

The outcome of the case seemed still less encouraging when Constable Cecil Harris was shot and wounded twice as he challenged two thieves at the back of shops in Forest Gate in the small hours of 4 May. 'When we were running away,' one of them told the police, 'Mickey said: "It's a good job I hit him. We would never have got away if I hadn't had the gun."' The speaker was forty-six years old, his accomplice seventeen. Before the month was over, Henry Paterson Kay, a police radio car driver, had been shot in the stomach when he answered a call to a gunmaker's factory in East Acton, where three teenage thieves were on the premises, the youngest being fifteen.[24]

5

One day, it was thought, there must be justice, or more probably vengeance, exacted from post-war villains. That was certainly to prove true. When it happened the precipitating cause was a single crime committed by those who were teenagers during the war and therefore young professional criminals by the time the 1950s began. Planned robberies were more often the preserve of elder brothers than of the teenage delinquents whose crimes were usually confined to vandalism or violence inflicted to pay off a grudge. By contrast, one robbery in 1952 was to have consequences which far outweighed the importance of the acts which constituted it.

On 14 March 1952, Herbert and Beryl Whiten went to bed as usual in separate rooms of their suburban house in Honey Lane, Waltham Abbey, on the semi-rural fringe of north-east London. Mr Whiten was a nurseryman and there was a child in the house at the time. They heard no car draw up, nor was there any warning of an intruder. Mrs Whiten was startled from sleep by the sudden flashing of a torch in her face. 'There was a gun at my head,' she recalled, 'and five men round my bed. A man had his hand on the sheet of the bed. He was holding the gun. He said: "Wake up, lady, and answer the questions."'

It was the worst nightmare of the comfortable middle class in the post-war years, waking to the voice of a stranger in the dark, torch-light in the eyes and a gun in the hand of the intruder, the threat of injury or torture, the victim isolated from help in the hours that lay ahead. The figures in such crimes were anonymous. The five young men standing round Mrs Whiten's bed, at 2 a.m., wore trilby hats with scarves across their faces. Two or three were wearing the familiar post-war belted raincoats. A man who seemed to be the leader held a Luger automatic pistol, a weapon preferred by the professional armed criminal because it was able to fire wartime Sten-gun bullets, still in plentiful supply. With the light shining on their victim, the questions began. Where were the money and valuables? Locked in the safe. Where were the keys? Not in the house. Herbert Whiten kept the keys with others that he used for his business, in his office at the nursery.

One man ripped the phone wire from the wall to isolate the victim more effectively. Herbert Whiten lay asleep in another room. Four of the men went to wake him, leaving the fifth to stand guard over his wife. Presently this man relented and asked, 'Would you like a cigarette, lady?' Mrs Whiten declined.

One of the others woke Herbert Whiten with the torch and two others subdued him. The fourth said, 'This is a hold-up,' as they tied his wrists to the bedrail above his head. They hooded him with the bedclothes, closed the curtains and turned on the light. The safe was in his room and he could hear them as they began to 'mess about' with it.

No witness had seen the large American car, a Buick, pull up quietly outside the house in what was now the small hours of 15 March. Fortunately the thieves were not to know that. There was also the unexpected presence of a child who would either have to be left behind and allowed to talk or be kidnapped. It might have reassured the captives to know that three of the five masked figures were professional criminals and not likely to use gratuitous violence. The man guarding Beryl Whiten was the same George Albert King, 'Ginger' King, who had led the ill-fated Mayfair fur robbery at Blundells in January 1946, had shot at a policeman and gone to prison for seven years. Two weeks before his arrival at the Whitens, he led a Post Office van robbery at gunpoint, kidnapped the driver, drove the van away and broke it open. The stolen mailbags yielded ninety-one packets containing £6,651.[25]

Surprisingly, it seemed that the robbers believed the story about the safe keys being at the nursery office. They could have taken Mr Whiten there to get them, leaving his wife under guard. The couple would guess the consequences if they had been lying, though they had separately told the same story. A professional thief knew the importance of getting in, doing the job, and getting out as quickly as possible. To drive to the office, get the keys and return would prolong the task dangerously close to dawn in the short May night.

Whatever the reason, the five robbers made off, settling for £4 in cash, some Scroll biro pens, and a handsome cigarette-lighter. The sequel was far more curious than anything in the raid so far. Their Buick car was found next day, abandoned and overturned three miles from the crime. It could hardly have been abandoned deliberately because there was a well-fingerprinted bicycle lamp inside. Before the wreck was discovered, a policeman patrolling nearby saw a man on foot, whom he recognized at once as 'Ginger' or 'Cat's-Eyes' King from Stoke Newington, currently wanted for the Tottenham mail van robbery. In a most unprofessional blunder,

King had inadvertently alerted the police on the day after the van robbery, when he paid £100 of traceable money into his Post Office savings account.

Though King was still only twenty-eight, he was a sad figure. If he was averse to violence in the house at Honey Lane, there may have been good reason. The alias 'Cat's-Eyes' had nothing whatever to do with keenness of vision. He was in the last stages of valvular disease of the heart and suffered from night-blindness. This professional getaway driver could only steer a car after dark by keeping its outer wheels on the cat's-eyes which studded the centre of the highway, steering along them and navigating by their rhythmic bumps under the tyres. He followed this reassuring rhythm, holding to the curves of the road without actually being able to see where he was going. Not surprisingly, he frequently came off the cat's-eyes. On this occasion he had come off the road and overturned the car.

As if to compound his misfortune, he fled from the wreck into the arms of Sergeant Norman Strachan, investigating the Tottenham robbery of 29 February. Of the haul at Waltham Abbey, King's share was the Scroll ballpoint pens. Found in his pocket at the police station, they were identified as belonging to Mr Whiten. 'Ginger' King was put on an identity parade and Mrs Whiten identified his as the voice which had said, 'Would you like a cigarette, lady?' Kindness, not violence, had been his undoing.

The other four men got away with £4 and a cigarette-lighter between them. Such was the modest total behind the next day's headlines of 'armed robbery'. Yet though King was not the brightest star of the underworld, he showed a dogged loyalty and refused to name his accomplices. Standing trial alone, at Chelmsford Assizes on 19 June, he was sent to prison for twelve years. The length of the sentence was immaterial. He died in the prison hospital at Pentonville on 11 September that year.

Even his loyalty was unavailing. The overturned Buick was registered in the name of Cyril Burney, one of the four robbers, though it was not owned by him. It had been bought for £200 a few weeks earlier by Niven Scott Craig, a young man with a criminal record, one of the masked figures at the Whitens' house. The other two robbers were neither identified nor caught. By dawn, the police had fingerprints from the cycle lamp and began a hunt for Burney and Craig. Burney was also on the wanted list for an £800 fur robbery at Wembley.

Burney was able to survive on the proceeds of the fur robbery. Of Niven Craig there was no sign. He bleached his hair and kept out of sight. If there was a leader among the five men, it was he, a true post-war professional. His background was middle class, his intelligence keen, his courage and daring unquestioned. Now twenty-six years old, he had been nineteen at the end of the war and his list of convictions was impressive. Yet as a boy he had won a scholarship at the age of ten to Archbishop Tenison's Grammar School in South London. After convictions for juvenile offences and while still under age, he joined the Gordon Highlanders, only to be court-martialled in Austria in 1947 for armed robbery. Sentenced to five years' imprisonment, he escaped from his escort, reached Italy and staged four more hold-ups of military vehicles at pistol-point. He had been discharged from the Army and released from a military prison in 1950.

A dark smartly dressed young man with a David Niven moustache in civilian life, he was known in the underworld as 'The Velvet Kid' and admired for his dash and daring. In the summer of 1952, he also remained the man whom Scotland Yard could not catch. One of his trial judges, Mr Justice Hilbery, described him as 'a very exceptionally dangerous man . . . cool and cold-blooded'. As for the robbery of the Whitens, Lord Hilbery paid him an unwelcome tribute by refusing to believe he was not the organizer and leader of the attempt, the figure with the gun and commander of men of 'rougher material'. His record set him apart from the likes of 'Ginger' King or Cyril Burney. He was a young man whose panache and daring might be admired by the young. In this lay his greatest danger.

Craig and Burney evaded capture for six months, until the police received information about the sale of stolen furs, which led them to a West London house, used as a private hotel. It stood in Kensington Gardens Square, just behind Whiteley's department store in the Bayswater shopping street of Queensway. Burney had been trying to dispose of the furs stored in his room but without always detecting the inside label with its pinprick code.

Before dawn on 14 September, at 3.35 a.m., armed officers of the Flying Squad surrounded the house. Detective Inspector Garrod and two sergeants moved quietly up the stairs to Room 5, where Burney had been located, and knocked on the door. There was the sound of a window being opened. By the time that Burney had climbed out and shinned down to the basement area, Detective Sergeant Cook was waiting for him. There followed what the police described as a 'terrific fight' with the robber, who was 'eventually subdued'. Reluctantly, he told Sergeant Cook that he was 'Jimmy Johnson', a painter. Three fur capes, a fur coat and several suits were found in his room. When confronted with the coat he had been trying to sell, he said indignantly, 'Who shopped me?' Then thinking better of this, he added earnestly, 'I never stole it. I was going to get £10 for selling it.'

Craig was either a heavy sleeper or perhaps thought that the noise from the basement area had nothing to do with him. The two sergeants went to Room 4 and tapped on the door, which had been locked. The sequel was reminiscent of the arrest of Donald George Thomas. 'The door was opened by a woman,' said Sergeant William Lewis. 'I pushed past her into the room. I saw Craig lying on his back on a bed. As I entered he sat up, his arms folded across his knees. He immediately put his right hand under the pillow and I jumped for the head of the bed. I put my hand under the pillow and took from his hand an automatic pistol.' When Lewis asked Niven Craig whether the Luger automatic was loaded, the reply was, 'Yes, and there is another one up the spout.' Niven Craig's girlfriend added that, as Lewis drew the gun from under the pillow, he said amiably, 'Now what would a nice boy like you want with a thing like this?'

Craig and Burney pleaded not guilty to charges of armed robbery and illegal possession of firearms. Burney simplified his own case by admitting that he was not 'Jimmy Johnson' and that he had dealt in stolen furs. Craig's alibi for the time of the Whitens' robbery was that he and his fifteen-year-old brother, Christopher, had been staying with a friend in Norfolk, who confirmed this in court. The story was not believed and both defendants were convicted. Mr Justice Hilbery turned to Craig. 'From my observation of you I have not the least hesitation in saying I believe you would shoot down, if you had the opportunity to do so, any police officer who was attempting to arrest you, or indeed any lawful citizen who tried to prevent you from some felony you had in hand.' He sent both men to prison for twelve years. 'Ginger' King had died in prison a month earlier but the press did not forget that his blunder in leaving his fingerprints everywhere had linked his friends with the robbery. Referring to Niven Craig, the *Daily Herald* banner of 31 October startled its readers with the assurance that 'Dead Hand Jailed Coldest Gunman'. King was 'a dead gunman who refused to squeal while alive' but whose carelessness had now jailed 'one of Britain's most cold-blooded criminals'. Craig's photograph was printed over the caption, 'Young Dangerous Baby-Face'. Neither of the two men now convicted was given leave to appeal, though Craig argued that the only direct evidence against him was his ownership of the over-turned Buick and this in itself did not prove that he was at Waltham Abbey.[26]

After his conviction for the armed robbery at Waltham Abbey, two policemen involved in the case were said to have walked from the courtroom, one remarking to the other, 'At least we've put that bastard away for a few years.' Standing nearby was an interested spectator of the case and a witness of these words. He was the younger brother of the convicted man. To any member of a family, such words might have caused anger and even violent thoughts. In the case of an older brother who was admired as only a younger brother could admire him, they might inspire a resolve to avenge the hero who was disparaged in this way.

The police force would pay dearly for its cavalier remark, if indeed it was accurately overheard. The consequences were about to embroil the government, Cabinet ministers, the judiciary and the entire country in what the journalist Kenneth Allsop described as an emotional turmoil equalled only by the national mood during the defeat and evacuation of Dunkirk in 1940 or at the sudden death of Britain's most beloved monarch of modern times, King George VI, in February 1952. Three days after Niven Craig's conviction, through the damp November air of South London on a Sunday night, a schoolboy's voice uttered words which were quoted, cited, debated and questioned for years to come. 'I am Craig,' they began. 'You've just given my brother twelve years. Come on, you coppers. I'm only sixteen.'

9

No End of a Lesson

THE AUTUMN OF 1952 marked the bitter climax of a campaign
for curbing youthful criminality, followed by the opening of a
hostile gulf between the generations of war and peace. The nation
had heard enough of youth clubs being wrecked, decent children
from decent families displaying their scars in court, cut by razors
and marked by bicycle chains. Policemen were threatened, attacked,
even killed in the line of duty. A post-war coming-of-age had created
an underworld of its own that was said to be beyond the compre-
hension of its elders.

Worse than these crimes was the attitude of many courtroom
professionals. When delinquents were brought to justice, probation
officers spoke optimistically of their essential good nature. They
were told 'to go away and not do it again'. Perhaps it was no co-
incidence that next to its report of the Waltham Abbey trial, the
liberal *News Chronicle* printed a report of a Mothers' Union
Conference under the headline: 'Mothers Say: Flog Thugs'. Yet the
days when that might have been possible had gone for ever.

Throughout the autumn, demands for the restoration of such
punishment of delinquents, and meanwhile for the use of such punishment in the home, rose in volume. During the Conservative party
conference at Rhyl in October, Lady Maxwell Fyfe, wife of the
new Home Secretary, Sir David Maxwell Fyfe, warned mothers
to birch their unruly young. The *Daily Telegraph* headlined news
of a petition in Liverpool as 'Parents Want Birch Restored'.
Though the right rather than the left in British politics supported
such measures most strongly, the fear of a country about to be
submerged by violent crime crossed political divisions. If
the *Daily Telegraph* warned, 'Wave of Crime: A Challenge', the

left-wing *Daily Herald* echoed it with 'More Action Demanded to Meet the Challenge of the Thug' or 'Women Go in Fear After Dark'.

In November, the Magistrates Association threatened to embarrass the government by holding a vote on the restoration of flogging. A move to restore it was promised by a private member's bill in the House of Commons. Sir Waldron Smithers and Sir Cyril Black supported the motion, as did a public 'town meeting' at Wimbledon, the British Housewives League and the Conservative Women's Advisory Committee. The nation had taken fright at uncontrolled violence and was in a mood to defend itself. That autumn a cosh was exhibited in the House of Commons. A cosh and a knuckleduster were demonstrated by the Lord Chief Justice at the Old Bailey for the benefit of jurors. The abolition of the cat-o'-nine-tails and the birch by the Criminal Justice Act four years earlier seemed in retrospect a prescription for anarchy.

At the height of the protests, there was little appetite for the inconvenient truth that crimes for which flogging had been available until 1948 were now falling rather than rising. Before the trial of Niven Craig and Cyril Burney was over, Earl Howe and Lord Goddard attacked the abolitionists again in a House of Lords debate on 22 October. Lord Howe complained that he could 'hardly pick up a newspaper' without reading of yet another outrage. 'I say that women and other defenceless persons are less secure today in this country than they have been for two generations.' The land was ruled by 'the revolver, cosh, bicycle chain and razor'. Lord Goddard added that his postbag was filled every day with letters 'asking me what I am going to do about reinstituting flogging to prevent the reign of terror which exists in some places'.

The Conservative government, brought to power in the 1951 election, seemed deaf to this. The liberal-minded might complain that hangers and floggers were a reactionary mob. If so, it was a mob now led by the Lord Chief Justice. The reign of terror, as he called it, was resolutely enforced by the weapons of war, which Earl Howe had enumerated. 'Who Has Guns For Sale? New Police Probe', was the *Daily Telegraph*'s headline on 4 November.

However, coshes and guns were not just available for purchase, they might easily be improvised. A cosh need be no more than a length of rubber tubing or hose filled with lead shot. A firearm might be an antique which could be bought by anyone from a curio shop or a harmless starting pistol from a sports shop, either of which could be 'enabled' to fire a small projectile. A handgun from a distant war, long buried in the history books, was still potentially lethal. A kitchen knife might kill, if a stiletto or a sheath knife was not available.

The young, who were rarely heard in the debate, reserved much of their scorn for the police. 'You won't get me into court,' a fifteen-year-old rifle thief had told the police at Hull in August. They had come to arrest him and he had tried to frighten them off by firing an 'enabled' starting pistol at them in the family kitchen. Such boys seemed never more aware of their youth than when calculating that they were below the age at which they could be imprisoned or hanged. Before the autumn was over, men and women would wish aloud for the lowering of the age for such penalties.[1]

A zeal for action rather than inquiry marked the public mood. Yet those whose role was to enforce the law frequently complained that violent films or magazines corrupted the young. By a moral irony, even this argument was turned against the righteous. If such corruption was possible, it immediately became the young criminal's explanation and defence. He was the victim of a greedy and unscrupulous film-maker or publisher who had propelled him towards his crime. A seventeen-year-old was accused of murdering a nightwatchman during a robbery in January 1949 by beating him repeatedly over the head with a monkeywrench, then stealing his watch and wallet. The boy protested that his crime was entirely the result of having just seen *The Three Strangers*, written by John Huston, starring Sydney Greenstreet and Peter Lorre. The film's principal characters were three lottery winners coming to grief as a result of greed and bad luck. 'A man hits a woman over the head with an idol and kills her,' the seventeen-year-old pleaded. As a result of that scene, 'Something came over me.'[2]

A fifteen-year-old who had inflicted grievous bodily harm on three women in separate incidents told the same court, 'After watching a dramatic type of film, I walk out into the cold air and it seems to affect my brain. I feel the urge to attack girls at this time.' A ten-year-old boy who had stabbed to death a nine-year-old girl told Southampton Juvenile Court, 'I have seen stabbing on television . . . I watch all the murders. I like the way they track them down and question them.' An eighteen-year-old bank robber claimed, 'I have seen it all on TV and thought how easy it would be.'[3]

Not surprisingly, the law sought to discredit such explanations. 'Now let us put out of our minds', said Lord Goddard, 'any question of films or comics or literature of that sort. These things are always prayed in aid nowadays when young persons are in the dock, but they really have very little to do with the case.'[4]

On Monday 3 November it seemed that the worst fears of public, police and judiciary had hardened into reality. Millions of newspaper readers at breakfast or on the train to work unfolded the pages to read a story which the *Daily Mail* headlined as 'Chicago Gun Battle In London – Gangsters With Machine Gun On Roof Kill Detective, Wound Another'. Even those who were gloomily accustomed to lesser crimes of violence wondered how an outrage of such proportions could have taken place.

2

On the previous day, the dull routines of an autumn Sunday oppressed the impatient young in South London, as in towns and cities throughout the land. Dance halls were closed, city centres and amusement arcades seemed far off. There was little for many teenagers to do but meet in small groups at the street corners of town centres. Some spent the day conventionally with their families, others found escape in the cinema, whose doors opened on Sunday afternoon to those over the age of sixteen. The Methodist flour-miller J. Arthur Rank owned much of the British film industry. He was anxious not to lure younger children from their Sunday School. A further moral precaution was taken by local watch committees who ensured that the films shown on a Sunday should be suitably bland or moralistic.

Two teenagers, as the troublesome age group was now being called, went separately to the cinema that afternoon. The elder was nineteen-year-old Derek Bentley, who lived with his parents, brother and sister at their home, 1 Fairview Road, almost on a corner of the long arterial stretch of the London Road between Croydon and Streatham. His father ran an electrical repair service at home. The son was tall and well developed, a bodybuilder, but mentally subnormal and virtually illiterate. His IQ was 66, his mental age ten and a half, and his reading age four. He was one of twins, the other of whom had died at birth. Twice in his childhood he had sustained head injuries, by falling from a lorry and when a ceiling fell on him during an air raid. At his local school he was a chronic truant.

Derek Bentley was also a petty thief in childhood but with no record of violence. He had spent two years at an approved school in Bristol, during which time his backwardness was treated without much success at the Burden Neurological Institute. He now seemed almost unemployable, having lost jobs as a Croydon Corporation dustman and as a road sweeper. He failed his National Service medical, being diagnosed with petit mal and as 'mentally substandard' for the Army. On Sunday afternoon, 2 November, in the long jacket and drainpipe trousers of what was soon known as a 'Teddy Boy', he sat through *The Lady from the West*, starring Betty Grable, at the Streatham Astoria. He went home with a slight headache, sank into a chair before the family television set and watched a programme of old-time music hall songs.

Christopher Craig, now sixteen, went to gangster films three or four times a week. On this Sunday afternoon he had taken his girlfriend to see *My Death Is a Mockery*. The lurid title disguised a moral fable of a British smuggler who killed a French policeman and was hanged for his crime. Unlike his friend Derek Bentley, Craig was armed. In his pocket lay a .455 service revolver from the 1914–18 war. It would fire .45 tommy-gun bullets, though not with great accuracy. At the garage where he had worked for a year since leaving school Christopher Craig had shortened the barrel of the gun to fit his pocket. 'Souvenirs' such as this Eley revolver were not uncommon. When the press headlined the youngster as 'Forty-Gun Craig', what this referred to in reality was the number of weapons that had passed through his hands as 'swaps' at school and elsewhere. He had not owned them all simultaneously. Only about ten of the guns had worked, though he had a supply of ill-matched ammunition, much of it picked up at the open rifle range of Caterham Barracks.

He was the youngest of ten children from a respectable middle-class family, living in Norbury Court Road. His father, a bank cashier, had been a captain in the 1914–18 war and a member of the Home Guard in 1939–45. Though Christopher suffered from 'word blindness' or dyslexia so that books had to be read to him, he was a bright child with a stable home background. He had one juvenile conviction for possessing a firearm without a licence, the result of a boyish escapade rather than a crime. More significant in his criminal career was his admiration for his brother Niven, 'The Velvet Kid', who had gone to prison for twelve years on the previous Friday.

Craig went home from the cinema and ate a meal. At 8.30 he rang the doorbell in Fairview Road to collect his friend. According to Craig, Derek Bentley on the previous day had purloined a bunch of keys from a Croydon butcher's shop, where he worked occasionally as an errand boy. If these fitted the street-door lock and the safe, the two youths might have the place to themselves on Sunday night and take whatever cash was still on the premises. Bentley subsequently denied stealing the keys.

The Bentley parents were not pleased to see Christopher Craig. William Bentley later insisted that he had been to Norbury police station on the previous Monday to ask Sergeant Reed if there was some means of keeping Derek away from the younger boy. Reed had previously talked to Mr Bentley and suggested doing this. Craig had then called on the next Saturday evening but Derek had been out at the cinema. A younger Bentley son, Denis, claimed that Craig had shown him a knuckleduster with a vicious spike at one side, made at the garage. Mrs Bentley remembered Craig saying that the police had just given his brother twelve years and that they were not going to get away with it. She had advised the boy to get rid of the knuckleduster but he had run off saying that the police would never take him alive.

When William Bentley warned his son against Craig, Derek made light of it, saying, 'The bloke's barmy.' Whether he believed this or was merely reassuring his parents was never explained. In any case, on the Sunday evening, when Christopher Craig came to collect her son, Mrs Bentley told him that Derek was out. A little later there was another ring at the bell. This time there were two boys, one of them from the grammar school. Mrs Bentley allowed her son to go with them to the end of the road where Christopher Craig was waiting. He and Bentley boarded the bus for Croydon. Bentley claimed that he knew nothing of the gun in Craig's pocket. He certainly knew of the knuckleduster with the spike because Craig gave it to him. In addition, Bentley had a sheath knife in his coat pocket.

Whether or not Derek Bentley had the keys to the butcher's shop in Tamworth Road, running west from the crossroads traffic lights at Croydon centre, that was the direction the two now followed. Bentley wore his camel-hair overcoat, long jacket and drainpipe trousers. Craig was in a trilby hat, corduroy jacket and slim-legged trousers. Tamworth Road consisted of houses, shops, storage facilities, the Robert Peel public house and a cinema. There was a light on in the butcher's shop and signs of movement. Further on was an electrical goods shop but a courting couple in its shadows made that too risky. The two would-be shopbreakers examined a second-hand shop, known as 'Reeves' Corner', then crossed over and walked back to the largest commercial premises in the street, Barlow & Parker's confectionery warehouse. It was quite possible that it contained money waiting to be banked on Monday morning.

The building was in darkness. The only means of entry was by climbing an iron gate, scaling a drainpipe to the flat roof, and then smashing one of the glass roof lights to drop down into the top floor. Bentley's physical clumsiness was a match for his mental incapacity. He first roused the neighbourhood by walking noisily into a dustbin and then got stuck on the gate. At last he got over and followed Craig up the drainpipe to the roof. The noise attracted the attention of the nine-year-old daughter of Edith Ware in a house on the opposite side of the street. Within a few minutes the police had been called and a van containing Detective Constable Frederick Fairfax and three uniformed officers was on its way. Constables Sidney Miles and James McDonald, on patrol in a radio car, also picked up the message and headed for Tamworth Road. It was four minutes since the alarm call.

Bentley and Craig hid behind the brick stack of a lift shaft on the flat roof as the first policemen came up the drainpipe. PC Miles set off to fetch the keyholder of the warehouse, while DC Fairfax stepped on to the flat roof about thirty feet from the hidden suspects. He shouted, 'I am a police officer! Come out from behind that stack!' Craig shouted back, 'If you want us, fucking well come and get us!'

Fairfax rushed the stack, grabbed Bentley by the left arm and moved towards Craig, pushing Bentley at the same time. He warned them that the building was surrounded.

There were conflicting versions of what happened next, not least because it was dark on the roof and difficult for other officers to see precisely what was going on. Fairfax shouted, 'I've got one. There's another one on the roof.' Bentley then managed to break away. Though both defendants denied it, three policemen swore that they heard him shout, 'Let him have it, Chris!' Another policeman also said that the words were not used. Fairfax recalled, 'There was then a flash and a loud report, and I felt something strike my right shoulder which caused me to spin round and fall to the ground.' He judged his distance from the gun as six feet. Craig gave it as about thirty feet. With the barrel of the Eley sawn off, it would not have been accurate within six feet at that range.

Fairfax got up, grabbed at the nearest figure and knocked him down with his fist. It was Bentley, who put up little resistance. Fairfax dragged him up, holding him as a shield, and forced him behind one of the raised roof lights. He searched his captive, finding the sheath knife and the knuckleduster. Bentley said, 'That's all I've got, guv'nor, I haven't got a gun.' Now that he was responsible for

Bentley's life, Fairfax told him, 'I'm going to work you round the roof to that escape door over there.' 'He'll shoot you,' Bentley said. However, Fairfax managed to get him behind the cover of a well-head.

The distance between these two and Craig was such that the sawn-off revolver could still not be fired with any hope of accuracy. PC McDonald, a uniformed policeman, climbed on to the roof and Fairfax told him, 'He got me in the shoulder.' Bentley, who denied saying the words, allegedly added, 'I told the silly bugger not to use it.' Craig fired twice more at a uniformed policeman on an adjoining roof. McDonald asked Fairfax what sort of gun Craig was using and Bentley was alleged to have replied, 'He's got a .45 Colt and plenty of bloody ammunition too.'

Craig told his counsel that Fairfax had sent Bentley to go and take the gun from him. As he approached, Craig had said to him, 'Fuck off, otherwise I'll shoot you too.' Bentley had retreated. There was no corroboration of this exchange but, if true, it would clearly have told in Bentley's favour.

Guns were being issued at Croydon police station as the bells of a fire engine and two ambulances sounded in Tamworth Road. Sidney Miles returned with the keyholder, who unlocked the warehouse. Leading the way to the staircase, Miles went up to roof level. He unbarred the well-head door, kicked it open and sprang out on to the flat surface. There was a single shot and his colleagues saw him fall backwards with blood on his face. By a terrible fluke, the sawn-off revolver had found its mark at a distance of thirty-nine or forty feet, hitting Miles just above the left eyebrow and killing him instantly. A second bullet hit the edge of the doorway.

'I am Craig!' a voice shouted. 'You've just given my brother twelve years. Come on, you coppers. I'm only sixteen.'[5]

3

'I'm only sixteen' was less contentious than 'Let him have it,' but did it mean 'I'm not old enough to be hanged' or 'I'm only sixteen but I'll take on the lot of you'? In the confusion, it scarcely seemed to matter. According to the police officers' evidence, there was another shout, 'Come on, you brave coppers! Think of your wives!' Bentley said to his captors, 'You want to look out. He'll blow your heads off.' Craig remembered calling out, after Miles fell, 'Is he dead?' Bentley shouted back, 'Yes he is, you rotten sod!' Fairfax and a uniformed constable now tried to get Bentley off the roof for his own safety. He shouted to Craig, 'They're taking me down, Chris!' He later explained that he had done this so that Craig would not shoot at the well-head while he was being taken through it.

The guns issued at the police station had arrived in a dispatch bag and were being issued as Bentley was taken down the stairs. The fire brigade had put up an extension ladder and run out hoses in case, as at the Siege of Sidney Street, the cornered gunman should set fire to the building. It was now about twenty minutes since the break-in had begun. Craig continued to fire but Fairfax, armed with a .38 revolver and his police training, was a match for him. As Fairfax ran in an elusive semicircle, Craig was sitting on the parapet guard rail, feet stretched out in front of him, holding the revolver in both hands as he fired. It was, he said later, like being 'in a film or something'.

At length, Fairfax heard his antagonist's weapon click without a shot being fired. It clicked several times. Craig swung his legs over the guard rail and stood upright on the parapet. 'Well, here we go,' he said. 'Give my love to Pam.' Then he dived head first, like a swimmer. He fell twenty-two feet, his fall broken about eight feet above the ground by the wooden frame of a glasshouse. He was not dead but had fractured his spine, his breastbone and his left wrist. He was still conscious. 'I wish I was fucking dead,' he said to the first policeman to reach him. 'I hope I've killed the fucking lot.'

Controversy seemed to obscure most items of the evidence. Three policemen had heard, 'Let him have it.' One police witness was sure it was not said. The bullet that killed Miles was 'of very large calibre', presumably Craig firing .45 ammunition from his .455 Eley. It might also have come from a .38 fired by police marksmen on surrounding rooftops, if there were any marksmen there. This, in turn, depended on how long the drama on the rooftop lasted, whether it was twenty minutes, as police evidence suggested, or forty-five minutes as suggested by the defence. Was there time for two marksmen with rifles to arrive from Scotland Yard before Miles was killed? When Miles set off to collect the keyholder, it was not known that the suspects were armed. When he returned and was killed, the dispatch bag of weapons had only just arrived from Croydon police station. Craig's revolver held six bullets and it seemed that ten or eleven shots were fired. There was disagreement as to whether some came from other guns or whether he had time to reload his revolver more than once, since it was found with six bullets in it when it misfired.

Such details were irrelevant to the public mood. When Craig's counsel, John Parris, met Bentley's counsel, Frank Cassels, he claimed that Cassels summed up the general reaction to the murder. 'I think both little fuckers ought to swing,' he said simply.[6]

Both youths were charged with the murder of Sidney Miles. Bentley was unable to grasp that he could be guilty of a murder which was committed when he had already been under arrest for fifteen minutes or so, and which perhaps he had indirectly tried to prevent. He made a statement or, rather, a statement was compiled from his words. He had difficulty in signing it, misspelt his Christian name as 'Derk' and asked how to spell it correctly. Craig showed no more remorse to the policemen who guarded him in his hospital bed than a prisoner of war might to the enemy who had captured him. 'You're coppers,' he said to Constable John Smith. 'Ha! The other one's dead with a hole in his head. I'm all right. All you bastards should be dead.' Later he gave an explanation. 'That night I was out to kill because I had so much hate inside me for what they did to my brother.'

Public reaction was swift in the week following the murder. On Wednesday, the Croydon coroner praised the 'fearless police', in particular Sidney Miles who had laid down his life. The appearance of his widow and two young children at the hearing added to the poignancy of his death. At his funeral, the Archdeacon of Croydon spoke of the wave of current armed robbery, women in fear, policemen who might find a gunman where they had expected a petty thief. 'This is not England, the England we have known and for which men and women have laid down their lives.' Most of this was true.

Yet cases of armed robbery in London, which had stood at forty-six in 1945, had dropped to nineteen by 1950, a figure that was to be repeated for 1952. Figures for the murder of policemen on duty in England and Wales in the half-century to 1952 totalled sixteen, far less than most people supposed. A more alarming statistic was that a quarter of those killed in the fifty years had died since 1948.

Craig, who had killed Sidney Miles and was known to be too young to hang, was the direct target of public hate and the object of most interest. He was a youthful, unrepentant and, in his suicidal dive from the roof, almost a romantic figure. Like his brother, the qualities which he showed in the Croydon rooftop fight would have been admired had they been employed against the Germans ten years earlier. As it was, the feelings of the crowds ran strongly against him. When he was carried on a stretcher from an ambulance to the magistrates court, there was jostling in the crowd and shouts of, 'Let's kill the little bastard!'

The trial was to be presided over by the Lord Chief Justice, who had dealt briskly with other teenage delinquents in the previous week. A pair of teenage brothers who had robbed two other boys at the point of an airgun and an air pistol were brought before him. 'Nowadays', Goddard told the court, 'the cane is never used at school. It would have done them good if they had had a good larruping. What they want is someone who would give them a thundering good beating . . . I suppose they were brought up to be treated like little darlings, and tucked up in bed at night.' He also dismissed appeals by two fifteen-year-olds who had held up another boy with a knife, regretting that he could not pass a more severe sentence than committal to an approved school, to which they had already been sent. With Goddard on the bench, the nation might feel that in the Bentley and Craig trial it was going to witness a vengeance long overdue.[7]

4

The facts of the case had seemed plain and the Lord Chief Justice lived up to his reputation. The prosecution evidence of the fight on the rooftop and Craig's subsequent comments were damning. When the jury heard, 'All you bastards should be dead' or 'I shot him in the head and he went down like a ton of bricks,' there was no hope for Craig and little for Bentley.

On behalf of defenceless shopkeepers or householders who feared to open their doors to strangers or to venture out at night, the Lord Chief Justice interrupted Craig's evidence with hostile interrogations on more than twenty occasions and Bentley's on ten, showing the jurors the type of youths they were dealing with. When Craig described how he had gone with his father to learn how to shoot as a pastime, Goddard barked: 'Did you know that firearms could kill people?' 'Yes, sir.' 'Let us get on to something that matters.' On the question of remorse, Goddard demanded, 'You were asked if you had ever shown any remorse or expressed any regret to anyone for having killed this young policeman.' 'Well, it is all I think about in prison, sir.' 'You may think about it. You were asked whether you had ever expressed any regret to anybody.' 'Who is there to express it to, sir?' 'You saw plenty of policemen because they were watching at your bedside.' 'I was hardly conscious half the time, sir.' 'Hardly conscious! Don't talk such nonsense.' This was what many of the public wanted to hear.

There was a long interruption as the knuckleduster with the spike was displayed and Goddard asked Craig, 'I want to know what you put this dreadful spike in for.' Craig protested that it was there already and Goddard concluded, 'A dreadful weapon!' He also intervened to inform the jury that Craig's elder brother had been arrested and convicted after carrying a gun.

Bentley's performance in the witness box was pitiful. He could not read the oath, let alone the statement handed to him. He could only attempt to rebut the evidence against him by reiterating, 'All untrue, sir.' As he was led back to the dock, Goddard's clerk, Arthur Smith, described him as looking like 'a zombie'.

Goddard's summing-up was little more than a direction to convict. The high point was when he produced the knuckleduster – 'Have you ever seen a more horrible sort of weapon?' – and promised the jurors they should have it with them in the jury room while considering their verdict. Bentley had denied knowing that Craig was carrying a gun but if he knew it then, under the law of 'constructive' murder, he was as guilty as Craig. The official transcript records Goddard as saying, 'If you find grounds for convicting them, it is your duty to do so.' Craig's counsel, John Parris, and several journalists reported hearing, 'Unless you find grounds for not convicting them, it is your duty to do so.'

The jury was out for an hour and a quarter. They returned verdicts of guilty but with a recommendation to mercy in Bentley's case. Christopher Craig was sentenced to be detained, 'until Her Majesty's pleasure shall be known'. He was a model prisoner, released in 1963 to continue a law-abiding life which had been interrupted by a year of teenage violence. As a matter of law, Derek Bentley was guilty, though he had done physical harm to no one. Goddard put on the black cap and passed the mandatory sentence of death. It seemed that the autumn of anger and fear had produced a felon upon whom physical punishment more severe than the cat-o'-nine-tails or the birch could be inflicted. His appeal was dismissed and his execution was arranged for 28 January.[8]

5

The public, or a large part of it, had not got what it wanted. Perhaps it was a caricature to describe Derek Bentley as a clumsy halfwit but his abilities extended little beyond cleaning and maintaining his bicycle or practising with a morse code set given to him the previous Christmas. The bedroom, which for reasons of domestic space, he still shared with his Uncle Albert, contained his toys and clothes. There was a wall pin-up of a starlet in blouse and shorts, but above it hung a framed text, 'Casting all your care upon Him, for He careth for you.' As the first days passed of the 'three clear Sundays' allowed to murderers in the condemned cell before their execution, a feeling gathered through the country that something had gone terribly wrong with the process of vengeance.

The press began to carry stories and photographs of the Bentley family in their desperate attempts to have the jury's recommendation to mercy implemented. Their dress showed a painstaking dignity and they had a natural pride. They were part of that London working class which had 'done its bit' during the war and shown that London could 'take it' without giving in. Apart from this son, who had never shot or stabbed anyone, they had children to be proud of. Now they petitioned those in positions of power who alone could reprieve him from the gallows of Wandsworth prison. They visited him every day with news of home and urged him not to despair, promising that at Christmas next year they would all be together with him.

His appeal was dismissed on 13 January. 'I shall now rely on public opinion to save my son,' William Bentley told the press. Petitions were circulated, while a mass of letters and telegrams arriving at the Home Office were 3–1 in favour of a reprieve. This roughly matched the proportions of letters arriving at the *Daily Herald*, which were 4–1 in favour. Elsewhere, 'Bentley Must Not Hang' car-stickers began to appear. Mr Bentley circulated a petition, hoping to gather 1,000 signatures. In no time he had 100,000. Lost in a labyrinth of bureaucracy and legality, he struggled on as the execution date of 28 January drew frighteningly close. By now, the story was in every paper and reporters from Europe, the United States and the Commonwealth had taken it up, their attention playing on the bewildered and uncomprehending youth. The mood of public vengeance faltered or, rather, many of its supporters drifted away.

Mrs Bentley, whose health was too poor for her to take an active part in the efforts to save her son, wrote a personal letter to the Queen. It did no good. Ironically the family, in a gesture of patriotism, had already chosen the week of the Coronation in 1953 for the wedding of their daughter Iris. It was Iris and her father who now led the active campaign.

It seemed that the Home Secretary, Sir David Maxwell Fyfe, had made up his mind from the start, though he later wrote with some self-pity of his lonely and unhappy position. He feared that a reprieve would antagonize the Lord Chief Justice, the police force and a number of his Cabinet colleagues. Moreover, public opinion wanted young criminals severely dealt with and there seemed no better opportunity than this. Four days before the execution date, one of his subordinates sent a letter through the ordinary post to Mr Bentley. It arrived two days later. Sir David Maxwell Fyfe had considered 'all the circumstances of the case' and had discovered no reason for advising the Queen to interfere 'with the due course of law'.

William Bentley said that he would hear the screams of his wife and daughter for as long as he lived. They were sedated for the short remainder of Derek Bentley's life. When they visited him that day, he said, 'As long as you keep your chin up, I'll keep mine up whatever happens.' Presently, he added, 'Help me, please help me.' On the following morning, a message relayed from him by his sister Iris appeared in the *Daily Telegraph*. 'No man's death is on my conscience. I know I did wrong in going with Chris Craig, but I killed nobody. I never intended killing anyone. Please help me.'

With twenty-four hours to go, 200 Members of Parliament gave their support to a motion urging the Home Secretary to reconsider his decision. How could there be no 'circumstance' justifying a reprieve when the jury had recommended mercy? Moreover, as R. T. Paget pointed out in the House of Commons, the Commissioners of Criminal Law as far back as 1839 and a Royal Commission of 1878 had both recommended that such offences as Bentley's should be removed from the category of murder. Indeed 'constructive murder', which made a second party guilty if he or she knew that murder or serious injury by the principal offender was a possible outcome of the joint enterprise, was soon to be abolished by the Homicide Act 1957.

On 27 January, the night before Bentley's execution, the scene in the House of Commons resembled a surreal nightmare. When the motion with the support of 200 MPs was to be debated, the Speaker ruled it out of order. It was unconstitutional to debate a sentence until it had been executed. 'While a capital sentence is pending, the matter should not be discussed in the House.' Whether Bentley should be hanged could only be discussed after he had been hanged.

Sydney Silverman, who had tabled the motion, protested to the

Speaker that 'A three-quarter-witted boy of nineteen is to be hanged for a murder he did not commit, and which was committed fifteen minutes after he was arrested. Can we be made to keep silent when a thing as horrible and as shocking as this is to happen?' The Labour opposition benches supported him while advocates of the death penalty among the Conservatives jeered.

It was of no use. A deputation, including Aneurin Bevan, now a senior Labour frontbencher, Sir Lynn Ungoed-Thomas, a former Solicitor-General, and three MPs went to the Home Secretary. That did no good.

At 10.30, William Bentley left the House of Commons to find a crowd of three hundred in Whitehall chanting, 'Bentley Must Not Die!' These were described as the articulate middle-class young, angry at the injustice being committed in their name. One contingent marched on Downing Street with a petition addressed to the acting Prime Minister, Anthony Eden. Another gathered on the Embankment and asked Mr Bentley to lead them in a march to Buckingham Palace. He declined. 'My family and I thank you from the bottom of our hearts. We shall always be grateful to you. But nothing more can be done. My son now is in God's hands.' The crowd stood bareheaded and sang 'Abide With Me'. Elsewhere there was a disturbance in the Charing Cross Road, where a man was arrested for distributing placards: 'Stop the Killing of Bentley'.

Derek Bentley dictated a final letter to his parents, written down for him by a warder of the death watch. He thanked them for all they had done for him, talked about his sister's forthcoming marriage, his bicycle, the television sets his father now sold, and his pets. A newspaper had taken a photograph of his pets and he had kept a cutting in the condemned cell, until the authorities confiscated it because newspaper cuttings were forbidden.

Next morning at nine o'clock a crowd of eight hundred gathered outside the gates of Wandsworth prison. These were not the ghouls who stood there as sex murderers or psychopaths were executed. They attacked the prison gates without much effect. There were shouts of 'Murder!' At nine o'clock, they stood bareheaded and again sang 'Abide With Me' and 'The Lord's My

Shepherd'. In the condemned cell, the hangman guided Bentley to the gallows trap, revealed as a metal partition on one wall slid aside. It was said that Bentley wept silently and sobbed, 'I didn't say it. I didn't tell Chris to shoot that policeman,' though some years later the hangman denied this. Albert Pierrepoint, who had sent so many to their deaths, was also asked what he thought this had accomplished. His answer disconcerted those who had preached the importance of capital punishment as a deterrent. 'Nothing but revenge,' he said.

When an officer came out to attach a notice to the prison gate, confirming that Bentley had been hanged, there was a scene of disorder. Among yells of 'Let's get the murderers!' the crowd seized and smashed the notice, pelting the police and prison officers with coins and apple cores.

In a matter of weeks the campaign for a restoration of flogging and harsher treatment of the delinquent young had gone badly wrong. A bill for the reintroduction of flogging was heavily defeated in the House of Commons on 14 February 1953 by a majority of 159 to 63. For many young middle-class adults of the 1950s, public figures like Goddard and Maxwell Fyfe were discredited. No less discredited was the system of capital punishment, which would be curtailed four years later and discontinued in 1964. As for the example which Bentley's execution might have set to the young, in the year that followed his death there was a continuing fall in the rate of most crimes. Only the incidence of armed robbery, which his punishment might have been expected to deter, increased by one per cent.

6

For the rest of their lives, his parents and his sister Iris fought to clear the name of Derek Bentley. It was half a century later when he received a royal pardon. There was no doubt that, as the law stood in 1952, he had been guilty of 'constructive' murder by setting out on a joint enterprise with Craig which ended in the death of Sidney Miles. The fact that Bentley had already been under arrest for fifteen minutes did not relieve him of responsibility if Craig went ahead with a crime. Had he been able to prove that he did not know Craig was carrying a gun, that might have saved him from the gallows. As it was, the disputed comment, 'I knew he had a gun but I didn't think he would use it,' sent him to his death. If he made the remark, which he denied, did he mean, 'I knew he owned a gun but I never thought he would bring it with him that night,' or 'I knew it was in his pocket but I never thought he would shoot at any one'?

A more general question for the appeal judges half a century later was whether the trial had been fairly conducted and whether Bentley should have been hanged in the light of the evidence. The jury who were 'judges of facts but not judges of law' plainly thought his life should be spared, by making their recommendation to mercy. Yet a reprieve was never likely. Bentley's counsel reported the Home Secretary as saying that this 'young man' was one whom the country could 'very well do without'. In the outcome, the reputations of both Lord Goddard and Sir David Maxwell Fyfe were indelibly stained by their part in the proceedings.[9]

The young who were supposed to have been taught a lesson by Bentley's fate more often responded with suspicion and contempt for the patent injustice condoned by their elders. In 1958, Karel Reisz's documentary about a South London youth club, *We Are the Lambeth Boys*, recorded such comments as, 'What about that Craig and Bentley, then? One fellow was in the copper's arms, wasn't he? And the other fellow had the gun and he was free. And he shot him. But the other fellow that was in the copper's arms got hung. And that kid'll be out.'

Far worse, Bentley became an unlikely icon. Hardly more than a week after his execution, a boy who appeared on charges of shop-breaking, stealing a gun, and going equipped with housebreaking tools by night, had been constantly 'reading and talking' about his hero Bentley. In March a girl of fourteen who also hero-worshipped Bentley had made her way from Salford to his parents' house, as to a shrine, equipped with a gun and a razor, as well as press cuttings of the case. She had 'no time' for the police. In another sphere, Iris Bentley attended a Conservative Political Centre conference on crime and punishment. When the speaker, Dr John Spencer of the London School of Economics, claimed that delinquency began at home, she stood up and interrupted to tell him he was talking nonsense.[10]

Whether or not Bentley appeared as a tragic hero to some of his generation, it was true that during the next ten years a violent underworld of youth, of which the Lord Chief Justice and others had seen him as representative, developed a culture of its own. Its gangs fought, injured, sometimes killed one another. As thieves and robbers they dispensed violence with a childish and casual ruthlessness, showing no apparent perception of the extent of physical harm they inflicted. In the decade that followed, they acquired an identity and culture of their own. As criminals they were amateur and opportunist, though no less dangerous for that. Even the last adventure of Derek Bentley and Christopher Craig had been marked by an entire lack of purpose. They had tried one set of premises after another, hoping to break in: the butcher's, the electrical suppliers, the second-hand shop at Reeve's Corner, finally the Barlow & Parker warehouse. They set out with a revolver and a knuckleduster but without the simplest tools for burglary. They would have been the despair of a professional thief.

Even when armed, Craig and his companions sometimes had no more resolve than naughty children. Before his brother's trial, he had persuaded a sixteen-year-old grammar school friend to come with him to a house in South Croydon. They were to rob an elderly butcher and his wife on a Saturday evening, 18 October. 'I had nothing to do and was fed up and browned off,' said the second boy, 'and I agreed to go with him. I was wearing my dad's trilby and I had a white scarf over my face.' The pair went by local bus, armed with one gun each. At the house, they knocked, pushed the butcher's wife to the floor and confronted him with their weapons. Craig said: 'Give us your wallet.' Mr Howes replied, 'There's nothing in it.' He put some coins into a bag and added, 'Take these and get out.' Mrs Howes brushed the guns aside, saying, 'They're toys!' She also tried to pull off Craig's mask. The two adolescent gunmen then ordered the couple into the sitting room so that they could be tied up. Neither moved. 'Get off these prem-

ises,' said Mr Howes, and the gangsters went. Their fathers' tril-
bies were restored to the hatstand. The haul in this 'armed robbery'
had been £4.[11]

It was an open question whether those who were previously
prepared to use guns against the police were any less likely to do
so after Bentley's execution. Nine days later, twenty-eight-year-old
Robert Sanders was carrying out a wage robbery in Hackney with
Thomas Jenkins, brother of the hanged murderer 'Harry Boy'
Jenkins. Sanders, who was a violent career criminal, had just escaped
from Wakefield prison where he was serving a fourteen-year
sentence for possessing a firearm with intent to endanger life. He
and Jenkins were surprised by uniformed police and a detective
constable. The constable who was chasing Sanders called out, 'Stop!
I am a police officer.' Sanders turned and shouted, 'Keep away
from me, you bastard, or I'll put a bullet through you!' He fired
without further hesitation, the bullet narrowly missing the detective's body and lodging in the belt of his raincoat. It was hardly a
warning shot.

Sanders was one of the toughest professionals. When sighted, he
and his two accomplices were about to stage a major wages robbery
in Chatham Place, Hackney. He had a lot to lose if arrested again.
In the event, he was sent to prison for life. With his record and his
reputation, it was a sentence he might expect. When it was
pronounced, he merely faced the dock, bowed, and said, 'My lord
is most gracious.' Yet while Bentley's fate might not alter the resolve
of a man like Robert Sanders, surely it would put the fear of God
into teenagers who were neither hardened by prison nor motivated
by plans for major robbery. Such was the hope.[12]

It faded quickly. Only six months after Derek Bentley's execution, there was to be a fatal and notorious encounter on Clapham
Common between two groups of teenagers. It was provoked by no
more than petulance in a trivial exchange of words. A fifteen-year-
old boy, walking with his girlfriend, asked four members of another
group to let him through on a pathway across the common. The
youths had blocked the path by sitting on one seat with their feet
on the seat opposite. One of them said, 'Walk round the other side,
you flash bastard!' The fifteen-year-old went back to tell seven or

eight friends. As the larger group closed in, one of them shouted, 'Get the knives out!'

A general mêlée followed and one of the smaller group ran home, bleeding from a knife wound in his shoulder. Another also managed to run away. The other two ran to the edge of the common and jumped on a bus which was making slow progress through the traffic. Instead of giving up the pursuit, those who had attacked them sprinted after the bus and caught it at the next stop. They dragged off the two fugitives and set about them on the pavement with fist and flick-knife blade, in full view of the mesmerized passengers. No one intervened. One victim escaped again, though with a stab wound in his stomach. The last, John Beckley, also escaped briefly, but was caught by his attackers. Presently they ran off, leaving him on the ground. As they ran, these teenagers shouted at the bus passengers, 'If you don't keep your nose out, you'll get the same.' Their ages were between fifteen and twenty-one.

Seventeen-year-old John Beckley lay bleeding to death on the pavement. He had been stabbed six times, and had suffered a major wound in the face from which he was bleeding copiously. From this confused encounter, it was eventually possible to make a case against a twenty-year-old in the larger group, Michael John Davies, whom witnesses had seen running off, apparently closing a knife. He was reported to have said afterwards, at a coffee stall, 'I only tried to run the knife up and down the fellow's face.' Davies was convicted of murder but, though he lost appeals in the Court of Criminal Appeal and the House of Lords, he was reprieved and subsequently received a free pardon. The truth was that no one could be sure who, among the half dozen that attacked him, had murdered Beckley. Despite the resolve in Parliament, the press, the public and the judiciary during the previous autumn to teach young thugs 'no end of a lesson', it scarcely seemed that the example of Derek Bentley had so much as entered the minds of John Beckley's killers, in the excitement of the chase.[13]

The problems of juvenile delinquency were now more vigorously discussed than their solutions. Some of the best-known work came from America in Frederic Wertham's *The Seduction of the Innocent* (1953) and *The Circle of Guilt*, published in England in 1958 with a preface by the English educationalist G. A. Lyward, subject of Michael Burn's *Mr Lyward's Answer*. Persuasive though Dr Wertham's exposition was, it relied very largely on the belief that juvenile delinquency, including murder and violence, resulted from corruption of the young by cinema and horror comics. Mr Lyward, by contrast, saw delinquents as 'confused conformists'. The way forward was for a society to nourish its children and direct them towards good rather than to poison them by materialism. One of his shrewdest insights was to suggest that the war and post-war society had produced a race of the 'under-individualized', a phenomenon seen equally in gangs or pop culture and, at its worst, in a combination of the two.

A more material explanation of post-war gang culture and delinquency was evident, for example, in the North London boroughs where violence on the streets was common by 1950, as it was south of the river in Bermondsey, the Bricklayers' Arms, and the Elephant and Castle. Areas of North London were no less grimy and gaslit than twenty years before, though the people were healthier. There was domestic overcrowding, which made it difficult for children to separate themselves from parents in the home. Outside the home, the opportunities for recreation were so limited that by the beginning of 1950 it was said that there was not a single open space of grass in the whole of Islington, Finsbury and Holborn where a ball could be kicked. The only two 'football pitches' in this area, the size of a provincial city, were on gravel.

Against this background, the cynics asked why it was, if the young could be placated by dances, coffee bars and football pitches, the great sport of the gangs seemed to be in wrecking youth clubs or vandalizing whatever facilities were provided. Perhaps, in this view, they simply found wrecking and inflicting injury more fun than the palliatives on offer. If so, all that had been done might prove too little and too late.

Almost at the end of the decade, a new Lord Chief Justice, Lord Parker, described the rising British crime wave of the 1950s to Canadian radio listeners in September 1959. He did not speak of organized crime as it had appeared in the past nor even of gangsters who specialized in smash-and-grab, protection rackets or armed hold-ups. He spoke of the 'high-spirited boy who does not merit a long term of imprisonment', but might get one anyway so that 'his comrades and others will be deterred from such behaviour'. Back in England a month later, addressing the annual general meeting of the Magistrates Association in London, Lord Parker added a warning. The crime wave was going to get worse, simply because there had been an immediate post-war rise in the birth rate. By 1962, a million teenagers would be reaching the age of criminal activity, bringing with them an extra 300,000 potential felons.[14]

10

'Who Are You Looking At?'

ON 4 NOVEMBER 1953, a sixteen-year-old barrow boy's helper
from Mitcham appeared at Brighton juvenile court. He had
come to the seaside with a gang of London youths to fight local
teenagers at the Aquarium Dance Hall. They had come solely for
the excitement of combat and, if any substance motivated them, it
was adrenalin. Fining him £5 for assaulting a Brighton youth, the
chairman of the court told him, 'Going about in gangs, and hitting
people over the head with chairs will not be tolerated in this town.'
At his hearing, the boy wore black peg-top trousers, a long grey
jacket with a velvet collar and six bright buttons. The press described
him quaintly as an 'Edwardian'.

The same term was used a number of times in the following
months, as the new fashion in clothes spread. Others in the same
age group disliked the effeminate length of hair and the pretentious
suits. In May 1954 two eighteen-year-old labourers went to a dance
hall at Twickenham. They approached a group of youths dressed
in the new fashion and threatened them. A plain-clothes policeman
intervened and told them to behave themselves, so the two labourers
attacked him instead. 'I saw the Edwardian boys there and I wanted
to beat them up,' one of the assailants explained later. 'I hate
Edwardians.'[1]

Even by the following month, the descriptions of those involved
in such violence were less arcane. A young railway fireman, twenty-
three years old, was accused of stabbing a ship's steward several
times in a fight at Southampton. He appeared at court in a velvet-
collared jacket and drainpipe trousers. This time, he was called a
'Teddy Boy'. For the next decade, the term encompassed participants in gang fights, robbery, assault and murder, as well as those

who led relatively blameless lives. For some who had to deal with the delinquents, the clothes alone were a passport to infamy. In July 1954, the Acton magistrate told a youth convicted of insulting behaviour, 'Get rid of that suit and try to become a decent member of society.'[2]

It was little consolation to know that these groups fought one another with a savagery equal to anything they showed the public. Gang fights became to them what cricket might have been to their elders and betters. No reason was needed to stage them. 'Coming down the dance hall for a fight?' was as common an invitation to a friend by 1953–4 as 'Coming to the match?' If the fight was an alternative sport, this was reflected in the successors of the Teddy Boys who criminalized the role of the football fan in the 1960s.

Sport requires a venue. By the end of 1954, seaside towns in easy reach of the main cities were a natural weekend choice. Before that year was over, the dance halls had had enough. The manager of the Regent in Brighton, one of the biggest, put up a notice in his foyer, announcing: 'No Edwardian Dress.' This followed a fight between two gangs in which knives and razors had been used. 'The known Teddy Boys who seek to get in by changing their clothes will not be admitted,' he announced. 'A security man will watch out for them.' Other battlegrounds were not hard to find. Within weeks there was a major fight between rival gangs at a Shoreditch fairground.

Having been banned from dance halls which had suffered their visits, the neighbourhood gangs turned their attention to those not expecting them. So, for example, in February 1956 twenty-three teenagers set out from south-east London in a uniform of 'Edwardian' suits and black duffel coats to wreck what was called 'a respectable dance' at the Civic Hall, Orpington. They formed a line across the floor, forcing girls away from their partners, starting fights and assaulting the sedate Master of Ceremonies, among shouts of 'Come on, let's get him!' The struggle lasted until the police arrived and ejected the intruders. As he was marched out, a seventeen-year-old garage hand, who was later identified as the ringleader, screamed back at the Master of Ceremonies, 'We'll be back and do you, bouncer! We'll cut you to pieces!'[3]

Almost as soon as the first autumn of notoriety was over, violence matured into murder. In February 1955, a young soldier on demob leave jeered at the fancy clothes of Teddy Boys in the Blue Kettle Café, Islington. He was chased outside by a dozen of them, stabbed three times in the neck by an eighteen-year-old Cypriot, and bled to death from a wound in the throat. In April, another youth was killed by a five-inch flick knife in a gang fight at Forest Gate. Fatalities were not confined to the Teddy Boys themselves. The following month, a sixty-year-old man was killed in Camden Town when he remonstrated with a group of them who were 'molesting' a young girl. He was knocked down, half-conscious. One of them then kicked him to death as he lay on the ground, while the others stood by giggling. An intensive police search of all-night cafés, milk bars, lodging houses and pin-table arcades in the area produced a suspect who allegedly confessed, 'Yes, I was the one who hit him. My mates didn't touch him.'[4]

It mattered very little that such criminals might be regarded as moral outcasts. The exhilaration of the Teddy Boy often depended on being a pariah who made war on society. He was two years ahead of his middle-class rivals, those 'Angry Young Men' identified with John Osborne and his mouthpiece 'Jimmy Porter' in *Look Back in Anger* (1956), whose advent intrigued the quality press. Anger or frustration rather than crime was their stock-in-trade.

It would have been absurd to classify every Teddy Boy as a criminal and yet each seemed capable of crime, when the clothes were right. The working-class youth who spent his days as a garage hand, a storeman or a clerk became a threat to law and order as the sun went down. In the evening or at the weekend, his act of 'putting on the agony, putting on the style' admitted him to a world in which gangs fought one another for little reason, sometimes to the death. The individual youth was amiable enough. As a gang member he appeared capable of offences which defence lawyers hopefully described as 'out of character'.

Despite the remorseless publicity which attended them, the vices of these youths were not a novelty. Almost exactly two centuries earlier, Samuel Johnson in his novel *Rasselas* (1759) had described such young men of 'spirit and gaiety'. No less than in the dance halls and seaside resorts of the 1950s, 'their mirth was without images, their laughter without motive; their pleasures were gross and sensual, in which the mind had no part; their conduct was at once wild and mean; they laughed at order and at law.' In common with other aspects of human nature, it seemed that not much had changed.[5]

The Teddy Boy cult had a good many harmless hangers-on at one extreme and a number of vicious criminals at the other. The latter yearned to prove themselves by extreme violence. Among such tribal fights of the Teddy Boy era in the East End of London were those to which the combatants came by their own transport, frequently setting out from the Regal Billiard Hall in Eric Street, Mile End. One such destination was the Britannia public house in Chapman Street, Stepney, frequented by a gang known as the Watney Streeters. On the night of 28 August 1956, most of these habitués fled at the arrival of the visiting team, who took revenge on one man too slow to escape, Terry Martin. They used a bayonet, a machete and a crowbar to put him in hospital. The leader of the attack was later arrested, in possession of a Young America revolver and with dumdum bullets in his coat pocket. He was a young boxer named Ronald Kray. With his twin brother Reggie, he ran the billiard hall and these outings, as if challenges to other gangs were the sole passport to manhood. In that belief, the twins were two among thousands.[6]

To the majority of Teddy Boys in their late teens or early twenties, the established order from which they had defected was a common enemy. From time to time, this hostility involved the taking of a life and the making of a martyr. In December 1958, a young scaffolder, Ronald Henry Marwood, drank ten pints of brown ale at his first wedding anniversary. He then joined a gang fight outside Gray's Dancing Academy in Seven Sisters Road, Holloway, where youths from two 'Edwardian' groups were wielding knives, bottles, knuckledusters, bicycle chains, hammers and hacksaws. As usual in the culture of the Teddy Boy, the fight had started on a pretext that was slight to the point of absurdity. One nineteen-year-old felt insulted because another flicked a piece of paper at him. A young policeman saw the scuffle and intervened, seizing hold of one of Marwood's friends. There was a struggle between the three, during which Marwood stabbed the policeman fatally in the back with a ten-inch knife.

After a trial for affray, youths whom the Recorder described as 'deliberately looking for trouble' were jailed for periods of six to fifteen months. Marwood was tried for murder, convicted, sentenced to death and hanged. The Homicide Act of 1957 had restricted the application of the death penalty to specific categories of murder but killing a policeman on duty remained one of them. There were objections to his sentence, largely because the Homicide Act was seen as anomalous. Yet none of these went beyond the familiar type of protest.

To many Teddy Boys, the condemned man became a hero, one of their own, an elder brother at twenty-five. Seventy of them surrounded Tower Bridge police station, chanting, 'Revenge for Marwood!' and 'Coppers are bastards!' They tried to rush the doors and force their way in as extra police were called, one of whom reported, 'For a few moments it looked a decidedly dangerous situation, where anything might happen.'[7]

If Marwood's fate was intended to curb the belligerence of gang culture, there was little evidence of its impact. Four months after the execution, there was trouble outside Wimbledon town hall after a rock 'n' roll dance. About 150 youths staged a small riot. Local police became uneasy and orders were given to move them on. There was 'pushing, shoving, and fighting' round the town hall steps until uniformed police had moved on most of the dancers. Five of them, led by a seventeen-year-old, stood their ground. His reply to the policeman who struggled with him did not suggest that Marwood's hanging had inspired a new respect for authority. 'I am not fucking well moving for any copper,' the youth shouted. 'You will get done if you don't push off.'[8]

Had it not been for the Homicide Act of 1957, which failed to save Marwood, many Teddy Boys who stabbed a rival through the heart or the throat in a dance hall fight would have gone to the gallows. This incongruous legislation was unpopular with the judiciary and doomed from its inception. It ordained death for murder by firearms or explosion; killing a police or prison officer on duty; killing in the furtherance of theft; killing in resisting arrest or escaping from custody. Other murders were punishable by life imprisonment.

The manner in which Teddy Boys escaped the gallows, as neither Bentley nor Marwood had done, was demonstrated a month after Marwood was hanged, when Terence Cooney, nineteen, was convicted of stabbing to death eighteen-year-old Alan Johnson during a brawl between 'The Dagenham Boys' and 'The Canning Town Boys' at the Woodward Hall, Barking. The killing also confirmed the extent to which gangs like the young Krays' had established themselves in their own areas, and were prepared to travel a little distance for the fun of fighting one another. Cooney, a Dagenham Boy, had bought a knife in a pub just beforehand, in anticipation of a fight at Barking. Others were armed with iron bars, bicycle chains and broken bottles.

'Dance hall' was a courtesy title. Music at the Woodward Hall was provided by gramophone records from 8 p.m. to 11 p.m. No alcohol was served, though nothing prevented dancers going to a nearby pub. After 10.30 admittance was free. At about 10.45, a gang of Dagenham youths burst in and asked who was from Canning Town. As the Everly Brothers sang 'Problems' on the record player, a boy who said he was from Stratford was knocked down and given 'a kicking'. Canning Town youths gathered at one end of the hall and the Dagenham gang moved in on them. Fighting broke out among the 200 dancers, some of the girls finding refuge in the toilets and others trying to run outside. At 10.50, the dance organizer went to get his seven bouncers and called the police. Cooney and Johnson were fighting alone, a fist fight during which Cooney drew his knife and stabbed Johnson three times, including a fatal wound through the heart. The brawl overflowed outside the hall, where those with no knives or iron bars tried to protect themselves with dustbin lids. When the police arrived the gangs had scattered, except for fourteen youths who were continuing the fight outside, leaving a litter of weapons on the dance floor. Alan Johnson lay dead on the floor in a pool of blood.

Because Johnson was not a policeman and no firearm had been

used by Cooney, the sentence for murder was life imprisonment. In parallel with the murder trial, there were prosecutions for affray. During these, a sixteen-year-old defendant was set upon in a café by four of the opposing gang while another witness who feared intimidation was warned by the court that if there were any repercussions he must go straight to the police. Those who remembered the pre-war world associated witness intimidation with the Lewes racecourse fight of 1936 or the Wandsworth Greyhound Stadium stabbing of the same year, not with a dance that belonged to the culture of the church hall or the youth club. Intimidation was now to become increasingly common, even among those who were little more than children. Six years later, there was a trial of defendants on charges relating to armed robbery, firearms offences and conspiracy to defeat the course of justice. The proceedings took place among allegations of witnesses being told they would be 'cut up' if they dared to give evidence against the accused. The oldest defendant in this case, the leader of the gang, was seventeen and the youngest fifteen.[9]

The habitat of the Teddy Boy was illustrated by the topography of the Barking murder. Woodward Road was a two-mile stretch of uniform pre-war council housing with churches, a library, and the brick hall whose posters advertised 'Non-Stop Rock 'n' Rolling' and 'Rock 'n' Cha-Cha. 2s. 6d. Every Tuesday 8–11'. With its plain brick and cement, it was a monument to post-war austerity, offering bare floorboards with chairs ranged round the walls. Once it had been a plain wooden hall where dancing was more genteel. By now, the residents of Woodward Road had had enough of the youths and their music. A petition had been organized against the noise of rock 'n' roll. There was also apprehension at the aggressive youths who showed their new affluence by coming from other towns in large but dilapidated cars to fight the locals.

Violence had not diminished during the first five years of Teddy Boy rule which preceded the murders in Seven Sisters Road or Barking. That scores of other incidents did not involve murder was a matter of luck. One of the last and most vicious London battles, from which 200 other young people fled in terror, was between the

'Finchley Mob' and the 'Mussies' of Muswell Hill. It took place more than two years after the Marwood and Cooney murders, again giving the lie to the assurance that such gang violence was a passing phase. As the principal defendant told the police, the Finchley battle was merely the latest in a North London gang war that had been 'going on for donkeys' years' and had included murder in its casualty list. By sheer good fortune, murder was not done on the night of the battle, but in the wake of the fight fifteen of the attackers from Muswell Hill, aged fifteen to twenty, were convicted of riot and sent to prison for a total of eighteen years.

At this stage of the 'war', on 4 April 1962, the Mussies had decided to do grievous bodily harm, or worse, to Vic Green, an eighteen-year-old window cleaner and leader of the Finchley Mob. His elder brother had been stabbed to death at a Wood Green bus stop six years earlier, when he was nineteen. The twenty-year-old leader of the Mussies told the police in justification of the present assault, 'Vic Green has been shouting off his mouth that he would do a few fellows in Muswell Hill. We have had fights before.' He heard that Green and fifty of the Finchley Mob were at a dance. Scooter-boys were sent out to collect the Muswell Hill gang from pubs and youth clubs. Twenty-two of them, armed with bayonets, knives, bicycle chains, broken bottles and wooden clubs with projecting nails caught the bus for Tally Ho Corner.

The dance was just ending as the attack began. The Mussies first wrecked the hall. They found Green and told him, 'You're the one we're after.' He was hit across the head with an iron bar, stabbed in the back and through the lung with a four-and-a-half-inch throwing knife. Had he died, it would have been difficult to argue that his attacker did not intend murder. Five others of the Finchley Mob were stabbed and taken to hospital. The organizer of the dance was unable to stop the battle in which seventy or eighty youths were involved or to stem the panic among the terrified girls present who were trapped without warning. At the first opportunity, the other dancers fled.

The police had no difficulty in identifying the attackers. The leader of the Mussies was woken at home in the small hours to be told that six Finchley boys were in hospital and he was under arrest. 'Can't it wait until morning?' he asked plaintively. 'I only had a good punch-up.' 'They have been asking for it,' said one of his lieutenants. 'I only used my fists,' said another indignantly.

In the aftermath of the Finchley brawl, Vic Green's sister suggested that the problem of gang violence was a symptom of the manner in which these boys were deprived of affection by a post-war generation of parents, so attracted to material possessions and the need to have more of them than their neighbours that they had no time to make a home. It was a derisive echo of the famous claim by Harold Macmillan, as Prime Minister in 1957, 'Most of our people have never had it so good.' It was also one of many assertions that such bloodletting was the fault of someone other than the wielder of the knife.[10]

2

Whatever the explanation of his conduct, on the television screen and the printed page the uniform of the Teddy Boy remained synonymous with criminality. In 1954, the first autumn of occasional notoriety, a girl in drainpipe trousers and jacket knocked down a wages clerk in Hammersmith and stole the bag she was carrying, which proved to be empty since the clerk was on her way to the bank rather than returning from it. Before long, few people needed to be reminded that Teddy Boys had been swiftly followed by Teddy Girls. Nor was it merely a matter of style. Crime among teenage girls was to escalate disproportionately in the course of the decade.

The girls who aped the gangs had first come to public notice in the summer of 1954, when two of them fought each other with knives in the street, 'over an argument which we started in a dance hall'. Two other girls of sixteen, bob-haired and in drape coats, explained in court that they carried cut-throat razors in their waistbands because they had seen young men at dance halls in Wimbledon carrying knives from chains on their belts. 'We thought it would be nice to carry them,' said one girl. 'We carried the razors in case any fellows got fresh,' said the other.[11]

Fashions in clothes changed but the criminality they cloaked did not, as the decade of the Teddy Girls merged into a general spread of juvenile violence. By 1964, Hoxton High Street was described among those who lived in the area as a 'stone jungle', in which girls contributed to juvenile anarchy. When four of them attacked a group of schoolgirls after dark in April 1965, ripping their clothes, smashing their heads and faces against a wall among shouts of 'Strip her! Tear her clothes off!' a young woman who was bathing her baby said that she did not even bother to look outside because she was so used to the same sounds, night after night. In the event, the victims managed to escape to the doors of several flats, begging for sanctuary. The porter of Hathaway House added that he had told several children to stop playing football on the lawn outside. In response, they scarred his face with a steel dog-comb.

Some attackers were caught. Later that month four girls, three of them fifteen and one sixteen, were convicted at the Old Bailey of a violent robbery on a student teacher. Judge Aarvold, the Recorder, sentencing them for their 'horrid and hateful offence', told them: 'As this trial has proceeded, no one who could see you could fail to be impressed by the sullenness of your four faces. It reflects the emptiness of your unhappy lives which is only relieved by you making pests and nuisances of yourselves in the streets.' No one, he added, had tried to teach them the happiness that came from self-discipline and self-respect. They also needed to be taught a sense of right and wrong. Such provocative comments from the judge caused a riot in the dock. The fifteen-year-old ringleader was removed, screaming abuse at all involved in the case, an outburst in which she was joined by a friend in the public gallery.[12]

No police force, no government, could have been prepared for the advent of this cultural phenomenon, cohesive and rebellious youth wedded to petty and murderous criminality for its own sake. It was far easier to deal with those professional gang leaders who might drink in the same bars or clubs as CID and Flying Squad officers, with whom there might be a grudging mutual recognition. The new threat to social order was quite different. Teddy Boys were alien to established criminal culture and there were many thousands of them. A number had criminal records but the majority of the new assailants and even of the killers had not committed a known crime until there was a dance hall fight and the button of a flick knife was released.

Press and television soon uncovered a rich vein for social investigation. The BBC, urging the nation to understand rather than condemn these 'deprived' youths, screened a 'Special Inquiry' programme, introducing a debutante from Kensington to two Teddy Boys from Pimlico, hoping to show how much they had in common. It was intended to establish their equal difficulty in being one of more than 3,000,000 bewildered young people in Britain between the ages of fifteen and nineteen, growing up in the stressful 'Atomic Age'. 'We want to know all about them,' the corporation insisted. In April 1959, the Scouts' Chief Commissioner for Lancashire belatedly joined this campaign to understand a generation of violent gangs, whom he saw as sharing the Boy Scout's longing for adventure. 'I think of Teddy Boys as lost Scouts.'[13]

While such arguments sought to appease or reform the new delinquency, others offered an encouragement to persist in youthful rebellion. Even the most aimless violence and vandalism were soon fuelled by what passed for criticism of the status quo. The advent of the Teddy Boy had been accompanied by a famous exchange in the 1954 film of *The Wild One*, a classic of teenage motorcycle hooliganism starring Marlon Brando and Lee Marvin. 'What are you rebelling against?' 'What have you got?'

The question and answer were simple and revelatory. However, there was little danger that they would influence a post-war generation in England. The British Board of Film Censors was so apprehensive of the film's effect on the restless British youth of the 1950s that it banned the film outright.

As it happened, the film which many British cinemas were banned from showing in 1956 and which brought town centres to a halt as gangs of youths fought or celebrated was nothing like this. It was a musical and had seemed harmless enough. The board of censors had not thought it necessary to cut or ban *Rock Around the Clock*. The ease with which rock 'n' roll fuelled Teddy Boy enthusiasm and aggression came as a shock, if only because popular music had never caused violence on this scale before. There was worse to come in makeshift dance halls during the years ahead. A single week in September might have acted as a warning.

Rioting first broke out during the weekend of 8–9 September 1956, when the Gaumont British cinema chain began to show the film in London. There were disturbances in town centres, as well as outside Gaumont cinemas. There was chaos in some of the cinemas themselves, as staff and police tried to eject youths and their girl-friends who were scrambling over the seats and jiving in the gang-ways. The film was screened first in the London area and the worst outbreaks that weekend were at Stratford, Leyton, Brentford, Twickenham and West Ham. Jivers were removed from the Gaumont, Chadwell Heath, outside which 120 of them were later found by the police still shouting, whistling and jumping over the ornamental gardens opposite the cinema. It was a relatively mild beginning.

On Monday night, a youthful audience left the Trocadero in the Old Kent Road, where Teddy Boys and their girls had been jiving between the rows of seats. A crowd of a hundred or more, singing and dancing, stopped traffic and began to hammer on the roofs and doors of the trapped cars. Similar disturbances occurred at the same time in Peckham and Woolwich. It was too late for the board of censors to intervene and the responsibility fell on local authorities. An anxious Watch Committee at Blackburn banned the showing of the film. The Chief Constable of Preston advised the Gaumont to withdraw it.

Next morning, Brighton Watch Committee also banned the film as being 'likely to lead to disorder in view of the miscon-duct and publicity which has attended the showing of this film in other towns'. By the afternoon, Birmingham magistrates had followed this example, on the urgent advice of the Chief Constable. That night, there were further disturbances at Carshalton, Greenwich, and at Lambeth, where fifty youths in a large crowd threw milk bottles and fireworks in the street. At the end of the first week in London, the film would move to provin-cial cinemas and was promptly banned throughout Berkshire. On that final Saturday evening in London, 15 September, a crowd of 1,500 brought the Elephant and Castle area to a standstill as it was shown there for the last time. At Woolwich, there was jiving in the street, lighted matches showered the crowd, and bottles were thrown in front of cars. Stockport and Gloucestershire also decided on a ban.

Bans in the provinces sometimes did no more than shift the problem of public order from one town to another. After the film was withdrawn in Berkshire, fans went in greater numbers to see it at High Wycombe in Buckinghamshire. Among their leaders they brought the self-styled 'King of the Teddy Boys', a twenty-five-year-old storeman from Reading who had been convicted the month before for causing actual bodily harm. He had been banned from most cinemas and dance halls in his own town. 'In my opinion he is a hooligan and a menace to the public,' said Chief Inspector Woodward. 'His general tactics are to remain in the background while he eggs on his Teddy Boy associates – usually from a very safe distance. He is known throughout the town as "Mad Charlie".' The visit of Mad Charlie to High Wycombe with twenty-two friends and hundreds of fans ended in a sentence of six months being imposed upon him for assaulting a police inspector.[14]

To anticipate such violence or disorder in general was, by its nature, difficult. In the following September, for example, a large crowd of Teddy Boys invaded a fairground at Dagenham just before it closed for the night. There had been no previous trouble here and, as usual, they had not been expected. The invaders were 'shepherded' out again by fairground staff and two policemen. It seemed that the incident was over but once outside the ground the crowd of 150 turned upon the two policemen, who held their position desperately with their truncheons drawn and called up reinforcements. Another battle followed, in which the youths pelted the arriving police with bottles and lumps of concrete, injuring seven of them as they tried to arrest the ringleaders. It was only possible to seize half a dozen of the crowd and these were not the leaders. The fines of £5 or £6 imposed for insulting words or obstruction were scarcely a deterrent.[15]

3

The image of the Teddy Boy had often been defined in public perception by tales of violence and murder. The nation and its legislators were appalled by the details of such cases as the 1953 Clapham Common murder or the stabbing at the Barking dance hall. Casual and aimless savagery of this order had previously been rare at any level of crime. Men and youths had killed for gain or for some well-established and easily recognized motive. They had not done it for a laugh or as a sport or, in taking the lives of others, put their own lives at stake for profitless excitement. Just as there had been alarm after 1948 that the abolition of flogging had exposed the public to violent crime with no effective deterrent against the perpetrator, so now there was unease that the defence of capital punishment might be withdrawn.

The Royal Commission on Capital Punishment reported in September 1956. It had been expected to recommend the raising of the minimum age for hanging from 18 to 21. In the event, the members were split and made their recommendation for raising the age by only one vote, which was no effective recommendation at all. Members of the minority insisted that it would be 'dangerous' to spare eighteen- to twenty-one-year-olds, when the wave of crimes by youths between seventeen and twenty-one had apparently not passed its peak.

It was not only in felonies as grave as murder that the public and its legislators confronted a criminality which seemed evil to the point of perversity. There was a sardonic cruelty in some instances, which suggested more than anything the culture of James Hadley Chase or Mickey Spillane – the deceitful heroine shot through the stomach by Mike Hammer and left to die with the comment, '"It was easy," I said', or the prisoner fatally injured when skewered to a tree by Slim Grisson with the dismissal, 'Take your time, pal.'

In the year after the rock 'n' roll disturbances, a man was walking home through East Moseley. The pavement ahead of him was blocked by a group of Teddy Boys, 'shouting and pushing each other'. As he tried to walk past them, one of them asked him if he was swearing at them. 'I've not said anything to you, cocky,' the thirty-eight-year-old man replied. They beat him almost unconscious and threw him through a plate-glass window, running off as two other men came to help him. Five days later, two more Teddy Boys were with their girlfriends near Teddington Lock, where the water was twelve feet deep. They asked a boy of fourteen if he could swim. When he said he could not, they threw him in and walked away laughing.

Murder might all too easily become a sport in such cases, as it did in reality among a group of youths in Southwark. At one point the police suspected that thirty were involved but it is more likely that there were no more than a dozen. The sport was beating up elderly tramps who slept in derelict buildings, in this particular case the Fountain public house near the Elephant and Castle. It was a hazard of the game that such sport might get out of hand.

Alexander Brown, one of the tramps who sheltered on the premises, had previously been beaten up by five of the youths. He was in the derelict pub when he heard them come in again and he hid under a coat in a corner of an upstairs room. They searched the building and he heard one boy say, 'There's a tramp over there.' Someone knelt on him and began hitting him hard with a brick, while the old man screamed for help. After a while, the boy stopped but one of the others said, 'Let's give him some more.' They came back and kicked him for a while. Presently they went downstairs and found another tramp, Joseph McGourty. They treated him to a more systematic and vigorous beating round the head, using the brick, until they had caused fatal contusions of the brain and haemorrhages elsewhere. Though he was still just alive when a policeman found him, he was incoherent and died without regaining his speech. The police questioned their thirty suspects but the killers were not identified. The coroner's jury returned a verdict of murder by persons unknown.[16]

With the advent of West Indian immigration, the newcomers offered a supply of easy targets. In 1958, the Dance and Social Club in Cable Street, Stepney, joined those venues where victims could be found for attacks with fist or knife – members of the coloured community being singled out in this case. Elsewhere, teenage youths formed themselves into groups to go on what they unselfconsciously called a 'nigger hunting expedition'. Nine of them who were jailed for four months had gone on 'a manhunt through the streets of London. They hunted as a pack to give what one of them called "a proper belting" to any coloured man they met.' Two others in a similar case had taken Greek Cypriots as their targets.[17]

Girls were not exempt from the attentions of the violent young, who sometimes left them marked for life. Within a month, one youth had said to a girl of sixteen in Walthamstow, 'I have a present for you,' and stabbed her in the back; a nurse who refused to go to a dance with two youths who accosted her in Brighton was held by one while the other slashed her face, neck and arms; a girl of fifteen was similarly attacked in a Godalming street. To make matters worse, in November 1957 the Home Office had announced an increase in crimes of violence during 1956 of 21 per cent. In the 14–17 age group, they had increased by 38 per cent in that year alone.[18]

As the 1950s merged into the following decade, public attention was more readily drawn to stories of moral nihilism or vandalism than to the protests of misunderstood teenagers. In the behaviour of the youthful gangs, vandalism had won publicity since the day in 1954 when the newly designated 'Edwardians' made a modest debut in the headlines after wrecking a weighing machine in spectacular fashion in front of holidaymakers at Herne Bay. In its later forms, it seemed a more direct attack on public life, or at any rate on public amenities.

So, for example, the wrecking of phone boxes, which had never been quite out of fashion, assumed serious proportions by 1962. Gangs from the suburbs now came to central London and to the centres of other cities to relieve the boredom of a Sunday evening. One antidote to tedium was to put banks of telephone kiosks out of action. On 8 April, for example, twenty wires in telephone kiosks at Victoria Station were slashed. By reporting this prominently, the press ensured that the epidemic would spread. On the following Sunday evening, 15 April, thirty kiosks were put out of action by wire-slashing at Piccadilly Circus underground station and eighty more in nearby areas of the West End. From there, the nuisance became more general. These cases were merely the first instances of such attacks. By 1966, the Deputy Chairman of London Sessions warned 'phone wreckers' that any who were brought before him could expect to be sent to prison for 'at least eighteen months'.

In an age before mobile phones and when millions of households still depended on the public call box, such vandalism was a serious matter. In the wake of the damage caused during that spring, the press was able to report that long queues had formed for the phones still working. The disruption continued on such a scale in the following months that the Assistant Postmaster General eventually had to admit in the House of Commons that spare parts had run out. Despite the threat of an automatic eighteen-month sentence at London Sessions, the current sentences in magistrates courts were four or six months. Moreover some wrecking remained the preserve of the small-time thief with burglars' tools and an eye to the coin box.

The appeal of vandalism which put public life and safety at risk spread to much younger children. The principal problem was no longer one of Teddy Boys who put their lives in peril by riding on the running boards of suburban trains. In April 1965 two eleven-year-olds readily admitted that they had put a tea tray and other objects on the electric line between Broad Street and Richmond. When asked to explain themselves, one boy said, after being reproved for his confident smile, 'I thought there might have been an accident.' The chairman of the court asked him, 'Do you mean you really wanted an accident in which people would have been killed or crippled for life?' 'Yes,' said the infant. This followed a crash on another line on 29 March, when two men were killed and fifteen people injured after a train was derailed on 'hooligan mile' near the London suburban station of Elm Park. The driver was one of those killed and his wallet, containing £30, was stolen.[19]

For ten years, the violence of the young had been characterized by dance hall fights with fist and knife and a series of murder or manslaughter cases which accompanied them; the wrecking of youth clubs; robbery with violence of those who were waylaid on pavements or footpaths, and pitched battles between gangs. As the decade of the 1950s ended and violence among the young increased steadily, casual and vicious criminality became less of a short-term post-war problem and more of a long-term social change.

4

From time to time, as in the case of Derek Bentley, it seemed that the courts were prepared to hit back on behalf of the public. They now did so with more accuracy than in 1953 and cases which might have caused disquiet passed almost without comment. In June 1960, four youthful robbers, two of them twenty-three years old, the others seventeen and eighteen, lay in wait in a Hounslow alleyway for the next person to come along. The time was 11.30 p.m. and the suggestion had been made, 'Let's jump somebody.' It was a crime which might have happened anywhere and at any time.

The 'somebody' proved to be a twenty-three-year-old engineer, Alan Jee. As he turned into the alleyway, Terence Lutt, the seventeen-year-old who also weighed seventeen stone, punched him, knocking him down. As Alan Jee fell, he covered his face with his hands and shouted, 'What do you want me for?' Norman Harris, one of the twenty-three-year-olds, described what happened next. 'The lads held him down and I put my hand in his inside pocket to get his wallet, but there was nothing in there at all. Me, Darby, and Lutt were holding him down, and Forsyth was standing above us.' Darby was the other twenty-three-year-old and Francis 'Flossie' Forsyth was eighteen. As they held down their victim, Harris noticed that there was blood on his hand. 'I realized "Flossie" had put the boot in.' The boot – or in this case the pointed winkle-picker shoe – had been put in with great energy. When Forsyth was asked to explain why, he said simply, 'The fellow was struggling, so I kicked him in the head to shut him up.'

In his Italian shoes, Forsyth did more than shut him up, he systematically kicked his victim to death as if stamping on an insect. When the police came to arrest him as a suspect, Alan Jee's blood was still on the pointed toes of his winkle-pickers. Norman Harris and Forsyth were sentenced to death for a murder committed in the furtherance of theft. Darby persuaded the court that he had not taken part in the attack, although he was present, and was sentenced to life imprisonment for non-capital murder. Lutt was too young to hang.

All the appeals in this case were dismissed and the fate of the two killers facing the gallows remained in the hands of the Home Secretary. It might have been thought an important case: it was almost forty years since an eighteen-year-old had been hanged, in 1922. Moreover, the present Home Secretary, R. A. Butler, was known as a liberal with a distinguished record as the architect of the 'Butler Act', the Education Act of 1944, which had set up a new and enlightened pattern of post-war schooling. For him to consider a reprieve would have been automatic, but it would normally have been supported by a representation from the condemned man's legal advisers. Forsyth's lawyers could see no basis for such an appeal. 'On the law as it stood', said one, 'I could see no reason for a reprieve. His youth was not a factor.'

No one said, in so many words, that Forsyth was a worthless youth but the implication was plain. It was a contentious judgement. On the day of his execution the *Evening Standard* cartoonist Vicky, perhaps the most famous of his age, raised a storm by publishing in the paper a cartoon of the Old Bailey's statue of Justice, her dress besmirched with shameful black at what had been done in her name.[20]

One factor in his decision was Butler's dismay at the growth in violent crime, which neither government nor police seemed able to control. Addressing the Conservative Women's Conference a few months later, on 19 April 1961, he confessed that 'No one occupying the high post of Home Secretary could be anything but aghast at the present situation over crime, or feel unsympathetic with the lonely, the old and those in dread of the thugs, crooks and criminals we must master . . . We are facing a crime wave without parallel for many years.' The death of a youth like Forsyth seemed a price worth paying if it helped to turn the tide or placate public anger. 'Surely they can't hang a boy of eighteen?' Mrs Forsyth had pleaded on behalf of her son. But they could and did.

What moral or rational appeal could be made to youths who asked a boy if he could swim and, when he could not, threw him into twelve feet of water and walked away? Or to those who stood by laughing as an old man was kicked to death because he asked them not to molest a young girl? Or to children who tried to derail a train in the hope of seeing its passengers killed or crippled? Or to a young man who believed he had a right to maim, perhaps to kill, when someone threw a piece of paper at him? Or to other youths whose sport was to beat out an old tramp's brains with a brick?

Legislators and pressure groups did their best to remove what were claimed to be evil influences. Not least among these were so-called 'Horror Comics' and crime comics imported from America, often as ships' ballast. In 1955, their importation was banned under the Children and Young Persons (Harmful Publications) Act, with sentences of four months' imprisonment for those who sold them. An important influence on the legislation had been Frederic Wertham's study, *The Seduction of the Innocent* (1954), which dealt with the effect of the comics on children who were illiterate, educationally backward or emotionally disturbed. His subjects enjoyed such comic series as *Crime Does Not Pay* because, as one of them explained, in order to learn that crime does not pay you first have to read about it. Meantime, they lived in a comic-book world where a mother-heroine explained to her children, 'I brought you kids up right – rub out those coppers like I taught you,' the children replying, 'Don't worry, ma! We'll give those flatfeet a bellyful of lead.'[21]

Yet the fashion for horror comics had passed almost as soon as the legislation reached the statute book. Television and cinema were regularly warned of the corrupting effects of their violence on the young. Yet in as well-documented a case as that of Bentley and Craig, Bentley's cultural fodder before the attempted robbery which ended in murder had been a Betty Grable film and a television programme, *Songs from the Shows*. Neither he nor Craig had come across such authors as Mickey Spillane or James Hadley Chase, since neither of them could read. The film which Craig had seen on the afternoon of the murder might have taken as its motto, 'Be sure your sins will find you out,' while according to his father at the trial, the boy's only knowledge of books related to the most famous and moralistic children's author of the day, 'the books of Enid Blyton that he gets other people to read to him'.[22]

More to the point, it was rock 'n' roll which accompanied riotous conduct in 1956, as it did stabbings at Grays, Barking, Finchley and elsewhere. Yet music could hardly be censored and there was a growing desire among adults not to be alienated from the young. By the 1960s, there were those who admitted that their music was not the music of young people but, they asked, who were they to say that the Beatles, in their way, were not the equal of Bach or Beethoven?

As the decade of the 1950s closed, it was not necessary to be a paranoid pessimist in order to see no cure for the nation's ills. Traditional beliefs and moral principles would certainly not have an easy time of it in the years ahead. Perhaps, after all, it was as simple as the rationalist philosopher A. J. Ayer made it sound in 1968, when he reflected that the world had become a nastier place for everyone since fewer people believed that they might go to hell.

11

'If the Coke Don't Get You . . .'

I

A T 9 A.M. ON 10 November 1960, Francis Forsyth was hanged at Wandsworth prison. His body was taken down an hour afterwards. Three minutes later, seventy miles away, his childhood friend twenty-year-old Victor John Terry staged what became known, rather too grandly, as 'The Worthing Bank Raid'. The target was a sub-branch of Lloyds Bank on the western outskirts of the seaside town. The raid was carried out with the aid of an inexpert twenty-year-old getaway driver, Alan Hosier, and seventeen-year-old Philip Tucker who went into the bank to assist. Terry's girlfriend, eighteen-year-old Valerie Salter, waited in the stolen car and took no active part.

Against the two robbers was a young clerk behind the counter and an elderly 'bank guard' who had gone into the cloakroom to fill the kettle for tea. He came out face to face with Terry, who was standing by the safe. Terry drew a long single-barrelled shotgun from under his coat. John Pull, the guard, lifted his hand just above his head, a mannerism of his before speaking, and may have touched Terry's arm. Terry drew back and fired. The charge of shot entered the guard's left eye and he fell dying. Terry only disputed this to the extent of saying, 'He grabbed the gun. It was pointing at his legs. I had my finger on the trigger – it went off. All I remember is seeing him fall down.'

Terry grabbed from the counter a bag of money, containing £1,372, and ran after Tucker to the car. Hosier then lost his way and the four occupants abandoned the car, leaving the shotgun in it. They could hardly carry the gun with them in the aftermath of the robbery. All four of them caught a bus to Worthing, where Hosier and Tucker hired a taxi. These two then aroused the driver's suspicions by giving him a ten shilling note for the 2s. 6d. fare and telling him to keep the change. Seeing the first report of the shooting, he contacted the police and told them about his two spendthrift passengers. Terry and Valerie Salter had already gone back to her house to hide the money. When they returned to the seafront to meet the other two, they saw them being questioned by police officers on the promenade. Though Terry and his girlfriend fled from Worthing with the money, by bus and taxi, they were recognized and caught in Glasgow a few days later.

Apart from the fatal shot, fired by accident or with intent, the bank robbery differed little from dozens of such attempts in the decade to come. Terry, a small-time criminal now made famous by murder, had grown up like Forsyth and his friends in the Teddy Boy culture of West London with periods of absence in Borstal. Yet the bank raid murder had one ingredient unknown in most previous Teddy Boy crime. People who read the headlines and the press reports during the trial soon talked knowledgeably about 'Purple Hearts', 'French Blues', drinamyl and amphetamine sulphate, as well as the improbable uses of Benzedrex inhalers, which could be bought from any chemist.

Victor Terry, handyman at the Dome Ballroom in Worthing, staked his life on a defence of 'diminished responsibility' under the Homicide Act of 1957. He claimed that he had acted under the influence of drugs, for which he had to thank a 'drug ring' operating in Worthing. In 1960 it was still possible to regard as ludicrous the suggestion of a drug ring operating in this seaside town of retirement homes and middle-class summer visitors. It was as if Lucky Luciano had been found occupying a bed in a local rest home.

For Terry, it was neck or nothing. He was addicted to pep pills in the form of 'Purple Hearts', or drinamyl tablets, derisively named after the American medal for gallantry. Amphetamines had been on the market since the early 1930s but their availability had been progressively restricted and drinamyl had been put on the poisons list in 1957. Even so, Purple Hearts were still relatively easy to acquire and had become the first general drug of working-class youth. Terry had also used Benzedrex inhalers.

Psychiatrists were called in his defence, as well as witnesses who had seen him taking drugs. Detective Inspector Albert Buckley of the local CID admitted that there was, after all, a drugs ring in Worthing. A director of the Dome Ballroom described Victor Terry at work, sitting at a desk with seven Purple Hearts in front of him, tossing them in the air, catching them in his mouth and swallowing them. When Harry Roberts told him he was a 'nutter' and that it was a week's supply, Terry laughed and said, 'I've already had seven during the day.' Another witness, who admitted convictions for housebreaking and actual bodily harm, had worked with Terry in a Worthing coffee bar, where an obliging chemist sold Purple Hearts and Preludin tablets at five shillings for twenty.

When these tablets were hard to get, Terry had used 'strips', breaking open Benzedrex inhalers which contained five of these 'blotting-paper' tissues. Each tissue contained fifty milligrams of Benzedrine. Dr Felix Brown, a psychiatrist who examined Terry, tried his subject's method of boiling a strip in water, drinking the water and following it with half a pint of beer. He reported palpitations, sweating and general restlessness.

Without drugs, Terry's emotional state was far from benign.

> When I get into one of these moods I have to destroy. I know it is wrong but I cannot stop it. I used to do anything I could to hurt people, anything. I went around smashing things. I wanted to smash anything. Nobody liked me. I never got any love from my parents. In eight years the hate inside me gathered up. It is getting serious now. I think one of the gangsters went into me. I am controlled by someone else. It is like a voice you can hear inside. I only get like this when I am upset.

A second psychiatrist, Dr Arthur Paterson, explained that the gangster whom Terry believed had possessed him was the American mobster 'Legs' Diamond. Mr Justice Stable interrupted him to say that if Terry believed any such thing, 'he is as mad as a hatter'. 'In my view,' replied Dr Paterson, 'he is mad in the medical sense.' Despite this, it was never likely that a defence of being possessed by 'Legs' Diamond would succeed in an English court or that Terry's plea of drug addiction would save him. He was convicted of capital murder, sentenced to death and hanged. His was a derelict's world of tablets bought in coffee bars or the interiors of inhalers boiled up as a narcotic soup. Yet one of the new American 'Beat Generation', Jack Kerouac, author of *On the Road*, was already using inhaler strips soaked in Coca Cola or coffee. The poet W. H. Auden had been dependent on them for many years. Victor Terry stood at a meeting of the ways. He was an early representative of the new proletarian drug culture and yet his confession to Dr Felix Brown of uncontrollable urges to harm or destroy, to 'smash up' people and objects alike, seemed familiar as Teddy Boy behaviour.[1]

2

As the Teddy Boys, who had not been part of a general drug culture, gave way to the Mods and Rockers of the 1960s, who were prepared to explore it, the police and public opinion were ill-prepared. The new scourge had come upon the country very quickly. Drugs were the vice of the young and disproportionately associated with famous names in pop music. In October 1960, as Rector of Glasgow University, Lord Hailsham, who was Minister of Science in the Macmillan government, warned his audience of a new age, led by 'popular idols with the bodies of gods and goddesses and the morals of ferrets'. The use of drugs became a topic of debate and a subject of concern. Yet there had been an historical period, well within many living memories, when what was now denounced as evil had not even been illegal.

The opiate laudanum was a universal and freely available painkiller in Victorian England, leaving addicts like Coleridge and De Quincey in its wake. Opium in the form of morphine was widely used in the 1860s during the American Civil War, creating some 50,000 addicts among the wounded of both sides. Its rival analgesic was cocaine, derived from the coca leaf and thought to be less addictive. The trade in such substances was still unregulated and Sherlock Holmes appeared to commit no crime by injecting himself with cocaine. It required a world war to bring about the control of these drugs in 1916, under Regulation 40B of the Defence of the Realm

Act 1914, which made them available only on prescription and placed their import under licence. This was followed in 1920 by the Dangerous Drugs Act, controlling the manufacture, supply and possession of opiates and cocaine. An amending Act in 1923 provided for the registration of addicts, of whom there were very few. In 1936, the League of Nations publicly apologized for a report which suggested that there were 30,000 drug addicts in Britain. As the report was withdrawn, the Home Secretary announced that the correct number was 2,000, and that 'most of those are known to the authorities'. Even this seemed an exaggeration, judging by the Home Office's own figures two years later. In 1938 it knew of only 519 drug addicts in the country, 246 men, 273 women.

Among other drugs in the 1930s, marijuana or what was called 'Indian hemp' and later 'cannabis' was generally seen as the preserve of bohemians, 'toffs', and the nightclub set. Few people got closer to it than reading the Fu Manchu novels of Sax Rohmer. The Scotland Yard 'Drug Squad' was disbanded, only to be formed again in June 1939, following reports that cannabis rolled in cigarettes was being sold to the young in the dance halls of Brixton, Bermondsey and the Elephant and Castle. A few months later, the coming of another war put a stop to this.

For almost twenty years after 1945, the misuse of drugs was not regarded as a prevalent criminal activity, either with respect to opiates or amphetamines. The number of convictions throughout the country for the possession of cannabis cited in the Wootton Report of 1969, for example, suggested some justification for post-war complacency. In 1947, there had been 42 convictions for possession. This figure rose to 51 in 1957. In 1967, the last year for which figures were available to the report, the number was 2,393. By 1967, it also seemed that drugs offences were almost doubling year by year. In London during 1965–6 total crime figures dropped slightly, if only because homosexual conduct and some forms of abortion ceased to be criminal. Arrests under the Dangerous Drugs Act rose from 459 to 790.

Drugs were a politically sensitive issue. There was no doubt that the rise in cases of possession or sale of cannabis coincided with the mass migration of workers and their families from the West Indies. Whether this was a matter of cause and effect or whether an increase would have occurred in any case, as with amphetamine abuse, was a question of opinion or prejudice. It was certainly true that cannabis could be grown in England and that innocent householders threw the stale contents of the canary's cage into the garden, not realizing that bird food contained seeds from which the plant would grow. By the 1960s, householders who were less innocent had begun growing the plant among vegetables on their allotments.[2]

In February 1954, a defendant who had followed the mass murderer Christie as tenant of 10 Rillington Place appeared at Marlborough Street magistrates court. Like most of the recent arrivals in the area, he was a West Indian. In this case, he was convicted and jailed for possession of cannabis. The police also gave evidence of a connection between drugs and prostitution. He had sub-let rooms to 'coloured men and white women', and had produced £200 in cash to buy the lease of the property, a sum not accounted for by any legitimate income. This was frequently the basis for a charge of living on immoral earnings but might equally apply to drug dealing. The Marlborough Street magistrate's outburst was an increasingly common indictment of the combined evils of drugs, pimping and criminal migrants. 'Very often such people as you get hold of these little white girls and supply them with Indian hemp. Then the girls become the sluts we see in court and later some of you live on their immoral earnings. Thank heaven there are many of your people who are grand folk.'[3]

The further argument, that cannabis was merely recreational and that people should be allowed to smoke it if they wished, was put forward by a film director at the West London police court in the following February. He described himself as an escapist and a dreamer who needed to relax. This got short shrift from the bench. 'If he had seen the animal-like people – that is a gross insult to animals – who smoke this stuff, he would not talk so much rubbish.'[4]

3

Until 1962, Teddy Boys were still smashing up youth clubs and their occupants, whether in rural Somerset or central London, where the 'Mussies' and the 'Finchley Mob' dealt out grievous and mutual bodily harm on a regular basis. Spite and envy, perhaps enlivened by alcohol, were sufficient stimulants. By 1963, however, the abuse of amphetamines among the young had gained such ground that new laws were needed to prevent it. In February, a helpful High Court ruling confirmed that it was an offence to be in possession of amphetamines 'suspected of being stolen or unlawfully obtained'. On the heels of this, the Drugs (Prevention of Misuse) Act provided a six-month prison sentence for unlawful possession of these pills, which had been easily available six years before.

By Easter that year, the world of youth had also begun to change in other ways. 'Mods' who rode scooters and 'Rockers' on motorcycles ruled where Teddy Boys once held sway. Now that the troublemakers were motorized, the British Medical Association prudently set up a committee to investigate drugs and road safety. The difference between the two groups was in part social and economic. The scooter-riding Mods represented a breed who were more likely to be the sons of bank managers or accountants, rather than the offspring of council estates and manual workers. An eighteen-year-old Mod who was arrested at Great Yarmouth for standing on the sea wall and shouting incitement, during the violence of August Bank Holiday Monday 1965, had actually been declaiming to his gang, 'Friends, Romans, countrymen, lend me your ears.'[5]

The new rivals had come of age at Easter 1964, in a battle at the chilly East Coast resort of Clacton-on-Sea. There had been previous violence near the town, involving groups of youths and the use of shotguns as well as fists, but this had been at holiday camps away from the centre. Indeed, the seaside violence at the end of March 1964 was far less serious than in the Teddy Boy gang fights at Finchley or Clapham. On the other hand, Mods and Rockers showed themselves equally capable of bloodletting. A twenty-two-year-old merchant seaman, George Monk, was stabbed to death in a fight between the two groups, during a 'Beat Dance' at Grays, Essex, by assailants carrying Purple Hearts. Nor did the assailants always require scooters or bikes, as in the following May, when petrol bombs were thrown outside a Wimpy Bar in central Harrow during a gang fight, while traffic swerved to avoid the explosions and pools of flame.[6]

After the Clacton fighting, the shock proclaimed by press head-lines was promoted by news that the violence had engulfed respectable families on holiday, as well as by reports of wholesale availability of Purple Heart tablets. One witness claimed to have been offered tablets for sale by three different vendors within his first fifteen minutes on the seafront. As for the violence, the press denounced the riders of both gangs as 'Wild Ones', in homage to the Marlon Brando biker classic of 1954, which England had yet to see.

The disturbance at Clacton may have been exaggerated in court proceedings and press reports. What was not exaggerated was the availability of amphetamines among the gangs and the inability of legislation or policing to prevent this. Despite the new laws and penalties of 1963, Purple Hearts or French Blues were still freely traded in the cafés and coffee bars of the West End, though the price had jumped from 6d. to 9d. each. One café trader boasted of being in the market for 40,000 of them. Their effects were also noticeable. On Sunday 4 May, forty or fifty youths came out of an all-night club, Le Discotheque, smashed up the washroom of Waterloo Station, broke glasses in the Long Bar and tried to force open the station's cigarette machines.

At Whitsun 1964, there was trouble at Margate and Brighton. Three youths were stabbed at Margate, and one had a starting pistol fired in his face. Once again the fighting seemed worse, if only because it was more public than most Teddy Boy violence. A hundred police tried to clear Margate beach while holidaymakers looked on. At Brighton, 2,000 Mods and Rockers arrived to settle their differences. On Whit Monday, police reinforcements were called to Brighton, Hastings and Eastbourne, while fighting broke out at Southend. The worst trouble was at Margate where some 3,000 Mods and Rockers descended, fighting one another and the police on the beach, storming the Dreamland amusement park and smashing plate-glass windows in the town's shopping centre. The Mods, who outnumbered the Rockers on this occasion, had adopted a scooter-rider's war cry, which echoed through the nation's bank holidays for several years to come, 'Ziggy-zaggy, ziggy-zaggy, oy, oy, oy!'

As shouting and screaming teenagers surrounded his court, fifty of the culprits were dealt with by the Margate magistrate as 'sawdust Caesars, who can only find courage like rats in hunting in packs'. At a similar hearing in Brighton, one defendant was recovering from a drug overdose and could not appear, while another admitted that he had taken Purple Hearts but could not remember an incident in which he had smashed the leaded windows of the Brighton Hippodrome. The magistrate remarked that in all these cases only one defendant had expressed the least regret for his conduct.[7]

A consequence of the Brighton cases was the discovery of a shop in the town where it was possible to buy 'special aspirins' in any quantity. These were Dexedrine pep pills, of which the owner of the shop had bought 13,000 from 'an unknown source'. Since the Pharmaceutical Society accused him of 'nothing more nor less than peddling drugs at the expense of the health and well-being of young people', he was remarkably lucky, on conviction, to escape with a fine of £100. He was not part of youth culture himself, merely a forty-six-year-old entrepreneur who saw a means of making easy money from the unwary. Not for the first time, the gullibility of the young was exploited to assure them that they were part of tomorrow's culture and of an overdue rebellion against the old order, when they were in fact filling the pockets of those who had little interest in an order of any kind except their own.[8]

For those who had no friendly supplier of drugs or who wanted to set up in business themselves, the easiest method was to steal books of prescription forms from doctors' surgeries or cars, and forge an order for drugs, a problem which had reached 'serious proportions' in London during 1963. An enterprising schoolboy in Streatham found a still more direct method by breaking into a chemist's shop to steal several hundred tablets as well as liquid morphine and opium. He was fifteen and had been addicted for some time. He kept his supplies in the left luggage office at Oxford Circus underground and in a lavatory at Streatham Hill station, drawing on them as necessary. 'He sold his loot to pupils at his school, at a bowling centre, and a dance hall. He uses the profit for food and lodgings as he has run away from home.'[9]

Brighton became a centre of the drug problem. The disorder

there had continued during Easter 1965 with fighting between youths and helmeted police. In March, the council ordered the closure of a basement café in Hove, which the police swore was devoted to trading Purple Hearts and 'petting parties' among those aged thirteen to seventeen. This use of coffee bars as venues for drug dealing prompted the same council in January 1966 to hold a poll, asking for the town's approval to promote a parliamentary bill which would allow it to curb and if necessary close down such places. The citizens backed the proposal by 94 per cent to 6 per cent. Given the size of its population, the drug problem now seemed worse here than anywhere else outside London. To make the point of how easily drugs could be bought in the town a young Methodist minister, who had worked with addicts, produced a glass phial of cannabis and showed it to his congregation during a sermon at Dorset Gardens Methodist Church. He was prosecuted by a police solicitor who grudgingly admired 'the defendant's motives' and he was given a conditional discharge.[10]

Brighton was close enough to London to be a main staging post in the supply of drugs to much of the South Coast. It had a lucrative retail outlet in the new University of Sussex, to which both cannabis and LSD were supplied. As yet, amphetamines remained the most common of the working-class youth's short cuts to Nirvana. The method and route of supply were simple. In April 1967, for example, eight Londoners, two of them juveniles, four of them seventeen years old and one of them a barrister's clerk, pooled £550 to buy amphetamines at Bethnal Green tube station. They sold some of these at the Green Gate public house in Plaistow, then set off for Brighton with the rest of the tablets hidden in an old van. Unfortunately, a twenty-one-year-old who appeared to be leader of the group took twenty of the tablets to celebrate his arrival on Friday evening and was seen by the police, behaving oddly on Brighton seafront. He and another youth were arrested. Ill-advisedly, two of the seventeen-year-olds went to the police station next day to inquire what had happened to their missing friends. A policeman noticed the van nearby and found another of the group asleep in the back with 32 tablets in an envelope and between 500 and 1,000 still unsold, under the spare wheel.[11]

With London as a centre of supply and Brighton as a staging post, towns like Eastbourne or Hastings were soon easy targets. An eighteen-year-old Brighton scaffolder was told that the Eastbourne court had been 'all too often called upon to sentence youths from Brighton'. The scaffolder dealt in 'French Blues', as amphetamine sulphate tablets were known, in the Continentale Coffee Bar, Terminus Road. 'A group of youths and girls were coming from Brighton with a drug commonly called "French Blues",' the prosecutor explained, 'being sold at 1s. 1d. a tablet, 11s. for ten or £5 10s. for 100. Some were sold to persons from Hastings for 1s. 3d.'[12]

Drug dealers, to appear more appealing, presented themselves as amusing amateurs, young people with a sense of adventure and mischief but no true flair for crime, figures of folk legend or pranksters rather than real criminals. Behind these provincial purveyors were the London suppliers. Behind them again were men who resembled less and less the high-spirited prankster. Three months after the arrest of the Londoners who had taken amphetamines to Brighton in their van, a Scotland Yard Drug Squad operation brought to court a gang in July 1967 who had unwittingly sold pills to Jeremiah Fallon, an undercover Drug Squad officer. The ringleader of the group was a forty-four-year-old café proprietor from Tottenham, who went to prison for five years. His accessories were a man of sixty-seven from Stepney and another of fifty-one. Drugs, whatever effect they might have on those who used them, were mere commodities to these professionals.

Fallon had visited the Tottenham café as a 'buyer' and the first two men had driven him to a road in Finsbury Park. They opened the boot of a parked car and produced forty-six tins containing 46,000 dexamphetamine tablets in two shopping bags. 'You have seen them now,' said Frederick Russell. 'Eleven hundred quid's the price.' Fallon agreed and Samuel Levy, the sixty-seven-year-old, added reassuringly, 'There's plenty more if you do business with us.' As they went to prison, the Chairman of Middlesex Sessions added, 'This is quite the foulest trade ever.'[13]

The Brighton experience persuaded other towns near London to deal more robustly with the circulation of drugs among the young. Southend had become another seaside target. Superintendent Jack Crickitt of the borough's CID made a night raid on the Harold Dog coffee bar during an April weekend at the beginning of the 1967 holiday season. He took with him a number of women officers, police dogs and a 'mobile police station', which drew up outside and was equipped for strip searching. Roads and alleys round the coffee bar had been sealed off. Despite the fact that it was the middle of the night, twenty-one of the girls caught in the raid were between fourteen and sixteen years old. These and more than a dozen others, as well as the male suspects, were taken into the mobile police station, stripped and searched for drugs, although by this time most of the amphetamine tablets had been abandoned and lay scattered on the café floor among other 'substances'.

The parents of the twenty-one young girls were then phoned and summoned to come and collect their daughters. Among 'Schoolgirls Stripped Naked' headlines, Crickitt waited for the complaints to come in. What he got instead was public thanks from one of the fathers, whose daughter had told him she would be staying safely with a friend for the night and had even given a reassuring description of what they would be doing.

Within a fortnight, the Harold Dog coffee bar had been raided four times. The young girls were no longer to be found there. 'It appears our efforts are having the desired effect,' Crickitt said modestly. On the fourth occasion there was a crowd of youths in the coffee bar with some older girls. A series of fights broke out as the police tried to search them. Some who refused to be searched were taken to the mobile police station. A crowd of their supporters gathered at the cordon which sealed off the building. 'They whistled and shouted to excite the police dogs and when asked to leave they threatened personal violence to the police.' After the fight which followed, the ringleader was sent to prison for three months and three other defendants went to a detention centre for the same period. However archaic he might seem to a new generation, Superintendent Jack Crickitt emerged as a hero in Southend.[14]

Seaside towns within reach of London had seen some of the

worst drug problems and it was not surprising that Crickitt's aggressive approach to adolescent children should have been welcomed rather than resented by their parents. Their sons, and even more so their daughters, seemed potential victims of such dramas as 'The Mad House Murder', which had occurred across the Thames estuary in Margate two years earlier. The nickname was given to a boarding house, frequented by adolescent drug users from Birmingham and the Midlands. In this case, the naked body of a sixteen-year-old, Shona Berry, known as 'Toni', had been found in a park in September 1965. She had been strangled. In the publicity of a murder trial, the details of her life became generally known. She had had intercourse with a man the night before her death and then gone back to her parents' house. She returned to 'The Mad House' next day, Saturday, 'coming down' from the effects of amphetamines.

She spent the afternoon at the Tahiti Club coffee bar, another rendezvous for adolescents. A few hours later, a girl of thirteen found her crying in a Margate club because she needed more drugs. At the Excel bowling alley she managed to get some. She went to the park at 1.30 a.m. with a twenty-seven-year-old mechanic, who had had intercourse four times with a girlfriend as well as consuming four pints of beer and fifteen tablets. She had teased him, saying, 'Come on, little boy, be a man,' and he had 'grabbed her by the throat'. At Kent Assizes on 16 November, he was convicted of her murder. The thoughts of many parents echoed the helpless words of her father. 'I didn't know all that was going on. Who did?' Certainly not those in Southend who had believed their daughters were safely in the homes of friends they were visiting.

On 10 November 1966, Renee Short, the Labour Member for Wolverhampton North East, warned the House of Commons that the age at which children began experimenting with drugs had fallen alarmingly. Those between the ages of eleven and twelve were 'now experimenting with drugs of all kinds'. She demanded to know what instructions had been given to teachers to watch for signs of this. The answer was that very few teachers would have known what to look for and perhaps not many would have suspected what was going on. In the autumn of 1969, it was thought that there might be as many as 600 children taking drugs in Bromley and that 'Pot and Pill' parties were sometimes attended by a few and sometimes by as many as 150 to 200 young people. Yet if this was the new culture of the young, it was bridging the class divide. Among drugs seizures in April 1970 was a confiscation of cannabis from the tuck-box of a public schoolboy at Sevenoaks. The expulsion of pupils from the nation's leading schools, for smoking cannabis, became a sad but familiar news item.

A worse consequence of childhood experiments was illustrated in headline cases. Terence Bowell had started taking drugs in 1959 at the age of fourteen. He achieved a brief fame eight years later when he was found dead on a concrete floor with a bottle of lemonade beside him and surrounded by cigarette butts. His pockets were empty apart from a pawn ticket. Whatever road he was travelling had led him only to a dilapidated block of council flats in Paddington. He had become addicted to both heroin and cocaine and three times in the previous nine months had been taken to Paddington General Hospital suffering from an overdose. Little else was known about him and the coroner's jury returned an open verdict.[15]

Amid so much propaganda on both sides, it was increasingly difficult to determine what proportion of the young had fallen victim to drug pushers or embraced a new morality. At an early stage, following the Whitsun Bank Holiday riots in 1964, a snap survey of Mods and Rockers was carried out in Brighton to establish the extent of the moral threat. The questions were asked in cafés and dance halls, as well as in the street, among the age group 14–21. Of the Mods of both sexes, 62 per cent said they had already taken drugs, compared with 42 per cent among the Rockers. Of the girls, 28 per cent of the Mods said that they had had sexual intercourse, compared with 73 per cent of the boys. The comparable figures were 12 per cent and 60 per cent among the Rockers. The 'new morality' of the decade had apparently taken root more easily among the liberated middle class than among their working-class contemporaries. A drugs survey of youth club members was more encouraging. Only 16 per cent had taken drugs. Yet those who took heart from this figure were to be disappointed. Two and a half years later, a similar questionnaire among club members aged between fifteen and twenty-five, in December 1966, revealed that 63 per cent had now taken drugs at least once and 23 per cent took them regularly.

In April 1969, the medical director of the National Addiction and Research Institute warned his members at an open day that the problems of drug addiction, not least as they affected the youngest victims, had become much worse within the past year. In June, Kent County Council asked its Chief Constable and Children's Officer to suggest by-laws that might close down amusement arcades which were being used to sell drugs to the very young, particularly in the coastal resorts. The Children's Officer agreed that such arcades had become 'focal points for undesirable elements' but warned the committee that closing them would merely drive the problem under-ground. Westminster Council Public Control Committee had already announced in April that the spread of amusement arcades in Soho would be curbed for similar reasons. Yet narcotics which had been sold in such places might now be traded as easily at a designated level of a multi-storey car park. The 'war against drugs' would continue, of course, but forty years later there were still to be very few signs that it could ever be won.

4

In parallel with the use of amphetamines or cannabis, hallucinatory drugs were more pretentiously publicized and played a more dangerous part in the culture of youth. In 1953, in his sixtieth year, Aldous Huxley had acted upon William Blake's suggestion that 'If the doors of perception were cleansed, everything will appear to man as it is, infinite.' The 'cleansing' in Huxley's case had been accomplished by means of mescalin, a drug long known to the Indians of Mexico and the south-western United States. The result, he reported, was not to depict a world of mere fantasy but to enable him to see the world before his eyes as Adam had seen it on the first morning of creation, a heightened visual awareness and a 'sacramental' vision of reality. His experiences were recorded in *The Doors of Perception* (1954).

By 1957, Oxford undergraduates were experimenting with mescalin, confirming Huxley's account of visual awareness and sometimes adding that the drug had the effect of 'slowing down time', so that an afternoon might seem to last for weeks or months. There was little agreement as to whether the doors of perception had truly been opened upon a mystical experience or whether this process was merely an abuse of the functions of the adrenal glands.

Mescalin never became a popular drug, if only because others were easier to obtain, or at any rate to manufacture. The best-known hallucinogenic drug was to be LSD, lysergic acid diethylamide, discovered by two Swiss chemists in 1938. Its hallucinogenic properties were accidentally tested in 1943 by one of the discoverers, Albert Hoffman, who reported his voyage into a world of dazzling colours and moving shapes. The substance was later thought to have uses in treating schizophrenia and, by the CIA, in assisting the interrogation of prisoners. Elsewhere in the 1950s, it became a palliative in terminal cancer and in treating alcoholism. Not until 1963, in doses dropped on sugar cubes, was it much used in America by those seeking hallucination for its own sake.

A curiosity of LSD, which also made it unwelcome to those who enacted or enforced the law, was that its presence in the body after death was often difficult to trace. At the Old Bailey, on 8 December 1969, when one man who was accused of killing another claimed that death was caused by the deceased taking LSD, the court was assured that there was no way of telling whether this was true or not.

LSD was a dangerous substance, not least because of the extreme difference in its effects on individuals. It was many times stronger than mescalin and, as Huxley wrote in 1962, in the hands of its new apostles who had no more than 'vulgar minds', or in the case of Dr Timothy Leary talked 'nonsense', it was a danger to weaker spirits who might be tempted to try it. It was a door that led sometimes to heaven and sometimes to hell. Howard Marks, who was to make a career as a cannabis dealer, was given his first LSD sugar cube for £3 in 1965 and was assured that it was like a trip to Paris, only cheaper. Instead, he suffered the 'horrors' of what the press soon sensationalized as 'the vision of hell drug'.

LSD was banned in America in 1966, after a New Jersey wedding party ended with the bride being found naked, stabbed by a pair of scissors and strangled. Stories circulated in England of those who took the drug, entered a magic world in which they believed they could fly and jumped to their deaths from tall buildings. Some of these tales were intended to scare but others had a basis in fact. The body of a twenty-year-old man from Walthamstow was found naked on the ground outside a chapel in Highgate Road, Kentish Town. A young woman drew a witness's attention to him, mentioned that he had tried to fly from the roof of a building on the opposite side of the street, and then disappeared before anyone could question her. The dead man had frequented the Blues Club, in Greek Street, Soho, and it was assumed that he had bought LSD from someone there. The St Pancras coroner remarked that if the mysterious young woman gave him LSD herself and knew its possible effects, she would very likely be guilty of manslaughter. In a similar case, a young Leeds financier who took LSD jumped from the roof of his hotel. He survived the fall to the street with severe damage to his legs but his jump caused fatal injuries to a passing motorist.[16]

If one well-publicized case was likely to deter the potential user of LSD, it was that of an American visitor, Robert Lipman, who was tried in 1968 for the murder of Claudie Delbarre, an eighteen-year-old West End club hostess and prostitute. They had gone back to her room with some 'great acid from America', intending to have intercourse. First, she had said, 'Let's take some acid.' He cut a blue pill in half and they shared it. His trip began almost at once. When it ended, the girl was face down on the bed, the corner of a towel in her mouth and bruising round her head. She had died of suffocation, following blows to the head and a cerebral haemorrhage. Lipman's defence was that after taking the pill they had put on some 'very strange music', like something from a science fiction film. A strange feeling swept over his body and 'there was no more me'. It was as though he had been shot out into space and had become an electric car which ran on specific lines, vertical and horizontal.

Then I plummeted down towards the earth, which opened up. I myself went right down to the centre of the earth. I found myself in a pitful of snakes. There were many snakes – I don't know how many. They were very large and they were entwining themselves around me and fire was coming out of their mouths. I realized I was in hell, fighting for my life, trying to pull them off me. I thought I was dying.

It was in this struggle that he must have killed the girl. The jury found him and his story credible. He was acquitted of murder but convicted of manslaughter and sent to prison for six years. As a defence in a murder trial, his story made Victor Terry's plea of being possessed by 'Legs' Diamond sound almost reasonable. However, a combination of scientific evidence and the demonology which now surrounded the infamous narcotic was enough to persuade the jury of his lack of intent. Had such evidence been available eight years earlier, it seemed possible that Terry might not have died on the gallows but would have gone to jail for manslaughter after the Worthing Bank Raid.[17]

By 1967, after the possession of LSD had been made criminal in the preceding year, Scotland Yard's Drug Squad began to locate the first 'factories' and the first illegal producers. On 13 November, six men and a woman were charged following the discovery of LSD worth £250,000 at a house in Islington. Those arrested were scarcely the most characteristic members of a criminal underworld, though their crime was extremely serious. They included an antiques dealer, a pharmacist and an artist. This and other cases gave LSD the reputation of being a drug designed for middle-class recreation. It was also possible to manufacture it in very large quantities.[18]

The Islington house was by no means the only factory in London. A second one was found five months later in the apparently deserted basement of a building in Clapton Common, where three men had been manufacturing the drug for the past three months. Once again, they seemed otherwise respectable and were given bail. By the time of their trial, two of them had left the country and only the 'sales manager' remained to face the court. Because LSD could be manufactured rather than imported, its share of the drugs trade and the sums of money involved began to escalate. In January

1969, another raid in London yielded ingredients that, when turned into tablets, would allegedly have been sold to its users for £5,000,000. In a bigger series of investigations in early September, the Drug Squad carried out simultaneous raids in Kent, Kilburn and Hampstead, arresting two men and two women as leaders of a major LSD 'ring'. Even this was to seem small-scale by the 1970s.[19]

In 1974–7, before the fashion for LSD began to fade, Detective Chief Inspector Dick Lee of Thames Valley Police was to lead the hunt for a major source of manufacture and supply in an investigation which became known as 'Operation Julie'. The target was an LSD factory in West Wales. This undercover operation ended in March 1977, after 800 officers had arrested 120 suspects. Six million doses of LSD worth a potential £100,000,000 were unearthed, as well as £800,000 in Swiss bank accounts. It was crime on a scale which ought to have been the work of the Mafia or, at least, of major gangs in Britain.

Seventeen defendants were sentenced to a total of 120 years in prison. Nine had had a university education, two with medical degrees, one was an accountant and one a social worker. Most were of previously good character. It was a graphic reminder of the extent to which drugs had criminalized this area of society and had extended the territory of the underworld to include those who were inclined by nature and upbringing to be law-abiding. Some who were involved in this conspiracy boasted a political idealism, which seemed entirely compatible with the liberty they sought for others to choose LSD or not. Timothy Leary had argued the point that governments have no right to interfere with an individual's control of his or her personal metabolism.

Throughout this period, LSD was the characteristic drug of the literate and articulate, linked to Huxley's experiments with mescalin. It had subsequently created a philosophy of drugs as the religion of the future advocated in America by Timothy Leary, Allen Ginsberg of the 'Beat Generation' and Kevin Kesey, author of *One Flew Over the Cuckoo's Nest* (1962). Robert Lowell, author of *For the Union Dead* (1965) and widely regarded as America's leading poet of the mid-century, had taken it at their suggestion. Even without such resonance in England, it seemed a natural choice of the intelligent and the versatile who often proved the most difficult to catch and, particularly, to convict.

Universities in an age of rebellion, often more apparent than real, were a natural market for drugs. Student life at Sussex offered cannabis, as well as LSD in the form of 'Purple Haze' and 'Strawberry Field'. An Oxford cannabis ring in the autumn of 1967 was run by an American Fulbright scholar. At Ipswich Quarter Sessions on 25 June 1969, the Recorder, sentencing two students for taking drugs, denounced the University of Essex as 'a university littered with unemployed, drug-ridden layabouts', and suggested that police should be called in to search the campus. The Student Council nervously insisted this would 'only make things worse', and that there were only between a dozen and twenty regular users among 1,500 students.

Twenty users in 1,500 students seemed an underestimate. Yet in that same summer, 150,000 fans crowded into the Isle of Wight Pop Festival to hear Bob Dylan. The police reported that they had arrested twenty-five for being in possession of drugs. If the percentage of young people who told pollsters that they were taking drugs was at all accurate, then those who were detected bore very little relation to this or to the figures suggested at Essex. The estimate for the number of undergraduates who were smoking cannabis at Oxford in 1967 was 500, not counting a number of the younger dons, and seems more likely to have been accurate.

5

Whatever the correct figure, the famous casualties of drug addiction were widely reported. Joshua Macmillan, a Balliol undergraduate and grandson of the former Prime Minister, was found dead at Oxford after an overdose of the Valium he was taking to help him recover from heroin and cocaine addiction. As a rule, the most dangerous period for a heroin addict was in giving up the drug. In a number of cases, those who had stopped taking it for some time decided to have one last fix. Because their tolerance to the drug had been reduced, a dose which would not have killed them while they were fully addicted did so now. It also killed swiftly. In September 1969, the manager of the Lady Jane boutique in Carnaby Street had been 'cured' of heroin addiction after a spell in the Maudsley Hospital, having first taken the drug at fifteen. But, as a friend said, 'He took heroin. He liked it. He liked to fly,' and he tried one last flight after a period of abstinence. It killed him with such rapidity that the needle was still in his arm when he was found.[20]

In April 1969, after a number of cannabis prosecutions involving the Rolling Stones, their drummer Brian Jones who had previously been convicted on drugs charges was found dead at midnight at the bottom of his swimming pool. The gallery owner Robert Fraser, who had been prosecuted in the same case as Mick Jagger and Keith Richard, died of an overdose. At his appeal the Lord Chief Justice had issued the standard warning: 'Heroin has been termed a killer and it must be remembered that anyone who takes heroin puts their body and soul into the hands of the supply or the supplier.' This was echoed in the summer of 1969 when there were a number of deaths from a far stronger drug, 'Chinese heroin', alleged to have come to the market by way of the Chinese community in Soho. It had been smuggled from Hong Kong and was one of the first indications of the Triads' involvement in smuggling drugs into Britain. One of those who was killed by it in September was David Goldberg, a jazz drummer well known from television appearances. Though he had been a heroin addict for a long time, an injection of Chinese heroin killed him so quickly that he too died with the needle still in his arm.[21]

Drug taking among undergraduates had a certain cachet, not least when its exponents appeared to be dicing with death. Such nonchalance was far removed from the grimness of drug abuse in the 'new towns', built as the prestige development of post-war Britain to rehouse London's slum-dwellers. The bright world of their estates and shopping precincts had been blighted by an increase in addiction to hard drugs. In Crawley, the total of addicts was estimated to be eight times the number known to the police. This had been calculated in December 1967 from the large number of cases of jaundice related to the use of unsterilized needles. A week later, Stevenage reported an increase in drug offences and violence for 1966–7 that was two and a half times the national average. Welwyn Garden City was added to the list, when the press produced a fifteen-year-old girl who was already a heroin addict.

Drugs and juvenile prostitution were soon associated, in a shadowland of new towns that had failed the young and old cities in decay. The experience of some adolescents in this area was a match for the destitute lives of young Victorians. A girl of thirteen described her ordeal in 1969, by the end of which year she was pregnant and suffering from venereal disease. When arrested during a 'disturbance' in a transport café near Luton, she was under the influence of a strong sedative used by heroin addicts. She had run away from home and met a woman who took her to a house in Luton. There she had sexual intercourse with six men and was given £10. She survived in an area of the town described in police evidence as 'cafés and houses in Luton, many frequented by coloured persons, where the girl met her friends, obtained the tablets, and had intercourse'.

A man from Rhodesia gave her drugs in tablet form. She did not know what they were. 'I took two of the pills. I felt I was walking on air. I thought I would pass out.' This was at the Rhodesian's house, where his wife was present. She could not remember anything else for two days, which may have been the intention of those who were making use of her, but then she woke up, still in the house of the same man, who 'had a beard, did not work, and was a poet'.[22]

A girl of sixteen suffered a similar experience, though not as a prostitute, by leaving home to join her boyfriend and the Hell's Angels. Two of the boys took her for a walk in the park, where they offered her some capsules and yellow tablets. 'I had some and had a good lift. After that we left the park because I thought I was going to crash.' That night she slept with the one who had become her boyfriend, while another slept on the floor. 'When I woke up I realized that one of them must have taken advantage of me when I was crashed.'

Next morning she took sixteen more pills and spent that day with the same boys. 'I was so crashed out I really didn't know what I was doing.' She returned briefly to her mother next day, then went out with her boyfriend and 'crashed' twice in the streets of Croydon. 'I'm not accusing this boy of raping me. I'm not definite about it. I can't say that he did. I've had intercourse with four boys but not every Tom, Dick and Harry.' Such experiences suggested that whether or not these drugs merely enriched the consciousness or significantly damaged the brain, they were the answer to a sexual predator's prayer.[23]

The voices of the casualties had been less often heard or publicized than those of the enthusiasts for the new culture. Yet by no means all of them were self-pitying. The daughter of a dental surgeon emerged from a fortnight in Holloway, in June 1967, with a warning for womankind. 'If any girl is on drugs, I suggest she spends a fortnight in Holloway as I did. There you can see some of the dregs of humanity who are hooked. It was such an eye-opener for me that I don't ever intend to go back.'[24]

Not all had her self-reliance. Indeed, some who had done no worse than smoke cannabis sounded a note of despair far deeper than the girls from Luton or Croydon. In August 1967, a girl of eighteen who was addicted to the drug walked into Brighton police station with an appeal which again echoed the helplessness of Henry Mayhew's mid-Victorian underworld a century before.

> I want someone to help me. I cannot give it up . . . I have been smoking choc for the past two years, particularly when depressed. It lifts me up. I now realize I cannot go on like this and I want someone to help me. About a week ago I went to London to a house in Coldharbour Lane, Brixton. There is usually a negro there who sells the stuff. I have been going there for about two years . . . I went up there and bought £2 worth of choc. I have smoked most of it during the past week and I have not given any away or sold any.[25]

It seemed a long way from a pro-cannabis article, 'The Love Generation', in *Queen* magazine a fortnight before, quoted in the House of Commons by Alice Bacon, which attributed to one of the Beatles the comment that 'God is in everything . . . I realize all this through weed.' Cannabis might yet prove to be the exception to the destructive effects caused by other drugs, though the experience of the girl in Brighton scarcely suggested that.[26]

At the beginning of January 1969, a sub-committee of the government's Advisory Committee on Drug Dependence, under Baroness Wootton, would probably have recommended the legalization of cannabis. They were prevented from doing this by the government's adherence to an international agreement to ban the drug. The sub-committee had found that, on the evidence before it, the harmfulness of cannabis was too slight to justify heavy prison sentences. Moreover, the belief in a likely progression from using cannabis to using harder drugs had been exaggerated. Occasional use of cannabis appeared to have no long-term ill-effects. Two years earlier, the Dangerous Drugs Act had fixed the maximum sentence for both smuggling and possession of cannabis at ten years. The Wootton sub-committee recommended that the present laws should be relaxed and that the maximum sentence on indictment for possession should be reduced from ten years, which was never imposed anyway, to two years.

On 10 January 1969, Lady Wootton told an audience in Holland that smoking cannabis was a form of protest by young people, who saw their elders drinking whisky and could not understand why cannabis should be any more harmful. The press had already reacted with dismay to the publication of her report. In the circumstances, the suggestion that cannabis smoking was a youthful and understandable protest against the habits of an older generation was not well-timed. When the Wootton Report came before the House of Commons there was almost universal condemnation of its suggestions. James Callaghan, as Home Secretary, promised reassuringly to 'call a halt to the advancing tide of so-called permissiveness'.[27]

The threat was not so much permissiveness as lawlessness. The criminal had never been stronger than when governments created laws which were rejected by those whom they were intended to protect. The American experience of prohibition in the 1920s was generally cited as a conclusive example of this. Though nothing in England had created a monster on the scale of Al Capone, the gaming laws and restrictions on betting had spawned the bookie's runner, the illegal bookmaker and the thugs who 'protected' him. Drinking laws had created the private clubs and clip joints of Soho. The battle-lines in the so-called drugs war undulated a little in the years and decades ahead. It seemed a struggle that neither side could win, unless governments were to give way and relax the law. The first significant movement in that direction was the reclassification of cannabis from Class B to a Class C drug in 2003.

12

Immoral Earnings

I

IT WAS NOT at all surprising that prostitution should have increased during the 1939–45 war in London, the major ports, and areas like Manchester or the South-West where there were high concentrations of Allied servicemen. In 1943–4, a million US troops as well as British and Commonwealth forces were in place for the assault on Hitler's Europe. Few of these men had taken a vow of celibacy and fewer still kept one. Jealous of their transatlantic rivals, British servicemen responded with the well-known wartime description of female undergarments, 'One Yank and they're off'. The gang leader Billy Hill cynically described a new sexual morality in the blacked-out West End. 'Women flocked from all over to walk the streets, to haunt the hotel lobbies, bars and clubs. Good-time girls became brazen tarts, ordinary wives became good-time girls.' It was estimated that the number of prostitutes in London tripled during the course of the war.[1]

From the end of the war until 1959, when the Street Offences Act attempted to sweep prostitution out of sight, the customs of the trade altered little from what they had been for a century or more. However deplorable its existence, this was essentially a conservative profession. Apparent innovations often proved to be a revival of something familiar long ago. When the women were ordered off the streets at the end of the 1950s, Frederick Charles Shaw sought to help them and their clients alike. From his premises in Greek Street, Soho, he issued five editions of *The Ladies Directory*, including names, addresses and telephone numbers of the advertisers. He also included photographs and what the House of Lords, upholding his conviction, described disapprovingly as details of the more unusual 'services' which others were prepared to perform. Welcome or not, the book seemed a novelty. In fact, *Harris's List of Covent Garden Ladies* had been issued as a Christmas annual at least as far back as the 1790s and its publishers had run into much the same trouble as Mr Shaw.[2]

As the law stood at the end of the war, prostitution was not a criminal offence but soliciting customers in a public place and causing them annoyance was punishable by a fine of £2 and the inconvenience of a police court appearance. A prostitute who solicited in Mayfair would earn about £100 a week, twenty times the average wage, though she might be obliged to give most of it to her 'protector'. The £2 fines were a mere nuisance, as a parking ticket might be to the motorist of the future. Indeed, the government introduced parking tickets once the girls were removed from the streets and their contribution to the exchequer came to an end.

The protector might be a pimp or a ponce, though the words were often used indiscriminately. A pimp solicited for his girl, a ponce might leave her to solicit but would take a share of her income, probably about half, for protecting her from rivals or other 'protectors'. The task of defending her chosen 'pitch' in a particular street was usually left to the prostitute herself. Pimps and ponces were said to be despised by other professional criminals, perhaps because they were frequently of foreign origin, Italian, Maltese or, later, Caribbean. This was also a reflection of the values of an age in which a man who lived on a woman's money was generally regarded as hiding behind her skirts.

The law reflected this prejudice, dealing more harshly with the pimp or the ponce than with the woman herself. It was an offence punishable with imprisonment for two years under the Vagrancy Act 1898 to live upon a woman's immoral earnings, the trade of the ponce. Unusually in English criminal law, a man who was shown to be living with her or was 'habitually' in her company had to prove his innocence of the charge of living on her immoral earnings, rather than requiring the prosecution to prove his guilt. This was to be an important consideration when Dr Stephen Ward was tried and convicted of living on the immoral earnings of Christine Keeler and Mandy Rice-Davies, in the wake of the 'Profumo

Scandal' of 1963. Even before that, it brought down Alfredo Messina in 1951, prominent among so-called 'white slavers'.

It was also an offence, under the Criminal Law Amendment Act 1885, to keep a brothel, punishable with a fine of £100 or three months in prison for a first offence and thereafter with a fine of £250 and six months in prison. To procure a girl under twenty-one to have sexual intercourse with a third party or to attempt or incite such procurement was punishable with two years in prison. This was probably the most contentious provision. It appeared to mean that if a man asked a friend to introduce him to a girl aged between sixteen and twenty-one, with whom he subsequently went to bed, he might be guilty of inciting procurement. More was also to be heard of this in the Ward case.

Under these haphazard regulations, prostitutes lived for the most part in an atmosphere of mutual tolerance and good humour. Others might regard them as 'fallen women'; their traditional description of themselves had been as 'gay women'. 'I ain't gay,' protests Kitty to Walter in the famous Victorian diary, *My Secret Life*. 'What do you call gay?' 'Why, the gals that come out regular of a night, dressed up, and gets their livings by it.' In the post-war world they also spoke of themselves as being 'on the game', while their earlier trade description of 'gay' found another use in America.[3]

Many prostitutes worked alone. The cliché of the razor-wielding pimp waiting in the shadows was usually an image of fiction. The authoress of the most graphic autobiography of prostitution, Sheila Cousins in *To Beg I Am Ashamed*, lived without a protector and easily saw off the only man who tried to sponge off her. A second group had either a pimp or a ponce. Prostitutes in certain areas were always at risk of being attacked, robbed, even murdered, and a protector on call, who might also be a lover, appeared a sensible insurance. Others simply employed a maid who intervened if a client became difficult or outstayed his welcome.

None of these women, the great majority, matched the lurid accounts given of a third group, who lived in 'white slavery' according to such documentary accounts as Albert Londres' *The Road to Buenos Ayres* (1928) or in Evelyn Waugh's parody during that year of 'The Latin-American Entertainment Company Limited' in

Decline and Fall. Yet what was described as white slavery existed after the 1939–45 war, as much as before it. It worked upon the principle of internationalizing prostitution. French or Belgian girls might be brought to England, English girls sent to France or South America. They worked directly for some of the most powerful and ruthless entrepreneurs of the underworld. In pre-war England, Max Kassel, 'Max the Red', had been one of the best-known, though he was Latvian by origin and had spent most of his life in France, Venezuela and North America, supplying girls to brothels in South America. After the war, until 1950, there were few successful rivals to the Messina brothers.

As a rule, the 'white slaves' who were shipped from one country to another were already prostitutes, rather than innocent teenagers. Some who came to England had been bought from previous 'owners' in Paris or Brussels. It was common for them first to go through a form of marriage with a man who was paid for his services and who would give them, as the husband of a few hours, the nationality of the country for which they were destined and a right of residence there.

They were slaves in the sense that they arrived in a land where they had no friends or acquaintances, seldom very much knowledge of the language. The laws and courts would be an intimidating mystery. In this new environment they would be entirely dependent on the 'protector' or 'souteneur', who provided them with a room, clothes, a watchful maid or pimp, and who furnished them with necessary documents and paid their fines. He was their only 'friend', perhaps a temporary lover, and they had little hesitation in doing as they were told. In their new country, they had nowhere to run to and no money of their own, even if they had chosen to abscond. The journalist Duncan Webb described the Messina family in post-war London ruling their women by persuasion, threat, blackmail, the use of the knife or the razor. While this was true, the list represented a descending order of frequency. Persuasion and threat were usually sufficient.

Murder was sometimes necessary, if only to set an example. Before the war, three girls were found strangled in Soho in a matter of months during 1936 – Josephine Martin, Jeanette Cotton and Leah Hines, the last with copper wire, presumably as a final warning to the others who were controlled ultimately by a gang in Paris. It was thought by the police that the killer had come from Paris on a false passport, carried out the murder, and was back in France before the crime was discovered.

In the post-war world, the shooting of Margaret Cook near Regent Street in 1946 was believed by Scotland Yard to be a gangland killing, as was the Soho shooting of Rita Barratt, 'Black Rita', in 1947, and the stabbing of Rachel Fennick, 'Ginger Rae', with a 'Mediterranean' knife in 1948. Duncan Webb confirmed in 1953 that the Messina brothers were in the habit of hiring 'a Corsican cut-throat from the slums of Montmartre', bringing him to England on the overnight ferry, employing him to stab or wound the victim and to leave the country within an hour or two. Such deaths almost always remained unsolved crimes.[4]

2

Until the law changed in 1959, the main territory of prostitution altered little. Street walking was often a relatively quiet backwater, some women with men pimping for them or ponces protecting them but most without. In the West End of London, the areas round Piccadilly and Regent Street were occupied by those who thought themselves aristocrats of the profession. East of Piccadilly Circus and Wardour Street, and north of Regent Street, was the terrain of what one aristocrat called the 'baggier' type of women and the shabbier men.

On the pavements and in the pubs of the Euston Road, Paddington, and round the Elephant and Castle, the prices asked were in shillings rather than pounds. The most disliked by other women seem to have been the French, brought over to England by their ponces. They were hard-bitten professionals, who spoilt the trade in Soho by undercutting others, charging only ten shillings or a pound instead of the post-war tariff of twenty-five shillings. As one Englishwoman remarked sourly, the 'French tarts' who occupied Bond Street at night were shapeless as sacks and waddled on legs like 'classic pillars'.[5]

Mayfair prostitutes operated in Curzon Street and Shepherd Market, while the Messina brothers had their pitches in Maddox Street, running between Regent Street and Bond Street, and Stafford Street, off Piccadilly. Their less successful sisters stood alone or in groups along the terraces of the Bayswater Road from smarter Lancaster Gate to run-down Notting Hill. The advantage of this was that clients could be taken into Hyde Park, just across the road, saving the cost of a hotel room or a flat. Among other areas, Paddington was preferred for its 'short-time' hotels in the long Victorian terraces that ran beside Brunel's railway terminus. Similar accommodation in the West End lay in the little streets behind St Martin's Lane. In the expansion of prostitution during the war, the profession spread west and north, into the quieter side roads of Kensington, Earl's Court and Maida Vale.

A curiosity which hardly survived the disruption of the war was what might be called the neighbourhood prostitute, who remained at home in a working-class area, like a seamstress or laundress, available by arrangement to those who knew her and made use of her services, the bachelor, the widower or the inexperienced. There was a 1940s music hall joke in which a boy went to his father to confess a sexual indiscretion. His father asked if it was Mrs Smith and the lad shook his head. Was it Mrs Jones? It was not. Was it Mrs Robinson? No. The father, exasperated and disgusted, told him to leave. Outside, a friend asked if the father had forgiven him. The boy shook his head, 'No, but he gave me three very good addresses.' In reality, the cricket writer Neville Cardus recalled how a member of his childhood household in Manchester, Aunt Beatrice, fulfilled this role when she 'joined the oldest of professions and became an adornment to it', though she also brought home a stout gentleman who proved to be the Turkish Consul.[6]

3

So far as the professional underworld controlled London prostitution before 1959, its enforcers were the Messina family. Giuseppe Messina, the father of the five brothers, had been born in southern

Italy, married a Maltese and had become the owner of brothels, first in Malta and then in Egypt, at Alexandria. Salvatore and Alfredo had been born in the Maltese brothel but Eugenio or 'Gino', Attilio and Carmelo were born in the house at Alexandria. In 1936, at the age of twenty-nine, Gino Messina came to England and saw opportunities far beyond the prospects in Egypt. During the next few years, his brothers joined him, Attilio masquerading as 'Raymond Maynard', Salvatore as 'Arthur Evans', Carmelo as 'Charles Maitland' and Alfredo as 'Alfred Martin'. Gino himself became 'Edward Marshall'.

The girls brought over to England from France and Belgium by the brothers were first married to English husbands, which gave them British nationality and right of residence. Marthe Hucbourg described how she was married in France to Alfred Watts, a widower sixty-three years old and a drunkard, whom she had never met before and who agreed to the arrangement for money. She did not expect to see him in London, but he was needed when she was charged with keeping a brothel and possessed no documents to ward off deportation.

After soliciting for a while in Soho from a flat in Carnaby Street, as Marthe Watts, she began an affair with Gino Messina while working in the Palm Beach Club in Wardour Street. The love affair did not preclude Gino acting as her ponce and, when he believed she was disloyal, beating her with electric flex. 'Have you tasted the electric wire yet?' another girl asked her knowingly. She also became subject to the Messinas' 'ten-minute rule', which required each client to be sent packing at the end of that time to make room for the next one. Gino's violence was not reserved for girls who disobeyed him. He also served six weeks in prison after a bespectacled special constable pointed out that his car was parked in a 'no parking' area. Gino Messina punched him in the face, smashing his glasses and drawing blood with the broken glass.

In the later stages of the war, Gino Messina first ordered his girls not to take customers from military units arriving in England from the United States. Then he changed his mind and decreed a fourteen-hour day. They would work from 4 p.m. each afternoon until 6 a.m. The reality of the 'gay woman' and the 'game' was that Marthe Watts' total of clients on V-E Day reached forty-nine.

In the post-war world, Gino had twenty girls working directly for him. They earned on average about £100 a week from a dozen clients a night and paid £50 each week to him. A wage for workers generally was reckoned to be about £5 a week. Even while he was in prison, from 1947 to 1949, his girls put by the money they 'owed' him. After Gino fled from England in 1950, they dutifully sent their earnings to a variety of hotels in Europe. Marthe Watts calculated that between 1940 and 1955 she had earned £150,000 for him on the streets of the West End. Her contribution alone was the modern equivalent of a winning ticket in the National Lottery.

In the first years of peace, the tax-free income of the Messina family in London was said to be £1,000 a week, well over a million pounds a year in modern terms. This money was systematically laundered so that their empire included restaurants, property and Rolls-Royce cars, as well as Mayfair brothels and those who worked in them. Gino was in a position to put his hand in his pocket and pull out enough cash to buy a substantial house in Berkeley Square, which he did in 1947. His transactions were so swift that it was impossible for the police to keep effective track of them – or him. If there was a shadow over his prosperity, it was not cast by the law but by the knowledge that rivals in the under-world were beginning to regard the Messinas as the target for a takeover.

These rivals included fellow Maltese, known in the slang of the underworld as 'Malts' or 'Epsom Salts'. In March 1947, a gang led by Carmelo Vassalo began driving round the pitches of the Messina girls in Maddox Street and Stafford Street, demanding protection money from them and promising to 'carve them up' if it was not paid. Though it was later said that the Messinas had fabricated this story to get Vassalo and his friends convicted, the police had also been present. Detective Inspector Watts, who arrested Vassalo and his companions on 15 March, confirmed at the Old Bailey that there was 'gang warfare between the defendants and the Messina brothers. I arrested the five men after I heard threats and demands for money coming from inside the motor car where they were. They were making the demands from the women who have already given evidence.'

If the Messinas felt safe, it was because they had little to fear at this stage from the police. Inspector Watts admitted that he knew the brothers 'not personally but by reputation'. He was asked, 'Their reputation is that they are men who keep women on the streets of London?' 'They are reputed to be so.' After twelve years of learning no more than this, it hardly seemed that Scotland Yard was about to take action. On the following day, as the screams of their women filled the courtroom of the Old Bailey, Carmelo Vassalo and three others went to penal servitude for four years, Michael Sultana for two years.[7]

The Vassalo threat was removed. So was Gino Messina. In the course of his evidence, Inspector Watts pointed out that Carmelo Vassalo had 'an injury to his left hand'. It was alleged that this had been inflicted by Gino Messina. Because Messina's trial on this charge was also in progress, Inspector Watts could not reveal that there had been an encounter between the two gangs on 14 March, the day prior to Vassalo's arrest.

On that evening, Vassalo and three companions were driving along Jermyn Street at about 11.30 p.m. 'I noticed three men coming out of a restaurant,' he said, 'Messina was one, the others were his brothers. They were round their car and made some remarks. Messina spat at our car.' Though they had passed the parked car, Vassalo ordered his driver to turn back, in order to settle accounts with the others. By now Messina was in his own car, making a challenging gesture to Vassalo to follow him. They drove to Kensington Church Street and stopped outside Winchester Court, owned by Gino Messina. The brothers got out and walked towards the building. 'As I got near the doors,' said Vassalo, 'they swung round and a knife came from between them.' The knife was thrust towards his stomach and instinctively Vassalo grabbed at it, cutting off the tips of two of his fingers.[8]

Vassalo's maimed fingers were still bandaged six weeks later when he gave evidence of the attack. It was on the day following the fight that he had stepped up his campaign of threats and intimidation against the Messina girls. Gino Messina was committed to the Old Bailey, convicted and sent to prison for three years for grievous bodily harm. The press and the police spoke of a vice ring smashed, of Gino stripped of his gold watch, gold bangle and gold tiepin on arrival at Wandsworth prison. His life had been one of extraordinary luxury. It included fifteen Savile Row suits bought at £45 each on the black market in an age of clothes rationing, Rolls-Royce cars, a privately chartered plane, Park Lane parties even while on bail, weekends in Brighton with a selection of his girls, and the four-storey house in Berkeley Square bought a few months earlier, for cash. Now he had been toppled and several senior Metropolitan Police officers had attended the trial to witness his fall.

Anyone who inquired a little further knew that the empire had not been smashed. It continued to make money as it had always done. Gino, a model prisoner, came out of jail with full remission of sentence to a pot of gold that his girls had put by for him. This was not the end of his career in London. Nemesis, when it came, was swift but more devious. By 1950, after three years of official inaction, the five brothers were sure that the police had preened themselves on a triumph in Gino's case, had believed the newspaper stories of a vice ring being 'smashed', and saw no need to look further.

By 3 September 1950 even Gino's trial and the prison sentence which followed it were little more than a memory. The threat from the Vassalo gang had evaporated and the good times rolled again. He celebrated his release from prison by treating himself to an £8,000 yellow Rolls-Royce. Then, with an abrupt spin of Fortune's wheel, the destruction of a family which had controlled the vice trade for sixteen years followed within a few hours. It was accomplished by the front page of a mass-circulation Sunday newspaper, the *People*, boasting a sale of 4,500,000 copies. Most of the page on that Sunday morning was taken up by a single feature, containing photographs of four of the five brothers and a main headline, 'ARREST THESE FOUR MEN'. Only Alfredo Messina was not mentioned.

For good measure, the lesser headlines added, 'They are the emperors of vice of London: The Messina Gang exposed'. What the police had neglected to do for three years was accomplished by Duncan Webb in as many months, working underground. His feature was documented by details of rents, leases and properties relating to the Messinas and the use of the premises for 'immoral purposes'. A small feature at one side, complete with photographs, exposed the bogus marriage racket by which the girls gained British citizenship. In this case, one of the high-earning Messina girls, the French-born Janine Gilson, had gone through a wedding in Gibraltar with an Englishman who thought it was to be a genuine marriage and was prepared to tell the story of his betrayal.

Webb pointed out that the gang members were known to the police and had been named in Parliament. Nothing had been done. He appealed to the public for action, adding with measured irony that he now offered Scotland Yard a dossier 'that should enable them to arrest four men'. Unable to avoid action any longer, the Yard set up an investigation under Superintendent Guy Mahon. It moved too slowly. A week later all four Messina brothers named in the article had left the country. They moved through Europe, from hotel to hotel with Webb in pursuit, beyond the reach of the English law. From a distance they controlled their London empire through Marthe Watts and others who remained loyal. The money 'owed' to them was put aside.

The nationwide publicity given to the activities of the gang by the *People* had one result that was not expected, though it might have been anticipated. The brothers were out of sight but their girls were natural celebrities and remained on public view as they earned their livings. In London, families visiting the West End, who might otherwise have gone to view the changing of the guard outside Buckingham Palace, now made their way to Maddox Street or Bond Street to watch the girls parading on their pitches. 'On Saturday and Sunday men, women, and the children as well, gathered to admire us and watch our movements,' said Marthe Watts.[9]

For reasons that were never clear, Alfredo Messina *alias* Alfred Martin was the only brother not to feature in Duncan Webb's article. He also appears to have been the most ostrich-like. Because his name was not mentioned, he assumed that nothing was known about him. He had ample time to make his escape but saw no need. Two months after the appearance of the article Superintendent Mahon was put in charge of an investigation. Still 'Mr Martin' of Harrowdene Road, Wembley, paid no attention. He held a British passport, having been born in Malta, and saw no reason why he should not buy a portion of British justice, if necessary, as he bought everything and everyone else.

It might have been wondered whether the immunity of the Messinas over so long a period had a sinister explanation. The Commissioner of Metropolitan Police, Sir John Nott-Bower, acknowledged this suspicion in his 1956 report, when he denounced 'vague allegations of corruption and other malpractices' against his officers. The truth in his view was that the existing law gave the police too few powers in dealing with the vice trade. It was extremely difficult to get at the landlords of premises and those behind the nuisance of pavement soliciting. For the most part, individual policemen performed a thankless and often futile role in arresting prostitutes on the street, having to prove that they had been solicit-ing and that they had done so to the annoyance of the public, seeing them pay a £2 fine at worst and return at once to their pitches.

The problem for the Commissioner was public indifference. Members of the public were rarely prepared to give evidence in such cases. Proof of annoyance thus depended on the opinion of the officer making the arrest as to the attitude of passers-by. The hours and the nature of the work also made the job of policing the laws against prostitution very unpopular. As a result the members of the Vice Squad were frequently changed. It was hardly a recipe for success.

In the case of Alfredo Messina, six months passed and still there was no knock at the door, no whispered announcement of 'Two gentlemen to see you.' Then came a telephone call, on behalf of Superintendent Mahon, requesting an interview. On 19 March 1951, Mahon went to interview Messina at home. The charge was to be that Hermione Hindin, who shared the house, had been a prosti-tute for thirteen years and he had been living on her immoral earn-ings. Hermione Hindin had not even retired. Messina thought the police had lost interest in him but he had been under observation. He was seen driving her from Wembley to Maddox Street at about 6.30 p.m. and collecting her in the small hours of the morning. She had been watched soliciting on the pavement and consorting with known prostitutes at the Running Horse public house in Davies Street, Mayfair, where they took their 'tea break'.

Mahon and Detective Sergeant Albert Foster arrived at Messina's house just before lunchtime. Messina offered them a drink and both accepted. Hermione Hindin brought a tray with Black and White whisky, soda and ice. There was concern at Scotland Yard over the discovery that someone had leaked confidential police information to Messina, following a Vice Squad interview with a former constable, Charles Roper. Mahon asked first of all how this information had reached him. Messina said simply, 'I know many people and they tell me what is going on.' He added for the superintendent's benefit, 'Let's be friends. We are men of the world and can't afford to fall out. I am going to give you a lovely lunch with turkey and champagne.'

Messina admitted that he owned the house, that he did no work because at fifty he was an invalid, and that Hermione Hindin lived with him. Mahon asked, 'Do you know she is a prostitute?' At his trial, Messina would express shock and astonishment but now he said amiably, 'You seem to know all about us. Between men of the world, I don't deny it.' Mahon warned him of the consequences. 'As you are living with a prostitute the onus is on you to prove that you are not living on the earnings of her prostitution.' Messina offered the two policemen another drink. Mahon and Sergeant Foster accepted again.

Messina said to Mahon, 'I would like to speak to you alone,' and the superintendent told Foster to leave them. Messina became confidential. 'Now we are on our own I can talk. I have got a lot of money and can help you. Will you take £200 to square up the matter?' Mahon asked him what he meant but Messina said, 'I will go and get the money,' and returned about a minute later. 'There you are, Mr Mahon. There is £200 for you to square up the matter and do nothing more against me.' Mahon went to the door, called Sergeant Foster, and said, 'He has just given me this money and requested me to take no further action against him.' Messina looked at the wad of notes and said, 'I did not give it to him. He must have found them somewhere in this room.'

Foster had discovered a 15cwt safe in the kitchen. When opened, there were passports for Messina and Hermione Hindin, as well as £222 in cash. On top of the oven was a roast turkey and the table was laid for four. Yet the convivial lunch was never eaten. Messina was arrested and taken to Wembley police station. He was charged with living wholly or in part on the earnings of the prostitution of Hermione Hindin for eight years and subsequently charged with corruptly offering £200 to Superintendent Mahon for showing favour to him.

In Messina's version, he was dismayed to learn that Hermione Hindin was a prostitute. As a fifty-year-old invalid, he spent his evenings quietly at home and had entirely believed her stories of going to visit her mother or to the cinema. He and Hermione Hindin denied the story of the attempted bribe. In their version, Mahon had induced them to open the safe. The superintendent had knelt down, pulled out £200 and taken it to the sitting room. Messina had followed, saying, 'Don't be silly, Mahon! Put it back!' Mahon was laughing. He went out into the hall and shouted to Sergeant Foster, who was searching the upper floor, 'Bert! Bert!! Come down! I am going to charge him with bribery.'

At the Old Bailey in May 1951, Alfredo Messina was convicted for the first time in his life. The jury found him guilty of living on immoral earnings and attempting to bribe Superintendent Mahon. Jailing him for the maximum of two years with a £500 fine, Mr Justice Cassels concluded, 'You thought that so far as the police of this country were concerned money could do anything. You are an evil man.' On his release, Messina settled in Brentford and died there in 1963. Because he had been born in Malta, he held a British passport and could not be deported.[10]

Of the four exiles, Attilio Messina slipped back into the country and set up home at a cottage called 'The Hideaway' at Bourne End, though keeping a number of London properties. He was caught in October 1951, after a police search. At Bow Street on 31 October, he was charged with procuring a woman to be a prostitute in 1945 and living on the earnings of prostitution on 'various days' in 1946, 1947 and 1948. These charges were then dropped and he was convicted of living on the immoral earnings of Robina Torrance, a Messina girl, his mistress during the six months since he had returned to England.

The Bow Street magistrate remarked that Attilio Messina was not in any poverty, yet he had allowed the woman he was living with to go out soliciting and, when she returned, had taken a share of her earnings from her. In his case, old habits had died hard. He went to prison for the maximum of six months. In 1953, the British government tried to deport him to Italy, his father's birthplace, but the Italians refused him. Later they relented and both Attilio and Salvatore were admitted. In Belgium, Gino and Carmelo were charged in 1955 with offences relating to trafficking in women, as well as carrying firearms and possession of false passports, which may have been used to make secret trips to London. At Tournai in June 1956, Gino was sent to prison for seven years and the ailing Carmelo for ten months. Gino was freed in 1959 and entered a new and more promising profession of supplying London with drugs from Afghanistan.

By no means all who lived on the earnings of prostitution made headlines in the Sunday press or received much coverage when they came to court. Yet the money involved, even among small fry in the mid-1950s, put to shame the average wage of most people, which was now about £10 a week. When Coppel Kovenskie, *alias* Charles Kay, was charged with living on the immoral earnings of a woman in Pont Street, Westminster, it was the Marlborough Street magistrate who could not credit the sums involved. 'Many people, including myself, at one time did not realize what big money there is in vice.'

The defendant had insisted that he was merely the caretaker at the flat and thought that the woman was a photographic model who posed for a two guinea fee. He took her earnings from her every day, handed her back a third of the amount less 'incidental expenses' and gave the rest to his employer, a woman who lived in Earl's Court. The annual gross takings were between £7,800 and £9,300, fifteen to twenty times the average wage, 'out of this comparatively unknown flat and one young woman'.[11]

As it happened, the reign of the Messinas in London was not quite over by 1952. When the Italians refused to accept Attilio the following year, he returned to business, though for the next seven years he had to report to the police weekly, as an alien. In April 1959, he stood in the Old Bailey dock as the last of his victims told their stories. He was to be convicted of procuring Edna Kallman to be a prostitute for the past twelve years and living on her immoral earnings for the past ten years. In that time she had handed him a total of £40,000. 'Who is she?' he had asked innocently, when Detective Chief Inspector John Du Rose charged him. He insisted that he had made the money as a successful West End antique dealer. What he had, it proved, was a second-hand shop in Fulham with a very few pieces of the most ordinary furniture in it.

Edna Kallman told her story. Messina in his car had picked her up in the Edgware Road as she was walking home one night in 1947. He later took her to dinner and she spent the night with him at one of the family's flats in Winchester Court, Kensington Church Street. He had set her up in a flat in Egerton Gardens, Knightsbridge, in May 1949, keeping her indoors for three months. The bargain was that she would be trained by someone he knew to 'make easy money' as a prostitute. 'This would last about eighteen months to two years and it would be a means to an end. Then he and I would have a life together.' He also took care of her Post Office savings book, which had £250 in cash folded into its cover. The book was returned but she never saw the cash again.

At first she worked as a Mayfair prostitute from a flat in Shepherd Market, returning to Egerton Gardens each night, then at other Messina addresses in Three Kings Yard and New Bond Street. She did as she was told because

> I had had a really good hiding in Egerton Gardens . . . I was absolutely terrified of him. That he would put me out in the street in my slippers and reduce me to nothing. He threatened, if I had any ideas of getting away from him, he would cut my face. I had some nasty blows on the jaw which a doctor had to attend to.

Messina had brought other girls to the Egerton Gardens flat but they had not proved satisfactory in training. 'The first girl was there about six days. I heard him hit her and I heard her crying. He said he was putting her out. She immediately packed and left.'

For Miss Kallman, he arranged a pitch where he could watch her from his window. He phoned her flat in Shepherd Market at night to ensure she was still working. She was allowed to visit her mother and stepfather in Derby only under supervision. Their letters were sent to his address and read by him first. To begin with, she had made £120 a week but her health had deteriorated over ten years and by 1959 she was making only £50, of which she was allowed to keep £7. He took her to a doctor who advised her to take a month's rest. Attilio Messina told her that this was 'rubbish' and ordered her back to work.

In the end, in an outburst of temper, he promised to 'deal with her' next day, after she called a policeman to get rid of a difficult client. Without waiting, she fled to Derby and stayed with a friend. Messina followed, went to her mother and stepfather and explained ingratiatingly that he and their daughter had had 'a silly row'. He managed to locate her and a car with two men in it began driving past the house. On 20 February 1959, in the middle of the night, she slipped out, went to the police and told them her story.

At the Old Bailey, when Attilio Messina applied for bail, Detective Sergeant Denis Welsh of the Scotland Yard Vice Squad warned the Recorder that Edna Kallman was in terror of the defendant being free. 'The main witness in this case has in fact disclosed, should Messina be at large, she herself will go missing and we will have great difficulty in putting her before the court.' As it happened, Messina gave up the struggle and pleaded guilty. Others were to follow in his footsteps but he was the last of the dedicated professionals, whose calling was the vice trade and to whom it was a hobby and relaxation. He had few interests but his work. In his flat, the police found a copy of the classic 1928 account of white slavery, *The Road to Buenos Ayres*. Passages had been underlined in pencil and one chapter was marked with the comment: 'The whole chapter worth reading twice.' If what he and his brothers practised was not white slavery, it was hard to know what would be.[12]

4

Vice abhorred a vacuum and the disappearance of four Messina brothers opened the way for other contenders. Yet the tyranny of the brothers was followed by anarchy rather than succession.

Following the death of George VI in 1952, England prepared for the coronation summer of Queen Elizabeth II in 1953. Duncan Webb, still the scourge of Soho, reported that 150 foreign prostitutes had arrived to join the festivities in West End Central alone, vanguard of a legion beyond the control of a single protector or his gang. Such immigrations had often preceded great events. Early in 1937, Scotland Yard had set up its 'Anti-Vice Squad', officially known as the Clubs Office, with the object of cleaning up the capital before the Coronation of King George VI and Queen Elizabeth on 12 May that year. Criminal court records showed the same targeting of vice before the Great Exhibition of 1851, and even before the Coronation of Queen Victoria in 1837. In 1953 the organizer of these unwelcome immigrants was Antoni, or Tony, Rossi, a shabby drunkard from the East End in a greasy trilby, hardly the pattern of a gangland boss.

Among inheritors of the Messina estate, even while Attilio was still trading alone, were both Tony Rossi and Anthony Micallef, a brother-in-law of the Messinas with seventy-four convictions to his credit. Micallef, like Rossi, was small fry, his principal investment a brothel at the Norfolk Hotel, Trebovir Road, Earl's Court. Duncan Webb kept a solitary surveillance and Micallef was sent to prison, though set free on appeal with a fine of £100. As a means of letting flats to prostitutes Tony Rossi had been a partner in a Soho estate agent's. He retired to the East End because, as Webb put it, 'I had Rossi by the unfortunates.' The firm was left in the capable hands of the 'respectable' Mr Bernie Silver, of whom far more was to be heard by the Vice Squad.[13]

So far as there was an attempt to control prostitution in the mid-1950s, it was undertaken by Tommy Smithson, a former boxer and merchant navy stoker. Yet at twenty-six he had crossed too many paths. Brought up in the East End since the age of two, he was stubborn, stoical, not clever enough to deal with opponents and stupid enough to trust his own hands rather than to have men who formed a bodyguard. His aim was to offer protection to the Maltese and those who gave prostitutes a licence to trade. Unlike the Messinas, he allowed his attention to wander to other sources of protection revenue in clubs and illegal gambling. He told Philip

Ellul, who soon afterwards turned against him and shot him dead, 'When I want anything I get it. The only difference between Billy Hill and me is that he takes ten shillings in the pound and I'm cheaper. I only take five shillings.'

As sole challenger to men established for ten or twenty years, Smithson played too dangerous a game. When Detective Superintendent Albert Webb was asked whether he was a man of 'ruthless violence', the answer suggested he was no match for his competitors. 'He had a long criminal career and two convictions for violence. I have looked through his record and I can see no evidence anywhere that he ever used a weapon. When he committed violence, when he was convicted, he did the damage with his fists and feet.'

In protecting the Maltese, Smithson crossed Billy Hill and Jack Spot. Good-humouredly, they invited him to negotiate a settlement at the Black Cat factory in Camden Town in 1953. Hill and Spot were there with a companion who told Smithson they knew he was carrying a gun and he must hand it over. He did so. A furniture van then drew up from which a number of men ran out and began to attack him murderously with knives and razors. The wounds inflicted were so deep that it was said he should have bled to death or lost a limb. Both sides of his face were slashed and he was dumped, perhaps left for dead.

Smithson was found in Regent's Park, near Park Village East, before he bled to death. Patched up and stitched up, he resumed business, never telling the police what had happened. For that he was said to have been respected. Another version of events was that he threatened to go to the police but was persuaded not to by a gift of £500 from Jack Spot and a share in a dice club, subsequently raided and closed down. He moved from the East End to Emperor's Gate, Kensington, and let it be known that he was setting up as a fence. In the territory he had sought to conquer there was, in truth, no place for him.

On the morning of 25 June 1956, he was found lying in the gutter outside a house in Maida Vale, owned by a Maltese he was protecting and described as 'a Maida Vale brothel'. His last words to those who found him were reported as, 'Good morning. I'm dying.' In a short while he was dead. The shooting had the characteristics of an underworld murder, one bullet hitting him in the arm and then a fatal shot entering his neck. The press could now write of Chicago slayings in Maida Vale.

It was not at all a Chicago execution. The search for the killers was brief and there was no wall of silence on the part of criminals great or small. By 10 a.m. a number of young women were 'helping police with their inquiries' at Harrow Road. The two principal suspects headed for Manchester, read their police descriptions in the papers, and returned to give themselves up. Three Maltese appeared in court, though no evidence was offered against Joseph Stammitt. Not only did Philip Louis Ellul, a labourer, and Victor Spampinato, both of Stepney, surrender at Scotland Yard, Ellul said, 'Sure, it was me that shot him. He was going to do me if I didn't get out of London and I don't stand for that.' Spampinato added, 'I was with him when he shot him. He is my friend and what he says is OK by me.'

Their defence was that Smithson had needed money for the legal expenses of his girlfriend, in trouble over a forged cheque. He had demanded it from George Caruana who had paid him protection and owned the Maida Vale house. There was a fight in which Caruana was cut and Ellul threatened. Ellul then went to the Maida Vale house for a showdown with Smithson. 'You've wanted me for a long time, Tommy,' he said and, as Smithson came towards him, drew a .38 automatic pistol and shot him in the arm. Ellul then went out of the room with Smithson after him, shouting, 'I'll get you in the East End tonight.' As Smithson closed on him, Ellul fired the second shot and hit him in the neck.

At the end of the trial, Spampinato was acquitted and Ellul sentenced to death with a recommendation to mercy. He was reprieved. Spampinato sold his story to the press. Believing his acquittal meant he could never be tried for anything to do with Smithson's death again, he recorded an interview which was handed to the police. In this, he alleged that he and Ellul had been offered a contract to kill Smithson by a man who said, 'This punk has got to be exterminated.' They stalked their prey and cornered him in the house in Maida Vale. Ellul had a .38 automatic and Spampinato a knife but Ellul insisted on doing the killing. As they entered, he shot Smithson in the arm, then the automatic jammed. After a struggle with the mechanism, Ellul cleared the gun and shot again, hitting Smithson in the neck, after which thick blood, 'like liver', came from his mouth. Spampinato added that he had really enjoyed himself.[14]

Ellul had been convicted of the murder and by the law of evidence Spampinato's version, given in the absence of Ellul, could only be evidence against himself. It sounded unconvincing, if only because no one wanting to issue a contract on Smithson would have entrusted it to these two. Spampinato went on to become a wine bar tout in Malta, and Ellul on his release went to the United States. Such control as there was over prostitution in central London passed to six other Maltese and the 'estate agent', Bernie Silver, who now called themselves 'The Syndicate'.

5

The Syndicate's power was far more limited than that of the Messinas had been, if only because the world they fought for was changing rapidly. The government had set up an advisory committee under Sir John Wolfenden, Vice-Chancellor of Reading University, to inquire simultaneously into the two contentious topics of homo-sexual crimes and prostitution. A major reform of the law on homo-sexuality had to wait until 1967 but, in the wake of the report, the Street Offences Act of 1959 sought to prevent the public nuisance of having prostitutes on the pavements and thereby turned most of them into 'call-girls'. The mass availability of the telephone as much as moral determination by the authorities made the change possible. Fines of £60 for pavement soliciting and possible imprisonment under the new law accelerated it.

Typed or handwritten postcards in glass cases outside newsagents shops, from Bayswater to Bloomsbury and Pimlico to Camden Town, had always advertised goods wanted and for sale. Now the cases were crowded with offers which coupled innocence and inti-macy with a phone number. It was a novelty and, for some time, furniture buyers who rang a number offering 'Large Chest For Sale' engaged in fruitless negotiations. Fetishism, preferred skin colour, lingerie or 'costumes', sadomasochism or high colonic irrigation were coyly alluded to. Many advertisers claimed a stage-dancing past as 'Ex-Windmill' girls. It would have been possible for plain-clothes officers to ring every number and bring the offender to court but lack of manpower and realism prevailed. It was not quite clear what offence the call-girl was committing and unless prostitution could be stamped out completely, which had never yet happened in human history, a compromise might as well be accepted.

It was at this point that Frederick Charles Shaw sought to do good to others and himself by producing his *Ladies Directory*. He went about it prudently by first going to Scotland Yard to ask if what he was proposing to do would be legal. 'Look, officer,' he said to a detective constable, 'I am going to publish this book. I am trying to make money out of this because since the new Act has been brought in the girls need a bit of publicity.' Unfortunately, it was Mr Shaw who got the publicity. Scotland Yard was non-committal when he asked for an opinion, saying that it was 'not in a position to advise' him whether he should publish the directory or not, but then prosecuted him when he did.

As in the case of the call-girls, it was not clear what he should be charged with. An initial attempt to try him for living on immoral earnings was thought unlikely to succeed. A charge under the new Obscene Publications Act would bring a tribe of 'expert' academic witnesses who would talk endless nonsense about the social value of the publication. As it happened, most witnesses were prostitutes who advertised in the book and were called for the prosecution. 'I do striptease, massage and correction,' said one of them brightly.

In the end the conviction in this case was for conspiring to effect a public mischief or to corrupt public morals. This was a new offence, not covered by Act of Parliament, but an addition to the common law if the defendant were found guilty, as Shaw was. As a conspiracy under common law, it also carried a theoretical maximum sentence of life imprisonment. Someone had it in for Mr Shaw. He was sent to prison for two years, but then appealed to the House of Lords on the grounds that there had been no such offence as conspiring to corrupt public morals when he published his book. The Lords ruled that there had not been one then but there was now, and sent him back to prison.[15]

On 28 October 1960, charges of living on the earnings of prostitution were brought against two of Frederick Shaw's former employees, who had optimistically published *The Ex-Showgirls and Models Christmas Club*, in imitation of *The Ladies Directory*. One protested to the police, 'I looked upon what I was doing as legal because we were not charging for advertisements. We were charging for books at a lower rate than they cost us to produce.' Despite this philanthropic intent each man went to prison for two months.[16]

For all these setbacks, and the possibility that a zealous police commissioner might prosecute them for the same conspiracy as Mr Shaw's, many of the new call-girls did well. There was an attempt in 1958 by the 'St Marylebone Vigilantes' to get rid of them by offering evidence of their activities to the police but this offer was not taken up. Sometimes the activities were investigated, as when the Vice Squad raided flats in New Bond Street and Curzon Street. Two plain-clothes members of the Vice Squad paid £15 each to see three obscene films at the Curzon Street flat on 12 October 1959. They arranged to go back on 23 October, when their hostess promised them a new projector and clearer images. A search of the flat revealed 70 obscene films and 1,000 obscene photographs, the objects of their visit. The flat also appeared to be a warehouse for the pornography trade, containing obscene photographic pictures, letters, typewritten stories and obscene books.[17]

As standards of censorship relaxed, however, the call-girl as projectionist was not much needed. What had once been called blue films were easily obtainable and might even be seen on the night shift at secret locations in major industrial plants. Small wonder, it seemed, that the country's output was in such poor shape. In the summer of 1966, security officers at the car plant of Fisher & Ludlow in Castle Bromwich, which had 12,000 employees, heard the men of the night shift clapping and cheering in the mess room of D block annexe. Two nights later the block was raided at 2.30 a.m., as the last hundred men were leaving and the film show ended. The reason for the enthusiasm on the previous nights was that one of those said to be organizing the show appeared as the male lead in one of the films, 'with a woman'.

The firm admitted that there had been 'trouble of this sort before' but that warnings had been given. Two years later it was the turn of the Southend Vice Squad to raid the 'second house show' in the plastic injections shop of the Ecko radio factory at Prittlewell. 'There was one show after midnight in the shop and that went off all right,' said a disappointed patron. 'It was while the second show was on sometime after 3 a.m. when the police burst in. They took the name of everyone there and confiscated all the gear.'[18]

The truth was that the blue film show had long been a staple of the vice trade. Several years before the war, Scotland Yard announced that films 'of an obnoxious character' were being smuggled by steamer from France, through small South Coast ports, as well as by plane. They were mostly shown in the provinces. The police believed that they were exhibited at 'certain hotels' and a two-hour show was held in a garage for twenty people. Each member of the audience 'paid highly for the "privilege" of seeing the pictures'.[19]

6

As the call-girls adapted to their new conditions, other young women did less well. The unsuccessful could not afford a Kensington flat or a Notting Hill bedsit, if only because their patrons, indirectly, could not afford it either. They hung around in cafés or bars, picking up clients, until the proprietors turned them out. In the East End and the dockland areas, they or their minders took over the worst and most decayed slum properties. In a censure motion on the Labour-led London County Council on 1 March 1961, the leader of the Conservative opposition, Sir Percy Rugg, reported of Stepney that

> The situation in this part of London is tragic enough when prostitution seems to thrive in the most appalling circumstances without any kind of physical comfort and only hidden from the road by a wall of some kind. If there is a floor inside that is all that is wanted.

Stepney was a running sore and three years earlier, in July 1958, Lady Henriques had asked the government to give the police more powers to deal with prostitution on the streets and in the cafés of the area. Her plea had contributed towards the framing of the Street Offences Act that year.

Prostitution had disappeared largely but not entirely from the public eye in other areas. The destitute, the under-age runaways, the addicts of hard drugs, still plied their trade wherever they could. In Aldgate there was organized prostitution still run by Maltese pimps. They included Caruana and 'Big Frank' Mifsud, business partner of Bernie Silver, but also John Borg and Emmanuel Buttigieg, known as 'The Farmer' because he kept rabbits and goats behind his house. Buttigieg's houses ran twenty-four hours a day with two girls in each. The idea that self-respecting gangsters despised this trade and declined to profit from it was rubbish. Much of the money from this area was passed to the Kray twins.

There was sometimes bloodletting between the slum ponces themselves. In 1969 Borg took a fancy to one of Buttigieg's womenfolk and there was a quarrel. On 20 February just after midnight and with snow falling heavily, a man went to a café of Buttigieg's in Leman Street just as it was closing and asked him for a lift. The two men went outside with his daughter Cincha. As Buttigieg was getting into his van, John Borg was waiting to fire three bullets, two of them hitting him in the chest. Cincha ran back, screaming that her father had been shot. Two teenage boys in the café went to the door, only to be met by a man with a gun who ordered them back inside. Borg went to prison for ten years on a conviction for unlawful killing. On 24 April 1978, he died in his turn, blown to pieces by a bomb which destroyed a minicab office and adjacent flats in Hackney, belonging to the procurer and murderer John Gaul.

Despite the contempt felt by most other professional criminals for pimps and ponces, some of the girls might have wished that they could have had a protector at hand. Between 1959 and 1965, there was a series of eight murders of prostitutes, sometimes called 'The Towpath Murders' – though this title was also applied to two earlier killings of girls who were entirely respectable – or 'The Jack-the-Stripper Murders'.

The first victim was Elizabeth Figg who was found by a willow tree in Duke's Meadows, near Chiswick, on 17 June 1959. She was wearing a torn dress but very little else and she had been strangled. She had not been known to the police as a prostitute. The murders that followed were at irregular intervals, though it may be that there were other killings in which the body was not found. The victims had few acquaintances in London and their identities were hard to establish among a variety of names they used.

The second body, that of Gwynneth Rees, who had come from South Wales and lived in Stepney, was not found until November 1963 on a rubbish dump near the Thames at Mortlake. She had two convictions for soliciting, though her family in Barry believed her to have a respectable job in London. The third body, that of Hannah Tailford, was found in the Thames at Hammersmith in February 1965. The cause of death was drowning, though other evidence and the absence of all clothing but a pair of stockings pointed to a criminal attack. Like her predecessors she had used a number of names, presumably in the hope of relying on them in court and avoiding the penalty of going to prison on a third conviction of public prostitution. In April, the body of a fourth victim, Irene Lockwood, was found in the river at Chiswick.

In the following month, a fifty-four-year-old man, Kenneth Archibald, went to the police and confessed that he had murdered Irene Lockwood on 7 April. Investigation identified him as caretaker at the Holland Park Tennis Club. He had served in the merchant navy, the Army, enjoyed reading P. G. Wodehouse and did odd jobs for an electrical repair firm. He was a solitary man, though after the tennis club closed for the evening, he and others ran an illegal drinking club on the premises, 'Kenny's Club'. A card for this club was found among Irene Lockwood's possessions when the police searched her flat. Apart from that, as the prosecution admitted, 'The case against him rests simply on a series of confessions he made to the police three weeks after the body was found.'

It was true that Archibald had stolen a deaf aid from a department store, that he was helping to run an illegal club and that £30 was missing from his employers. These items hardly amounted to proof of murder. His confession was one that anybody could have invented. He had gone with the girl from a pub to the side of the river for a 'short time' at about 11 p.m. She wanted £4 in advance. He refused, there was a fight, he must have lost his temper, put his fingers round her throat and strangled her. He removed her clothes because he had been in the pub with her. If the clothes were found someone might connect him with the girl.

The police were used to false confessions in serial murders. They ought to have treated Archibald with greater caution. Yet there had been four murders and no doubt someone on the case was nearing desperation. As a matter of fact there had been a fifth murder, three days before Archibald went to the police. He had not confessed to that nor appeared to know anything about it. At the Old Bailey, he pleaded not guilty and the jury acquitted him on the second day. Why had he confessed? He could only say that he was fed up and depressed – and that he had 'a lively imagination'. Three more murders of prostitutes followed, in July, November and the following February. Then they stopped altogether and the mysteries were never solved. At the inquest on the final victim, Detective Superintendent William Marchant said, 'I regret to say that at the moment there is no real suspect for the death of this woman.'[20]

The problem was that other prostitutes were frightened and co-operative in the aftermath of each killing but then went back to their twilight lives, moving from room to room and changing from name to name, until they vanished from the view of those who tried to protect them. In this series of murders, it might be doubted whether Elizabeth Figg, whose death pre-dated the next by four years, was a victim of the same killer. That the remainder were victims of the same murderer rather than a 'copy cat' was probable in the light of the evidence.

7

The Thames-side murders brought prostitution into the public eye as the normal lives of call-girls seldom did. Yet there were other and less hazardous ways of conducting business, increasingly associated with the growth of clubs. The 'nightclub' with its hostesses and other employees or hangers-on went back to the 1920s and Kate Meyrick's Forty-Three Club in Gerrard Street. In January 1955, Scotland Yard had stepped up the post-war campaign against what it saw as vice when Chief Superintendent Hewlett, two superintendents from Tottenham Court Road police station and fifty officers from West End Central raided ten establishments in a few days and took the names of 300 patrons in an attempt to frighten them away.

Almost without exception, clubs who employed hostesses made much of their policy that the girls were not allowed to date the customers. Having said this, most of them did no more about it. It was some relief when, in April 1960, the High Court ruled that for a hostess to smile at a prospective customer did not constitute insulting behaviour under the Metropolitan Police Act 1849.

Those whose establishments might have led to girls enticing men or men picking up girls were resolute in their defence of the propriety of such institutions. 'These girls at £15 a week were artistes,' the owner of Jane's Club told the Marylebone magistrate on 10 December 1959. He denied that they sat on the customers' knees wearing only G-strings or allowed men to undress them. They were never completely naked. In October 1960, to demonstrate their social conscience in such matters, the Nell Gwynne, Casbah and Panama clubs set up the Theatre Clubs Association, claiming to represent 250,000 members of the public, to enforce decorum before the law did it for them. From now on G-strings or sequins were to be a minimum dress requirement.

The members of such associations were not the problem. Elsewhere, for example, some of the dancers were very young. A fourteen-year-old girl was making £9 a week as a striptease performer in a West End club, having left a secretarial school because it was 'like a jail', and not liking the work she had then found in a coffee bar. Another fourteen-year-old was found in Foubert's Place, Soho, where hostesses served drinks on commission. She too had been performing as a striptease dancer, also for £9 a week, and was now suffering from 'a serious disease'. What the police called 'filthy photographs' and 'obscene' correspondence to a hostess were also found at the club, whose secretary was fortunate to escape with a fine of £115 for unlicensed music and dancing.[21]

In October 1960, when the owner of the Geisha Club, Old Compton Street, Soho, whose performances 'went beyond striptease', was fined £250, the prosecuting counsel seemed puzzled that the rules of a gentleman's club did not apply in respect of membership. 'Anybody could complete a form of membership', he complained, 'with no question of a proposer or seconder.' In the following month, another owner of strip clubs, Freddy's Club in Frith Street and the Tropicana in Greek Street, was allegedly guilty of 'an absence of frank communication between solicitor and client'. What this meant in plain English was that the defendant had fled abroad at the first sign of trouble.[22]

The limit on striptease itself was enforced in December 1960 with the prosecution of Soho's Raymond Revuebar, which claimed public support in the shape of 47,000 members. The acts objected to included 'Bonnie Bell the Ding Dong Girl', who danced with a minimum of little bells which customers were allowed to ring while she called out 'Dinner time . . . Supper time . . .', 'The Whip Sensation of the Century', in which a man whipped a woman while she lay on the floor, and Julia Mendez who danced with a snake coiled round her.

The club owner was to be convicted and fined £5,000 at London Sessions in April 1961. Yet it was the magistrate who perhaps asked the most pertinent question. When Sergeant Albert Corry described the performance he had witnessed, he explained that there was an audience of about 200 people and that he had attended the performance on five occasions. The Marlborough Street magistrate, Paul Bennett, inquired: 'Is it necessary for the police to go five times to these clubs to make sure of what they see? It is the one thing I never understand about these cases.'[23]

A fine of £5,000 on a club that was said to be taking £3,000 every week was hardly severe. On the other hand, where the circumstances warranted it, club owners were sent to prison. The owner of the Keyhole Club in Masons Yard was sentenced to a fine of £3,000, three months in prison and a further year in prison if the fine was not paid. In this case, however, the line between performance and prostitution seemed hardly visible. Special performances had been put on at 12.30 a.m. for clients paying £6 a ticket to participate in what the Chairman of London Sessions called a 'stew-house of vice'.[24]

The most important of the clubs were perhaps those that were never heard of in such circumstances, somewhere between the Revuebar and a dining club or nightclub with a floor show. One of these in 1958 was Murray's Cabaret Club, which had existed since the 1930s and where the showgirls who put on two nightly stage performances talked to the customers between them. In that year, one dancer was the most famous the club was ever to acquire, Christine Keeler. She first appeared there at sixteen in sequins and tiara, walking around with no clothes on, as she later described it to Lord Denning. Despite the policy of forbidding the girls to date the customers, which may have been merely a means of protecting the customers' reputations, there was nothing to prevent it. It was at Murray's that Christine Keeler first met and danced with Dr Stephen Ward.

What happened among the actors of the impending scandal between 1958 and 1963 was largely a matter of private and even secret association between them. It was the summer of 1963 which revealed to most people a world behind closed doors. It seemed that the entire nation became knowledgeable as to the roles of a mistress, a kept woman, a courtesan, a call-girl and a street walker, or those of the lover, the exploiter and the ponce. The involvement of the security services, a Soviet naval attaché, Cabinet ministers, the great and the powerful added seasoning to the dish but without the sex they were nothing. For readers and viewers, that summer was the voyeuristic thrill of a lifetime. It was perhaps the last time, for many people, that the newspapers were something to look forward to.

There had never been such a chance to see, through the journalist's peephole and the camera's eye, such a world of commercialized sex in high places, illicit couplings, erotic perversions, sexual secrecy, arts of procuring, a dance of predators and prey. Those who had never expected to read a government document in their lives hurried out in the autumn to make a best-seller of Lord Denning's report on 'The Circumstances Leading to the Resignation of the Former Secretary of State for War, Mr J. D. Profumo'. Millions bought copies of those newspapers which published every word of it. This was 'What the Butler Saw' on an astonishing scale and, ultimately, a turning point in the history of the vice trade. But rather than a mere peephole, the floodgates soon opened upon what was called, misleadingly, the Profumo Scandal.

8

Though the events of the scandal were precipitated by the conduct of the Minister of War in the Macmillan government, his part in what followed was almost incidental. Millions of other men must surely have felt how easily what had happened to him might have happened to them. His affair with an extremely pretty and engaging teenager had been over for more than a year before anyone who mattered knew that it had taken place. On 22 March 1963 he told the House of Commons, quite correctly, that he had known Christine Keeler though he had not been in touch with her since the end of 1961. He also added, incorrectly, that there had been no impropriety between them. In a later age, it would have been argued that whether they had been to bed together or not was no one's business but theirs and that the question of impropriety was a private matter. In the event, that question forced his resignation on 5 June. This marked the tragedy of an able and distinguished politician, who then turned that tragedy into a personal victory during his ensuing years as Warden of Toynbee Hall in London's East End.

With the departure of John Profumo, the man at the centre of the summer drama in 1963 was to be Dr Stephen Ward, a gifted osteopath and portrait painter, fifty years old. He had West End consulting rooms in Devonshire Street and a flat in Wimpole Mews. Among his contemporaries, he had known a good many of the famous, both as patients and as sitters, though he seldom knew them quite as well as he hoped the world would believe. There was a hint in him of Frank Harris, socialite and philanderer of an earlier generation. Harris had once recited to Oscar Wilde a list of all the houses where he had been the guest of a society hostess. 'Once,' said Wilde.

One aristocrat whom Ward certainly knew well was Lord Astor and, on Lord Astor's estate at Cliveden, he enjoyed the use of a cottage at a peppercorn rent. On the weekend of 8–9 July 1961, his guests at this cottage included Christine Keeler, who was then nineteen and lived with him at his flat in Wimpole Mews, and Captain Eugene Ivanov, the assistant Naval Attaché at the Soviet Embassy. In politics, Ward was naive but claimed a sympathy with the Soviet Union. He and Ivanov had discussed how they might find out if or when the British and Americans were going to arm West Germany with atomic weapons. Ward, despite his fifty years, also seemed adept at attracting girls in their teens and some were present when his party went to make use of the open-air swimming pool on the Cliveden estate. While they were there, a group of Lord Astor's guests arrived, including John Profumo, who saw Christine Keeler for the first time. The affair between them lasted for about five months and was conducted, in part, at the flat in Wimpole Mews. A number of other girls, including Mandy Rice-Davies and Vicki Barrett, who was a professional prostitute, either stayed at the flat or made use of it during this period.

The central figure in this ménage was Stephen Ward himself, politely described at the time as a 'deviationist' in sexual matters. He certainly picked up pretty girls of sixteen or seventeen and seduced them. That he procured them to be mistresses for his influential friends was possible, though at his trial the jury acquitted him on the two charges which related to procuring. That he attended parties which some might call 'orgies' was true and, indeed, these sometimes involved whipping or 'other sadistic practices' to which he was not averse. Perhaps more important still, he was Svengali to his young protégées.

Trouble began for the principal actors at the end of 1962, when a story reached the Labour MP George Wigg that Stephen Ward had asked Christine Keeler to find out from John Profumo when the Americans would deliver atom bombs to West Germany. George Wigg judged that this must be for the benefit of Captain Ivanov, who had always warned his English friends to be careful. 'Anything you say goes back to Moscow. Look out what you say.' Ward ridiculed the story, saying that the Minister of Defence would 'jump out of his skin' at such a question from the girl. Yet by the end of January there was a further threat to stability as Christine Keeler began negotiating the sale of her story to the *Sunday Pictorial*.

This was a story bearing the whiff of an underworld that smoked and dealt in cannabis, sold sex and, when necessary, shot or stabbed. In October 1961, Stephen Ward had taken Christine Keeler to the Rio Café in Westbourne Grove, where reefers were being smoked and where she met a West Indian, Lucky Gordon, who sold her some 'weed'. She subsequently left Stephen Ward and lived for a while with Lucky Gordon, then with another West Indian, Johnny Edgecombe, a convicted criminal. There had been a fierce argument between the two men and Edgecombe had slashed Gordon's face at the 'All Nighters' Club in October 1962, leaving a wound that required twenty-seven stitches. Christine Keeler decided the time had come to leave Johnny Edgecombe. During this period, Mandy Rice-Davies, who was then seventeen and had been the mistress of Peter Rachman, a notoriously unscrupulous property owner, went to live with Stephen Ward in Wimpole Mews.

In December 1962, Christine Keeler was visiting Mandy Rice-Davies at Ward's flat. While she was there, Johnny Edgecombe arrived in a minicab, wanting her back. He demanded to be let in and, when this was refused, tried to break the door down. Failing in this, he drew a gun and first fired several shots at the door lock, then fired in the air as Christine Keeler was looking down from the window. The police were called and he was taken into custody.

When his trial came on, Christine Keeler was to have been the principal witness for the Crown. Instead, she went to Spain and forfeited her £40 surety. In the absence of her evidence, Edgecombe was acquitted of shooting with intent to murder or cause grievous bodily harm, and of slashing Lucky Gordon. He was convicted of possessing a firearm with intent to endanger life and, perhaps in the light of previous convictions for stealing, living on immoral earnings and possessing dangerous drugs, was sent to prison for seven years.[25]

In consequence, rumours circulated in the Inns of Court of well-placed people who had paid to have Christine Keeler spirited out of the country during the trial, so that famous names should not be mentioned in her evidence. Once the trial was over, Stephen Ward's memoirs appeared in the *Sunday Pictorial* as 'The Model, MI5, The Russian Diplomat And Me'. These did not mention John Profumo and, again, that seemed to the public to be the end of the matter.

There followed what Lord Denning called two uneasy months until the Profumo resignation on 5 June. When that happened, Lord Denning, as a High Court judge, was asked by the Prime Minister to undertake an inquiry into the events leading to the resignation and into any danger to national security. 'I was determined', said Harold Macmillan afterwards, 'that no British government should be brought down by the action of two tarts.' Lord Denning found no danger to national security.

Yet he was not the only one to make inquiries. Though the security services had no further interest in Stephen Ward as a purveyor of secrets to the Soviet Union, Scotland Yard now interested themselves in the possibility that Christine Keeler and Mandy Rice-Davies had, in the technical sense at least, been earning a living as prostitutes and that, since they had both been residents at Wimpole Mews, Ward had been living on their immoral earnings. 'I am not, and never have been, a prostitute,' Christine Keeler told the court at Ward's trial and it was true she did not appear or behave like most people's idea of one. Moreover, it might seem absurd that a man with Ward's profession and income could be guilty of living on the two girls' earnings. 'If anything, she was living off me,' he said of Mandy Rice-Davies. But the law, of course, would require him to prove that he was not taking money from them.[26]

Ward's trial on three charges of living on immoral earnings and two charges relating to procuring took place at the Old Bailey in July, long before the more general scandal was forgotten. It did little to allay the rumours that were circulating of a Cabinet minister and his passion for little boys, of another minister who acted as a submissive maidservant at parties in a mask and apron, or of orgies involving members of the Cabinet and other public figures in the Cliveden swimming pool. The proceedings once again did much to inform the innocent. There was a two-way mirror in Wimpole Mews, so that guests in one room could watch a couple in bed without the couple knowing it. Until this trial it seems doubtful if most of the country had even heard of a two-way mirror. Then there were Mariella's Chelsea parties at which girls were whipped, or stories of chastisement meted out to England's finest by prostitutes at a pound a stroke.

Ward was depicted by his detractors as the spider at the centre of a web of seduction and depravity. Yet he was acquitted of both charges of procuring and of living on the immoral earnings of Ronna Ricardo and Vicki Barrett, two known prostitutes who had testified under police pressure at the magistrates court. However, he was convicted of living on the immoral earnings of both Christine Keeler and Mandy Rice-Davies. Common sense might suggest that he did not live on such earnings, for he gave or lent them money when they were his tenants at Wimpole Mews. Yet they had paid him rent with what were judged to be the proceeds of prostitution and he could not prove otherwise. Ward never knew that he had been convicted on these two counts. He was free on bail and had gone home after the judge's summing-up to take an overdose of drugs. He died on 3 August without regaining consciousness.

There was little doubt that the events of the summer had made members of the government seem individually absurd and collectively inept. The names of Cabinet ministers had been pinned to the worst of the rumours. They might not be true but many people, not knowing otherwise, assumed that they were. In this predicament, it seemed that the 'Establishment', as the newly popular term was, had looked for a scapegoat or an object of retribution and that Stephen Ward was a perfect fit. His conviction was probably not a disaster for the government but his death certainly was. He had been hounded to it, according to this argument, and was in danger of seeming a martyr to moral bigotry, as Oscar Wilde had been.

The Denning Report and the trial of Stephen Ward merely compounded the scandal. Lord Denning reported that there was no truth to the slanders and deplored the 'trafficking in scandal for reward' that had been permitted. A significant section of the public felt once again, in the courtroom riposte of Mandy Rice-Davies, 'He would say that, wouldn't he?' It was one occasion when no one was to be given the benefit of the doubt by public opinion.

There were many convictions for sexual offences after 1963 and yet there was a major shift in public attitudes. Men and women had seen the behaviour of their ruling class revealed in detail. They had seen what many regarded as an act of vengeance on Stephen Ward, while those who had brought about the scandal went unpunished. When their turn came to sit on a jury in a case of prostitution or brothel-keeping, where they felt that all concerned had been willing participants, they might recall that their leaders had behaved as badly or worse. They might acquit, where in a time of moral deference they would have convicted. In 1967, when certain forms of abortion and homosexual conduct were legalized, there was significant hostility to both. Those who disliked the legalization of homosexual conduct might feel that whatever the legal position of prostitution, it was a matter between a man and a woman. Perhaps they declined to criminalize it when what had lately been indecent conduct between two men had the sanction of the law and when extra-marital sex of all kinds had become not so much a problem as a fashion.

Vice was increasingly left to get on with its business, so long as it did not impinge on society or engage in conduct that was generally abhorrent. The events of the summer of 1963 were not forgotten but often remembered with nostalgia, as an older generation had looked back on the last golden summers of Edwardian England before 1914. At the time, however, it was uncomfortably evident that the government had been made a laughing stock before the entire nation and that the nation had made a show of itself before the world.

There were stern rebukes and calls for moral renewal. But national self-respect was not entirely crushed. Peter Ellis noted this in *Weekend* for April 1963, as all the trouble began. England might have lost the Ashes, industrial productivity might have nosedived, the nation's sportsmen were guaranteed to finish last in any international event. Yet despite gloom and shame, 'Our safe-breakers are the best in the world.' For all the other setbacks, there were few robbers who could beat an English robber at his best.

Four days after Stephen Ward's death, the summer scandals were wiped from the headlines. On Thursday 8 August, the nation woke to news of the greatest theft in British criminal history, carried out the previous night. At lunchtime it was known that £1,000,000 in used banknotes had been seized. Excitement grew as the total reached £2,595,997. Only £349,000 would be recovered. The haul would have bought an estate of suburban houses and forty years later would equal some £30,000,000. While their compatriots had sniggered or tutted in front of their television screens that summer, a group of dedicated professionals had gone for 'The Big One'. Their fame would eclipse the most lurid fantasies of Cabinet ministers in masks and pinafore aprons or Russian spies in Lord Astor's swimming pool.

13

Robbing the Mail

I

A T 6.15 ON Wednesday 7 August 1963, the overnight mail
train left Glasgow for London. It made a number of stops to
collect further mailbags, the last at Rugby, before the non-stop run
to Euston. Among its registered mail, it carried an exceptionally
large number of used banknotes. These had been paid into the banks
on Tuesday after a busy three-day weekend over the August Bank
Holiday. Banks throughout the country routinely returned to their
head offices in London those notes which were surplus to their
normal trading requirements. Parcels of £1,000 or £5,000 were sent
by registered post. Of the £2,595,997 only the numbers of 1,579
notes had been recorded.

Although mail also travelled in the guard's van of many passenger
trains, the mail train had no passenger coaches. It was hauled by a
diesel engine with a luggage wagon immediately behind it. Next to
the wagon was the HVP or High Value Packet coach and then ten
more coaches either used as mobile sorting offices or carrying mail
already dealt with. There were seventy-seven Post Office workers
on the train. A corridor ran through the rear ten coaches but the
High Value Packet coach and its five sorters were sealed off from
these and from the forward part of the train. A communication cord
ran through the entire train so that anyone could stop it in an emergency.

The train reached Rugby on time, picking up registered mail
along the way. It left for Euston at 2.17 a.m. At 3.03 it was forty
miles on, six minutes beyond Leighton Buzzard and approaching
Sears Crossing in Buckinghamshire. Jack Mills, the driver, saw that
a 'dwarf' signal ahead of him was at amber. This allowed him to
proceed but warned him that the next 'home' signal was at red.

The train reached the red 'home' signal but Mills and his fireman could see a further signal at green. This contradiction suggested a fault in the signal showing red.

David Whitby, the fireman, got down to call the signal box from the trackside phone. When he picked it up, the phone line was dead and he saw that its wires were cut. A man, whom he assumed to be one of the sorters, appeared and told Whitby to follow him. As he did so, Whitby was seized by several men in balaclava masks and rolled down the far side of the embankment. A hand was clapped over his mouth. A voice in the dark said, 'If you shout, I will kill you.'

The rest of the robbery was almost a formality. The rear ten coaches were quietly uncoupled. Jack Mills, who tried to resist the masked men on his footplate, was savagely coshed and permanently injured. A former train driver hired by the gang proved unable to manage the engine. Mills, whose head streamed with blood, was ordered to take the uncoupled front portion of the train half a mile forward to Bridego Bridge, where a strip of metal had been lodged across the track to ensure that it would stop. Only the baggage wagon and the High Value Packet coach were still attached to the engine. The guard and the sorters in the ten rear coaches assumed that the train had stopped routinely for the Sears Crossing signal. When at last they looked out, the engine and its two wagons had vanished. This first phase of the robbery took about two minutes.

At Bridego Bridge, the High Value Packet coach was attacked with sledgehammers and axes by more than a dozen waiting robbers. This was not the usual coach, which would have been better protected. There were three normal HVP coaches, but all were out of commission with one fault or another. Well-timed sabotage seemed likely. As the first window was smashed in, the five GPO sorters tried to barricade the doors with mailbags. A voice shouted, 'They're barricading the doors. Get the guns.' No guns were carried by the attackers but the bluff worked. A second window went in and several masked figures carrying coshes climbed in. Resistance in the HVP coach was soon over, the sorters lying face down at one end, as they had been ordered. Fifteen robbers formed a human chain to pass 120 mailbags, weighing more than a ton, down to a lorry parked on the quiet country road by the bridge. When the loading was complete, the lorry and the robbers disappeared into the night.

By now, the guard from the rear of the train had begun walking along the track, where he met a sorter with a GPO inspector from the front portion of the train coming back the other way. The guard used his lamp to stop a passing train. He reached Cheddington at 4.15 a.m. and phoned news of the robbery to Buckinghamshire police. Scotland Yard was called at breakfast time. Deputy Assistant Commissioner George Hatherill ordered a search of all empty houses, farms, and abandoned army or RAF camps within a thirty-mile radius of Sears Crossing. Police vans with loudspeakers toured the area, inviting information from the public.

It was reasonable to assume that the robbers had gone to earth somewhere within the area of the attack, as a precaution against early discovery of the crime and an inevitable police cordon, cutting them off from London. Among other informants in the next five days, John Maris, a herdsman, thought he had seen suspicious movements at the remote buildings of Leatherslade Farm, near the little village of Brill, several miles north of Thame and about ten miles west of Aylesbury. He and the local policeman called there. They found the farm unoccupied but there were several vehicles apparently abandoned outside and in one of the cellars lay some empty mailbags with postal and banknote wrappings. The robbers had long since fled but the shelves of the larder were stocked 'like a supermarket', as one officer described it. Upstairs were sleeping bags, blankets and pillows, all that might be needed if a long stay were necessary. The gang had evidently returned here direct from Bridego Bridge, presumably shared out the booty, and then left surreptitiously, one by one.

The organizers of the robbery had aimed at military precision, as if in imitation of the recent Jack Hawkins film, *The League of Gentlemen* (1960), in which a group of ex-servicemen led by their commanding officer staged a City robbery, using the lessons and methods of war. Bruce Reynolds, who saw himself as 'The Major', was dressed for that part, including a sand-coloured beret of the

Special Air Services with its badge and motto, 'Who Dares Wins'. The preparations were so businesslike that there had even been a preliminary robbery, apparently to finance the attack on the train.

Almost nine months earlier, on 27 November 1962, three BOAC security men had escorted a steel strongbox, measuring three feet by two, a few hundred yards from Barclays Bank at Hatton Cross to Comet House at Heathrow Airport. The box contained £62,500 for the airport's own bank. The three guards travelled in a car, followed by a security van, followed in turn by a radio car. The convoy drew up outside Comet House, the strongbox was transferred to a trolley and wheeled in. A lift, which was to take the guards and their box to the second floor, was not yet at ground level but they could hear it descending.

As the lift touched the ground floor, the doors opened, and five men in masks and balaclavas, carrying iron bars and pickaxe handles, sprang out at the guards. At the same time, three more attackers, two dressed as bowler-hatted 'City gents', came down the stairs. Two of the guards were knocked unconscious and the third overpowered. The robbers wheeled the money out to a van and two Jaguar cars, one containing a uniformed chauffeur with a woman sitting next to him, and set off at racing speed round the back of the airport hangars. They reached a locked but disued gate giving access to the A30. A man driving past saw them cutting the chains from the padlock with bolt-cutters. He tried to reverse his car into one of the escaping Jaguars. By this time, however, both getaway cars and the van were away, leaving skid marks on the tarmac and churned up grass at its verge, heading for London on the Great West Road. The whole drama was over in no more than two minutes.

A number of suspects were arrested. However, the investigation was not made easier by having to dress all those on identity parades in similar costumes: dark suits, bowler hats and false moustaches. Three men, including Gordon Goody and Charles Wilson of the future train robbery, were picked out. False moustaches and chauffeur hats were found at Goody's address. Both men were tried but acquitted early in 1963 for their part in the airport robbery; only the third defendant was convicted.[1]

By contrast, the aftermath of the 1963 robbery recalled Winston Churchill's colourful phrase, 'a panorama of ineptitude'. It was said that a team had been paid to wipe Leatherslade Farm clean, if necessary burning it to the ground. They failed to arrive. Fingerprints remained, including those of the racing driver Roy James. On the walls of his workshop, someone had scrawled the telephone numbers of Bruce Reynolds, Gordon Goody and Ronald Biggs, all well-known to the police. Bruce Reynolds was the reputed leader of the so-called 'South-Western Gang'. Fingerprints at the farm identified him, as well as Jimmy White, John Daly and Ronald 'Buster' Edwards, reputed leader of the 'South-Eastern Gang'. This indicated that a 'team' had been put together from various gangs and that, if the plot had leaders, Goody and Reynolds were the two most likely. Among other discarded items was Reynolds' SAS beret.[2]

Though the robbers had gone to earth, it was only a week later when the arrests began. This would have happened even without the evidence at the farm. A woman in Bournemouth rented a garage to Roger Cordrey, who insisted on paying three months in advance. He peeled the money from a very large wad of banknotes. The observant lady remembered the train robbery and phoned the police. Cordrey and a companion, William Boal, were questioned and Boal's shooting brake was searched. It yielded two bags stuffed with banknotes and a pillowcase full of banknote wrappers. Cordrey's house and flat were also searched. There was £141,000 in cash. For the police to say that they were not satisfied with the suspect's explanation of where so much money had come from was an understatement.

Buster Edwards, Bruce Reynolds and Jimmy White remained at large, even while the trial of the other principal defendants was proceeding at Aylesbury Assizes from January to March 1964. Seven men, including Charles Wilson, Ronald Biggs, Roy James and Gordon Goody, received concurrent sentences of twenty-five years for conspiracy to rob a mail and thirty years for armed robbery. Most of those in court were astonished by the severity of these terms as Mr Justice Edmund Davies announced them. Even a murderer's life sentence was in practice little more than ten years.

Long ago, however, Lord Goddard had insisted that the only remedy for the softer punishments implemented by the Criminal Justice Act of 1948 was longer sentences.

Among the three fugitives, Jimmy White grew weary of life on the run and gave himself up in 1966. By now the deterrent sentences had made their mark and he went to prison for only eighteen years. Buster Edwards, who surrendered by arrangement in the same year, received fifteen years. Last of all, in November 1968, Bruce Reynolds was tracked down to a house in Torquay, though he had spent most of his time as a fugitive in Europe, Mexico, the United States and Canada. Of his reputed £250,000 share of the mail robbery, he had only £6,000 left. Reynolds had a fair claim to being the mastermind and he went to prison for twenty-five years. If he was not the mastermind, at least he and Gordon Goody were the brains of the operation.

Others facing thirty years in prison sought desperate remedies. On the night of 12 August 1964, three of Charles Wilson's friends took ladders and scaled the outer wall of Winson Green prison in Birmingham. Their names were never revealed but, according to Bruce Reynolds, they were led by a Special Forces veteran of the Korean War, who was also a veteran of an Irish Mail robbery and the London Airport robbery of 1962. The three made their way to Wilson's cell, opening doors with duplicate keys which had somehow come into their possession. They overpowered the duty warder, gagged and bound him. Wilson put on the civilian clothes they had brought and the party left, locking the doors behind them to delay suspicion and pursuit. Wilson was caught again in Quebec in January 1968 and brought back to complete his sentence.[3]

Ronald Biggs made his escape from Wandsworth prison. His rescuers were led by Eric Flowers, a childhood friend who had been finishing a sentence in Wandsworth when Biggs arrived there. On his release, Flowers bought a furniture van and cut a hole in its roof, mounting what was described as a turret on top of it. During an exercise period in the prison yard, the van parked alongside the twenty-five-foot wall. The rescuers went up through the turret, level with the top of the wall, and threw a flexible ladder down to Biggs, who was waiting for it. Two other prisoners followed him, uninvited, as he scrambled up. From the top of the wall, they jumped to the van and down through the hole in its roof, landing on a mattress positioned to break their fall. They left in a waiting car.

Though hunted by the police and the press, found and lost again in Australia and then found in Brazil, Biggs remained at liberty for thirty-six years, until age and ill-health obliged him to return to England and prison in 2001. Even if crime did not pay in his case, at least this foot soldier of the robbery had enjoyed half a lifetime of freedom, to the frustration of those who sought to bring him back to captivity.

The story of the train robbery was one of which neither press nor public could hear too much. The events surrounding it seemed to justify the interest. Even during the trial itself, Mr Justice Edmund Davies had taken the unusual step of ordering the police to carry out round-the-clock surveillance on the families of the jurors while the verdict was being considered. Thirty-six officers were drafted in after a juror had been offered money to try and sway his colleagues towards an acquittal. In November 1965, as if to keep the pot boiling, a tip-off suggested that a thirty-strong rescue team was planning to get Roy James and Thomas Wisbey as well as Gordon Goody, the 'brains' of the crime, out of Durham Gaol's maximum security wing. It was reported that armed troops would now guard the men and, subsequently, that the 1st Battalion of the Lancashire Regiment had a machine-gun emplacement on the ten-foot high roof of a building in the prison. Public excitement was scarcely cooled in the following February, when the Chief Constable of Durham told the press that a full-scale military attack to free Goody was possible, 'even to the extent of using tanks, bombs and what I believe are known as limited atomic weapons'. Tanks could breach the prison wall and 'a couple of tanks could easily have come through the streets of Durham unchallenged'.

The reason for this scenario of tanks and tactical nuclear weapons, as well as the assurance that there was no likelihood of an early move from Durham for the three men, became apparent two days later. All three had been transferred to Parkhurst on the Isle of Wight within hours of the interview, well before the public or the press knew anything about it. The story told to journalists had been what was later known as 'disinformation'.

2

In 1963, opinion was divided between those who saw the train robbery as a cavalier Robin Hood crime and others who regarded it as a vicious assault, in which the greatest price was paid by the engine driver, Jack Mills, who had been brutally attacked, never worked again, and died in poverty seven years later. Though leukaemia was the immediate cause of his death, it did not help the robbers' case or enhance their Robin Hood image when some of them suggested that he was merely shamming or work-shy.

The division in opinion was delineated by Mr Justice Edmund Davies, in sentencing Roger Cordrey. 'Let us clear out of the way any romantic notions of daredevilry. This is nothing less than a sordid crime of violence inspired by vast greed.' He also called it 'a crime which in its impudence and enormity is the first of its kind in this country. I propose to do all within my power to ensure it will also be the last of its kind.'[4]

His second comment was open to question. The size of the robbery undoubtedly set a record, yet its admirers and detractors were wrong in regarding it as something quite new. In many respects it was an end rather than a beginning. There were to be greater robberies in the near future, larger sums of money would be stolen, but the idea of robbing railway trains or the mail in this way was soon as remote as Billy the Kid. Before the motorway age of the 1960s and the huge development of road freight, cash and even smaller consignments of gold or diamonds went by registered mail. This meant that it travelled by train. For almost twenty years after the war it was a temptation to the professional and the amateur alike.

There had been so many robberies of the kind in those twenty years that it was not surprising when some of the apparently ingenious elements of the 1963 plan proved to be mere copies. To stop the train in the first place, the robbers had put a glove over the green light of the 'home' signal at Sears Crossing. They had then wired a battery to the amber light of the preliminary 'dwarf' signal and another to the red light of the 'home' signal. Yet similar methods of stopping a train had been used at least twenty years earlier, certainly during the Second World War in South London. Those robberies were not violent and the aim was more modest. According to the railway police in 1942, by covering the green light at a junction and shining a light through red glass, it was possible to halt a train in the near total darkness of the blackout. This allowed wartime looters to swarm aboard and steal supplies of rationed or controlled goods. Neither the engine driver nor the guard, at opposite ends of an extended line of goods wagons, had much reason for suspicion until it was too late.[5]

As recently as 1960, there had been a series of mail robberies, two by the so-called 'Red Light Gang', between Victoria and the Sussex coast. Mailbags were routinely carried in the guard's van of these passenger trains. A passenger corridor passed down one side of this van, divided from the contents by a mesh partition with a locked gate. On the night of 20 September 1960, three men travelled as passengers on the 9.28 p.m. train from Victoria to Brighton. Their accomplices used a strip of metal to short-circuit the green signal at Patcham Tunnel. The train stopped at the red signal, 'faked' by these accomplices. The three men on the train, disguised in capes, entered the guard's van with a duplicate key and overpowered the guard. The leader was carrying a cosh. He told the guard to keep quiet and he would not get hurt. They threw him on to the floor and tied his wrists to an iron ring on the side of the van. Then they tied his feet. The raiders jumped down from the stationary train with six mailbags containing £9,000 in banknotes. The strip of metal was removed from the contacts on the signal, which changed to green, and the train went on its way. The guard was found, still tied up, by a porter at Preston Park, Brighton.

To compound the railway's embarrassment, a journalist repeated the process next day, without criminal intent. The lock of the guard's van was of so common and simple a type that the key with which he opened it had been bought at a garage for ten pence. The click of the lock opening was drowned by the sound of the train's wheels. The month before, robbers had got away with £7,500 from Victoria and had attacked a guard at Haywards Heath. Then, on 29 November, the 'Red Light Gang' reappeared, as the 7 p.m. train from Ore and Hastings travelled to London. At Battle Bridge Lane, near Redhill, the green signal had been put out of action by simply resting a penny across the short-circuiting wire. Even before the driver stopped for the faked signal, three masked men had entered the guard's van, overpowered its sixty-one-year-old occupant, tied him up, gathered twenty-four registered packets, and disappeared down a railway embankment in the darkness.

There were 150 passengers on the train who, apparently, saw nothing suspicious. Yet though the robbers left no fingerprints at the scene of the crime, they had been careless when sitting in their seats. The train was meticulously examined, fingerprints collected by the railway police and then checked by Scotland Yard. Two sets belonged to known criminals, one of whom had planned previous railway robberies and had been released from prison recently. The hunt lasted for more than a month. Then the Flying Squad raided a house in Chingford, where traveller's cheques from the robberies, as well as other stolen property, were found under the floorboards. The two wanted men, as well as three other men and a woman, were arrested. The three principals went to prison for terms of four to seven years.[6]

Yet the battle of the mail trains during the autumn of 1960 had not been one-sided. On the night of 11 November, the latest of a number of attempts was made to rob the Euston to Holyhead Irish Mail, while it was approaching Rugby. A locked door between the passenger section of this train and the front mail van was opened with a duplicate key, while the guard was on his way to the rear van, and three men went in. A fourth man kept watch beyond the door for the guard's return.

The intruders had brought a very large suitcase. They stooped over the mailbags and began to rip the canvas. Next to them was a small compartment for the guard to sit in, though they had already checked that he had left for the other end of the train. However, after two or three minutes Terence O'Malley, the leader of the robbery, walked across and looked into the compartment. He turned to the others and shouted, 'Get out quick! It's the law!'

The three men in the van rushed out through its door with O'Malley in the rear and several officers of a special squad of British Transport police close behind. There was a brief fight, ending with the arrest of the intruders. They went to prison for periods of five to ten years in January 1961. 'Fair enough,' O'Malley said, 'I've had a good run.' He had been jailed for four years in 1955 for stealing mail from the Euston to Holyhead train and after his release had been recognized again in 1959 by railway police in the Midlands. From then on he had been watched by officers from a special squad of plain-clothes railway police under Detective Inspector Bob Kerr.[7]

O'Malley and his accomplices had made a habit of travelling from London to the Midlands, carrying large light-coloured suitcases, and then travelling straight back. They soon attracted attention and were so closely watched that even the 'porter' who carried O'Malley's suitcase for him at Rugby was a railway detective. This detective informed Inspector Kerr that the suitcase seemed to have very little in it. When O'Malley deposited it in the left luggage office at Euston, it was opened and, as Kerr expected, had nothing but another light-weight suitcase inside it.

After this, a disguised radio van was parked outside O'Malley's London home to track his movements. Even when he took his wife to a Blackpool holiday camp in the summer of 1960, his neighbours in the next cabin were Kerr's detectives. There had been fourteen robberies on the line between London and Birmingham in that year, totalling £17,000 and including one haul of £14,000 in diamonds. They stopped after the arrest of the 'Irish Mail Gang'.

The post-war age of mail robbery ran from the Eastcastle Street hold-up in 1952 to the more famous robbery of 1963. Security in the mail, as in most other forms of carrying money, had been minimal in 1952 and improved very little in the immediate future. A total of 629 mailbags had gone missing in 1952, followed by 738 in 1953. It was a disquieting number, though the Postmaster General pointed out reassuringly that it was still a mere fraction of the

350,000,000 bags that had been sent. Yet theft remained so easy that in November 1953 a thief on the 3.25 a.m. train from London Bridge to Brighton had been able to saunter along to the unattended and unlocked guard's van, rip open a mailbag, help himself to £9,000 in banknotes and stroll away. The loss was not discovered until the train reached Redhill, by which time he had had ample opportunity to leave it.

Mail robbery was out of fashion by the end of the 1960s, yet the lack of security during its heyday had made it a temptation even to amateurs. Bags lay unattended on empty platforms in that more trusting age. Vigilance was so slack that in February 1953 two bullion boxes of silver coin were wheeled away from Paddington Station with the connivance of a porter. At Liverpool, an opportunist almost got away with a swindle which would have netted him a £60,000 dividend from Vernons Pools, now worth over £1,000,000. He travelled from his home in Sheffield to Liverpool on a Saturday afternoon, carrying a suitcase with a false bottom. The passenger train had no registered or high value mail but millions of weekly forecast coupons were on their way to the football pools firms, in this case to Vernons' office at Liverpool. Every mailbag on the train would contain at least a few. It was easy for the swindler to purloin one of the smaller bags and stuff it in his case while the guard was on the platform at an intervening stop with the van unlocked.

At Liverpool, he waited until the football results edition of the evening paper came on the streets and filled in his coupon with a winning line. It was simple enough to untie the mailbag in his suitcase, extract and open a Vernons envelope, already time-stamped before the matches were played, and slip his own coupon inside. The time-stamped envelope was gummed, resealed and returned to the mailbag, which he tied up again. Returning to Lime Street station, he walked down an unguarded platform, where the incoming mailbags lay. He put down his suitcase and released the bag from it, then picked up the case and walked away. With very little effort he had outwitted the vigilance of those guarding the mail. Unfortunately for him, he was a veteran claimant of race-track and football pools winnings to which he had no right.

Gambling was his profession and in the previous five years he had claimed winnings of £121,566, of which he was entitled to only £2,199. When his name appeared as the winner of £60,000, Vernons were suspicious and the envelope was examined. The culprit admitted his guilt and went to prison for five years. Had he found a trustworthy accomplice whose name was unknown to the pools promoters, he would probably have made his fortune in a single afternoon.[8]

This football pool forgery was one of many cases which showed the difficulty of guarding the railway system, to most of which the public necessarily had access. It was impossible to protect tens of thousands of miles of track or a thousand of the most vulnerable signals. Who would have thought it necessary to mount a day and night guard at the Sears Crossing signal in rural Buckinghamshire – and what good would a solitary guard be anyway? As for the main stations, sacks of mail were piled on platforms to which even the most dim-witted thief, especially wearing a borrowed porter's uniform, could find his way. Though there were mail trains which travelled through the night and acted as mobile sorting-offices, most of the mail, including registered mail, was carried by a thousand passenger trains every day. On most of these trains there was no one to protect the consignments except the guard who might be duped and, if necessary, overpowered.

Keys which would open the guard's van were distressingly easy to borrow or duplicate with the aid of a single dishonest employee. Railway pay before, during and after the war was poor. In 1939, the National Railway Staff Tribunal admitted that such commodities as butter, cheese and jam were beyond the means of railway workers and that fresh fruit was 'a luxury'. Not surprisingly, industrial relations in the industry were abysmal and morale poor.

In 1961 the problems of security and public access were well illustrated by a crime which, in itself, was relatively minor. On 28 March, the 9.47 p.m. suburban train left Waterloo for Teddington. At Clapham, an invalid in a wheelchair was lifted into the guard's van, accompanied by a male nurse who said gratefully to the guard, 'Thank you very much.' The invalid appeared to be 'really ill', head hanging down and hands twitching, with a rug over his knees. As the train left Clapham for its next stop at Earlsfield, the same invalid sprang from his wheelchair and joined the 'nurse' in attacking the guard. They knocked him to the floor and then tied his hands and feet. His cap was pushed over his eyes as he lay face down but he could hear them opening the mailbags amid such exchanges as, 'Here you are, there's another one,' answered by, 'It's got a green label, that's no good.'

Four minutes from Clapham the train stopped at a red signal, faked by other members of the gang. The invalid and the nurse threw their bags of registered mail from the train, jumped after them, picked them up and sprinted across Wandsworth cemetery to a car waiting on the main road. A search by the railway police found, unsurprisingly, a strip of metal by the track, used to short-circuit the green light of the signal. In response to the crime, British Railways Southern Region pointed out that to have an extra guard specifically to protect the mail on every train and others to protect the signals would mean employing a financially ruinous workforce of many thousands. The mail must take its chance.

The Post Office itself depended upon the honesty of its employees even more directly. Once again, the fact that a few of those working in the service were corrupt served only to highlight the honesty of the underpaid majority. Yet in the security of the mail, a few criminally inclined postmen could cause damage out of all proportion to their numbers. Most sums of money and acts of dishonesty were relatively small. Sometimes they were sufficiently ambitious to reach the status of a major crime.

In February 1954, the headlines reported a jewel robbery in the form of a daring one-minute grab behind Regent Street, outside the premises of the Goldsmiths' and Silversmiths' Company, which incorporated the royal jewellers, Garrards. A van from the Western Post Office in Wimpole Street was parked unattended but locked, while the driver and his assistant went into the nearby buildings. On their return, the driver told his assistant that a mailbag was missing, no doubt stolen by a thief with a duplicate key. This explanation was not at all hard to believe. The cutting of duplicate keys for Post Office vans had been publicly reported as part of the plan for the Eastcastle Street hold-up two years earlier.

In the present case, the driver of the van had a brother, a labourer who lived in Camberwell. After two weeks of investigation without results, Detective Sergeant Herbert Sparks of the Flying Squad concluded that the crime was probably an inside job. He detained the postman's brother as he was leaving a café in Camberwell and told him that he was under arrest. This suspect proved to be the weak link. As so often in these arrests, the man's anger at being 'grassed up' overcame the commonsense need for steady denial. Instead of denying all knowledge of the crime, he asked aggressively, 'How did you get on to me? I am wild over this. I have been shopped.'

He had not been shopped but because Sparks then encouraged him to think that he had been, the story of the robbery came out. The driver had left the van unlocked and the brother had taken away a mailbag containing packets addressed to West End jewellers. He was disguised as a postman in the driver's coat. This brother had then gone to a local fence, who ran a coffee stall in Peckham, and who was now 'shopped' in his turn. The fence had received the contents of twenty-two registered packets from the mailbag, including gold watches, pearls, a clock and silverware.

At the Old Bailey, the postman went to prison for five years, his brother for four years and the fence for twenty-one months. The Recorder added a few words for the benefit of any other amateur, or indeed professional, who thought that robbing the mail was easy. 'Perhaps it is not sufficiently widely known among those who might contemplate attacks on Her Majesty's mailbags that the offence of stealing a mailbag is punishable by as much as imprisonment for life.' Indeed, in July that year Lord Chief Justice Goddard reiterated the warning when two men who had ambushed and robbed a mail van in Surrey were sent to prison for fourteen years.[9]

3

As the prestige and rewards of mail robbery declined, it was wage-snatch gangs and safe-blowers who dreamt of 'The Big One' which might make their fortunes. In their isolated and maverick worlds, cat burglars, forgers, dopers of greyhounds or fixers of horse races shared that dream. All these classes often forgot the lesson of history that major crimes, like major wars, are far easier to get into than to conclude successfully. As in the case of the famous train robbery, the aftermath was decisive. Yet wage-snatchers and safe-breakers plotted coups to set them up for life or, in the case of the wage-snatchers, even for a foreseeable year or two of leisure. Others believed that they had used theft as a way of quitting crime and going into legitimate business, financed by the proceeds. It seldom seemed to be the result.

The rewards of theft in the last quarter of the century would dwarf the 1963 train robbery. They included an estimated £8,000,000 from the Bank of America vault in Mayfair in 1975; £3,500,000 in silver bullion hijacked en route for London docks in March 1980; £7,000,000 from the Security Express headquarters in Shoreditch on 14 April 1983; the £26,000,000 Brink's-Mat bullion robbery at Heathrow in November that year, and a sum estimated at between £30,000,000 and £40,000,000 in jewels, bullion and cash from the Knightsbridge Safe Deposit Centre in 1987. To most people the sums were meaningless and some totals could only be estimated. With strongboxes in a vault, for example, it was impossible to tell accurately what the total might be. Those whose boxes contained proceeds of theft, drug dealing, tax evasion or money laundering were unlikely to invite questions by admitting the true value.

Most of those responsible for such robberies were caught, even if the cash or bullion was not recovered. Once caught, they went to prison for long terms. By the 1980s, the gentle days of the quiet-as-a-ghost railway robber or the patient lock-picker were no more than a memory. The guardians of Security Express and Brink's-Mat were subdued by threats of castration or were doused in petrol and shown a lighted match. Those with a knowledge of the past might lament how far the underworld had degenerated since the Bidwell brothers removed over £100,000 from the Bank of England in 1873, some £25,000,000 in modern terms, and did it so kindly that the bank was unaware of its loss for several weeks. To such men, the Security Express and Brink's-Mat robbers would have seemed like ham-fisted bruisers with no sense of style, a disgrace to the profession who, if they were caught, deserved to be.

14

Cosh and Carry

FROM THE END of the war until the 1970s most urban robbers saw their target as cash in transit. They coveted money carried on foot or in a car by a couple of wage clerks, even in an armoured truck. A minority, more skilled and ambitious, aimed at cash or valuables in a safe or a strongroom. A night or an entire weekend of skilful wrenching, hammering, burning or blowing might be spent in extracting the contents.

Street robbery of whatever kind was the most common form of violent theft. For a quarter of a century after the war, Britain at the end of the working week was a wage-robber's dream. It was an age when bank accounts remained a middle-class privilege and the great majority of workers expected to be paid weekly in cash. Those who were responsible for organizing the collection and delivery of the cash learnt, year after year, to come to terms with the more rapacious and violent post-war world. In December 1956, American Express lost £12,000, almost £200,000 in modern terms, when their wage-carriers were attacked on foot at 10.30 a.m. on a pay-day morning outside the National Provincial Bank in Ruislip High Street, en route for a major USAAF base. Two of these robbers were caught and sent to prison for seven years. Eighteen months later, the American Express wage-carriers were attacked again on foot. It was also 10.30 a.m., also on a pay-day morning outside the same National Provincial Bank in Ruislip High Street, en route for the same destination. On this occasion, however, the wage-bag was saved by a sixty-three-year-old USAAF master-sergeant. He saw a robber cosh the man with the money and swiftly coshed the robber in his turn.[1]

In the immediate post-war years, most firms were content to

allow wages to be fetched on foot from the bank each Friday by one or two male or female clerks, or even by odd-job men who were frequently in their sixties and had retired from other employment. Believing that streets which were familiar must also be safe, these sacrificial victims walked the same route or used the same vehicles, usually at the same time each week. They were invariably attacked when walking back with the wages or in the short distance from the bank to a waiting car. Yet even the robbery of other firms had little effect in persuading the rest to change their ways.

The post-war predators ranged from small-time thieves thinking big to the hard men who were prepared to take on an armoured truck. Some 'gangs' were in truth no more than a group of street-corner louts who saw an easy way to a few hundred pounds, at a time when £5 was a good weekly wage. The robbery was often casual, in the sense that the youths found themselves short of money and so planned and carried out the attack on the same day. These were the unskilled labourers of crime. When three wage-snatchers, aged nineteen to twenty-three, arrived outside the National Provincial Bank at Ealing Broadway on 31 March 1950, they had no idea that their movements had already attracted the attention of the CID and that the window cleaner working his way down the road was Detective Inspector Peter Sinclair. They had been identified because they were acting suspiciously and were recognized from previous convictions. None of them was armed.

When they were arrested for loitering with intent to commit a felony, the eldest admitted that they had come to snatch a wages bag from whoever came out of the bank with one. Surprisingly, his accomplices were merely 'two other men whom I know slightly'. The second youth insisted that the eldest was 'a stranger to me'. He explained that 'Me and Den were the lookouts. We were to give the tip to the big fellow Charles. He was going to take the money and we were going to meet on a bus and divide it.' It was not so much a plan as an opportunistic impulse to finance his weekend.[2]

Unlike a safe-blowing or a train robbery, wage-snatches required little skill and no finance. The pattern of the theft varied as little as the routine of the wage-carriers. A car would be stolen just before the attack. Weapons were carried by two or three men, usually coshes and iron bars, bags of pepper by the early 1950s or water pistols and plastic bottles filled with ammonia to blind the wages clerks and their escorts. Increasingly, as the banks employed security vans and guards in the 1960s, the professionals armed themselves with guns and the casual robbers turned to other forms of theft. Once the robbery was over, the thieves would run for their stolen car, where one man had been left at the wheel for a fast getaway, drive a short distance to where their own car was waiting, abandon the stolen vehicle and disappear with the loot. Masks were usually worn, at first no more than a scarf across the mouth and chin, then a nylon stocking drawn over the head with the features compressed to a gorilla-like distortion, finally rubber party-masks which added a bizarre malevolence to the attack.

Small-time thieves in the immediate post-war years usually came away with hundreds rather than thousands of pounds. Yet some were right to think big. On 1 December 1949, four men targeted three clerks from Colville's steel works in Motherwell, as they were about to enter a taxi with the firm's wages outside the Commercial Bank of Scotland. The robbery was over within seconds. Before the clerks could get into the taxi, two men in an adjoining shop doorway drew revolvers, held them up and snatched the three bags of money. They ran to a waiting car about thirty yards off and drove away. There were two more men in the car and it bore false number plates. The haul on this occasion was in £5, £1 and ten shilling notes. It amounted to £17,600 and its comparative value was the weekly wage of 3,500 workers, enough to keep all the robbers for the next twelve years. As time went by, it would seem incredible that a firm of such importance had trusted its wages to three clerks and a taxi.

When employers abandoned the practice of fetching wages on foot, the opportunity for the Friday gangs narrowed but most thieves proved themselves equal to the challenge. They became increasingly audacious, concentrating their attention on the short distance between the bank and the firm's car or even on a well-frequented route from a nearby bank or a wages office to the firm's main building. The office manager of Sir Robert McAlpine and his driver were coshed by two men with iron bars as they crossed a few yards of pavement from the Southwark branch of the Midland Bank, on the corner of Blackfriars Road and Stamford Street, in March 1950. An attaché case with £1,900 in wages for construction workers at the Bankside power station was snatched. A lorry tried to block the thieves' car some distance away, whereupon three men jumped out and scattered while their driver carried on. The money and the stolen car were lost in the maze of side streets on the South Bank.

During the 1950s the wage-carrier on foot was progressively replaced by 'bank cars' or 'wages cars'. The scheme was intended to protect money in transit, leaving only the few yards between the car and the bank at one end. Where possible, the car would be driven into the firm's premises on its return. The clerk with the wages was to be accompanied by two or three other employees, stalwart enough to see off any attack. Protected from the outside world, the money would be safe inside the car. Such was the plan.

It was a failure from the start, circumvented by the robbers in short order. As usual, they stole a car just before the assault. Using this, they rammed the wages car to a halt at the most convenient spot on its route. The vehicle which had appeared to offer protection now imprisoned those sitting inside it. Crouched in the damaged interior, it was impossible for them to get out, as the hooded figures of the robbers surrounded them, or to fight back while pickaxe handles smashed in the windows and showered them with broken glass. As an experience, it was said to be far more terrifying than being attacked on an open pavement. The attaché case was easily wrenched from the sitting clerk and, if the gang had noticed from observation that the case was usually attached to his wrist by a light chain, they brought bolt-cutters to cut through the metal links.

Worst of all, a false sense of security encouraged bank cars to carry larger sums of money, sometimes deliveries by the bank itself to two or three firms. In Sheffield, a four-man gang with coshes and jemmies got away with something far larger than an individual wages snatch when they grabbed £50,000 in 1959 from an Austin used to carry money between branches of William Deacon's Bank. All the attackers had to do was to force the car on to the pavement with their stolen vehicle, smash in the windows, beat the occupants with coshes, and jemmy open the boot. As so often, the robbery was over before any potential witnesses would have realized what was going on.

In its early stages, the idea of a wages van offered little improvement. Indeed, the first of these were three-wheelers normally used by dairies, which were more vulnerable than a car. Even a four-wheeled van was little protection against attack. A common form of robbery was to ambush a firm's van at traffic lights or else to ram it as bank cars were rammed, then to enter it by the doors at the back. These were easily jemmied open, while the driver and escort were imprisoned in the front seats. Once again, the rewards might be far greater than mere wage-snatches. On 15 May 1957 two robbers caught a British European Airways van at traffic lights on the Great West Road, on its way from Heathrow. Without harming the two men inside, they forced their way in at the rear of the van and came away with 600 gold bars valued at £20,119. It was the disposal of the gold which led to their arrests. They refused to reveal the whereabouts of the bullion. One man went to prison for eight years and one for seven. The Recorder of London Sessions remarked of the lost gold, 'It is very important that it should not be possible, where a robbery of this kind has taken place, that anybody should enjoy the proceeds of crime until a substantial interval of time has taken place before they can reap the reward of their efforts.'[3]

This so-called Brentford Gold Robbery was one of many which illustrated the defects of the average 'traveller's van' when used to carry money. There had been a similar robbery of £22,000 from such a vehicle in Ipswich, on its way to the bank from Ipswich Co-Operative Society shops. Two men in another van, their faces masked by Ipswich Town football scarves, drew alongside. At the time, both vehicles were moving at walking pace across a car park. The driver and his passenger heard the sound of their van's rear doors being forced open, then saw a man climbing into the back and throwing out bags of money to his companion. By the time the driver of the Co-Op van could get out, the thieves were back in their own vehicle, moving off. He drove after them, caught up and rammed the rear of their van, only to fracture his radiator and be brought to a halt. He was just able to see them return to the car park, jump on to two motorbikes with the bags of money and disappear.

323

Drivers or guards of such vans were no better protected than the occupants of wages cars. A van from the Handley Page Aircraft Company on its Friday run through Cricklewood in September 1960 was stopped by a black car which drew in front of it. Three men in the van were attacked by five others with coshes and pepper. The guards found themselves trapped in the vehicle, while the driver was seized from behind and pinned in his seat. 'If you give any trouble, you'll end up on a mortuary slab,' said one of the robbers breezily before he laid the driver unconscious with a vicious cosh-blow to the back of the head.

2

Despite the introduction of armoured trucks in the late 1950s, a limited number of bank cars survived through the next decade and with them the bank-car robbers, many of whom also failed to move with the times. In an age of Special Patrol Groups and Regional Crime Squads the Friday afternoon wage robbery was becoming an anachronism, a refuge for the maladjusted. One of the last and most humiliating attacks was in January 1968 in what might have seemed an easy assault. A bank car coming down Baring Street, Islington, was stopped by a red Jaguar which pulled out from the kerb and braked sharply causing a collision. Three men with sawn-off shot-guns jumped out of the Jaguar, surrounded the bank car and ordered its occupants to hand over the money or be fired on. The money was handed over in an attaché case. However, the thieves either did not know or did not care that most bank cars were now shad-owed by the police. In consequence, a police van with siren active and lights blazing roared down the street towards them.

The robber who was holding £8,000 in the attaché case dropped it. Two others jumped a wall and landed on the canal towpath, throwing away their weapons as they ran. The man who had dropped the money sprinted down the street, away from the police vehicle, past a Friday afternoon bus queue. Two miniskirted girls in the queue, carrying suitcases, threw the cases at him and tripped him up. Joined by a middle-aged woman in sensible tweeds, they ran across and all three sat on the struggling robber, indifferent to his screams of 'I'll kill you for this!' He was rescued by the police and taken into custody.

By 1968 attacks of this kind were the province of mavericks and amateurs. Bank cars were increasingly replaced by the vans of Securicor, Security Express, Armoured Car and their competitors. The cars that remained carried smaller sums of money than the security vans and the temptation to attack them had been considerably reduced after the introduction of the Special Patrol Groups in 1965. Yet encountering an SPG was not the worst that the robbers faced.

On 23 September 1965 there had been a £32,000 payroll attack at the junction of Rosebery Avenue and Havelock Road, off Tottenham High Road. As the bank car turned the corner it was rammed by an Austin pulling out from the kerb. An escorting police car was immediately behind and was in turn rammed by a second carload of thieves at its rear, driving it into the back of the bank car. Two policemen and four wage-carriers fought twelve robbers carrying knives and one armed with a pistol. One of a group of men resurfacing the road drove his steamroller into the battle but arrived too late. The thieves grabbed a case with £32,000 in wages, ran to a parked car and a Dormobile and drove off, leaving the wage-carriers injured and a policeman with a fractured skull.

The freedom of the robbers lasted for only a few hours. They had been identified by the three policemen. In the following year the ringleaders appeared at London Sessions and were convicted of armed robbery. The Recorder described their attack on the wages car as nothing less than 'armed rebellion' against the state. In January 1965 he had denounced 'criminals conducting war just like generals', in the case of a gang armed with axes, pickaxe handles and coshes who staged a violent robbery of £8,000 from members of a loan club in a South London church hall. The sentence for that had been ten years. In the later case of the bank car, the Recorder dealt with the three defendants as armed rebels by sending two of them to prison for fourteen years each and the third for sixteen years. From this point, those who thought wages an easy target had also to think of the SPGs and sixteen years as the tariff. A £2,500 share of cash was not worth the best years of one's life in prison.[4]

As bank cars and vans gave way to the armoured trucks of security firms, young pavement robbers tested the alternative of wage-snatches on a firm's premises. Because there was a risk of being trapped in the building, most of the youths went heavily armed.

Weekends when the money for annual holidays of larger firms would be in the office were a favourite time, and in the summer of 1970 the wage-office snatch seemed an epidemic. A masked gang burst into the accounts office of Hawker Siddeley at Walthamstow on Friday 17 July and came out with £18,000, the double wages for 750 workers. Next Friday, another £18,000 was taken by four men in masks, possibly the same gang. This time they smashed in the wages office door of Woolf Electrical Tools at Ealing. Two of them sprayed the female staff with ammonia, temporarily blinding them and putting them in hospital with burns. The others kept order with a sawn-off shotgun and a revolver. On the same afternoon, three robbers held up the wages office of the London Electrical Manufacturing Company in Hammersmith, escaping with £11,000.

Even firms of size and prestige were not safe from this series of attacks. On 4 September, the target was Sainsbury's head office in Stamford Street. At first sight, an attack on a well-known company by four men in white masks might seem preposterous. However, they were all carrying Sten guns, the British 9-mm sub-machine-gun of the Second World War, capable of firing 550 rounds a minute and of killing everyone in the building. The cashiers obediently lay on the office floor, while the men in white masks scooped £15,000 off the table into a sack. They escaped in a stolen Rover 2000 which was, predictably, found abandoned on the far side of the Thames.

Some wage robberies depended increasingly on deception. On 6 May 1958, a coach hired by the Westminster Bank from a private contractor was halted by a red van in Westbourne Park Road, Kensington. The driver was seized, bound and gagged, then forced into the van. His place and uniform were taken by one of the attackers. The coach stopped at the head office of the Westminster Bank in the City, where a bank messenger got on, carrying £11,835 wages for the Thames Board Mills. The bogus driver helped to load the money. There was a stop in Threadneedle Street where a second messenger got on, carrying £31,000 in wages for two firms at Purfleet, Van Den Burg and Jurgens. The coach reached Stepney, turned into a side street and pulled up. The red van drew up beside it. Five men from the van with pickaxe handles coshed the coach passengers, loaded £43,000 into the red van, put the coach driver back on his vehicle and drove off with the wages for about 3,500 workers.

As if to commemorate the first anniversary of this robbery, a British Railways van was targeted in Stratford, East London, on 6 May 1959. It contained four cashiers and three guards delivering wages. The driver was surprised to be overtaken in Angel Road, Stratford, by a Wolseley police car, which pulled in ahead of him and signalled to him to stop. There were two uniformed officers in the car, one of them from the railway police, and three in plain clothes. The senior uniformed officer identified himself as Chief Inspector Simpson of Scotland Yard. He told the van driver that information had been received of an armed hold-up, planned to take place a short distance ahead. The railway van was assumed to be the target and the police were lying in ambush. He then told the van driver to get into the back of the police car.

When the railway driver hesitated, Inspector Simpson took him firmly by the arm. A second policeman came to assist, and the driver of the police car said, 'Get him out – he's involved in the hold-up.' The van driver was pushed into the rear of the Wolseley and the other railway workers were ordered out of the wages van. The police then jumped into it and drove off. Too late, the railway van driver turned to one of his companions and said, 'Here, mate. We've been done. We've been robbed.' The only consolation was that the 'policemen' had picked the wrong wages run. This was not the main delivery and the van held only £1,366. Next day they would have got £50,000, the wages for 4,000 staff.

3

The conflict between banks who held money and robbers who were determined to get their hands on it resolved itself ultimately into an arms race. Most firms in the 1950s still stopped short of employing security guards to carry their payrolls. Yet the decade saw the introduction of such deterrents as the 'screaming siren' bag. When under attack, the clerk or guard could activate a device on the bag of banknotes which emitted a 'klaxon howl'. It was no true deterrent at all. In November 1957, the first gang to encounter it were attacking the wages car of Elliott Brothers, electrical and mechanical engineers of Lewisham. They coshed the wages clerk, cut his wrist chain and simply drove off, indifferent to the howling of the bag. Their haul was £11,200. In a similar attack, the robbers ripped out the cash and threw the wailing bag over a fence on to waste ground as they left.

An equally unsuccessful variant was the 'smoking bag'. The day after it went into use in June 1962, two thieves waited in a Jaguar outside an Ipswich brewery for a car carrying the wages and the cashier. Wearing duffel coats and hoods with eye-slits, they threw a hammer into the windscreen of the car, snatched the bag, and drove off unperturbed by the trail of smoke.

A more effective device was introduced by Securicor in 1961 as the 'dye-gun'. It was first used when three of the firm's guards were carrying £8,000 in wages by car from Gravesend to Maidstone on a foggy November morning that year. They noticed a black Jaguar keeping pace just behind them. The Securicor driver telephoned the other car's details to his London headquarters, who in turn informed the Kent police. Presently, the Jaguar drew alongside and forced the Securicor car off the road. Confronted by four wage-robbers, the Securicor men produced what looked like powerful firearms and activated them, spraying the attackers and their car with indelible yellow powder. The sight of the mystery weapon and its bursts of yellow powder unnerved the robbers who ran for their car and drove off.

In March 1961 the Metropolitan Police belatedly issued to firms twelve rules for carrying wages. Routes must be varied; wage-carriers must have an escort; escorts should be robust and reliable; the route should be known in advance and those taking it should not dawdle; they should walk against the flow of pedestrians to reduce the risk of being attacked from behind; draw wages only in normal banking hours; use several people to carry money, concealed on them and not in bags; if bags were used they should be chained to the body; alarms on bags or waistcoats made to carry money should be used; suitable transport must be employed and the vehicles varied; registration numbers of suspect vehicles were to be noted, as was the description of anyone who appeared to be keeping watch.

Such advice, like the screaming bag and the smoke bag, became redundant as more businesses turned to the security firms. In December 1962, Securicor, Armoured Car and Security Express formed the Industrial Security Association to promote standards acceptable to the police, the public and those whose money they carried. By September 1970, these vans were a familiar sight on the streets of towns and cities. They were also noticed in the columns of the financial press which that month described Keith Erskine's Securicor as a big name in British business. It was an apt, if ironic, comment on the progress of crime in the post-war world.

The time when security firms would run a number of the nation's prisons had not yet come. Meantime, the deployment of guards and armoured vans was a sensitive matter because the companies appeared to many people as private police forces – if not private armies. As it happened, they were not new. Securicor, the pioneer among the firms, was directly descended from Night Watch, founded in 1935. It then consisted of a patrol of twelve guards on bicycles who were paid to provide security at night for residential areas of Mayfair, Hampstead and St John's Wood. Even this was too close to a private police force or army for the Labour leader, George Lansbury, who described it as 'the first faltering steps down a road to fascism'. From 1953, as Securicor, the firm's speciality was industrial security. By the 1960s it was identified with bank deliveries and the carrying of cash in general. Its first important business rival, Armoured Car, appeared in 1957, followed by Security Express, a subsidiary of De la Rue.[5]

The existence of such firms would certainly not stop robberies but they would require robbers to use far more sophisticated methods or greater violence than most seemed capable of in dealing with the challenge of helmeted guards and armoured vans. But what would happen when armed guards and armed robbers faced one another?

The dangers of gunfire on the streets were illustrated in 1961 by an attempted robbery in Bow. The target in this case was a security van belonging to Glyn Mills Bank, with £100,000 in wages for six gasworks, some £1,250,000 by modern values. On 14 December, the van left Lombard Street carrying in the back two guards, a cashier and a policeman with an Alsatian dog. It reached Turner's Road in Bow at about a quarter to ten. Before it could turn into Bow Common Lane, en route for the North Thames Gas Board's works, a red lorry ahead of it stopped, then reversed at full speed into the front of the bank van, trapping the driver in his cabin. A moment later, another van rammed it from the offside and hemmed it in.

The four men in the rear of the bank van, with the £100,000 in six brown leather bags, felt the impacts and then saw the two windows in the rear doors of the van being smashed in. Chains were run through these two gaps and attached to a minibus parked behind the van. There was a loud tearing of metal as the minibus hauled at the chains and wrenched the doors clear. In crash helmets and gas masks, eight attackers confronted the two guards, the cashier and the policeman. The leading robber was carrying a 14lb sledge-hammer to quell any resistance. At this point one of the bank guards, who was standing astride the six leather bags of money, produced a .22 revolver and fired five shots at the gang. One of them shouted, 'Beat it, they're shooting!' and the thieves ran for their minibus. One of them was holding his arm but it seemed that none of the others had been wounded. Harry Wright, the robber who had been hit, was not caught but was said to have died of his injuries.

One guard had had a gun and used it. The other bank guard was also armed but had no chance to fire before the robbers ran away. However, as the hero of the hour said, 'We always carry guns.' The City policeman and his dog had leapt out in pursuit of the attackers but had been no match for the eight fugitives. There was no doubt that the guards had faced serious injury and, indeed, the robbers had brought their own brand of tear gas to smoke out the occupants if the van doors remained in place. It consisted of a gas cylinder attached to a container of cayenne pepper and face powder.

Though Harry Wright's fate was not yet known, questions were asked in Parliament as to how many security guards were permitted to carry guns and when they were entitled to use them. There were murmurs of the danger posed by 'Chicago in London', as the two sides shot it out in the streets. Archbold's *Criminal Pleadings*, the guide for most police authorities of the day, held that if one person attempted to kill another, on or near the highway, and was killed himself in the attempt, his killer was entitled to an acquittal. A man who faced death or serious injury to himself or others was justified in killing the assailant.

A more practical consequence of the gunfire in Turner's Road was that criminals who went armed in any case with sledgehammers, coshes and iron bars when they attacked wage-carriers now decided that they had better carry guns as well. It seemed the only way to match the new security and, even if murder were committed, after 1964 there was no danger of being hanged. A life sentence of ten or fifteen years was no more than some of the harsher terms being imposed for armed robbery. By now, the theft of money in transit had become the province of attackers who were prepared to plan and prepare in detail and go equipped accordingly, like the train robbers of 1963, rather than of opportunist thugs with a cosh and a stolen car.

4

In the end, the security firms got the better of their enemy, to the extent that their precautions became more than a match for all but the most resourceful and ruthless. Thereafter, successful robberies were usually of large sums of money and often the work of criminals as well known in the underworld as any of the train robbers. Yet it was frequently the ambitious robbers who were caught and the modest who escaped. A £20,000 payroll might be quietly and gradually spent whereas £200,000 of bullion was not to be disposed of without fencing, rumours and underworld blackmail.

Though they could not compare with the famous train robbery, the late 1960s saw two robberies which set new records, one for the biggest theft from a security van and another for the biggest bank robbery. On 1 May 1967, £711,000 in gold bullion, belonging to N. M. Rothschild, was taken in an attack on a Security Express armoured truck at Bowling Lane, Clerkenwell. The firm had already lost £250,000 in gold bars four years earlier, when thieves slipped in behind a security van at a Finsbury bullion broker, seized their chance to overpower the firm's guard, and drove the gold away in their own van. In 1967, the royal blue van was hijacked in Clerkenwell and driven off with its crew of three locked in the back. It was abandoned some hours later in Finsbury. The crew had been beaten and suffered ammonia burns. The 140 gold bars had been transferred to another vehicle in the garage of a disused service station in Holloway.

It was an unsatisfactory case, in that the full story was never told. Of the £711,000, sixteen bars valued at £97,000 were traced to Switzerland a month later. Six of the bars were recovered but ten, valued at £67,000, had already been melted down, or cut up, and sold. The proceeds were paid into bank accounts in England. Four of these bars with their numbers hammered out had been bought by a Swiss bank and sent for smelting to a foundry on the borders of Switzerland and Italy.

The small fry who were caught were very small indeed. There was no doubt that some had been involved in the payment of Swiss money to English accounts, the question was whether their involvement was innocent or not. Others were not arrested until three months after the raid. One of these had bought a Gelenkemp electric furnace soon after the robbery and traces of gold were still in it. There had been ample time to melt down and recast the bars into smaller ingots. A former speedway rider and his fiancée were arrested in August when the car in which they were travelling to France was found to contain twenty-six gold ingots in its chassis. The rider admitted receiving the gold but denied that it came from the robbery. He went to prison for four years, his fiancée for six months.

Two more men were arrested at Victoria Station on their way to Dover. One of them had forty-five gold bars hidden in a special waistcoat made by the speedway driver's fiancée. The bars could not be identified as Rothschild's. The carriers were charged with exporting gold which they knew to be stolen but there was still no proven link with the bullion robbery. Indeed, a further search turned up a small cache of military arms which suggested that this venture, wherever the gold came from, was connected with the purchase and smuggling of arms to Biafra during the Nigerian civil war.

As the result of an undercover police operation, one ten-inch gold bar in its original state and valued at £500 was recovered. Scotland Yard's detective inspector in the case was the future Chief Superintendent Jack Slipper – 'Slipper of the Yard' and hunter of Ronald Biggs. On 26 July, with Detective Sergeant Peter Boorman posing as a fence, he penetrated the bullion plot as far as an East End flat in Powerscourt Road, occupied by two alleged receivers who called themselves 'Tony' and 'Alf'. Boorman's cover was that 'My father is a jeweller in Victoria and is in a position to dispose of anything like this. He can supply the ready cash providing the goods are genuine. I have come to do the business because he doesn't like showing his face.' Tony then explained that he could supply the gold but that it was not on the premises. 'I can get only one bar at a time. If you don't mind I would rather meet some-where else.' It was also said that the gold had been buried and was still in bars, which suggests that some of it might not have been melted down before the end of July.

Two nights later, Slipper led a raid on the house in Pinner where the two receivers lived. The door was half opened by Tony, who then tried to slam it shut. By that time, Slipper's foot was in the gap and he burst through with Sergeant Boorman. Improbable though it might seem, Tony was alleged to have said, 'You have got me bang to rights.' The house was searched and the bar of Rothschild's gold was found. Asked by Slipper where it came from, Tony replied, 'I'd get my ears cut off if I told you that.' It was as far as the case went. One other man was charged a fortnight later with conspiring to rob the security van but no case was proved against him.[6]

The last major raid of the decade in February 1970 set a record for cash stolen from a bank building. At £237,000 it was still no match for the train robbery, though it had an additional importance in its creation of a species known as the 'Supergrass'.

Barclays Bank, Ilford, received very large deposits from a nearby

Tesco supermarket but not in every delivery. A man who had observed this also noticed that, when the large deliveries were made, a red Mini arrived at the bank first, as if to alert the manager. He passed this information to a friend whose relative worked for the security company. This informant and two of the guards then conspired with a group of nine professional robbers, including the future informer 'Bertie' Smalls. Smalls had recently received £10,000 as his share of a £70,000 haul from an armed robbery at the National Provincial Bank in Norfolk Square, Brighton, during the races of August 1968.

Despite the size of the Ilford theft, the robbery was straightforward. One man, dressed as a 'City gent', went in to write a cheque as the security van approached. He was followed by others who lay in ambush for the two compliant guards, one of whom lost his nerve anyway and ran off at the sight of trouble. The money was taken effortlessly and the robbers vanished. The treachery of the guards and their informant was soon discovered. They and three robbers were convicted and sentenced. The others remained at large. Two more of the nine were caught after police searched strongboxes following a Wembley bank robbery five years later.[7]

A year after the Wembley raid, Bertie Smalls did his deal with the Director of Public Prosecutions and became the first 'supergrass' or 'squealer' for the newly formed Robbery Squad. He had taken part in fifteen raids himself but, as he said, 'I can give you every robber in London.' He gave the squad thirty-two bank robbers, including two more for Ilford. The only judicial mishap was that one man sentenced to fifteen years for the Ilford robbery had not been there, according to Smalls who certainly was present and had no compunction in betraying his accomplices. The man's conviction was quashed, while others were less fortunate. As Smalls appeared in the witness box, the occupants of the dock sang to him 'Whispering Grass' and, more ominously, 'We'll Meet Again'.

5

With the Ilford robbery, a quarter of a century of post-war wage snatching, car ramming, blinding with ammonia and subduing by cosh, iron bar or starting-handle was at an end. The security firms were a deterrent to all but the most resolute and many of those would not in future remain at liberty to enjoy the proceeds of their ambushes. By 1970, each van was loaded within the firm's headquarters and prior information as to its route was restricted. Armoured vans were so constructed that the cash was virtually inaccessible from the street. The guard in the back dispensed it to a self-locking driver's compartment by a hopper or a miniature revolving door. The doors of the guard's compartment remained locked throughout the journey and an alarm was triggered by any attack on the van's outer skin. Cash was no longer the easy target it had been. Opportunists now staged robberies on banks during opening hours with members of the public present. They entered masked, fired a shotgun into the ceiling, vaulted the counter, took what they could and then fled to their stolen car. Little by little even these raids were frustrated as the new internal architecture of the banks closed such approaches with security screens and counter alarm buttons connected to police stations.

Terror, an apparent disregard for human life, and the corruption of guards or officials were the attacker's continuing advantages. Even fatal violence might be dispensed without compunction. Post-war judges in their sentencing and newspapers in their editorials still castigated those who had abolished the deterrents of flogging in 1948 and hanging in 1965. Had they not left the innocent at the mercy of those who would kill or maim as it suited them, who would blind young women in a wages office with ammonia or soften a guard with the promise of a mortuary slab?

Jack the Lad or the loveable rogue had been replaced by those with a chilling indifference to the pain, death or grief of others, an indifference that frequently verged on contempt. This new and psychopathic philosophy of robbery with violence was echoed in the words of Neil George Adamson, a thirty-two-year-old labourer who shot dead a police inspector and a nightwatchman during a raid on Sunnybrook Mills at Farsley, Yorkshire, in 1970. The watchman was a witness to the policeman's murder and so had forfeited his right to life under this criminal's code. 'I figured I would get no more for murder than attempted murder so I shot him. A dead witness can't talk.'[8]

Those who now read of threats of amputation or burning alive, blinding with ammonia, marking with a razor, nailing a foot to the floor, extracting teeth with pliers might have thought that the methods of the Third Reich came deftly to the modern gangster's hand. The famous quartet of post-war psychopaths appeared more plainly what they had always been, not freaks of nature outside the criminal world but central in its post-war development. The watchman who made a nuisance of himself by witnessing a murder and so had to be killed recalls Haigh's irritation at Mrs Durand-Deacon's buttock which failed to dissolve and threatened to give his murderous game away. The killer's contempt for the three Shepherd's Bush policemen, shot without compunction in August 1966, recalls Heath who, having butchered a nineteen-year-old Wren, held women to be debased and corrupt.

That all criminals were to some extent psychopathic was not the case, certainly not of the Victorian 'poor who fought back'. That an increasing number of them now shared the moral qualities of the famous post-war names seemed evident. When guns or knives were drawn, it was all the more alarming that the power of life and death in criminal matters lay not with the judiciary or the executive but with the underworld.

15

All the Way to the Bank

I

M ANY OF THOSE involved in hijacks and wage robberies had appeared so repulsive that it was easy to overlook another branch of the profession staffed by the ingenious, the patient and the skilled. It might have been added that they worked quietly, had not gelignite become the livelihood of so many.

During the nights of the immediate post-war years 'hole-in-the-wall' gangs, and those who came down through a ceiling or over the rooftops, developed alternative forms of robbery. Their targets were almost always unoccupied premises. They avoided violence, except in its milder forms, when having to tie up a nightwatchman, to whom they sometimes gave a cup of tea or a cigarette.

To attack a bank or a jewellers' shop from adjoining premises was nothing new. In 1863, Thomas Caseley had used this method to empty a Cornhill jeweller's 'burglar-proof' Milner safe, in an iron-lined room, lit by gas and constantly on view from the street. Though he defeated all these obstacles, he was caught when the jealous mistress of his accomplice turned informer. 'It is a pity you did not turn your talents to better account,' the Lord Chief Justice told him. 'It is a pity the police did not let me, my lord,' Caseley replied.[1]

During the Second World War, in a time of acute shortages, the hole in the wall had been used even in minor thefts of easily portable commodities like cigarettes or perfume, removed from manufacturers or warehouses. It was not, as a rule, used in peace-time for anything less than a bank, a post office safe, a jewellers or a furriers, unless the quantities were worthwhile. On the weekend of 20–21 November 1952, for example, a team of robbers in Leeds were still prepared to tunnel through two walls and the stone floor of a warehouse in order to reach 600,000 cigarettes. They had hoped for far more and even 600,000 must have seemed an indifferent return for all their efforts.

On a quiet weekend, a well-organized gang could get through a good deal of brick and stonework. Plasterwork and boarding were no obstacle at all. A jeweller's shop in East London was emptied in the same year as the Leeds warehouse by breaking into a next-door insurance office, containing nothing of value. It was guarded only by Yale locks, which yielded to a craftsman of gangland folklore, 'Celluloid Alf', later replaced by the plastic credit card. The robbers then hacked through a basement wall into the jeweller's cellar, through the cellar ceiling and the floorboards above, emerging within the otherwise impregnable strongroom.

An important ingredient of such robberies was nerve and bluff. A gang of nocturnal post office robbers in 1949 had rivalled Caseley by working at night in the brilliantly lit car showroom of Bernard & Allery in the King's Road, Chelsea, while passers-by stared covetously at the sparkling new vehicles. The thieves had watched their chance and entered the showroom with a skeleton key. Once inside they pushed a Ford van and a Jaguar car, like assistants working late, until the two vehicles were manoeuvred to a point where they concealed a section of the party wall. They chiselled through ten inches of brick and plaster behind the car and the van, forced the ancient post office safe next door with wedges and hammers, then emptied it of cash and stamps. Finally, they opened the showroom doors wide, and drove off in one of the new vans on display. The thieves calculated correctly that those who saw them enter or leave in this manner would feel a predictable response: 'It must be all right or they wouldn't be doing it, would they?'

The simple hole-in-the-wall method could hardly have survived the 1955 screening of Jules Dassin's gripping portrayal of robbery and treachery in *Rififi*, a well-illustrated instructional film showing how to burgle Mappin & Webb's Paris branch by overcoming both conventional and combination locks, sensors and exterior alarms. Until then, Thomas Caseley's hole-in-the-wall method prevailed, enhanced by the new power of gelignite in the Martin's Bank robbery of 1955, at the prestigious London address of 23 St James's Street.

On Monday morning 7 February 1955, the branch manager went down to the St James's Street basement to find it a wilderness of brick dust and plaster, from a hole blown through the reinforced twenty-two-inch wall of the strongroom. Inside the strongroom, the twelve-inch-thick steel door of the safe had been blown clean off and the safe itself was now empty of its £20,000 in banknotes, or some £250,000 in modern terms. The robbers had not left a single fingerprint or any conventional clue. It was little consolation to Martin's Bank that this safe-breaking was seen as a small landmark in the history of crime, the first time gelignite had been used to blow open both a bank safe and its strongroom.

Two of Scotland Yard's most famous names, Detective Chief Superintendent Greeno and Detective Superintendent Herbert Sparks, 'The Iron Man', were given charge of the case. It was evident that the thieves had entered through a basement window of the women's cloakroom opposite the strongroom, where the glass was broken. The window had iron bars but one of these had been bent aside by a crowbar, giving just enough space for a man to get through. It ought not to have been possible for anyone to reach this window from outside, except through the adjoining building, also owned by the bank and currently being renovated for leasing. The decorators had left on Saturday morning.

One or more of the robbers must have hidden in the empty premises and been locked in when the workmen left. It would have been easy to get into the basement of the disused building, from which a man could climb out and reach the barred cloakroom window at the rear of the bank. Once the robbers had smashed the glass and bent back the iron bar, they were in the basement of the bank itself. Only the twenty-two-inch strongroom wall was between them and the main safe. Unlike the ten-inch party wall of the car showroom in the Kensington post office robbery, twenty-two inches would have taken too long to dig through and might easily have brought down part of the structure on the heads of the diggers. The robbers had tried the novelty of blowing a hole with gelignite, using an electric charge and almost certainly having to take cover outside the building from the ferocity of the blast.

The same process was used on the steel door of the safe and, once again, it had been necessary for the thieves to take cover outside the building as the steel door was blown into the room. The noise would probably have been heard in the street, but against the busy traffic of St James's it could easily have been taken for a car back-firing. Some safe-blowing gangs would arrange for their 'chauffeur', as he was called, to drive noisily about the neighbourhood at the moment of the blast and it may have happened on this occasion. In any event, the safe had been blown by an expert who knew how to use the correct charge without jamming the lock.

There was no obvious clue to the identity of the robbers and by Monday morning they would have had time to pass the banknotes into safekeeping. The hole in the strongroom had been made as small as possible, perhaps for fear of bringing down the entire wall. The expert was therefore a man small enough to get through it and expert enough to blow the door off the safe without doing further damage. Herbert Sparks, whose knowledge of the underworld came from years of experience, thought of Alfred Fraser, a Cricklewood greengrocer, 'a persistent criminal and a very dangerous man'. Fraser had only been out of prison a few months after serving a sentence for an attempted safe-blowing at the Hounslow Labour Exchange. He was small enough and thin enough to be known as 'The Ferret', and skilled enough to have done the Martin's Bank job.

Fraser was put under surveillance. He now bought himself a Daimler limousine and began negotiating for a greengrocery business in Paddington. He was seen much in the company of 'The Monkey', another known criminal and impecunious with it, who had surprisingly bought himself a Riley Pathfinder and set off on a tour of expensive hotels. If Sparks had needed any further help, it came from the gangland stupidity of Fraser's response when he was detained for questioning. After all his expertise with the safe, he blurted out, 'It's a rumble. That bastard has been talking.'

In a search of 'The Monkey's' home, a pair of trousers was found, so thoroughly washed to remove tell-tale brick dust or plaster that even the turn-ups had been unpicked. Yet though they had washed themselves, scrubbed their fingernails and laundered their clothing, the robbers had not thought of cleaning the banknotes or the brief-cases in which they carried them. The cases were examined by the

Forensic Science Laboratory at Hendon. The dust inside them held tiny fragments of various woods as well as crystals of potassium alum. These came from the fireproof packing between the steel plates of the wrecked safe door. The dust had settled on the banknotes after the explosion and some of it had then fallen off in the briefcases.

In addition to this, a particle of paint in the dust contained six layers identical to those used on the bank's strongroom walls in recent years. A glove was found which 'The Monkey' had evidently used to avoid leaving fingerprints and also to clear jagged glass from the frame of the broken window. Tiny fragments of glass caught in the fibres of the glove were tested for density and refraction. They were identical to the glass in the broken cloakroom window of the bank. Fraser went to prison for ten years and his accomplice for seven. They were comparatively fortunate. Robbery apart, gelignite was too great a public danger to be regarded lightly by the judiciary. By 1957, the tariff for safe-blowing was fourteen years, in the case of a man who robbed Greenford post office.[2]

It was also in 1957 that Martin's Bank tried the novelty of suing a robber. The bank brought a successful action against Fraser for the loss of its money and the considerable damage to its building. He had no money to pay them but the costs of the hearing were awarded against him. 'I think it is a formality but the bank is entitled to that,' said Mr Justice Glyn-Jones reassuringly. In some future cases it was not to be a formality, where convicted robbers were found to have substantial bank deposits and the banks sued them. The matter was in part regulated by the Powers of Criminal Courts Act in 1973, which empowered the court trying the accused to order compensation for the victim from the assets of those convicted, without the necessity of bringing a civil action.[3]

Yet those who hailed the Martin's Bank robbery as the first in which gelignite was used to blow open either a strongroom or a bank safe were wrong. Two years before, it had opened the strongroom of Barclays Bank in the Sussex market town of Midhurst on a quiet weekend in April 1953. Indeed, the malleable explosive jelly had been used before the war on the safes of cinemas and department stores, though the blasting open of bank vaults was a post-war development. As an advance on picking locks or forcing a safe door with wedges and a hammer, it first came into its own during the 1930s in the hands of Eddie Chapman, later famous as a double agent – perhaps a triple agent – during the war.

Within a few years of the war's end, gelignite was all too easily available. In 1950, even schoolchildren in Dorset were stealing it from an unguarded supply as a dangerous plaything. Sticks of the putty-like material were found casually thrown away near a railway station. The county police warned parents of the appearance of the explosive, which might be mistaken for modelling clay, and the importance of keeping it in a cool place until help arrived.

In the case of the Barclays Bank raid, several residents of Midhurst heard something on that Sunday afternoon in April 1953. Understandably, they dismissed it as a car backfiring. The robbers had approached the rear of the bank like polo players from Cowdray Park, climbed a few garden walls and broken into the ground-floor office. In common with almost all banks at this time Barclays at Midhurst had no alarms and the intruders walked down to the basement without hindrance. They first blew open the strongroom door and then cut open the safes with an oxyacetylene torch, combining the two favourite methods of post-war bank robbery. Copper coins were left scattered on the floor but £6,000 in banknotes was missing and it was evident that the thieves had spent several hours on the premises.

Far worse was the violence of the explosion, during which they had presumably withdrawn to the ground floor or left the building altogether. The heavy steel door of the strongroom was twisted, its lock blown off, and the walls of the basement were pitted by the lethal impact of metal fragments. The police conceded that it was the work of an expert but anyone, robber or civilian, in the vicinity when the gelignite exploded might as well have been standing in the path of a machine-gun. An ill-timed explosion would have caused a public disaster with considerable loss of life. The power of gelignite was demonstrated repeatedly when, for example, it blew a safe door clear across the car park of the Rose and Crown public house in Wimbledon on the night of 5 July 1954 or buckled and twisted the six-foot steel doors of the National Provincial Bank strongroom at Hounslow in November 1967.

Scotland Yard tried to choke the threat at its source by tracking stolen consignments of blasting gelignite and those who either held or supplied it. This followed the successful blowing of the safe at the Catford Greyhound Stadium in February 1950. Gelignite was used again in two raids on Crystal Palace Football Club that year, for which a man was arrested in April. Another gang was sufficiently impressed by the Catford robbery to blow safes in the next few months at Dagenham Stadium, the Odeon Cinema at Hornchurch, the post office at Laindon, Essex, the Westminster Bank at Upminster, and Hitchmans Dairies at Dagenham. Their incompetence was such that they got £9 at the stadium, nothing at all at the bank or the dairy and only about £400 for all their work. Worse still, there was a watchman concealed in the tote at Dagenham, who called the police after the night sky was lit up by the fire which the safe-blowers had inadvertently started in the administration buildings.[4]

Prior to this, there had been a series of major thefts of blasting gelignite from quarries, beginning in 1946 and 1947. The material had never been recovered. In March 1950, there was a large theft from a store near Branksome Chine, Bournemouth, where gelignite had simply been left unwanted by a demolition firm in 1948. Another major theft occurred at Kent Works near Dartford in January 1953. Because it had so many legitimate uses in places that were not easy to secure, these thefts were innately difficult to prevent. Eddie Chapman, for example, had stolen all the gelignite he needed from remote and unguarded quarries in North Wales.

By 1955, deterrent sentences for possessing the explosive seemed the answer. Edward Rice, a fugitive from Strangeways prison in Manchester, was sent to jail for thirteen years for stealing it. He had already been serving a sentence of ten years for blowing the safe at the head office of Skyways, Stansted. Four days later, a lorry driver admitted stealing seventy sticks and seventy detonators, which he had hidden under the coal in his shed. More astute thieves hid the explosive where it was unlikely to be found in a search. A large suitcase loaded with it was found in the left luggage office of Paddington Station in May 1955 and identified as part of a batch used in recent London robberies.[5]

In October, Scotland Yard investigations caught a gang of four, whose car boot contained gelignite, a detonator, eleven skeleton keys and a jemmy. There was even gelignite in their kitchen refrigerator. 'You have got us bang all right,' one of the gang admitted in an apt turn of phrase. Three men went to prison for a total of fourteen years. In the same month, when the safe was blown at New Cross post office, the police warned the public that gangs were now using a more powerful and convenient form of 'plastic gelignite'.[6]

Unskilled and inexpert safe-blowers packed the keyhole with too much gelignite and merely succeeded in jamming the lock, as had happened at a Coventry bank the week before the Catford Stadium robbery. From time to time a major bank robbery was frustrated by the misjudgement of the explosives expert. An otherwise professional gang missed £25,000 by jamming the lock of the strongroom door at Barclays Bank, Bethnal Green Road, on the weekend of 23–24 August 1958.

It was equally true that those who were inexpert with skeleton keys snapped them in the lock, making it impossible to open the safe. This happened at the East Strand post office in the same month as the Midhurst raid. The robbers jammed the lock of the first safe, attempted to open a second with a meat skewer and then to prise money out of the telephone call boxes, in all of which they failed. It was a mingled display of incompetence and frustration.

The consequences of a bungled explosion were far more serious than snapping a key. Jamming a lock was by no means the worst penalty. On the night of 1 December 1958, thieves wrecked the interior of Wandsworth Town railway station, and possibly themselves, emerging with only £10 and nothing from the safe. In a £6,000 raid on the City Road post office, Clerkenwell, during the night of 3 December 1962, another set of safe-blowers wrecked the interior of the building, though they also blew the safe apart. Fortunately, it seemed that they set off the detonation from outside and survived to grab the cash from the shattered building before running. In other cases, incompetent safe-blowers failed to detonate at all and then fled. They left the putty-like explosive, ideal for fingerprints, packed into the keyhole of the safe for the police to find.

Those who used the explosive might put themselves in jeopardy in unexpected ways. In July 1961, a gang who stole a new car and blew the safe of Johnston's Service Garage at Newington Green in North London could certainly claim to be unique. Their haul in banknotes was a modest £1,800 but, in blowing the safe, they also shattered a small bottle which, unknown to them, contained liquid cyanide salts. In the explosion, the liquid had sprayed the banknotes. With some satisfaction the garage and the police were able to issue a public warning that the liquid drops on the notes would dry in the form of dust and become invisible. Those who handled the notes might feel a tingling in their fingers. Any of them who subsequently put their fingers to their mouths, as in the familiar lick-and-count motion, would die quickly but not quite painlessly.

The use of gelignite was always subject to human error. Sheer bad luck also overtook a number of those who used it. Few had such bad luck as John Vernon Rees, a member of the team which raided Lloyds Bank at Kingston-on-Thames on the weekend of 14–15 December 1957. The two safes in the strongroom were replete with takings from Christmas shopping and money banked by bookies after Hurst Park races. The thieves broke in by using a ladder and a pair of powerful bolt-cutters to deal with bars on one of the windows. They used the manager's office carpet to muffle the explosion and demonstrated the triumph of gelignite by blowing open the strongroom door, six feet high and weighing two tons. They also blew open the safe and left £25,000 the richer.

Rees might never have been caught but for a small accident in climbing out. He put his hand on the top of a wall, not realizing that broken glass had been cemented into it. His injury was not severe but he unwittingly left behind on the jagged glass a small fragment of skin from his finger. He was subsequently arrested on suspicion but without any other conclusive evidence against him. However, the fragment of skin had by then been conscientiously fingerprinted and was a match for his own, which earned him ten years in prison.[7]

Throughout the 1950s, safe-makers and locksmiths had been striving to stay ahead of criminal expertise. By the end of the first post-war decade, gelignite however expertly used was no longer a guarantee of a successful attack on a safe or a strongroom. On the last weekend of August 1959, there was an attempt to imitate the 1955 Martin's Bank robbery at the Westminster Bank in Station Road, Chingford. The gang's explosives expert blew a 2ft 6in hole in the wall of the strongroom, as cleanly as if it had been cut by a pick. A mattress soaked in water deadened the blast and it was one of the neatest jobs of its kind known to Scotland Yard. Once inside the strongroom, the thieves broke open individual deed-boxes of cash and jewellery but their main target was the safe.

Residents of houses nearby were woken at 2.30 a.m. on Sunday morning by a succession of three loud explosions at intervals and smoke was reported further down the road. No one thought it was anything but a gas main blowing up at some distance or perhaps a building on fire. Inside the bank there was gloom. The expert who had blown the hole so neatly in the strongroom wall should have had no trouble with the safe. Yet all he had managed to do was to jam the lock and immobilize the handle. In hindsight, the third explosion heard outside suggested that a second attempt had been needed on the lock of the safe. Even so, it did no good. How could a 'jelly man' have been so adroit in blowing the strongroom wall and yet prove to be such an apparent amateur with the safe?

Undeterred by this, two months later the gang chose a second target nearby, the National Provincial Bank in Church Road, Chingford. On the night of 31 October they climbed to the flat roof of the building from a lane at the back, forced a skylight, dropped their ladder down into the bank, and made their way to the basement. Rather than blowing a hole in the strongroom wall, they chose simply to blow open its door, which was no more difficult in itself than blowing the door of a safe. This time their expert failed even to do that. It made no sense, until the bank and the police told them why. In both these banks they had encountered a new 'anti-blow' device which responded to an explosion by throwing bolts behind the door of a safe or a strongroom, as well as immobilizing the handle. It was not lack of expertise which had stopped them during the first attempted robbery. Even so, on the second occasion they were able to blow a hole in the strongroom wall, by detonating gelignite in a ventilation shaft, and went on to loot the deed-boxes beyond it.

In this case, the gang were fortunate to have chosen the weekend before 5 November. The bank's neighbours suspected nothing. They had heard explosions at 11.30 p.m. on Saturday, when the gang failed to open the strongroom door, and at 6.30 p.m. on Sunday, when they blew a hole through its wall. The detonations were loud enough to rattle all the windows down the street. But Guy Fawkes Night was at hand and the disturbances were put down to what one resident called 'firework yobs'.

Even so, it took the police only a week to make an arrest, though this was not one that they relished. The first suspect to be identified by Chief Inspector Baker was a uniformed policeman who had asked to be put on a night beat which included the Westminster Bank at Chingford when it was robbed in August. His beat had also included the National Provincial Bank on the nights of its robbery in November. As suspicion hardened, his home was searched and £1,500 of the missing £18,000 was found, as well as sticks of gelignite in a pair of rolled-up trousers. After this, the rest of the gang had little chance. For his part, the policeman went to prison for seven years, one of four men sent down for the National Provincial robbery.[8]

2

The later 1950s saw an attempt to replace gelignite, against which more and more safes and strongroom doors were defended, by burning through steel with oxyacetylene torches or the more powerful thermic lance. Yet the change was neither quick nor complete. It took time to install new defences and many steel doors still yielded to explosives. For a time both methods were used in tandem. On a single weekend, 25–26 July 1959, three Midland Bank safes were robbed, at Finsbury Park, Stepney and Ilford, as well as the Walls Ice Cream depot at Wembley and American Express in Mayfair.

The gangs at Finsbury Park and Ilford blew their safes, the Stepney raiders used oxyacetylene equipment. As usual they left behind the empty gas cylinders and also a heavily bloodstained towel, suggesting

347

that all had not gone well. At the Walls Ice Cream depot the thieves used gelignite and at American Express the safe was burnt open with an oxyacetylene torch. The total haul was £40,000 and would have been far more, had not the Stepney gang burnt open the wrong safe and found bank records rather than cash.

The primitive use of oxyacetylene equipment in burglary went back to the first years of the twentieth century. The principle of using a gas-fed flame on metal preceded that. Its use was not uncommon by the 1950s and, as an early example, the post office safe at Wickford in Essex was burnt open by this method in July 1954. Yet the task of a safe-cutter might be daunting. Torches and thermic lances were difficult to use in a confined space. In other circumstances, the equipment would require an ample air supply, protective clothing and insulation against the drizzle of molten sparks, even breathing apparatus in a space as airless as a bank vault.

Few ordeals can have been worse than the oxyacetylene robbery of the Gestetner plant in the Euston Road during December 1963. The gang tricked its way into the building by ringing persistently on the back doorbell and overpowering the nightwatchman who answered. They tied the watchman to a chair and stole the safe – carried by four men and containing £6,000 in wages. To get it to ground level, they had to use the lift. To their consternation, the lift jammed between the first and second floors, trapping the safe and the robbers. With four men in this confined space, the cutter used his oxyacetylene torch to burn open the safe and extract the money. The four of them then crawled out through the lift shaft with their prize.

Burning a safe had more obvious disadvantages than blowing it open, which required only gelignite, detonators and an electrical charge. The gas or oxygen cylinders for an oxyacetylene torch might be so heavy that it would take two men to carry one. Conspicuous transport was needed to get to the scene of the robbery and the empty cylinders would frequently be left behind with the rest of the equipment. After more than ten years, many robbers had acquired a professionalism with explosives. They were reluctant to give them up unless it proved necessary. Even as more safes were burned open, the illegal market in gelignite remained active at the end of the

1950s. Scotland Yard believed that it was now organized by 'jelly masters' who sold the explosive to gangs for a cut of the profits of the robbery.

In some cases, both blowing and burning would be used. The gang which raided Bravingtons the jewellers in Brompton Road, Chelsea, on the weekend of 1–2 December 1962, in quest of £50,000 in gold and jewellery, used most of the post-war techniques. They broke into an empty shop next door and hacked their way with chisels from its basement to that of the jewellers' showrooms. The strongroom wall was formidable. They tried chisels at first but soon gave up. It needed gelignite and then oxyacetylene to cut the steel lining. On the far side, the gold and jewellery awaited them.

These thieves were on the premises for some time and, as an extra precaution, rigged up their own alarm system. A wire with a buzzer alarm ran between the men working on the strongroom wall and one of the gang sitting in the empty shop next door, surveying the street with his finger on the button. The explosions were so expertly muffled that not a sound was heard in the mews houses immediately behind the shop. Because it was a long job, they fetched chairs from elsewhere in the showrooms and organized breaks during which they consumed coffee and sandwiches. They left no clues, except for empty coffee cups, oxyacetylene cutting equipment, detonators and wires on the floor.

An increasing number of jewel thieves and bank robbers, like the rest of the nation's workforce, became more conscious of their rights to decent working conditions in the post-war world. They were entitled to a tea break and refreshments. One of the first instances, which came to light because the members of the gang were arrested, involved raiders at the Westminster Bank in Brompton Square, South Kensington, in 1958. They might have got clear before the policeman on his night beat noticed a broken window, had they not taken time off for the tea and sandwiches which they had brought.[9]

The routine problems of burning open a safe were illustrated by the Midland Bank robbery at Stoke Newington on 30 October 1958. It was in many ways a well-planned raid, timed for a Thursday night when the safe in its strongroom would hold £80,000, the wages of some 1,200 workers to whom the money was to have been paid out on the following day. This was also a bank known to pay the money in used notes, which could not be traced, rather than in newly issued currency. However, the robbers also believed that it had one of the new generation of Midland Bank safes protected by a 'porcupine' system, which was to be the undoing of the Chingford robbers a year later. If the lock was tampered with, steel bolts would be thrown, securing the safe door to its frame. Gelignite would not overcome this nor, probably, would an oxyacetylene torch. The safe door itself was made of laminated steel, reinforced by heat-resistant metals, including nickel-alloyed stainless steel and copper.

Undeterred by this, the robbers forced the padlock of a builder's yard behind the bank and used bolt-cutters to sever two inch-thick bars on a rear window. A slightly built member of the gang was able to get through the gap and open a boiler room door from the inside. Through this, the rest of the party carried heavy gas cylinders and other equipment. They brought with them a so-called 'heat gun' used by contractors in breaking up army tanks for scrap. It combined oxyacetylene cutting with a high-speed electric arc that generated a still fiercer heat. Its cost was, surprisingly, just £14.

It seemed that the gang must have worked from midnight until about 5 a.m. In addition to their other equipment, they had brought canvas screens which were erected to hide them and the flame of the acetylene torch from Stoke Newington High Street, as they attacked the strongroom door. They first burnt a hole through the six-inch thickness of the steel and then through a steel grille inside. They also used power tools at some point and fused the basement lights. Once in the strongroom, they faced the heat-resistant door of the safe and its lock. They left the lock alone and used electric welding equipment to cut a post-box 'slot' in the safe door. It was a long job and other members of the gang had to cool the hot steel with buckets of water. At length there was a hole big enough for another craftsman to put his arm through and manipulate the bolts manually from inside. The safe was not proof against this, since the makers had assumed that no one would ever be able to get at the interior mechanism.

When the robbery was over, the heavy gas cylinders and the canvas screens were left for the police to find and the robbers fled with their haul. In their wake, CID officers checked sales of the type of equipment used in the raid and a Wembley club owner went to prison as an accessory. He had bought apparatus for cutting armour-plated steel on behalf of one of his members, who preferred not to purchase it in person. That man had gone to ground. Another year passed before Scotland Yard received an underworld tip. The suspect was arrested after Flying Squad officers had surrounded and raided a boarding house in Earl's Court. On 3 March 1960, though he had meantime been sentenced to eighteen months on 25 February for possessing gelignite, he was acquitted of taking part in the Stoke Newington robbery, as his wife had already been. At her arrest, £8,000 had been found in her vanity case. Since she was acquitted, no charge against her had been proved to show that the money had been illegally obtained and it was returned to her.[10]

3

After so much ingenuity, the simplest way of robbing a safe was still to have either a set of keys or some form of inside help. Even in the 1960s, a set of keys would not only open safes and strong-rooms but would also turn off burglar alarms. As late as 1963, the safe gang who raided the Co-Operative Bank in Sheerness were able, quite simply, to turn the alarm off. At the other extreme, the showroom of Carringtons, the royal jewellers in Regent Street, was protected by an alarm system connected to Scotland Yard's Information Room, as well as by concrete floors and ceilings to prevent an attack from below or above. Yet its strongroom was emptied of £300,000 in jewels during the weekend of 20–21 November 1965 by a gang who used oxyacetylene torches to burn their way through the strongroom door. They had solved the problem of getting into the building and turning off the alarm system by using duplicate keys. Nothing was suspected until 7 a.m. on Monday morning, when Scotland Yard received an anonymous phone call to say that a number of men had been seen behaving suspiciously in Regent Street.

Little by little, alarm systems were introduced which could no longer be silenced by sabotaging the electricity supply in the street outside or by injecting foam into the metal box so that the bell was silenced. But they were not universally adopted and as late as 22 June 1964 a gang broke into the vaults of one of Glasgow's biggest jewellers, Edward & Son, by simply ripping out wires from a junction box adjoining the building, which silenced the alarm inside. They broke into the vault, blew three safes and left with £70,000 in diamonds and emeralds.

More sophisticated alarms were no guarantee of security. In November 1963, furs worth £35,000 were stolen from Arpad of Grosvenor Street, Mayfair, by a gang who came down through an eighteen-inch hole in the ceiling from premises above, unoccupied for three years. Arpad claimed to have 'alarms everywhere', presumably pressure pads and sensors. The skill with which the fur robbers had navigated these and had first entered the floor above without leaving any clue as to how they had done it, suggested that they knew the premises well. Six nights later, the same gang was credited with a £25,000 fur robbery at Bonham & Sons, auctioneers of South Kensington. The building had an outside alarm and another wired from the strongroom direct to Scotland Yard. The exterior alarm had been smashed with a wrench. How the intruders had broken into the steel and concrete lined strongroom without activating the alarm to Scotland Yard remained a mystery.

When they worked, even the most primitive alarm systems were a deterrent. In November 1960, Lloyds Bank in Commercial Road, Stepney, was entered during the night by a gang carrying an electric drill and bolt-cutters. They may have been an advance party whose job was to carry out preliminary work on the strongroom before the arrival of the gelignite expert who would blow the steel door off. As they approached the door, what the bank called 'a powerful hooter' sounded. The robbers fled, leaving behind their tools, but were not caught. Similarly, in October 1963, a trio of robbers in stocking masks were seen running from Lloyds Bank at Hackbridge, Surrey, after the alarm was triggered. It was one thing to have an alarm but another to ensure that the response was quick enough to catch the intruders. As in so many cases, the Hackbridge robbers reached their car and drove off long before the forces of law and order appeared.

Neither duplicate keys nor inside help was uncommon. A gang that depended on a dishonest employee was more likely to find one on the larger and less carefully vetted payroll of a large store than in the smaller and more carefully chosen staff of a bank. To check thoroughly the entire workforce of a major department store would have been daunting. In October 1961, for example, when Barker's of Kensington High Street was raided by a safe gang who appeared to have obtained duplicate keys, the number of employees was 2,400. The thieves had taken £26,000, which was close to the maximum for a store robbery. Though cash in the safes of leading stores might not equal the sums held by some banks or the proceeds of a jewel robbery, it was still a match for the bank safes at Chingford or Kingston-on-Thames.

In some robberies of this kind, the 'inside help' was speedily identified. On the night of 30 January 1959, thieves had raided the London headquarters of the Army and Navy stores in Victoria Street, where there was a night stoker on duty. They came away with £16,000. To do this they entered by a side door in Artillery Row, well concealed on a night of thick winter fog, and made their way unerringly through a labyrinth of basement corridors to the strong-room door. Before they reached the door, the passageway was sealed off by a steel roller-shutter with a padlock. They cut the padlock free with bolt-cutters and unlocked the fireproof steel doors beyond the shutter. They also opened the cashier's office with a key, though they made an attempt to force the door, perhaps again to protect their accomplice. They then cut the bars of an iron grille to reach the strongroom corridor, cut through a further grille of inch-thick iron bars with a hacksaw and entered the strongroom. The safe was eight feet high, ten feet wide and three feet deep. The man who blew it used gelignite in the keyhole, rammed home with putty. He retired almost forty yards down the passageway and detonated the charge with a torch battery. To carry away so much money in notes and coinage the robbers also stole twenty-six canvas holdalls from the store's display.

The thieves' knowledge of the maze of underground corridors and their careful preparation for the obstacles suggested that they must have been in the building before. The manner in which they had apparently tried to force the door of the cashier's office unnecessarily pointed to the involvement of the stoker. He was no match for police questioning and felt poorly rewarded by his partners. To Detective Chief Inspector Iredale of Scotland Yard he confessed, 'I have had £40 so far and have been promised another £800 to £900 later on if I keep quiet.' When he realized that £40 was all he was ever going to get out of £16,000, he admitted that he had let the two robbers in on previous occasions to work out their plans.

Inspector Iredale also heard that Eddy Knapp, market porter of Peckham, had been spending a mass of newly minted shillings in Covent Garden, many of which had been in the safe to pay the store's wages next day. Knapp's home was searched. Iredale found £150 in new shillings in a laundry basket and banknotes under the baby's bedclothes, still in their Army and Navy stores wrappers. In Knapp's garden there had been a recent bonfire but the metal fastenings of a number of canvas holdalls had not been consumed by the flames. Though two other members of the gang were still at large, both Knapp and the watchman went to prison in March 1959.[11]

A persistent problem for banks was that, however carefully they vetted their clerks, it was often necessary for workmen or auxiliary staff to be on the premises unsupervised. In the autumn of 1965, Detective Inspector John Swain of the Flying Squad received a tip-off that there was to be a raid on a City bank on a Saturday morning, its target identified subsequently as Lloyds Bank head office in Lombard Street. Presumably the aim was to get the thieves in before it closed for the weekend at noon, giving them almost two days to carry out what was likely to be one of the biggest bank robberies to date.

Observation was kept on the bank from surrounding buildings for several Saturdays without any sign of the robbers. Early on 6 November two bank porters, acting as cleaners, arrived at the bank and began to empty waste paper and other refuse into the bins outside. One of the men, Frederick Williams, had worked at the bank for sixteen years. Presently, as Swain described it, 'A car with three men in it drove by. Two sacks were thrown out from the vehicle.' On his orders, the car was followed and was stopped some distance away. The three men were taken into custody. Their sacks had been dumped next to the rest of the bank's rubbish.

Swain and his men continued their observation from windows overlooking the bank. Presently, Frederick Williams reappeared with another load of waste paper. He put it in the bins, then picked up one of the sacks left by the men in the car and carried it inside with some difficulty. Swain's men could easily see that an object just protruding from the neck of the sack was an oxygen cylinder. When both sacks had been carried in, the Flying Squad entered the bank and arrested the two porters. In Williams' pocket was a set of four skeleton keys which would unlock the grilles of the strongroom. In a cupboard next to the strongroom were the contents of the two sacks left by the suspects in the car: an oxygen cylinder, a gas cylinder and an oxyacetylene cutting gun.

The trials of the accused, as Lord Chief Justice Parker told the Court of Criminal Appeal in June 1966, left 'a very nasty feeling in one's mind'. There were persistent attempts to bribe successive juries to acquit the five defendants. It was still the law that a jury verdict must be unanimous. The first trial at the Central Criminal Court, for conspiring to rob the bank, ended when the wife of one of the five accused attempted to approach two jurors. At the start of the retrial, the accused men challenged sixteen jurors from the dock, 'and it became apparent that those who were being challenged were the ones who looked the most intelligent'.

After a few days of the second trial, counsel saw the judge in his room and reported that one of the jurors had been seen talking to 'a man well known to the police and with a long criminal record'. Information had been received from an undisclosed source that the juror had been offered a bribe and had said he would consider the proposition. That juror was discharged but on the next day another juror reported to the police that he had been offered £600 'to say not guilty'. Soon afterwards, a third juror reported that he had been offered £100 to find the defendants not guilty. One juror who insisted on an acquittal would make a conviction of the five defendants impossible.

Since two of the three jurors who had been approached had proved honest, the trial continued with a jury of eleven. At first this jury was unable to agree. At length, they found Williams guilty but acquitted the other four men. Williams went to prison for five years and his appeal was dismissed. Had the bank inquired more closely into his past, it would have found that he had previous convictions for both shopbreaking and housebreaking. Lord Chief Justice Parker in the Court of Criminal Appeal said that he had some sympathy with Williams, in the light of attempts to bribe jurors. 'One has the impression that the others got off because one of these attempts succeeded. Think of the strength of the case against these four who were acquitted.'[12]

Bribery of jurors and intimidation of witnesses had already been alleged during the trial of the Kray twins in 1965 for demanding money with menaces and in the trial of the Richardson brothers in 1966 on charges of violence, fraud and extortion. In an effort to prevent this, the Criminal Law Act 1967 provided for majority verdicts. Ten of the twelve jurors would constitute a majority. It was assumed that bribery of three jurors might be beyond the powers of the underworld.

Where there was no willing employee to supply duplicate keys, it might be possible to obtain them by force. At the end of 1945, Billy Hill had found that the easiest way to rob a jeweller or a safe was to kidnap an assistant who carried the keys, while he or she was on the way home, and commit the robbery before releasing the captive. The safe of Moorgate post office was robbed on 17 July 1954 by the more direct method of holding in her own home a supervisor who lived alone. Two of the robbers guarded her from 1 a.m. to 3 a.m., a time when she was unlikely to have visitors or phone calls. A third man took the keys to open the doors and the safe. He drove fourteen miles from her home in Kent to Moorgate, emptied the safe of £32,000, and then returned.

Seventeen years after Billy Hill had first organized the kidnapping of women on their way home, that method was still in use. It was simple and infallible, given reliable information beforehand. Nor was it any longer confined to London and major cities. On 23 November 1962, a twenty-six-year-old jeweller's secretary locked up the shop in Gabriel's Hill, Maidstone, at the end of the day's work. She was watched as she got on the bus to go home and the bus was then followed by a van. As she left the bus and began to walk along the darkened pavement, the van reversed into her path.

Two men seized her and pushed her into the back, where they and four others tied her hands and feet. It was too dark to identify them in the interior. They demanded the keys and details of how the jeweller's alarm worked. She thought it best to tell them. She was then driven to London by four of the men and dumped at Eltham. By this time, the other two men had opened the shop and taken jewels worth £20,000.

A more direct form of attack, requiring speed, precise timing and ruthlessness, was to kidnap the carrier of the jewels. In October 1961, Ansel Weingarten, a seventy-three-year-old diamond broker, was seized in Hatton Garden. He had come out of the Midland Bank just after 10 a.m., wearing a dark overcoat and grey suit over a special black waistcoat with secret pockets for diamonds and keys. He was said to be carrying polished stones worth between £20,000 and £30,000. Before passers-by could intervene, three men stepped up to him and within seconds had hit him over the head and bundled him into the back of a stolen van. It was so fast that a would-be rescuer noticed nothing until he heard cries and saw the victim's legs disappearing into the rear of the van, as the vehicle moved off. The attackers tied the diamond broker hand and foot. He was heard thirty minutes later, banging on the sides of the abandoned vehicle in a cul-de-sac off the Pentonville Road. The black waistcoat had been ripped open, the diamonds and his keys were missing. He was said to be in a state of shock.

4

Combination locks had seemed a sure method of defeating the robber and his inside help. Sometimes two bank officials would know half the combination each and each would also have a key to only one of two locks on the door of a strongroom or a safe. It might have seemed foolproof but it was nothing of the kind. The combination lock was not new, even in Victorian England, and it had never replaced the conventional key.

As a defence against robbery, a combination had a fatal flaw, which was psychological rather than physical. The immediate fear

of most of those who used such a lock was not that a thief would
discover its number but that they would forget it. It was a fear
which applied equally to burglar alarms operated by numbers. Some
of those who adopted these devices were content to leave them on
the factory setting, which they could always check if they forgot it,
as could the thief. Others were content with 1, 2, 3, 4, 5, 6 or
simple arithmetical sequences like 2, 4, 6, 8, 10 or even 2, 4, 8, 16,
32, 64 . . . An extremely popular sequence was a numerical version
of the custodian's birthday or that of a family member. Other combin-
ations related to games like golf or bridge. As for the modern
Raffles who listened to the tumblers with a stethoscope and opened
the safe door when he heard them fall, he was an invention of the
screen. The technique had been possible with the earliest and crudest
locks but not with their descendants.

The most famous combination lock robbery did not occur until
the Mayfair branch of the Bank of America lost many millions of
pounds from the strongboxes of its clients in April 1975. The mystery
of the vault's opening was easily solved when an electrician who
had helped to install alarm systems confessed that he had hidden in
the ceiling above the vault and, through a small hole made with his
screwdriver, used a spyglass to watch the fingers of the staff as they
turned the combination. He then passed the information to the
robbers.

These locks were used by banks in addition to conventional keys
rather than instead of them. Even so, by the end of the 1960s, locksmiths and safe-makers had made the attempts to rob bank vaults
increasingly unrewarding. In addition, the police had taken the offensive against serious crime with the creation of Regional Crime Squads
in 1964, to be followed by the Robbery Squad in 1972. With the
first 'supergrasses' in the early 1970s, criminal intelligence was a more
significant weapon than it had ever been and robbers were more
likely to find the Flying Squad or the CID lying in wait.

The immediate result was not that all thieves gave up robbing
banks. Some retired and others changed their methods, joining the
wage-snatchers who had also lost the easy targets on the streets.
For both professions, robbing a bank now meant entering with a
shotgun, firing into the ceiling to subdue staff and customers, and

vaulting the counter or the grille – or else ambushing a security van delivery. It was a career for the thug rather than the true professional, for brawn rather than brain. Though such robberies were successful at first, the banks and the security industry were largely effective in improving their defences. The sums of money involved in the Security Express or Brink's-Mat robberies might be much larger than their predecessors but such robberies faded from the headlines.

As security gained the upper hand in the 1960s, bank robbery and its rivals attracted the forlorn, the desperate and only in a few cases the ingenious. Yet ingenuity was not dead. After the failed but famous Heathrow robbery of 1948 and its successor in 1962, a team of experts removed £104,000 in diamonds, gold and dollars from the airport's Pan American strongroom in December 1968. There was no violence and, indeed, the robbery was not discovered until the following morning. Those guarding the cargo shed, which contained the strongroom, saw nothing. The strongroom door had three locks, each of which could only be released by a security guard and a supervisor using separate keys. One lock had been cut through but the other two had not apparently been tampered with. Yet a fortune in diamonds, gold and dollars was missing when the steel door was opened by security officers.

The plan had been meticulously researched. It was carried out when the cargo shed was exceptionally full of crates and piles of freight, caused by the Christmas rush and the threat of an American dock strike. Under normal conditions the theft would have been impossible. On hands and knees, the robbers could move unseen behind these unusual mountains of cargo. There had also been a moment in the routine when the security man on duty had to stand outside the shed, though never out of sight of its door, while he watched the loading of cargo on its way to an outward-bound flight. However brief this moment seemed, it was long enough for the robbers to get in or out.

Gentlemanly theft of this kind was largely an art of the past. The wage-robbers and the safe-breakers cast subtlety aside in a wave of attacks on banks and customers, in which guns were routinely carried and sometimes freely used. In the National Commercial Bank of

Scotland robbery in Glasgow, during April 1966, three masked gunmen set something of a precedent when one of them vaulted the counter grille and the others opened fire on the terrified bank staff without provocation, hitting two of them. On 17 November in the following year, robbers opened fire in Barclays Bank, Kensington High Street, having made customers sit on the floor with their backs to the wall. The following day, it was the turn of Barclays in Dulwich, where the manager was shot and a clerk coshed, and then Barclays again in Peckham Rye, where six masked men carried sawn-off shotguns.

There was a grim similarity in these attacks of the late 1960s, though some showed an occasional novelty. In December 1967, a silver-grey Jaguar with a railway sleeper tied across its radiator as a battering ram was driven over the pavement and smashed open the locked doors of Barclays Bank in Hemel Hempstead. The staff were counting money at the time. They stopped when two men jumped out over the car bonnet and fired automatic pistols into the ceiling. One man kept guard while the other collected the takings.

5

So much burning and blasting by professional gangs left out of account those who were the freelances and mavericks of post-war crime. In the age of gelignite, thermic lances and *Rififi*, it seemed that old-fashioned smash-and-grab belonged to crime capers in film comedy. Yet as late as 1964, the West End saw it at its most spectacular. The attack proved that a pre-war ritual could still be enacted among well-guarded shops and crowded streets by daylight, if carried out with panache. The shopkeepers in the fashionable stretch of Burlington Arcade, running between the crush of Piccadilly and the calm of Burlington Gardens, isolated from motor traffic, considered themselves the least likely to be targets of such a raid. The arcade was only fifteen feet wide and with no way in or out except at either end. A man had once walked in with a gun and held up a shopkeeper but even he had been caught. No sensible smash-and-grabber would attempt a raid on foot with the prospect of being trapped in the arcade or, at best, running with a crowd of shoppers at his heels.

Shortly before 10 a.m. on the morning of 27 June 1964, a Jaguar car turned into Burlington Gardens. It bumped up over the pavement and accelerated loudly into the arcade with horn sounding and headlights on full beam. Some people thought it was a stunt for a film but all fled or jumped from its path among a confusion of shouts and screams. The car braked, skidded, and came to rest after fifty yards, outside a shop belonging to the Goldsmiths' and Silversmiths' Association.

There were six men inside, black stockings pulled over their heads as they smashed in the jewellers' shop windows with sledgehammers. The glass broke with a sound like gunshots and no one attempted to 'have a go'. Instead, the bystanders took cover from fragments of flying glass. Three men at an upper window on the far side of the arcade threw down small furniture and ornaments but to no effect. In a moment more, the raiders with £50,000 in jewellery were reversing at full speed down the arcade, the car swaying erratically and smashing into shopfronts on its way. It reversed into Burlington Gardens, skidded into Bond Street and was found abandoned half a mile away in Carlton Gardens. As people so often said, it was all over before anyone knew it had started.

In a less ostentatious form of post-war robbery, the nimble and the audacious navigated the heights and chasms of rooftops or formed ladder gangs to raid country houses or found their fortunes in the sporting underworld. Their rewards often exceeded the proceeds of many bank robberies. At the end of January 1950, a weekend raid was carried out in Great Arbour Court, opposite the Old Bailey. The thieves took advantage of temporary scaffolding to climb to the third floor, occupied by a small firm in which a self-respecting professional thief could have little interest, Williams & Row, looseleaf ledger makers. They climbed to the roof of its office, smashed a wooden panel and let themselves down into the poky premises. Once inside, they were able to open a little window which gave on to the roof of Platform 1 at Holborn Viaduct railway station. They then worked their way thirty feet along the station roof to the barred window of Continental Express, forward shipping agents.

Having brought a hacksaw and with all the time they needed at a weekend, they cut through the iron bars, broke into the firm's Customs Room, where goods in transit were examined, chose the most valuable parcels and left by the same route. Ironically, their haul was scarcely reported but it exactly matched that of the famous Martin's Bank robbery five years later.

In this area of crime, the impact in 1955 of *Rififi* – which in French slang meant both 'violence' and 'a bungle' – was never in doubt. The British Board of Film Censors had no qualms in giving the film an 'X' certificate to keep out impressionable teenagers. It was a masterpiece of suspense in which during the robbery itself not a word was spoken on the screen for almost half an hour. Those who thought it an instructional film for the underworld were able to cite the manner in which the criminals surveyed their target, the chloroforming of the concierge, the duplicate key for the flat above the jewellers', the chipping of a hole in the floor, with an umbrella inserted and opened to catch fragments that might otherwise fall and trigger the alarm sensors, the silencing of the alarm itself by squirting thick foam into its box.

In reality at this date when George 'Taters' Chatham, an enterprising but often-imprisoned English burglar, wanted to silence an alarm in Mayfair before his night's work, he dressed as a repair man with the name of an alarm company on the back of his overalls. He propped his ladder against the wall and cut the clapper out of the alarm above the busy street, during office hours with the system switched off. It would be switched on and activated that evening but its days of ringing were over. No one gave him a second glance as he removed the clapper. Once again, it must be all right or he wouldn't be doing it, would he?

Many of the most successful robberies were also the simplest, not least when they were jewel thefts. In July 1956, for example, Mrs Mullen, the secretary to a diamond merchant of Holborn Viaduct, had collected £100,000 in diamonds, some £1,500,000 in modern terms, from a safe deposit. She was returning in a chauffeur-driven Rolls-Royce. At the junction of Farringdon Road and Cross Street, the car paused for a break in the traffic before pulling out. A tall young man stepped out, as if to cross the road at the junction, jerked open the rear door of the Rolls-Royce, grabbed the bag of diamonds, and ran. Before anyone could catch him, he turned into Clerkenwell Close, where an accomplice was waiting with a car. The robber jumped in and the car drove off.

As so often, it was disposing of the diamonds rather than stealing them which was the thieves' downfall. In this case, information was exchanged and twelve days later, at 5 a.m., thirty CID officers, ten of them armed, surrounded a house at Westcliff-on-Sea. They burst in and took away a man who was, not surprisingly, still in his pyjamas. Four months later, the robber went to prison for seven years and two accomplices for three years each.[13]

Not all the ingenuity of *Rififi* could compensate for the ineptitude of some of those who tried to imitate it. On the night of 16 December 1957, the coldest in London for many years, a hopeful gang climbed to the icy flat roof above the National Provincial Bank in London Road, Croydon. What followed owed more to Laurel and Hardy than to Jules Dassin. Climbing an eight-foot wall from the car park, the thieves forced open the first glass skylight. It gave way and they dropped down, only to find themselves in the booking hall of West Croydon station. Undaunted, they went out, climbed the wall again to the ice-covered roof and attacked another skylight. It also opened and they dropped down, this time into the station bookstall. Wilting a little, they climbed the wall a third time and forced a third skylight. The way was blocked by a metal security grille and a panel of armoured glass. In some desperation, they forced the last of the skylights and, finally, dropped down into the washroom of the bank. When confronted by the strongroom door, however, it was beyond their resources to open it. There were only a few loose coins in the tills and their chief prize was the staff's tea money which they took from the cloakroom. It was a refreshing reminder that *Rififi* was, after all, only a film.

As in the case of the 1963 train robbery, some of the elements in that film were not new. In March 1950, for example, raiders entered a five-floor office building in Great Portland Street from the roof and found some three-inch-wide navy-blue satin ribbon on the top floor. They knotted it at intervals for a hand-grip and, having torn up the floorboards, lowered themselves from level to level by means of this 'ribbon rope'. On other occasions a rope ladder was used, as in the Williams & Hutchins fur robbery of December 1964, usually secured by tying it to a radiator on the upper floor.

Inevitably, in the wake of the film, the press announced the first 'Rififi Robbery', in February 1956 at Lawrence's jewellers in Newbury. The thieves had climbed to the roof and cut a hole. They cut another hole in the ceiling of the living room below, quietly barricaded its doors and cut a further hole in its floor. Then they lowered themselves into the shop. They positioned the last hole so that they could not be seen from the street as they dropped into the showroom, which was lit all night and on view from the street through its grille. They were on the premises for five or six hours, choosing the most valuable items, yet the caretaker and his wife slept undisturbed. One reassuring piece of English amateurism was that they could not have staged the robbery at all had they not borrowed a ladder in the first place from the garden of one of the jeweller's neighbours.

The lesson that a ceiling is much easier to break through than a wall was not forgotten. As late as 1966, a so-called 'Pussy Gang' of fur thieves carried out two 'carbon copy' raids by this method. In the first, during the weekend of 8–9 January, they scaled the roofs of Great Portland Street, smashed the window of a betting shop and unscrewed its internal bars. They entered the shop and stood on cartons of betting slips to break through the ceiling and floorboards above them. They then emerged in the showcase of Millward's Fur Models, slid back a door to the main room and left with mink worth £36,000. They also found time to locate bottles of champagne in the bookmaker's refrigerator and drink them on the roof, despite sub-zero temperatures. On the weekend of 12–13 February, their second target was H. B. Swerling in New Bond Street. In this case, they entered unoccupied premises above and chiselled through the floor. Though the showrooms were alarmed, the gang navigated the sensors and pressure pads, leaving with a £23,000 selection of the best mink and sable.

Away from London and the West End, ladder gangs had been a scourge of the immediate post-war years, targeting country houses and their occupants. A series of thefts in the New Year of 1952 began with the removal of guests' furs worth £4,000 during a reception given by the private secretary to the future Queen Elizabeth, Lieutenant-Colonel Martin Charteris, at his home in Kenwood, North London. The ladder was put tidily away afterwards. The first man sent to prison for this robbery was not a Raffles of modern crime but a costermonger from Willesden. Ladder thefts in the early months of the year culminated in the loss of jewellery and furs by the actress Celia Johnson at her home in Oxfordshire, while she was writing letters downstairs and heard nothing.

Ladder crimes were discouraged by the conviction of George Pyser, again a street trader rather than an international jewel thief, who was removed from the dock at Surrey Quarter Sessions in March crying, 'Five years! Oh, no!' His job had been to hire cars and drive the gang to country houses. He pleaded with the detective inspector in charge of the investigation, 'If you get me out of this, I will tell you all I know about the team. I don't want bird. It will kill me.' Soon after his release from prison, he fell to his death from his fourth-floor Drury Lane flat into the basement area.[14]

In June 1952, Raymond Jones, known as 'Raymond the Climber', was also sent to prison, in his case for six years, for robbing Colonel Charteris. He had fifteen criminal convictions going back to the age of twelve. Alan Grant, the Willesden greengrocer, had already been sent down for seven years in February. The vogue for ladder robbery dwindled and died. Even the proceeds were unrewarding for many of its practitioners. Two men were accused of stealing jewels in Bristol worth £6,825 from Lady Monckton, wife of Sir Walter Monckton, Minister of Labour in the new Conservative government. The fence who admitted buying them claimed that they had first asked him for £15 for the jewels but that he had knocked them down to £7 10s.[15]

The more successful jewel thieves often worked alone. Few seemed more casual about it than Peter Scott, *alias* Peter Gulston. In a long career which alternated between temporary affluence and regular imprisonment his most impressive theft was of £180,000 in jewels from Sophia Loren, who was currently filming *The Millionairess* at Elstree with Peter Sellers in 1960. Using a bogus press card, Scott located her secluded lodgings, the Norwegian Barn in the grounds of the Edgwarebury Country Club. He entered by an open window while she and her husband Carlo Ponti were embracing one another downstairs, on Ponti's arrival from Italy. In the bedroom, a tallboy had been secured by a very large and obvious padlock. By removing the fastening, the padlock came away as well, opening the way to the jewel case. Scott left with the jewels and a pair of the actress's knickers, which earned a very public gypsy curse that she pronounced on the unknown thief.[16]

Many such forms of individual crime had an impressive history. The sporting underworld had thrived in the Victorian period and in the years before the Second World War. Much of its energy went into protection rackets and a lesser amount into dog-doping at the kennels of greyhound stadiums, which seldom seemed to be out of the news. To stage the big coup was another matter and it was always likely that it would have to be done on the racecourse rather than the dog track. One man who tried it held the attention of the public throughout most of the summer of 1953.

On 16 July, Francasal won the two o'clock race at the Bath July meeting, the Spa Selling Plate. Its fortunate owner, Maurice Williams, had backed it for £3,500. It was enough to keep him for life. There was nothing improbable about its win or in the show of confidence which the bet represented. The odds on the horse had stood at 20–1 that morning, which would have made Mr Williams a very rich man indeed, but by the start of the race they had shortened to 10–1.

Though he claimed to have £7,000 at home in cash, his London bookmaking firm, J. Davidson & Co., was not making money. The manager, Victor Robert Colquhoun Dill, known in the business as 'Colonel' Bob Colquhoun, had only seen him on a couple of occasions since Mr Williams appointed him manager after a brief meeting on a racecourse. Maurice Williams had placed his bet about half an hour before the race, through his own firm with instructions to lay the money off among other bookmakers. This was done and there was no reason whatever to impugn his honesty. However the other bookmaking firms, naturally wondering why so much money was going on an outsider just before the race, wanted to contact the racecourse on the bookies' 'blower', their direct line, in case they needed to lay off the bets in their turn. That might have been bad news for Mr Williams, particularly if the odds dropped further before the start of the race since his bet depended on the starting price.

Most unusually, the 'blower' to the racecourse was dead. There was a rumour on the course that it had been cut by lightning in Bath's traditionally stormy summer weather. Unfortunately for the rumour, the line ran up Weston Lane to the course and a roadsweeper had noticed two men with a lorry and a ladder at the spot. They put the ladder up against the hawser. One man went up and used a blowlamp on the cable. The other said reassuringly to Bert Glass, the roadsweeper, 'We've been having a lot of trouble with this cable. It's the damp getting through the lead covering. We'll have to weld it to keep the rain out.' The preposterous explanation that a telephone wire was being protected by having a gas jet turned on it stuck in the mind of Mr Glass.

The line had, of course, been severed. Indeed, on inspection it had been burnt through with an oxyacetylene torch. The Chief Constable of Bath talked of 'a huge racing conspiracy'. Mr Glass was able to describe a red lorry and a slightly built man, dressed for the races in a brown check coat worn over an open-necked shirt and brown trousers. The lorry was traced and Detective Inspector Glyn Evans set off for South Wales, where he arrested a scrap-metal dealer, Leonard Phillips, who had been brought to Ton Pentre police station to answer his questions. Phillips admitted severing the blower line and went to prison for three months in September. 'If I had known it was going to turn out like this,' he said glumly, 'I would not have done the job. It was chicken feed compared to what they got and I know what I am talking about.' It was not much consolation to Mr Williams, however, to know that before July was out the whole matter of the Spa Selling Plate fraud was being investigated by Detective Superintendent Reginald Spooner of the Flying Squad.[17]

Superintendent Spooner soon discovered that Mr Williams owned two horses, Francasal and Santa Amaro, both bought in France and virtually unknown in England. Francasal was described as 'a somewhat indifferent horse' and Santa Amaro as 'a good horse'. Far worse for their owner, Santa Amaro was shod with racing plates and Francasal with ordinary horse shoes. Faced with this, he admitted that he must have run Santa Amaro as Francasal but that it had been a genuine mistake. As for the cutting of the 'blower', he was as mystified as everyone else. It had absolutely nothing to do with him.

Accusations of switching were part of sporting life, even in the better-regulated post-war world of racing. They had been made in March 1950, over the alleged running of a 'ringer' at Haydock Park in November 1949, and in June 1951 concerning the entering of Stellar City at Alexandra Park in August 1949 as Peaceful William, known on the Turf as a 'crock'.

The first Francasal jury could not agree. A second jury convicted George Kateley, a bookmaker said to have devised the fraud, Maurice Williams, Gomer Charles, a Cardiff bookmaker who helped to finance the escapade, and Victor Colquhoun Dill, *alias* 'Colonel' Bob Colquhoun. All went to prison in March 1954. Yet however ingenious the fraud, like the Great Train Robbery it was nothing new. As far back as 1844, the four-year-old Maccabeus, which had won the St Leger, was entered as a three-year-old outsider Running Rein for the Derby. It won at a canter. Indeed, the race was so dishonest that there was even a second suspect runner, whom Running Rein disabled with a deft kick.[18]

Most criminal activity connected with racecourses and dog tracks concerned the 'protection' of bookmakers. It was the business of protection, rather than bank raids, train robberies, racehorse swindles or greyhound doping, which was the foundation stone of organized gangs. By the end of the 1960s, people who could not have recalled the name of a single bank raider or white slaver, who were uncertain whether Heath was Haigh or Craig was Bentley, or even what Ronnie Biggs had done, were suddenly knowledgeable about the lurid and unappetizing lives of such families as 'The Richardsons' or 'The Krays'.

16

Safety in Numbers

IN THE AUTUMN of 1937, the *Sunday Despatch* published a series of six articles on the British underworld by the thriller-writer Peter Cheyney, who was also a lawyer, former news editor of the *Daily Graphic*, and director of his own private inquiry agency. He had found no hierarchy of gangs in England on the American model. Men and women drifted in and out of criminality, while the underworld itself wandered from place to place. It merged easily with the society on which it preyed, at nightclubs, racecourses, dog tracks and gaming parties.[1]

There were gangs in many British cities outside London, though few boasted more than a local fame and fewer still were closely organized. None had the scope for protection rackets offered in London by Soho, the East End and surrounding racetracks. Crime figures were high in Glasgow or Liverpool but criminality did not necessarily equate to organized crime. Pre-war Glasgow had been dominated by rival sectarian gangs, who gave as much energy to fighting one another as to robbing the community. Yet most of the city's violent criminals belonged neither to the Protestant 'Billy Boys' nor to the Catholic 'Norman Conks'. In response to the gangs Percy Sillitoe, Chief Constable in 1935 and future Director of MI5, authorized 'the only sort of measures which were likely to be effective' in breaking them up. Following a pitched battle, in which the victorious police were led by Sergeant Tommy Morrison, 'Big Tommy from the Tollbooth', the leader of the Billy Boys, William Fullerton, went to prison and the pre-war gangs were dispersed.[2]

Arthur Thompson became a major figure of the post-war Glasgow underworld, both as robber and enforcer. Perhaps in tribute to the Billy Boys, he was described as manager of the Glasgow Hanover

Club. Thompson was also one of the few leaders outside London to enjoy cordial relations with such men as Billy Hill and the Richardsons. Even so, his power in Glasgow was not unchallenged. In 1963 he was accused of planting a bomb in a bookmaker's office but the case was dropped. In November 1965, he was freed from the dock of the Glasgow High Court when a man whom he was alleged to have slashed developed sudden amnesia and said, 'I can't remember what happened.' In August 1966, his enemies hid a bomb under the driver's seat of his car, to explode as he drove away from his well-fortified house, 'Fort Thompson', in Provanmill Road. He escaped with injuries but his mother-in-law in the seat beside him was killed. Martin, George and Henry Welsh, brothers from a rival family, were tried but acquitted. Three months before the bomb, Thompson had run one of their cars off the road, killing a family member and a friend as the vehicle smashed into a wall. He too had been acquitted.

In the early 1980s, Glasgow was also to be the scene of the so-called 'ice cream wars', which were fought with firearms and petrol bombs to determine which vans should have the right to trade on which estates. While it was true that drugs and stolen cigarettes were sold as well as ice cream, protection at this level was still short of the ambitions of major London gangs. These particular wars ended with two men going to life imprisonment in 1984 after murdering five members of a vanman's family in an arson attack on his home.

Elsewhere, the activities of gangs fluctuated according to circumstances. During the Second World War, for example, organized crime thrived in the three cities of the 'Black Market Triangle', Leeds and Liverpool as well as London. Liverpool docks in wartime were a natural target. Yet much of the crime was carried on by those who might not have been tempted in time of peace. F. H. Porter Ltd robbed the government of a fortune in 1940–41 by taking pay for 2,000 ship repair workers and employing only 800. A Ministry of Food supervisor ran a major racket in meat stolen from the docks. Proceeds from such thefts would make the combatants in the 'ice cream wars' seem pitifully underpaid.

Post-war Liverpool found its gang leaders in men like George Kelly, hanged in 1950 for the murder of the Cameo Cinema manager during a £50 robbery, or Edward Devlin and Alfred Burns, hanged two years later for killing a woman whose house they had burgled. So far as they had a regular 'racket', it was no more than petty theft or pimping in dockland, where they used very young girls and made do with the backs of cars as bedrooms. The same was true of ports like Cardiff where, despite the reputation of Tiger Bay, crime in the 1950s was at a relatively petty level of prostitution and pimping, some of this organized by Michael de Freitas who was to be the future self-appointed Black Power leader 'Michael X' in the 1960s. Cannabis smuggling and routine theft occasionally led to murder.

Such comparisons served only to illustrate that just as London accounted for a hugely disproportionate amount of the nation's crime, so it was the natural home for an ambitious gang leader. Even the American Mafia was prepared to talk business with the Krays of Bethnal Green, as it would never have considered doing with the small-time criminals of Liverpool or Cardiff.

By mid-century, there was no necessary division between London and the rest of the country. The Kray twins offered protection to clubs in Birmingham and Leicester. A career criminal like 'Mad' Frankie Fraser, a major figure in the metropolitan underworld, prided himself on being a 'respected citizen' of Brighton. During the war, Jack Comer had made his name in Leeds, having fled the London police after a gaming club fight in which he slashed the face of 'Edgware Sam'. Wartime Leeds was a city where clothes rationing and the garment trade combined to stimulate a prosperous black market. That market put a lot of cash into the pockets of many people. There were not enough goods to spend it on and so the city's gambling clubs were well patronized. At a gaming club in Chapeltown, Jack Comer saw the proprietor being threatened by a protection agent and stepped in to offer his services. Within a week or two, he himself was protecting three gambling clubs in Leeds: the Regal, the Carlton and the Economic. With the war over, Leeds was no longer the place it had been. Comer returned to his native Whitechapel, where he was better known as Jack 'Spot', being always on the spot when there was trouble to attend to.

So far as London had a modern underworld, its traditions and practices dated from the 1890s. Immigrants from Eastern Europe, notably Odessians and Bessarabians, had begun extorting money by threats against shopkeepers and coffee-stall proprietors in their own communities. Guns, knives and broken bottles were the means of persuasion. Shops and stalls were smashed, their owners beaten. It was very little different in Petticoat Lane during the 1930s, when stallholders without protection might find their stalls overturned and the contents smashed. Indeed, it was little different to Soho in the 1960s, when clubs that refused the protector's hand were gutted by a petrol bomb. Evidence had always been hard to gather. Superintendent G. W. Cornish of Scotland Yard pointed out before the First World War that the first victims and exploiters came from a common culture. Both had suffered under Tsarist police oppression. Much as they feared or despised each other, grievous wounding or destruction of property did not move them to cooperate with the law.[3]

By the outbreak of war in 1939, London gangs were well rooted in geographical areas. The Sabini family of Clerkenwell's 'Little Italy' were pre-eminent in racecourse protection from 1918 until the end of the peace. They never truly recovered from internment as enemy aliens in 1940. Their nearest rivals were the Whites of Islington and King's Cross, who also controlled part of Soho. There was rivalry in Soho between Italian and Jewish gangs, which surfaced in the 1941 murder of Harry 'Scarface' Distleman, for which Antonio 'Babe' Mancini was hanged. Elsewhere there were 'The Hoxton Boys', then a Hackney gang to the east, and the more loosely organized 'Elephant Boys' south of the river. Billy Hill, a young pre-war challenger, established a base in Kentish Town, thereby inviting trouble from the Whites.

In breaking up pre-war gangs, the Luftwaffe had done a more efficient job than Scotland Yard. After the blitz of 1940–41, post-war redevelopment laid waste much that remained of traditional territory. Many East Enders found themselves relocated in the 'New Towns', the planners' dream of a future in green fields. When the drug trade attracted attention in the 1960s, it was the New Towns rather than the East End which provided the worst examples.

2

The focus of attention in London for ten years after the war was on the rivalry of Billy Hill, Jack Spot and the Whites of King's Cross. In Hill's case it was a curious irony that by 1950 a self-styled 'Boss of Britain's Underworld', forty-one years old, had spent seventeen years of the past twenty-four in prison or Borstal. It might seem he had chosen the wrong profession, though he had acquired enough money by 1956 to leave Britain and live comfortably in Spain. Yet while he boasted of being in demand as an expert international safe-breaker, his convictions were for the less glamorous crimes of breaking and entering, smash-and-grab, and once during the blackout for robbery with violence.

Jack Spot was two years younger than Hill, yet both men were seen by a new generation of the 1950s as 'well past it'. Spot was born of Jewish immigrants in Whitechapel in 1912. He had taken part in the Battle of Cable Street and other street fights against Sir Oswald Mosley's British Union of Fascists. In Cable Street on 4 October 1936, he claimed he had dealt with the wrestler who was Mosley's bodyguard, hitting him over the head with a lead-filled sofa-leg. As a pre-war racketeer, he volunteered to protect East End clubs and cafés from trouble, a service many of them needed in some form. He also introduced protection schemes for Petticoat Lane stallholders, his Market Traders Association, after knocking out the previous provider. He worked with a burglar in the East End, his practical knowledge being put to use as a 'guv'nor' who sponsored thefts, including the London Airport robbery of 1948.

Unlike Billy Hill, Jack Spot had few criminal convictions. He had been bound over for housebreaking, served nine months before the war for inflicting grievous bodily harm on a member of the British Union of Fascists and was belatedly tried but acquitted for his attack on Edgware Sam. Almost all his adult life had been spent outside prison. To the public, he was a bookmaker whose stand was seen at race-meetings, point-to-points, and who appeared as the owner of clubs in Soho and Aldgate. Away from the public eye, he had controlled and protected bookmakers' pitches at courses like

Haydock Park and Pontefract before returning to post-war London from the North. There was a popular belief that racing authorities secretly liked to have a strong protection racketeer in charge rather than a succession of violent and contending gangs. At Ascot in 1946, there was a confrontation between the Whites of Islington and gangs loyal to Spot, from Aldgate and Upton Park. It culminated in an Islington man being chased down the track by one of Spot's men with a hammer, in full view of the occupants of the Royal Enclosure.

Of the three post-war gangs, the Whites had become the weakest but they remained long-standing enemies of Hill. Subsequently, both Hill and Spot claimed to have put them out of business. The two victors then behaved as if they were joint lords of London crime, though Hill went back to prison for three years, a sentence imposed for warehouse breaking in 1947.

Before his removal, there was a showdown with the Whites. According to Hill, he decided to unleash 'a night of terror' on his enemies on 9 July 1947. He described how he had mobilized 200 men, armed with razors, choppers, hammers, bicycle chains and iron bars. They were accompanied by women who walked through the streets with handguns and Mills bombs hidden in their handbags. The Whites sent out a peace envoy. He had been returned to Soho with his face slashed and a promise of similar damage to anyone who got in Hill's way.

To top this, Spot claimed it was he who had led the attack with a thousand men carrying Sten guns, bombs and revolvers. A more persuasive version from Chief Superintendent Peter Beveridge was that information reached Scotland Yard several months earlier of a forthcoming confrontation between Hill and the Whites. It was planned for Harringay Arena on the night of 17 April 1947, when Bruce Woodcock was a contender for the world heavyweight championship. Beveridge summoned Hill and warned him of the consequences of public violence. Hill, with surprising meekness, promised there would be no trouble.

A specific account of what happened later came from Hill, who claimed that he and his men ran to earth Harry White at an Islington flat in July. The door was broken down to reveal his older rival surrounded by his aides. White, whose son and heir died in 1943, had no appetite for a confrontation, let alone a fight. He looked at Hill and said, 'Okay, Billy, you're the guv'nor.' The Whites faded from the underworld, bequeathing it to Hill and Spot. Hill was then sent to prison, leaving Spot to mismanage the London Airport robbery of 1948.[4]

3

Billy Hill and Jack Spot were both distinguished by an overt contempt for the system of criminal justice, whether it was for or against them. Systematic intimidation of jurors had yet to come but once witnesses were subject to threats or bribery, jurors would become the next target. As an early example of their methods, Hill and several companions called on a rival gangster, Freddy Andrews, in Kentish Town on 27 December 1953. There was bad blood between the two, according to Frankie Fraser. It was just after midnight and the visit was a demonstration of gang law. Andrews claimed that when he answered the door, Hill lunged forward and slashed his face with a razor. In truth, it may have been done by another man while Hill was elsewhere, establishing an alibi. In any event, Andrews knew who was behind the attack. Contrary to the code of gangland, he identified Hill to the police as the man who had cut him.

In February 1954, Hill appeared at the Old Bailey to answer charges of wounding with intent to cause grievous bodily harm. It was inconceivable, in the case of a man he had admitted knowing for twenty years, that Andrews was mistaken as to whether it was Hill who had used the razor. By then, Hill had bought him off and promised to 'look after' him in future. In consequence, Freddy Andrews explained to the court, 'I thought I saw the prisoner Hill but I realize now it was not so.' The Recorder, Sir Gerald Dodson, asked, 'You want to say this man wasn't there at all?' 'Yes.' 'Are you finding it difficult to recollect what happened?' 'I know what happened.' 'Are you frightened of anybody?' 'Definitely not.' The only course was to direct the jury to acquit Hill. For the benefit of the world at large, the Recorder remarked of Andrews, 'You may think it is quite obvious he is either scared out of his life or is wilfully concealing the truth.'[5]

In the same month, a postman who had stolen £32,000 in jewellery and handed it to three men whose names were those of the accused, and who had picked out all three on an identification parade, also found himself in error and told the Old Bailey judge at their trial, 'They are not the men I handed the stones to at any time.' The three men were acquitted and the postman was charged with perjury. In May, in a case of grievous bodily harm, the Thames Court magistrate complained, 'This is another case where witnesses are "got at" and don't come.'[6]

Much worse followed, after a fight on 11 August 1955 between Jack Spot and Albert Dimes, a forty-year-old bookmaker who was a friend of Hill's and a survivor of the Sabini gang. On a Thursday morning in the most crowded part of Soho, Dimes and a friend were sitting on the wing of a car in Frith Street. Spot appeared and said to Dimes, 'I want a word with you.' The two men walked off and, according to Spot, there was a quarrel over the 'pitches' which he controlled at point-to-point meetings. Then there was a shout. More shouts followed and there were screams among the pavement crowds who were by now standing motionless and watching the drama. Spot was chasing Dimes with a knife. Dimes turned into the Continental Fruit Stores on the corner of Old Compton Street, 'trying to get something to defend myself with', and knocked over a box of fruit. Spot was close behind shouting, 'You want to be a fucking tearaway? How would you like this?'

The fight continued in the shop, the two men overturning fruit trays and boxes. Dimes, whose face was seen to be slashed from the left ear to the chin, was at the mercy of his attacker's knife. The shopkeeper's wife was trying to end the fight by hitting both men from behind with a greengrocer's brass scale-pan. Though Dimes was bleeding badly, he grabbed the knife from Spot and began stabbing in his turn. At length both men were exhausted, Dimes leaning against a girder, Spot sinking to the floor. The knife had just missed Dimes' abdominal cavity and twenty stitches were needed to sew up his forehead where the six-inch blade had cut him to the bone. Spot had four facial wounds, four in the left arm, one in the neck and two in the chest. Dimes was helped outside to a taxi which took him to Charing Cross Hospital. Spot managed to crawl to a barber's shop from where a policeman took him to the Middlesex Hospital.

The men were separately charged with causing an affray, later known as 'The Battle of Frith Street'. 'Why only me?' Spot demanded. 'Albert did me and I get knocked off.' 'Spotty does me up and I get pinched,' Dimes complained. 'That don't seem fair.' Yet Dimes refused to prosecute, loyal to the code, and Spot insisted to the police, 'It is our business. Leave us alone to settle it.'

The charges were brought by the police. Though the pavement crowds had dispersed, Spot was able to produce two witnesses at his trial in September 1955. Both swore that Dimes had started the fight. Christopher Glinski was an interpreter and eighty-eight-year-old Basil Andrews was a retired clergyman of the Church of England, who had spent thirty years as duty priest at Kensal Green cemetery. Andrews now lived frugally at a hotel in Bayswater, describing himself as 'a clergyman and an ex-public schoolboy . . . the oldest old boy of St Edward's School, Oxford'. Faced with such witnesses, the jury acquitted Spot and the prosecution of Dimes was then abandoned.[7]

On 27 September, the Home Secretary instructed Scotland Yard to report on discrepancies between the witness statements to the police and the evidence given in court in the case. The Yard had already received anonymous phone calls, denouncing the Reverend Basil Andrews as a liar and a well-known 'scrounger'. The inquiry was led by Superintendent Ted Greeno. On the same day, having sold his story to the *Daily Sketch*, Basil Andrews went to see Jack Spot's solicitors and then admitted that he had been nowhere near Soho at the time of the fight. He lived on a pension of £150 a year, could afford to eat only a Continental breakfast, morning and evening, and had been desperate for money. As for his perjury, 'It was very wicked of me. I admit it. I was very hard up and I was tempted and I fell. It is rather humiliating for me to have to tell you that I was desperately hungry.' A man who was once kind to him, Peter MacDonough, had approached him in the lounge of the Cumberland Hotel near Marble Arch and asked if he would like to make some money. The old man said that he was almost destitute and would very much like to make some. He was taken to see Spot's wife, Margaret Comer, whom Spot always called 'Rita', and her friends, Morris Goldstein and Bernard Schack, who were Spot's lieutenants. They offered the old man a total of £64 to say 'six words' in court and they treated him kindly. His new friends also showed him a magnum of champagne, to be opened if 'all went well'.

All did not go well. Stories about the previous activities of Basil Andrews began to circulate. In order to obtain £300 from a man of seventy-two he had presented to him a girl of sixteen, Barbara, as his niece who would inherit £100,000 at twenty-one. He was also alleged to have performed a bogus marriage for £300. He had contrived to borrow money from sympathetic clergymen and seldom repaid it, indeed his bishop had summoned him and given him a warning about this. Before long, he admitted to Scotland Yard that he had committed perjury in the case of Jack Spot.

Mrs Comer and her three companions were charged with conspiring to pervert the course of public justice. However, the Reverend Basil Andrews was more use to the Crown in the witness box than in the dock. He gave evidence, publicly hoping that God would forgive him, since he could not forgive himself. Rita Comer was fined £50, Peter MacDonough the intermediary went to prison for a year, Morris Goldstein and Bernard Schack, with previous convictions for unlawful wounding, were jailed for twelve months each. Christopher Glinski was also charged with perjury but acquitted in December. The disgraced clergyman concluded ruefully, 'I am told if I am seen by some of the gang I shall have my throat cut.'[8]

That was not the end of the battle between Hill and Spot on one side and justice on the other. As relations between the two men deteriorated, Spot was arrested in June 1956 on charges of causing grievous bodily harm to Tommy Falco, a forty-four-year-old bookmaker who was one of Hill's men and whose arm had been badly slashed. Spot was outraged. 'I am innocent,' he insisted as he was arrested. 'This is a diabolical liberty. I will get ten years for nothing . . . This is a frame-up.' Tommy Falco continued to insist that Spot had attacked him at 2.15 a.m. on 20 June 1956 as he left the Astor Club, off Berkeley Square, after the cabaret and was going down the steps into Curzon Street. He had needed forty-seven stitches in his arm. As Spot slashed him, Falco claimed that the attacker had said, 'This is one for Albert,' referring to Dimes.

Spot insisted, truthfully, that he had been at home in bed at Hyde Park Mansions, Marylebone, and had not left there until the following morning. Even the police at this stage admitted having a statement from another witness, describing a plot to implicate Spot falsely in the charge. This information came from Victor 'Scarface Jock' Russo. He described how Dimes and Billy Hill had offered him £500 to allow himself to be slashed and then to accuse Spot of the attack. Russo refused but heard that Falco had later agreed to act as victim.[9]

Even before his acquittal a last and more dramatic attack on Spot had occurred, fuelled by the festering animosity of Billy Hill. On the evening of 2 May 1956, Spot and his wife were walking home to Hyde Park Mansions. From the twilight, seven men appeared with razors, coshes, iron bars and a shillelagh. One of them inflicted a deep razor cut across his face, others clubbed him to the ground and then systematically kicked him senseless. By the time help arrived and an ambulance took him to St Mary's Hospital, Paddington, Rita Comer had also been cut, bruised and knocked down. As Spot fell, she had tried to stand between him and his attackers so that 'I got some of the kicks aimed at Jack's face.' Even now, Spot from his hospital bed at first refused to name his attackers, though in a witness statement produced at his trial he named Frankie Fraser and Robert Warren. Rita had less compunction; she named Billy Hill and six others. The police confirmed that Hill and Dimes had alibis. They were held for questioning but no action was taken against them.

The first two men to be tried for the attack were Fraser and Warren, a gaming machine installer. Bail was refused on the grounds that already 'There has been certain intimidation of witnesses in this case.' Jack Spot now claimed that he could not identify the men who attacked him, despite his earlier witness statements. There was no evidence that this was the result of intimidation. Frankie Fraser's fifteen previous convictions told against him. He went to prison for seven years, taking Warren down with him for the same period.

Three more attackers were then arrested, William 'Billy Boy' Blythe, Robert Rossi and William Dennis. Rossi and Dennis were jailed for four years each. Blythe was sentenced to five years but died in prison the following year.[10]

By now the reign of the men who had spanned the war was over. In 1956, at the age of forty-five, Billy Hill retired to Spain. It was said that his 'bottle' had gone. If so, perhaps he had reason to be grateful. At the time, a new form of imprisonment, 'preventive detention', was provided by the 1948 Criminal Justice Act. It allowed little remission and was frequently imposed for ten years. If he was caught and convicted again for any offence, most of the rest of his life might be spent in prison. Earlier he had expressed contempt for criminals who were afraid of doing their share of 'bird' but the lesson taught by more than half an adult life spent in prison seems to have borne fruit at last.

In the world that Hill left, Jack Spot's power dwindled. He became bankrupt and by the time he was fifty was working for a meat packer. Both men had helped to give the post-war criminal a new self-confidence and audacity. In this, the end justified the means. If the means were perjury, intimidation, extortion and falsehood, they were the currency of crime at mid-century.

The response to this, on the part of judges and juries, was evident in a prosecution that began even as the case against Spot's attackers was being heard. It concerned a feud between two families in the South London underworld, the Brindles and the Carters, the latter a family that had been loyal to Jack Spot. Johnny 'Scarface' Carter, a fruit trader from Peckham, was cornered by four men with a knife, hammers and a shillelagh as he was leaving the Tankerville Arms in Lambeth, on 15 April 1956. He ran down the street, into a garage and then upstairs into a private house. The four men cornered him in the bathroom and attacked him with such ferocity that he needed sixty stitches in his face and head. In many respects the underworld was a small place and one of those first accused but dismissed from the case was Frankie Fraser, who was brother-in-law to the Brindles. A few weeks later, Richard Frett and Ray Rosa were arrested for the attack. Mrs Carter, who had seen the assailants, identified both accused. Carter picked out Rosa but as he already knew Frett this second suspect was not put on the identity parade.

At the Central Criminal Court in the following month, Johnny Carter explained that he did not really know either of the accused, after all, and could no longer identify them positively as his attackers. Tina Carter, who had picked out both at the identity parade, agreed that the two men looked like her husband's attackers but she did not know for sure. The owner of the garage said that he had seen Carter chased upstairs by a group of armed men but was unable to recognize them. The case against the accused seemed hopeless until counsel for the Crown suggested to the jury, 'Carter now says neither of these men attacked him. You might ask yourselves if perhaps something has happened to make him a little more reticent about identification.'

The jury asked themselves and, next day, convicted both defendants. Mr Justice Donovan sent each to prison for seven years, as a tribute to 'the very wicked persons behind you'. The case sounded to him

> more like Chicago and the worst days of prohibition than London in 1956 . . . If gangs can go about cutting people up and then by some means or another their victim, after first identifying his assailants quite positively, can be given to entertain doubts in the witness box then a very ugly situation is developing and it can lead not merely to a breakdown of criminal law but to all law.[11]

It was a succinct summary of the legacy bequeathed by Billy Hill and his kind. In 1957, with Hill's departure for Spain, some of his own friends faced the consequences. Before a bookmaker of Warren Street went to prison for dishonesty in May, he refused to give the names of four alleged accomplices he had met in the street because he feared being attacked if he did. Judge Maude told the jury, 'There is no doubt that in London there are men who can terrify others. You know that as well as I do.' What had once seemed to the people of England like the folk customs of Chicago were now the law of the underworld about them.[12]

As for Johnny Carter, who boasted that 'With a razor in my hand I was uncrowned King of the Underworld,' he lost heart and gave up. At one time he claimed to be making £600 a week from robbery, protection and the racetracks. At length he found himself penniless and in June 1960 signed on at the Peckham Labour Exchange.

4

There was no obvious successor to Hill or Spot, yet the malign influence of organized crime remained evident. The most persuasive public example of this came four years after Hill's retirement and Spot's downfall in the murder trial of Jimmy Nash for the shooting of Selwyn Cooney. The charge followed a fight on 7 February 1960 at the Pen Club in Duval Street, Stepney. The club derived its name from a story that it had been financed from the proceeds of a robbery at Conway Stewart in Stepney, involving gold intended for making fountain-pen nibs. Billy Ambrose, the owner of the club, had taken part in this and had gone down for five years.

Jimmy Nash was twenty-eight and described as a steeplejack of Charing Cross Road. He was a minder at the Astor Club, one of an Islington family, friendly with the young Krays and with an eye on the clubs of Mayfair. On 7 February, he walked into the first-floor bar of the Pen Club with two minders and a girlfriend, Doreen Masters. At the bar he saw Selwyn Cooney, manager of the New Cabaret Club in Soho, owned by Billy Hill and his wife, Aggie. Cooney had been involved in a car accident with a driver who was the girlfriend of Nash's brother. Cooney had sent 'Blonde Vicky' a bill for the damage.

According to witnesses, Jimmy Nash crossed the bar, delivered a punch that broke Cooney's nose and said, 'That will teach you to give little girls a spanking.' In the ensuing fight, other witnesses described Nash as drawing a gun from the waistband of his trousers. He first used it on Billy Ambrose, now described as 'club doorman' who was trying to break up the fight, shooting him in the stomach. Cooney shouted, 'Don't let him get away!' and the witnesses were adamant that it was Nash who then shot Cooney in the head. Cooney's friend Johnny Simons, a bookmaker's clerk, also attacked Nash as he fled with his companions. As Nash went down the stairs, according to Simons, he was still waving the gun and shouting at those on the staircase, 'You want some too? Get out of my way!' At that point Simons hid in the doorway of the toilet.

Cooney, whose girlfriend Joan Bending was a witness, had died instantly, though his body was carried down to the pavement before anyone realized this. A few days later Nash gave himself up. When asked why it had taken him so long, he protested that he had merely punched Cooney because of things that Cooney had been saying. He had not shot him, had no gun, and had hoped that the police would have found the killer by now. 'The only time I have ever used a gun in my life was a Sten gun when I was under army training.' That at least sounded odd. He would have been far more likely to use a rifle.

To the public at large, the trial of Nash and his two alleged accessories, Joe Pyle and John Read, was probably of more interest than the incident at the Pen Club. All three men were charged with capital murder, since hanging was still the punishment for death by shooting. Billy Ambrose survived the bullet wound in his stomach. When Simons was asked why he had not identified Read and Pyle at the identity parade, he said simply, 'I was scared.' He had reason to be. He appeared at the Old Bailey trial with a two-inch razor slash down his face, the result of an attack in a Paddington café meant to deter him from giving evidence.

When Simons was given police protection and was no longer available to the persuaders, a twenty-three-year-old model who was his girlfriend, Barbara Ibbotson, was attacked. She was pulled into a car in Wardour Street on 16 March, cut and beaten to persuade her to reveal where the police were keeping Simons. At the beginning of April, three men broke into her flat while she was in the bath, forced her face under the water as if to drown her and slashed her with a razor. She left London the next day. 'My job depends upon my looks. Two attempts have been made to ruin them and I'm making certain there will not be a third.' By this time both Johnny Simons and Joan Bending, Cooney's girlfriend, had also been taken from London by their police guards. Fay Sadler, part-owner of the club and also present at the killing, had vanished. A police search had failed to find her.

The first murder trial opened on 21 April 1960, only to be abandoned after four days because a juror whose husband was on remand in Brixton let it be known through him that she had decided in advance to vote for the acquittal of the three men. Another juror also proved to have had a criminal conviction.

During the second trial, the Crown dropped the murder charges against the two accomplices on the grounds that the evidence did not show them to have had knowledge that Nash was carrying a gun. Nash accused Cooney of starting the fight by taunting him and saying that he was living on the immoral earnings of the girl who was with him that night. 'So you are another of those Nashes. You are just a lot of jailbirds, you, Ronnie and the rest. Who is the bird with you? Easy money for you?' Nash claimed he had heard two shots, one wounding Billy Ambrose and the other killing Selwyn Cooney, but had no idea who fired them.

To add to the complexity of the case, the defence produced a new witness, David Sammons. He gave evidence that he had been in the Pen Club on the night of the murder and that Johnny Simons had been in the second-floor bar at the time when Cooney was shot in the first-floor bar. If that was true, Simons' evidence was worthless. Moreover, Joan Bending had been so drunk that she had to be helped out of the first-floor bar before the fight took place. If this were true, in the absence of Fay Sadler, the prosecution case was almost unsupported. Yet Sammons had not said any of this before the magistrate.

Mr Justice Diplock questioned David Sammons before allowing him to leave the witness box. 'The first time you said Miss Bending was tight was the day before yesterday?' 'That is correct.' 'If your evidence today is right, you knew that she was drunk?' 'In my opinion.' 'Did you tell anyone that?' 'No.' 'Why didn't you tell that before?' 'I don't really know.' 'You realized that if you are right, Simons was telling a pack of lies?' 'I did.' 'In a murder trial?' 'Yes.' 'Did you realize that a man might have been hanged?' 'Yes.' Sammons added that he was shocked to read Simons' evidence in the press during the first trial but then saw that there was to be a retrial and so came forward. When Mr Justice Diplock asked him why he had not done so in the two months since the murder, he explained that he was unfamiliar with court proceedings and was 'lost in the surroundings'.

The jury acquitted Nash as the only remaining defendant in the murder trial. All three defendants were then tried for causing Cooney grievous bodily harm. Nash went to prison for five years and his minders for eighteen months each. A month later, Johnny Simons who had been under day and night police guard was flown abroad to begin a new life under a new name.[13]

In the aftermath of the case, there was much discussion of the threat posed by the new post-war gangs. Their power over witnesses seemed awesome and their influence on jurors was disturbing. Protection rackets were increasingly their business and firearms the means by which they enforced their demands. In Mayfair, Soho or the East End, the gaming clubs, coffee bars, striptease clubs, street-corner bookmakers, betting shops and public houses were a prize to be fought for. Ironically, only if one gang could impose its law on the rest was there likely to be peace.

Their methods were familiar from films depicting organized crime in America. A messenger would first be sent to suggest protection to the owner of an establishment. If the owner refused, trouble would follow a week or two later. At first, this would usually take the form of a fight breaking out among the customers and the club or café being wrecked. It took about five men to do it and the wreckers would have gone before the police could get there to intervene.

None of this was new. In 1952, in an earlier gang war, there had been a staged fight by six men, including a veteran of the 1948 London Airport robbery, at the Madeleine Club in South Molton Street, Mayfair. These were not boisterous merrymakers or casual hooligans. They carried coshes and knuckledusters. At the Madeleine they broke up chairs, tables, a telephone and a drum from the band. They smashed champagne bottles and glasses, then discharged the soda water siphons over the girls who worked in the club.

There were also racial protection rackets in which, for example, Cypriots terrorized Cypriot café owners in Soho. In 1960 it was the turn of the owner of the Granada Café in Berwick Street to be attacked by his compatriots. When he refused to join their scheme, despite the promise of 'all the protection you need', he was given an ultimatum to think the matter over. At 1 a.m. on 1 September, fifteen men smashed up his crockery, tables and chairs. Two days later came a phone call saying that next time they would smash the counter and his head. At 2 a.m. on a subsequent morning, their leader came looking for the proprietor, saying, 'Where is he? I want to break his neck and smash his face.'

Some of those who were attacked resisted the intimidation. The outcome of that at the Rio Grande Club in Berwick Street in 1957 was a visit by fifteen attackers who fired shots, wounding the cloakroom attendant. Two of those among the gang were named by the attendant and the doorman but when the case came to court they were no longer able to identify them.[14]

Even so, it seemed by 1962 that Scotland Yard might be winning the protection battle against the thugs. The CID commander in the West End, Chief Superintendent Ronald Townsend, heard of a new and extremely dangerous gang in Soho. He gave the job of surveillance to a team under Detective Sergeant Harry Challenor. 'Tanky' Challenor had a distinguished war record, having served in the Special Air Service behind enemy lines and won the Military Medal. In the Soho operation, he brought to trial five men, led by a twenty-three-year-old docker from the 'Little Italy' of Clerkenwell, known in Soho clubs and coffee bars as 'The King'. The King in this case was accused of 'terror tactics' and demanding money with menaces from Wilfred Gardiner, whose striptease clubs included the Phoenix in Old Compton Street and the Geisha in Moor Street. Gardiner told Challenor and the court that he had been threatened or assaulted on thirteen occasions by his 'protectors', their threats reinforced by an iron bar, a flick knife, and turpentine substitute as a means of setting fire to his clubs. He was also threatened with having his face slashed and was told that he would be shot.

Mr Gardiner paid at first but eventually went to the police. When the men were arrested, even the smallest fry with a cut-throat razor in his pocket was scornful. He looked at his victim and said to Challenor, 'I suppose he put you on to me. He doesn't know what is coming to him. He will have to get more than your lot to look after him. His days are numbered.' At the Old Bailey, sentences were imposed on five men of seven years, six years, five years, three years, and fifteen months respectively. There were gasps from family and friends in the public gallery and screams from some of their womenfolk. Judge Maude was unimpressed. 'Woe betide anyone else who should injure Gardiner as a result of this case. Any further recurrence of blackmail in the heart of London will be followed by sentences double the length of those passed today.'[15]

The police were elated and the press was jubilant. At last it seemed that someone was prepared to face up to the dim-witted thugs. Contrasts were drawn between Harry Challenor with his distinguished record in the Army and the Metropolitan Police, as opposed to the gang leader, whose public distinctions included convictions for petty theft, assaulting women and carrying housebreaking implements.

After so much celebration, it was all the more disheartening when Harry Challenor was diagnosed in the following year as suffering from paranoid schizophrenia. On 25 October 1963 he was found to be certifiably insane. On 4 June 1964 he was unfit to plead at the Central Criminal Court to charges of conspiring to pervert the course of public justice by carrying out unlawful arrests, making false statements, and fabricating evidence between 10 July and 23 October 1963. Most famously, he had planted pieces of brick in the possessions of eight people arrested after a demonstration against the Greek military junta during a state visit by the King and Queen of the Hellenes in July 1963. He was also alleged to have punched one of the defendants several times while the man was in custody at West End Central police station.

No one had thought him ill when he worked a 102-hour week on the Soho cases and once walked fifteen miles home to Sutton at the end of the day to 'toughen up'. Yet these were early symptoms of his illness. 'If I don't go out and break the villains,' he had said, 'I will not hold up my head in the West End again.' When he was at length required to explain his conduct he told his superintendent, 'It is very hard, sir. These villains are doing their best to crucify me and I feel as if my hands are tied behind my back.' It was a tragedy with many dimensions, since there was no doubt that he had previously been a courageous soldier and a most effective CID officer.

The period of the offences alleged against him and that of his illness came the year after the Soho protection case but it was plainly unsafe to allow those convictions to stand. All five were quashed, Lord Chief Justice Parker ruling that it would be oppressive to require the defendants to face a retrial. In further cases, including that of two men convicted of carrying explosives and four others concerning the carrying of offensive weapons, a Home Office tribunal cleared Challenor of planting either substances or weapons but the convictions had none the less to be regarded as unsafe in law. In the case of four more men accused of conspiring to intimidate witnesses, Challenor was already known to be ill when it came to court and no evidence was offered by the Crown. Finally, Challenor had arrested a West Indian and two women in July 1963 for conspiring to get money by false pretences from a Swiss man in a Soho 'clip joint'. The jury failed to agree at the first trial and the Swiss visitor did not appear at the retrial, so that the defendants were acquitted. However, Challenor had allegedly punched the Barbadan on the mouth at West End Central and sung to him a hit tune of the day, 'Bongo, bongo, bongo, I don't want to leave the Congo . . .'[16]

Meantime, the consequences of resurgent protection in Soho were evident. In September 1964, the so-called 'Emperor of Porn', Jimmy Humphreys, had his strip club in Walker's Court firebombed and was one of those who now fitted steel shutters over doors and windows, as if acknowledging that this was a battle zone. In the wake of the attack the owner of the building had a number of telephone calls warning him that it would happen again unless he saw reason. Humphreys asked for police protection. Sooner or later intimidation would turn to murder and one man died in the destruction by fire of a Frith Street club in May 1966. The Keyhole Club in Old Compton Street was destroyed in November that year by a bomb left on the doorstep to explode at 3 a.m. Harry Roy, the bandleader, whose Directors Club in Bond Street had defied protection despite a number of attacks, had his premises set ablaze in the same month. The Americana Strip Club and a gaming club in Greek Street were burnt out in February 1967, the girls running from the Americana and trapped gamblers climbing, jumping or falling into the street. Unsurprisingly, the firemen reported a strong smell of petrol in the building. A Paddington club was petrol-bombed in September. A month later, shots were fired into the Mint Casino in Kilburn High Road.

After Challenor's downfall, protection also spread north and west in London, where betting shops either paid or faced burning and bombing. The man who helped to put an end to what he described in court during July 1963 as 'an extortion racket going on for some time in the north-west districts of London' was Detective Sergeant Leonard Read, universally known in the Metropolitan Police as 'Nipper'. The organizer of the racket was Patrick Ball, known in his turn as 'The Professor' because of his precise dress and appearance. Ball and his accomplices had been demanding protection at the modest rate of £10 a week from betting shops in Paddington and Shepherd's Bush. One owner, James Burge, had refused a knock-down offer of £5 and in retaliation his betting shop was firebombed a fortnight later. Two more betting-shop owners, Leslie Potter of Paddington and Sid Kiki of Shepherd's Bush, were under threat. It was arranged that Sergeant Read should pose as Kiki's clerk. When Ball arrived to demand protection again, Kiki would agree and hand over £10. Then the arrest could be made. When the moment came, however, Kiki forgot his part. Instead of handing the money to Ball when it was demanded, he shouted angrily, 'You can fuck off! I'm not having any of this!' The consequence, none the less, was that Ball went to prison for six years and his accomplices for three.[17]

As a result of 'The Professor's' fate, the betting-shop gangs became more subtle. Money did not change hands in the old and simple way. Instead, the collector would come in and ask for pink betting-slips, which would be given to him. He would not pay for them. If he had a winning ticket, he would come back for his money. If not, he would collect more pink betting-slips for the next race. This method of payment made it far more difficult for the police to prove a case in the manner they had done against Ball.

The gangs also remained prepared to deal with those who had defied them. On the night of 10 November 1964, Sid Kiki's betting shop in Netherwood Road, Shepherd's Bush, was firebombed. The damage was relatively slight but the occupants of the flats above and from an adjoining club fled the building. Nathan Mercado, the owner of the premises, had received a reward for his part in bringing Ball and his accomplices to justice, which now made him a principal target. Twenty minutes later, a Molotov cocktail was thrown at A. C. McLean's betting shop nearby, though most of the damage was external. Far more serious was the attempt, ten minutes after that, to destroy Prosser's betting shop in Du Cane Road, Hammersmith, by pouring about a gallon of petrol through the letter box and setting it alight. The petrol was seen and smelt as it seeped through the ceiling of the Delta Club in the basement. There was just time to get everyone out, seconds before the building went up 'in a sheet of flame'.

In the psychopathic philosophy of the gangs who operated in the East End as well as West London, neighbours of the betting shops had to take their chance. On the night of 30 April 1965, petrol was squirted through the letter box of a Lower Clapton betting shop and set alight. The owner, his wife and three children were in bed in the flat above and the possibility that they would all be burnt alive must have been present in the minds of the attackers. Fortunately, the owner's wife was lying awake and the flash from ignited petrol alerted her. After their escape, the owner recalled a telephone message a fortnight earlier, when a voice told him that if he stayed in business he would 'run into trouble'. The persistence of such gangs was shown in June that year, when it was the turn of the Copper Kitchen restaurant in Old Compton Street to be burnt out. It was the third attempt to destroy the restaurant that week.

Middle-class London, which may have thought itself immune to such ruffianly assaults, discovered its error when they reached Hampstead. On 19 March 1967, two men arrived and spoke to a club proprietor's wife about the need to pay 'protection money'. She knew what they were talking about and had them thrown out. She alleged that they came back a week later with thirty or forty companions and started a fight, though there had been nothing to fight about. One of the members, an accountant, described how stools, tables, chairs, bottles and glasses were hurled behind the bar, where the proprietor had taken refuge. Even so he was badly injured as the bar was stormed by men using a hammer, a billiard cue and a rifle butt. They tried to drag him over the counter, breaking his jaw in the attack and inflicting other injuries. When the time to give evidence came, he could not do it. His attackers took his wallet, as well as the club's cash register, which was thrown in the back of a car and driven away. 'Practically everything that could be broken in the club was broken,' said one member. When the case came to court, witnesses were allowed anonymity to the extent of writing down their names and addresses. Even so, one man's hands trembled so violently that he could not do it.[18]

Scotland Yard could only wait and hope that the victims of blackmail and extortion would turn to the police. Few of them did. In January 1968, a woman who owned a Soho nightclub offered the Yard full details of an attempt to extort protection money from her. In response, Detective Superintendent Arthur Butler created a special CID squad whose members would frequent two clubs in the area while remaining in radio contact with the police. The plan succeeded to the extent that the existence of the squad became known and this kept the racketeers clear of these clubs. It did not end attacks elsewhere. One man died and nineteen were injured when a petrol bomb was thrown into the Salamis restaurant and casino in Seven Sisters Road, Finsbury Park, in August that year. Three men died seven months later after an early morning blaze in Meard Street, Soho, at a building which housed the Golden Girl Club, the Haymarket Club and Kowloon Barbers. There was to be no way of curbing the rackets except by destroying the hierarchy of the gangs which sponsored them.

5

Following the abolition of capital punishment in 1964, murder and attempted murder in the underworld became more casual. Some attacks involved doorstep shootings or stabbings, where chance not only decided whether the wounds were fatal but even whether the right person was hit. On New Year's Day 1969, a man with no criminal connections answered the door of his flat on the sixth floor of a Hoxton tower block and was killed by a blast from a sawn-off shotgun. The police found no motive. Another doorstep attack with a sawn-off shotgun in South Woodford, during December that year, gunned down a girl of seventeen who merely happened to be visiting a friend.

It was not always possible to tell whether what seemed like a case of mistaken identity was truly that or merely a preliminary to demands for protection money. In January 1970 a gunman burst into the bar of the Royal Standard in Victoria Road, Hackney. The son of the woman working behind the bar saw the shotgun and shouted, 'Get down, mum!' before he and another man were injured by the blast. The gunman ran for a van and was driven away. The two men shot were singled out as victims without the least apparent reason, other than error.

Some doorstep attacks had a clear connection with the gangs. In December 1964, George Foreman, a betting-shop clerk, was shot on his doorstep in Vauxhall Street, Kennington. It was at first thought to be in mistake for his brother Freddie Foreman, one of the Krays' closest aides. The man who first knocked was Thomas Albert 'Ginger' Marks. George Foreman recognized him as an enemy and shut the door. There was another knock. This time it was Jimmy Evans, to whom Marks had identified Foreman. George Foreman was hit by the blast of a shotgun and thrown against the wall, seriously injured. Rumour had it that Evans' wife was having an affair with Foreman. In any case the feud could not rest there.

It was said that Ronnie Kray issued, or more probably authorized, a contract on Marks in support of his friend. On 5 January 1965 the press began asking, 'Has anyone seen Ginger Marks?' Scotland Yard was concerned at the disappearance of the man 'missing, believed shot'. He was last seen with Jimmy Evans in Bethnal Green, in the bar of the King's Arms, Buckfast Street, on the evening of Saturday 2 January. There had then been an 'incident' just after midnight, when two shots were heard nearby in Cheshire Street, close to the Carpenter's Arms. Bloodstains were found on the pavement, as well as a .22 cartridge case and a pair of spectacles which Mrs Marks identified as those of her husband. She had also received an anonymous phone call, telling her that Marks had been shot and taken away in a car. She had not seen him since.

Evans was subsequently tried but acquitted for attacking George Foreman. When arrested he asked anxiously, 'Can I have bail because if I'm put inside they will get me.' When possession of a firearm was added to the charge, he replied, 'Now you have done that to me, you will get no further information about Marks.' However, after his acquittal in the case, he revealed that he, Ginger Marks and others had tried to burgle a Bethnal Green jewellers' shop on the night of 2–3 January 1965. In Cheshire Street, a car stopped, containing Freddie Foreman and three other men. Someone called, 'Jimmy, come here,' presumably to Evans. Marks seems to have thought the name was 'Ginge', and he stepped forward. Three shots were fired from the car and Marks fell dying. Foreman and three other men identified by Evans were tried but acquitted of the murder in October 1975. In Foreman's account, Evans grabbed Marks, used him as a human shield against the bullets and then ran off.

Among others whose deaths were unaccounted for was the American-born Jack Buggy, whose bound and gagged corpse, shot twice in the head and four times in the body, was found floating in the English Channel, half a mile off Seaford in June 1967. Sid Kiki, one of Leonard Read's informants, had warned him in May that this foot soldier of the protection rackets was missing. Buggy had received a phone call on 11 May from 'Pinky' Lewis, telling him that someone had planted a bomb at the Mount Street Bridge Club in Mayfair. The two men were close friends, planning to run a pitch at Epsom races. Buggy went to the club next afternoon and was never seen alive again.

The Mount Street Bridge Club was a gaming club run by Franny Daniels, a former associate of Billy Hill, and by his nephew. A story circulated of three shots being fired there on the afternoon of 12 May and of Daniels then sending the staff home. The premises were cleaned and the carpet renewed. It was rumoured that Buggy had been shot because he was involved in retrieving £30,000 of Great Train Robbery money from a dishonest 'banker' in Australia but the motive was more probably connected with the rivalry of protection rackets. Franny Daniels and one of his club workers, Abraham Lewis, were belatedly tried for the murder and acquitted in November 1974.

A year after Buggy's death, it was the turn of a more famous name in the East End, Tony Maffia. He was found dead in his Jaguar car on 1 June 1968 with a tarpaulin over him. He had been shot twice through the head with a .22 Browning automatic. Shortly before his death, he had been discussing the purchase of counterfeit currency, and even the sale of his house, with John Jewell, a Manchester coalman whom he had met in Stafford prison. Jewell had tried unsuccessfully to sell Maffia £32,000 of forged currency which was being held by a man at the Albion Casino in Manchester. Maffia certainly left behind him a substantial fortune locked in deedboxes, including a bar of gold identified as coming from the 1967 Rothschild bullion robbery.

Jewell was convicted of the murder, having told an implausible story of three men in a Ford Zodiac who had sent him away while they talked business with Maffia. When he returned, the Zodiac had gone and so had Maffia.

The last and, in some respects, most celebrated gangland murder of the decade was that of David Knight, brother of the armed robber Ronnie Knight who was then married to the actress Barbara Windsor. There had been trouble between David Knight and Johnny Isaacs, leading to a bar-room brawl in Islington. Ronnie Knight claimed that he wanted to put matters right by taking his brother to the Latin Quarter Club in Wardour Street to meet Isaacs again, on better terms. When they arrived, in the small hours of 7 May 1970, there was no sign of Isaacs but presently another fight broke out. In the course of this the doorman, Alfredo Zomparelli, who worked for Albert Dimes, stabbed David Knight to death. At his trial, Zomparelli was sent to prison for four years on a conviction for manslaughter. After his release, he was 'executed' in his pinball arcade in Old Compton Street by two men disguised in dark glasses and false moustaches. They fired one shot through his head and one through his back. The accusation that David Knight had not been a mere visitor to the Latin Quarter Club but had been receiving protection money from it remained, in every sense, a dead issue.

Such headline cases stood out from mistaken hits, attempted killings, and assassinations of less important figures which made up a background tapestry of gangland murder. Little space was given to such deaths as that of Ernest Isaacs in 1966. A professional but not a major criminal, he was shot dead during the night of 23 May in the basement of his home by a man who waited for him there. Three bullets were fired through his body and one through his head from a gun with a silencer. For some time Isaacs had been a frightened man. A friend of George Cornell, a South London villain and target of the Krays, Isaacs lived in the Krays' territory and was terrified that he might be on their list. The coroner's jury could only find a verdict of murder by person or persons unknown. 'He was not an informer as such,' Detective Inspector Harry Howlett explained tactfully, 'but he would give information if it suited his purpose.' The superintendent added that witnesses were 'extremely reluctant to come forward'.[19]

Striking terror into witnesses was a weapon whose uses the leaders of the underworld had developed until it came as deftly as a flick knife to their hands. Those who saw themselves as rulers of that world in the 1960s began to seem like modern Medicis or Borgias, who could shape the thoughts of city states in the East End or South London to their policies and purposes.

The Crazy Gang

I

A GAINST THIS BACKGROUND of organized crime in the 1940s and 1950s, the gang leaders who became household names grew from youthful street fighters to become entrepreneurs of the underworld in the following decade. A revelation of that world at its worst came with news of a man being shot dead and several badly injured at 'Mr Smith's' gaming club in Catford in the small hours of 8 March 1966. The club had been the brainchild of Manchester businessmen who saw a chance to provide South London with comforts normally reserved for the West End. It had been opened by the film star Diana Dors in October 1965 and, predictably, attracted the attention of South London criminals. Protection in its usual sense might have been necessary. Even when Eddie Richardson and Frankie Fraser offered 'security', the owners were prepared to discuss this, though Fraser had a serious criminal record and Richardson was one of two brothers whose crimes would get a good deal of news coverage in the next two years.

The matter of security had not been decided when two groups took their places at tables in the club balcony on the night of 7 March 1966. One consisted of Eddie Richardson, Frankie Fraser and several companions. The other comprised men with criminal records who had already been keeping order of a kind in the club. They included William Haward, Henry Botton, William Gardner and Richard Hart. 'Dickie' Hart was a friend of the Kray twins, north of the river. Until almost 3 a.m. it seemed the two groups were getting on well, though members of staff had noticed William Haward's shotgun under his jacket and Hart's .45 automatic.

When Eddie Richardson decided to use his authority to put a stop to the night's drinking, an argument began and fighting broke out. Like two gangs of Teddy Boys in a dance hall, those concerned required little pretext. The fight spilled from the club into the street, waking sleepers in adjacent houses and prompting calls to the police. Residents reported a dozen or more men fighting in the road and the gardens, some covered with blood and lying in the gutter. There was hysterical laughter and gunfire. Witnesses saw one man grab another and heard him say as he drew a gun from the waistband of his trousers, 'Let me kill him. Let me kill him. This is the bastard that hit me on the head.'

By the time the police arrived, Dickie Hart was lying dead in a garden with his face blown off. Frankie Fraser had his thigh bone shattered by a bullet. Eddie Richardson and three other wounded men had been taken and dumped by their friends at accident and emergency departments of local hospitals, one in the children's section. The casualty total was one dead and four seriously injured. At the trial which followed, Frankie Fraser was acquitted of murdering Dickie Hart on the direction of the judge. He was found guilty of causing an affray and sent to prison for five years. On the other side, Henry Botton and William Haward were also found guilty of affray and sentenced to eight years and five years respectively. In the case of Eddie Richardson, the jury could not agree. At his retrial in September 1966, he was convicted of making an affray and also sent to prison for five years.[1]

Bribing the jury in such cases was now almost as much a part of the proceedings as any other aspect of the trial. One juror was approached twice and another had a milk bottle thrown through his window with a message in it. The bottle was thrown by Charles Richardson. His co-accused John Longman described himself as 'a professional frightener'.

Charles Richardson, rather than Eddie, was the power in the family. He was fourteen when his father deserted them and he had acted as a father in his turn to Eddie and a second brother Alan, later drowned in a boating accident. Though he had spent some time in an approved school for petty theft, he was known as a 'grafter'. After two years' National Service in the Army, part of it in Shepton Mallet military prison where he was a contemporary of the Kray twins, he set up the Peckford Scrap Metal Company in

1956, at the age of twenty-two. Eddie became a director. Thereafter, Charles Richardson had seemed far more a businessman who was occasionally dishonest than a hard-faced gangster. He was associated with insurance fires and long firm frauds, in which an apparently honest and successful company traded for a while and paid its bills, then ran up very large debts and vanished. He had also used his business enterprises to conceal his career as a receiver, though he went to prison for six months in 1959. The following year, faced with charges of receiving stolen metal, he left for Canada until the charges lapsed and he felt it safe to return.

To this point there was little to suggest that he might soon be regarded as one of the decade's public enemies or that he had done anything which might lead him to spend much of the rest of his life in prison. A moderate change of direction early on might have recast him as the businessman who had been wild and unscrupulous in his youth but matured into a useful middle age. Instead, he had gone to prison after interfering with witnesses and jurors in his brother's affray trial but the greater cause of his destruction lay in South Africa. He had chanced a good deal of money there in the search for diamonds, minerals or oil, including £200,000 to find deposits of perlite. This was an uncommon but strong volcanic rock, in demand for high-rise buildings. It seemed a shrewd investment.

He had also sent to South Africa a criminal associate, John Lawrence Bradbury, putting him beyond the reach of interrogation by Scotland Yard. On 29 June 1965, Richardson's South African business partner, Thomas Waldeck, was shot dead. Bradbury confessed to the murder. He was tried, condemned to death, and then reprieved. The name of Charles Richardson played a large part in the confession and details began to appear in the British press.

Bradbury described his childhood friendship with Richardson, how they had met again in 1960 and Richardson had employed him as manager of a couple of South London clubs. Then Bradbury discovered that Richardson had used his lorries for carrying stolen goods and protested, saying that he wanted to pull out of the club. According to Bradbury, he was visited at the club by three men, including Eddie Richardson who felled him with a knuckleduster. He was held down with his arm out straight and cut with a razor from wrist to elbow, the razor run up and down the cut. His face was repeatedly slapped during this ordeal and he was asked if he still wanted to leave the club. He said that he did not. Subsequently, he was accused of not paying £12 10s. which he owed. He was denounced for 'turning them over' and was beaten up in the warehouse by Eddie Richardson, badly enough to leave him with a cyst on one eye.

Bradbury claimed that he had also been present when one of the Kray twins' collectors was brought to the club after hours. The man had made the mistake of trying to collect from a club protected by Eddie Richardson. Eddie and several other men stretched him on the floorboards and nailed him down through both legs.[2]

Before these revelations could have their full effect, the Richardsons became involved in a business deal with James Taggart. During this they insisted that Taggart still owed them £1,200, which he claimed he did not. When he agreed to go and discuss the matter, he was viciously beaten and then made to clean up his blood which lay on the floor in front of him and the wall behind him. The beating was intended to put the fear of retribution into him. However, James Taggart decided that he was just as likely to be beaten up for no reason as for going to the police. Knowing that the Richardsons claimed to have bought off officers at Scotland Yard, he went to Welwyn Garden City on 8 October 1965 to tell his story to Assistant Chief Constable Gerald McArthur, commanding No. 5 Regional Crime Squad. After that, the Richardsons stood no chance.

There was no evidence that any police officer was in the pay of the brothers but McArthur worked on the principle that it might be so. On 29 July 1966, seventy men from West End Central descended on a number of addresses at dawn. Eleven suspects were now under arrest, including Charles Richardson and his wife. In the course of the trial Mrs Richardson was acquitted. Two other men, Eddie Richardson and Frankie Fraser, were by this time in prison for their part in the affray at Mr Smith's Club in Catford.

The trial was one of the longest in British criminal history, lasting from 4 April to 8 June 1967. For the most part, the prosecution case was a conducted tour of a chamber of horrors, perhaps a madhouse, allegedly presided over by Charles Richardson at his offices in Bermondsey or Peckham. Among other exhibits was 'the box', a hand-turned electric generator which could be attached to the genitals or other parts of the victims' bodies and used to give them electric shocks, sufficient to make them jump in the air. One man, Derek Harris, was said to have been attached to this for an hour. Charles Richardson had then pinned him to the floor with a knife through his foot. Then, for no apparent reason, Richardson apologized, gave him a glass of whisky, peeled £150 from a wad of banknotes, handed it to Harris and told him to go.

A good deal of violence was delegated to others. Frankie Fraser was responsible for hitting Benjamin Coulston repeatedly across the face until it was necessary to put him in a bath of water to wash the blood off. Fraser then tried, without success, to extract Coulston's teeth with a pair of pliers. Instead, Coulston was roped inside a tarpaulin shroud and allowed to hear the others talking about driving him to Westminster Bridge with a couple of weights. He was driven off, lost consciousness, and came round in the office again with Richardson saying, 'We've found out it was someone else who got the £600 and I am very sorry.' He then offered Coulston a glass of whisky but the man could not open his lips to drink it. He had a fractured skull and wounds that needed stitching. While he was still in hospital, the police arrived, gathering evidence. Coulston fled in terror from the hospital, still wearing his pyjamas.

At another extreme, when Jack Duval was brought in with eyes blackened, nose bleeding and bloodstains down his clothes, Richardson was almost fatherly towards him. 'Why can't you be a good boy? Why do you misbehave? Must you put people behind prison bars?'

Of the seven men convicted, Charles Richardson was sent to prison for twenty-five years, Eddie Richardson for ten years, to begin after he had completed his five-year sentence for affray at Mr Smith's Club. Frankie Fraser, company director of Hove, Sussex, and Roy Hall of the electric generator went to prison for ten years each, one other man for eight years.[3]

Alfred Berman, though convicted of demanding money with menaces and of assault, was set free. 'I have learnt since my arrest eleven months ago that the police are my best friends,' he said. According to Superintendent McArthur, Berman had been attacked by Charles Richardson while in custody 'and it has been necessary to transfer him to another prison'. He had also resisted Richardson's demands to provide a vast sum of money, 'which might have been used to defeat the ends of justice'. After that, life in prison had become 'very difficult' for him.[4]

Whether or not the means of defeating justice referred to bribery of witnesses or jurors, there was the usual evidence of such attempted persuasion. Before the Old Bailey trial, two men had been jailed for two years each, in December 1966, for an approach to a witness. In January 1967 a man and two women, one of them Frankie Fraser's sister, had been charged with conspiring to prevent a witness giving evidence. They were subsequently convicted. Benjamin Coulston, though a victim of torture, was currently an inmate of Canterbury prison and had been allowed out for the day to attend his mother's funeral. He had no police guard and claimed he was approached in a pub with an offer of £1,000 with £1,000 to follow if he made a statement that the evidence he had given at the magistrates court was untrue. Of this money, £500 with £500 to follow was offered by Frankie Fraser's sister. In March, two of those involved in this attempt were jailed for two years each and one for six months. By then, one of the key witnesses in the case was under police guard at a 'temporary home' in Hastings. The trial judge, Mr Justice Lawton, revealed during the proceedings that further approaches had been made to two jurors 'which seemed to indicate a material advantage might result'. Even a juror's seventy-five-year-old mother had been told that 'there had better be disagreement'.[5]

A good deal of 'nobbling' was not even expert, let alone subtle. A so-called 'small cog' was jailed in September. He had tried to get at a juror under police guard, a man who kept an off-licence opposite the La Paloma café in Stoke Newington. The 'frightener' had offered the café proprietor £50 to take a message to the man. He came back the next day, by which time the proprietor had told the police. This time the fixer said, 'I will give you as much money as you want if you will pass a message to Mr Baldwin. Forget about the £50 I mentioned. You can have as much as you want.' When asked what the message was, he said, 'I don't know.' As a rule, the approach was furtive and brisk, as a juror reported to an Old Bailey judge during a trial in 1964: 'When the others say "Guilty", you say, "Not guilty", and you will receive £100.' Within a few years, judges did not wait for an approach to jurors before ordering twenty-four-hour police surveillance. When the South London protection racketeer Billy Howard went on trial in April 1968, in the Craywood Gaming Club case, the jurors were told that they would be under surveillance throughout the proceedings, as a matter of course.[6]

Only after the trials of the Richardsons did the extent of the gang's network become clear, not least in respect of its ability to extort protection money from the proceeds of other criminal enterprises. An undercover squad of CID officers had shadowed their known associates. There seemed to be a regular weekly delivery from the car parks at Heathrow Airport to the letter box of a council flat on the twentieth floor of Draper House, a high-rise block in Southwark. The flat was occupied by a couple whose son had links to the Richardsons. Though it was a courtroom cliché, there had been what the prosecution called a 'gigantic fraud' run for almost six years by employees of Airpark Garages Ltd. The firm managed multi-storey car parks at Heathrow on behalf of the British Airports Authority.

The originator of the fraud had a simple and apparently foolproof scheme. Drivers were allowed to park their cars for up to twenty-four hours and would pay up to £2 on leaving, depending on the length of their stay. The ticket was collected and stamped as they left. It was only necessary for the attendant in the exit kiosk to manipulate the time-stamping mechanism or even to perform a little forgery so that the ticket recorded a stay of two hours and a charge of two shillings (or ten pence). The remaining £1. 18s. of the £2 charge went into the pockets of the swindlers. If no one in authority noticed this, it was because the used tickets were very seldom looked at anyway. The success of the fraud might be judged by comparing the takings for the last week before the conspirators were arrested, when they were £1,963, with the first week of honesty when they were recorded at more than double that amount, £3,983. This was corroborated by monthly figures of £8,800 before the arrests and

£17,000 after them. It seemed that the loss to the British Airports Authority had been running at about £100,000 a year, or £1,000,000 in modern terms.

It was not Scotland Yard or the airport authorities who discovered what was going on but the Richardsons. Money had become no object to the swindlers. At first it had been handed to them in envelopes. Then, as it became clear that the tickets were never checked after use, they were simply told to help themselves from the tills. No one bothered any longer to alter the time-stamping machines. They began to take cruises, buy cars and furniture, invest in Premium Bonds and even to buy houses. Some of them also began to enjoy the nightlife of West End clubs. They were noticed there as living beyond their probable means and, it seems, some of them talked indiscreetly.

The organizers of the fraud received a visit from the Richardson gang, who demanded £500 a week, at least a quarter of the proceeds. When the swindlers hesitated, they were told the story of the man who had been taken to a cellar in Soho, then stripped and beaten with wet towels until he saw the error of his ways. The car park men were not hardened to this sort of criminality and they gave in. One of the Richardsons' men was even taken on as a car park supervisor to make sure that there was no unfairness towards the extortioners. The money was collected weekly by Eddie Richardson or Frankie Fraser until both were arrested for their part in the Mr Smith's Club affray. After that, the weekly subscription was increased on the grounds that it was needed for legal expenses. The money was now delivered to the letter box of the flat at Draper House.

Detective Sergeant Peter Boorman, who was to play a major part in the investigation of the Rothschild bullion hijack in the following year, spent the autumn of 1966 on the roof of one of the multistorey garages with binoculars, a police photographer and long-range photographic equipment. The lenses were trained on the car park exit kiosks and their tills. Sergeant Boorman also used the car park himself. As yet, he did not know the names of his suspects but identified them by christening them after Snow White's seven dwarfs, beginning with 'Dopey' and 'Grumpy'. Then, walking through the airport one day, he noticed a child's toy for sale at the bookstall, 'Be a

Secret Agent'. It contained invisible ink. He used this to mark his car park tickets with the true times of his arrival. In the witness box of the Old Bailey, he asked if he might have a look at one of them, which had been seized at the time of the arrests. It was handed to him with the writing still invisible. To the consternation of court officials, he ignited his cigarette lighter but merely held it close to the ticket. As the heat warmed the paper, the secret writing appeared.

At the end of the trial, eleven of the thirteen defendants were convicted and prison terms ranging from twelve months to seven years were imposed. In December 1969, the British Airports Authority brought an action against the defendants and in some cases their wives for the money found on them or at their homes at the time of their arrests.[7]

2

While the Richardsons' natural territory was South London, the East End of the 1960s belonged indisputably to the Kray brothers. They too fought for control of protection but also strove for something beyond the reach of South London, a glamour which reflected on those who mingled with the famous. The twins, Ronnie and Reggie, had risen from being proprietors of the Regal billiard hall in Eric Street, Mile End, to their role as West End celebrities and owners of Esmeralda's Barn in Belgravia. They had rubbed shoulders and been photographed with a number of famous names, including Judy Garland, Sophie Tucker, George Raft, Jackie Collins, Stanley Baker and Billy Daniels. They were among the subjects of a 1960s cultural condescension by the middle class and its media, soon to be killed stone-dead by Tom Wolfe as 'radical chic'. The world première of Joan Littlewood's 1962 cockney comedy, *Sparrers Can't Sing*, starring Barbara Windsor, was screened opposite their club in Bow Road, before Princess Margaret and a distinguished audience. Though royalty kept its distance, much of the celebration took place by courtesy of the Krays.

Yet from every photograph, film stars or entertainers smiled out energetically and confidently, while the twins looked anxious and seemed to wish they were elsewhere. In the press, they were described as ex-boxers and later as East End businessmen who gave generously to charity. No one, it was said, ever appealed to them in vain. The local clergy knew and liked the family, whose roots were woven into the East End past. There were surviving grand-parents, beyond question the salt of the earth. With the parents and children, they were the folk who had seen off Hitler and his Luftwaffe. The young brothers, now doing so well for themselves, had become benefactors who would never let the pensioners go short of a party at Christmas.

The twins were born in 1935, four years after their brother Charles. They survived diphtheria and measles at the age of three, though it seemed that Ronnie was afterwards slower and more awkward than Reggie. Yet Ronnie was the reader of such novels as John Steinbeck's *Of Mice and Men*, the twin who learned from his reading to hero-worship Orde Wingate, Lawrence of Arabia and Al Capone. Some years later, he read *Mein Kampf* and developed an interest in Adolf Hitler. Their taste for violence was not essen-tially different from thousands of 1950s Teddy Boys, though few of those had in mind fights as vicious as some in which the twins engaged. Cutting or slashing was preferred to punching. Ronnie Kray was said to favour cutlasses or knives, rather than razors, because he could get more power behind them.

Their professional careers as boxers were early and brief, ending with conscription into the Royal Fusiliers for National Service at eighteen after appearances at the Albert Hall as lightweight contenders. Army discipline did little, except to keep them in the military prison at Shepton Mallet for a good deal of their time. They were dishonourably discharged in 1954. Ironically, in the gang wars which followed, Ronnie relished his nickname of 'The Colonel'. He planned attacks as if they were military operations and exercised a pseudo-military discipline over his followers. When trouble with the Richardsons threatened, two Browning machine-guns under the floorboards of the family home in Vallance Road, Bethnal Green, were among his impressive collection of weapons.

Back in civilian life, the twins had taken over the billiard hall and defeated the three reigning hard men of Mile End and Poplar

in a private bar-room fight. This earned them the rewards of protection in the area, from illegal bookmakers and gaming clubs – an
income known to the twins and their assistants as 'pensions'. In the
following year, at the 1955 Ascot spring meeting, they met Billy
Hill with Frankie Fraser, and Jack Spot who had already paid a visit
to the billiard hall. The twins were offered a pitch.

Having met Hill and Spot, whose active criminal careers were
drawing to an end, the twins felt only contempt for the old men
standing in their way. Within a year they had extended their control
over Hackney and Mile End, recruiting and rewarding those who
proved loyal to them. They found new targets for protection,
including used-car lots, where a refusal to pay might invite a night-
time visit from gang members with paint-spray cans and sledgehammers. Some of the money extorted was used to buy more general
loyalty. Among good causes, the twins pensioned the families of
'aways', as men serving prison sentences were euphemistically
known.

John Michael Barry, a club owner who was invited to contribute
to the Kray pension scheme, described the method of recruitment.
At 3 a.m. one morning, he received a phone call from the doorman
of his Regency Club in North London. He went to the door of
the club and saw the Krays' cousin, Ronnie Hart, holding a gun.
Hart was backed up by 'Big Albert' Donaghue and another gang
member, Dicky Morgan. The doorman was 'absolutely terrified'.
Barry was summoned to meet the twins.

> I went to see Ronald and Reginald Kray. I went to a flat in Bethnal
> Green. I can't tell you whose flat it was. I got the address by tele-
> phoning Ronald Kray at his home. This was the following day. Both
> the Kray twins were there. There were about ten or fifteen members
> of 'The Firm' as well.
>
> I told them it was Morgan, Donaghue and Ronnie Hart who
> entered my club. They got in by smashing two doors. I also told
> them that Big Albert told me that I was to join the pension scheme
> and got to pay £50 a week. Ronnie Kray said, 'I just want you to
> help us out for a while.' Ronnie Kray also apologized for the way
> they got into the club. I didn't have any more to say because I didn't
> have the chance. I just said, 'OK, I'll pay the £50.' I paid £50 for

about three weeks. I couldn't possibly keep it up so I saw Ronald Kray in a public house. I met him by appointment. Members of 'The Firm' were there when I spoke to him. I said, 'It is crippling us. Can you help us and let us pay less?' Ronnie Kray suggested I paid £20 a week to Hart and £20 a week to Albert for the time being – reducing the amount by £10. I kept it up until they were arrested.

The twins made sure that Barry knew he was in their thoughts. From time to time he was invited for a drink. 'I had no option but to go. I was frightened. I didn't enjoy their company.'[8]

By 1956, the balance between the twins had shifted. To this point, Ronnie had seemed the dominant partner. In November that year he was jailed for three years at London Sessions for the savage attack on Terry Martin who had the misfortune to be the only person in the bar of the Britannia, where Ronnie Kray had expected to fight the Watney Street gang. The violence inflicted on Martin with a bayonet and by kicks to the head seemed psychotic. Ronnie Kray's conduct during his prison sentence confirmed this. He had to be restrained in a straitjacket, and was certified insane, suffering from 'prison psychosis'. More specifically, he was paranoid and was transferred to Long Grove Mental Hospital in Epsom. He now swore his twin Reggie was not Reggie but a Soviet spy impersonating him and even had doubts as to the reality of his mother and their home in Vallance Road. At times he was convinced that one of his fingers was missing.

Ronnie was overtly homosexual. He was never treated for this and his most illuminating comment was simply that women were smelly and gave men diseases. Reggie was briefly married to Frances Shea, who committed suicide after a year, but it was said that the marriage was never consummated and there was evidence that he was at least bisexual. A gruesome story in Michael Connor's biography of the South London protection racketeer Billy Howard describes the twins in their car picking up a youth at night from the so-called 'meat rack' of male prostitutes outside the Regent Palace Hotel, near Piccadilly Circus. According to Howard, they broke into a house near Sloane Square and made use of the rent boy simultaneously, choking him to death in the process. They put his body in the boot of the car and, again according to Howard, disposed of it in Norfolk. Howard was employed to pay the owner of the house for the damage caused by a wild party at a mistaken address and to persuade him not to complain.[9]

By the mid-1960s, the Krays were spoken of as a great power in the East End and a growing menace to the West End. Though Reggie was jailed for eighteen months in 1960 for demanding money with menaces, he was released after nine months. By then the notorious landlord of the Stephen Ward case, Peter Rachman, had been warned by Ronnie that unless he paid his dues, the gang would put his rent collectors off the street. This problem was resolved by the transfer of a West End club, Esmeralda's Barn in Wilton Place, to the twins.

Yet the myth of an all-powerful gang had some odd discrepancies. John Dickson, who was one of their lieutenants, recalled that the 'Kray Gang' consisted of only about twenty members. It seemed less a widely extended criminal conspiracy than a coachload of social misfits. On the other hand, the Krays had campaigned for the hearts and minds of East London, the catchment area from which any future jurors and witnesses were likely to come. In the pubs where they drank, they claimed that they also sent in drinks to police officers in the other bar. The impression was that at least some of those officers were in their pockets.

They had got away with so much for so long that it must have seemed to them that they could get away with anything. Their powerful friends would aid them. When trouble seemed likely in 1964, Ronnie had been to see the maverick Conservative politician Lord Boothby, a voice familiar to millions of radio listeners and a favourite contributor to programmes like *Any Questions?* It was arranged that the two men should be photographed sitting on a sofa together. The bisexual Boothby had little idea of who Ronnie Kray was or what suspicions the photograph might suggest to the public. Then he realized, panicked, and went to considerable lengths to prevent its appearance in the *Sunday Mirror*, though to any rational person it appeared entirely innocent.

Sooner or later the Krays might demand protection from someone even more famous than themselves who was prepared to call their bluff. The comedian Charlie Chester had said that he would close his club rather than pay. Peter Cook and Dudley Moore of the Establishment Club were also approached. Billy Howard claimed that he had been to see Peter Cook who told him that the Kray twins were trying to force 'insurance payments' from him and that he had been to the police.

Howard advised the twins to keep clear. When Ronnie began to bluster, he was reminded that Cook and Moore were celebrities and so were their friends. If there was trouble, the twins could expect to find themselves deserted by the famous and outwitted by the satirists of the Establishment Club and *Private Eye*. They had a good deal to lose. Their homosexual conduct was still a criminal offence which carried a prison sentence. In the East End they were already referred to behind their backs as 'Gert and Daisy'.

By 1964, it seemed they had lost whatever judgement they once had. They had become involved in plans that were absurdly beyond their capacity. Among the wildest were a plot to rescue ex-President Moise Tshombe of the Congo from detention in Algiers, using their own military strike force, and building a major new city in Nigeria. Closer to home, the protection business ran into trouble. Their target had been Hew McCowan, owner of the Hideaway Club in Gerrard Street, Soho. In October 1964, two nights after his club opened, it was alleged that a man had 'caused a scene' there, occasioning damage to the value of £20. Shortly after this, McCowan was told by his business manager, 'It is a difficult area to control.' One of the twins had offered to introduce the partners in the club 'to someone to whom we could pay a salary to look after the door'.

There were two meetings with the Krays in a public house in the Whitechapel Road. 'It was more or less business. They would introduce people to the club for a percentage of the turnover.' In exchange, the Krays would provide a receptionist and a doorman 'to stop undesirable elements entering the club. We would pay a percentage of what the people who had been introduced spent in the club. It would be 20 per cent for the first month, increasing to 30 per cent and then 50 per cent.' When the 50 per cent was demanded, at the Grave Maurice, another East End pub, one of the partners recalled, 'We were a bit agitated over it and I used bad language to Ronnie and said, "You are a bastard."'

The agreement was never concluded. Hew McCowan went to the police and complained that the Krays had tried to blackmail him. At their trial, the defence produced a witness who swore that McCowan had offered him money to tell lies about the Krays. Instead, this witness had generously offered to get Judy Garland and the wife of Nat King Cole to perform in McCowan's club. A clergyman gave evidence that he had heard McCowan threaten the same witness that unless he gave false evidence against the Krays, he would lose the £40 a week that McCowan was paying him. The jury at the first trial could not agree. At a retrial, they acquitted the twins even before the final speeches of counsel had been made.[10]

This acquittal reaffirmed their belief that no one could touch them. For a year afterwards, they continued to prosper and opened a new club in Soho, the El Morocco in Gerrard Street, which had previously been the Hideway Club owned by the man who had prosecuted them. If the police made no effort to put a stop to their activities, perhaps it seemed to them that the police did not want to. The police were no nearer closing down their protection rackets. The twins' cousin Ronnie Hart, a member of the gang, described what happened to the 'customers' who still refused to pay their dues to the Krays. 'Either they get hurt or people are sent into the clubs to have fights and things like that but nine times out of ten, they get hurt.' A 'pension' was regular payment for protection but it was supplemented by 'nipping'. This was where 'you just go in and help yourself'.[11]

It was murder, not protection, which brought the Krays down at last. Two days after the murder of Dickie Hart in the affray at Mr Smith's Club in Catford, one of the Richardsons' men crossed the river on 9 March 1966 to have a drink with a friend at the Blind Beggar in Aldgate. George Cornell, *alias* Myers, was a natural enemy of the Krays, though Ronnie had lately spoken to him kindly on the phone when Cornell's daughter had been ill. The twins suspected Cornell of trying to poach on their territory north of the river but that was not necessarily a killing matter. More important, he had referred publicly to Ronnie Kray as 'a fat poof'. However shocking, both components of the phrase were entirely accurate.

To say that Ronnie Kray had become unpredictable in his reactions was an understatement. An old friend had tried to borrow £5 and said jokingly that, with all the weight he had put on, Ronnie looked as if he could afford it. Ronnie left the club, then came back, saying he wanted a private word with the joker, in the washroom. The culprit was found there later, so disfigured by Ronnie Kray's knife that it required seventy stitches to sew his face together. Permanent double scars down each cheek earned him the name of 'Tramlines'.

During Cornell's visit to the Blind Beggar in March 1966, Ronnie caught up with him. Kray and one of his aides, John Alexander 'Ian' Barrie, were both carrying guns. Barrie fired wide to empty the bar. Cornell then had time to say, 'Well, look who's here,' before Ronnie killed him with a single shot through the forehead. In a little while there were few people in the East End who had not heard the rumour that Ronnie Kray had killed Cornell. Yet not a single witness was prepared to talk to the police.[12]

Later that year, the widowed Reggie Kray was dragged further into danger by his twin. For some time there had been a plan to rescue Frank Mitchell, 'The Mad Axe-Man', who was serving sentences of ten years and life imprisonment concurrently in Dartmoor for robbery with violence. He might almost have been the dim-witted giant of crime comedy, except for the injuries he had inflicted in reality. He had been repeatedly imprisoned, adding to these terms by his escapes; he had also been flogged, held at Rampton and Broadmoor and certified as a mental defective. What value he possessed for the twins was not clear. Perhaps he was thought to be a useful heavyweight or, once the promise to liberate him had been made, perhaps it became to Ronnie a matter of honour and saving face. The escape was not difficult. The prison authorities had tried to pacify Mitchell by putting him on a casually supervised 'outside working party', which did not preclude him from meeting a woman by arrangement, out of sight of his guards.

The escape plan was activated on 12 December 1966 by the twins, their elder brother and fifteen accomplices. Mitchell was collected from the moor, taken by car to London, arriving almost before he was missed from the prison. Kept at a flat in Barking with all comforts supplied, including a hostess from Winston's Club in Bond Street, he was soon a liability. Naturally he wanted to go out and became restive. He was promised a safe-house in the country with Ronnie and Reggie, then, perhaps, a new life abroad. Predictably, he had fallen in love with the club hostess, hired or abducted to share his bed, and to her dismay insisted that she must come too. On Christmas Eve 1966, he was told it was time to leave for the house in the country. The girl would follow in a day or two. As he left, those in the flat heard shots from the street. The girl cried out, 'Oh, God, they've shot him. I've had it now.' As a matter of fact, she had not. After promising Reggie Kray that she would tell no one about Mitchell, she was released. According to Albert Donaghue, who turned Queen's evidence, Mitchell had climbed into the back of a grey van and two men had shot him dead. His body was burned. No one was ever to be convicted of his murder.[13]

The Krays had murdered at least twice and the law had not been able to touch them. In the course of 1967, another candidate for assassination presented himself. Leslie Payne, who had been instrumental in ousting Peter Rachman from Esmeralda's Barn and replacing him with the twins, was now thought to be talking to the police. The risk to the twins of doing their own killing was still too great but they had found willing deputies in the case of Frank Mitchell. Now the chosen hit man was Jack 'The Hat' McVitie, so called because he habitually wore a hat to cover his baldness. The Krays no longer scorned the drugs trade and McVitie was Ronnie's dealer in Purple Hearts. McVitie took a gun and £100 on account. His first attempt was a failure. Then he got drunk, took a handful of 'Black Bombers' and began to talk about killing the twins instead.

McVitie in his garrulous mood was a far worse threat than the grateful Mad Axe-Man had been. On the night of 28 October 1967, Reggie set out to find him. McVitie was not at the Regency Club in North London, where the Krays were 'protectors', nor at the Stoke Newington flat of 'Blonde Carol', where a party was ending. Reggie installed himself in the house, ordering Tony Lambrianou and Ronnie Hart to find and fetch McVitie for a party. As McVitie arrived, Reggie tried to shoot him through the head with a gun that jammed. McVitie then attempted in vain to dive through a window. Ronnie grabbed and held him, shouting, 'Be a man, Jack.' McVitie replied, 'I'll be a man but I don't want to die like one.' Ronnie impatiently told his twin to 'Do him,' and Reggie butchered the unreliable subordinate with a carving knife.[14]

The twins went to a flat owned by Harry Hopwood where they bathed while Ronnie Hart took their Mini and fetched fresh clothes from their Aunt May in Vallance Road. On the way, he threw the gun and the knife into the canal at Queensbridge Road. Ronald Bender meantime had driven McVitie's body 'over the water' to South London and disposed of it. The body was never found and a variety of stories circulated as to its destination, including its incorporation in the arch of a motorway flyover. Another rumour suggested that, like the unfortunate rent-boy, McVitie had been fed to the pigs in Norfolk. He may well have been dumped out at sea by a friendly and well-rewarded trawlerman.

The clothes the twins had been wearing were burned, as were the banknotes in their wallets. Even the ashes from these were swilled down the sink. Their rings and coins were washed. Meanwhile the living room where McVitie had died was cleaned and its contents destroyed. Like Mitchell, he vanished as if he had never existed. The two killers then left for a tour of Cambridge and the Eastern Counties. Once more, there were rumours and no evidence. This time, however, the newly promoted Detective Superintendent Leonard 'Nipper' Read was summoned by Peter Brodie, the Yard's Assistant Commissioner (Crime). 'Mr Read,' he was told, 'you're going to get the Krays.'[15]

3

The catch was that the Krays could be put away if someone was prepared to talk but no one would talk until the twins had been put away. Such was the deadlock in East London for some months. The breakthrough, when it came, was not in the East End but in Glasgow. There had been considerable police cooperation between London and Glasgow, as there had been between the Krays and the Glasgow underworld.

An authorized phone-tap in 1967 led to the arrest of a minor figure in the Kray network, at Glasgow airport en route for London. Paul Elvey was carrying a suitcase containing three dozen sticks of dynamite. When questioned, he at length admitted that the Krays had intended to use the dynamite to blow up a Maltese nightclub owner, George Caruana, an enemy of the 1950s Soho vice racketeer, Tommy Smithson, and in whose Maida Vale house Smithson had been shot by the Maltese, Philip Ellul.

Elvey named Alan Bruce Cooper as his mentor. When Cooper was arrested and faced with a charge of conspiracy to murder, he also gave way and admitted that he had been employed by the Kray twins on a contract killing. There was now a chance that gang loyalty would crack if it was attacked quickly. At 6 a.m. on 8 May 1968, Commander John Du Rose of Scotland Yard coordinated the assault. The twins were arrested at their flat in Braithwaite House, Shoreditch. The home of their elder brother Charles and those of eighteen other men were raided simultaneously by a hundred Regional Crime Squad officers. By the afternoon twenty-one suspects were in custody at West End Central police station. They faced charges of conspiracy to murder, grievous bodily harm and extortion. Though none of this related directly to the killing of George Cornell, Frank Mitchell or Jack McVitie, those who had played lesser roles in their deaths might now try to save themselves by cooperating with the police. Yet detailed evidence against the Kray brothers was so scarce for a further month that Leonard Read assumed the 'prime mover', as he described him in court, to be Charles Kray rather than his twin brothers.

For the time being, the press still referred cautiously to the twins as East End businessmen, charity workers and former lightweight boxers. Meantime, the police kept all prosecution witnesses under guard at houses outside London. On 13 May, Lennie 'Books' Dunn, who sold magazines and pornography from a stall in Aldgate, went to West Ham police and told them that his was the flat where Mitchell had been kept after his escape. The Krays had promised him money for the use of it and he had never been paid. He was soon to give evidence as 'Mr B'. Far worse for the twins, one of the principal figures in the gang, 'Big Albert' Donaghue, sought a deal and pleaded guilty to being an accessory to the murder of Jack McVitie. Donaghue had also helped to look after Frank Mitchell. He had taken Mitchell out to the van and returned. He and the club hostess, Liza, had heard the shots from the van as it drove off, after which Donaghue made a phone call to someone – presumably one of the twins – and gave the coded message, 'The dog has won,' to signify that the killing had been carried out.

By the time the first trial began on 8 January 1969, for the murders of George Cornell and Jack McVitie, the twins' cousin Ronnie Hart turned Queen's evidence and gave a detailed account of McVitie's murder. John 'Scotch Jack' Dickson, who drove Ronnie Kray and Ian Barrie from the Blind Beggar, was also to be a prosecution witness. As they left the pub, Ronnie Kray had said, 'I hope the bastard is dead.' The following evening, he had told another gang member, Billy Exley, who now gave evidence for the Crown, 'When I pointed the gun at him, George Cornell knew he was going to die.'[16]

More important in this case, the barmaid who three years earlier had failed to identify Ronnie Kray or Ian Barrie as being in the bar with Cornell and had told the inquest she had not seen the shooting, now gave evidence that she had seen the killing and recognized the two men. Why had she not said so at the time? 'I was terrified I would get shot like George Cornell did if I told the truth.' Though she had lied, it was easy for the jury to see why. That, in turn, cast the Krays as gangsters of calculated viciousness. If evidence of this were needed, it was provided by Ronnie Hart who described what the twins had called their 'pension scheme' and which was more bluntly termed extortion. As for 'nipping', it was more like wholesale looting. There had been a good deal of nipping at the Regency Club on the night of McVitie's murder.

The immaculately suited Krays sat in the dock of the Central Criminal Court as 'company directors', suggesting to the jurors that they must be far above such behaviour. Occasionally but significantly the mask slipped, as when Kenneth Jones QC for the Crown was questioning Reggie Kray's sister-in-law about his dead wife. Reggie jumped to his feet and shouted, 'What's this got to do with the case? Sit down, you fat slob!' He was removed from the dock, still shouting that the police were 'pigs' and 'filthy animals'. Indeed, the mask had already slipped before the magistrate at Bow Street, when Ronnie Hart gave evidence to the accompaniment from the dock of 'Liar! Liar! He is known as a liar in the East End!'[17]

Ronnie Kray's appearance in the witness box at the Central Criminal Court was at best tetchy and did him little good. Worse still, his character witness proved to be 'Mad' Frankie Fraser, serving fifteen years for torture and the affray at Mr Smith's Club. Fraser contributed nothing beyond having heard the name of another man who was supposed to have shot Cornell. His credibility was finally destroyed when he admitted his previous criminal record and having twice been certified insane. The twins were to be acquitted of the murder of Frank Mitchell. Meantime, Ronnie Kray was convicted of the murder of George Cornell with Reggie an accomplice after the fact. Both were found guilty of the murder of Jack McVitie.

The trial was presided over by Mr Justice Melford Stevenson, whose country home rejoiced in the name of 'Truncheons' and who was known for conducting court proceedings with an unusual degree of rigour. One of his first actions was to order 'protective surveillance' of all the jurors. After the three Kray brothers and all but one of the other defendants were found guilty, he began by sentencing Ronnie Kray. 'I am not going to waste words on you. The sentence upon you is that you will go to life imprisonment. In my view society has earned a rest from your activities and I recommend that you be detained for thirty years.' Reggie Kray received the same minimum recommendation and the accessories went to prison for terms of seven to twenty years. At thirty-six years old, the twins were not to have a hope of freedom until they were sixty-six. Even that proved optimistic. Ronnie Kray was to die in prison and Reggie was released at sixty-seven, in the final weeks of terminal cancer.

The reputation of the Krays was formed in part by what they did and in part by when they did it. They fitted neatly into a vogue for working-class history, in an age of 'history workshops'. Their downfall coincided with the popularity of such films as *Bonnie and Clyde*, which raised to cult status two violent small-town bank robbers of the 1930s Mid-West, Bonnie Parker and Clyde Barrow.

The Americans' murderous career was even said to have existen-
tialist significance and to be a 'meditation on the place of guns and
violence' in society. Their assaults on the personnel and property
of the banks chimed with a late 1960s taste for anti-capitalism and
student rebellion against the established order. For a mercifully short
period, radical young women adopted the 'hayseed' fashions of
Bonnie Parker in her knitted bonnet.

By December 1968, England had what the press called its very
own 'Bonnie and Clyde' gang of five men and a woman all under
twenty-one, four of whom escaped from prison while remanded on
charges of robbery, assaulting a prison officer and stealing guns. In
April 1969, four of its members, 'young men of promise', went to
prison for a total of twenty-two years after a series of armed attacks
on betting offices, sub-post offices and banks across the country.
They had been recaptured after staging an armed robbery at a
Birmingham bank, which might have brought them £18,000.[18]

In such circumstances, the Kray twins were not to be lightly
discarded as icons of the 1960s. Their stereotyped faces appeared on
souvenirs, following a joint portrait by the fashion photographer
David Bailey, and their views on clubland were respectfully sought
in television interviews. They were, at least, examples of that modish
type of the decade, the anti-hero.

The twins lived on in prison for three decades, unfailing objects
of curiosity. They showed little repentance, Reggie saying years later
that he did not regret the murder of Jack McVitie at the time and
did not regret it now. Ronnie died in Broadmoor in 1995. Reggie
was released in 2000 on compassionate grounds, shortly before his
death. Other families, including the Dixons and the Tibbs, tried
briefly and unsuccessfully to imitate what the Krays had done in
East London. The law was ready for them and their new order was
quickly destroyed.

During their long imprisonment, the twins remained kings over
the water, while Bethnal Green, Stepney and their neighbours underwent a change greater even than the blitz, principally with the arrival
of immigrants from Asia. Most of the indigenous post-war community had left London for Essex or Hertfordshire, Surrey or Kent.
Many who remained were elderly, impoverished and often resentful.

At the time of the row over Enoch Powell's 1968 warnings against mass immigration and his 'rivers of blood' speech, thousands of London dockers struck and marched with such banners as 'Enoch Powell says what everybody thinks'. On 1 May, they staged a running fight with anti-Powell students in Parliament Square.

Three decades later, to many of those who watched the funeral processions of the twins through the East End, it must have seemed as if their royalty were going to its grave. The crowds who lined the streets for Ronnie's cortège were said to be larger than for any funeral between those of Winston Churchill and Princess Diana. That might have been mere curiosity, had it not been for the waves of cheering as Reggie passed by and then stepped from his limousine, handcuffed to a prison officer. The heroes had come home. To many this nostalgia was incomprehensible. To the crowds, however, the twins with all their faults represented an old and fondly remembered culture, for those of that culture who still remained. They had been 'bad lads' and yet 'our very own'. How swiftly, it must have seemed, they would have dealt with the newcomers who did not know their place and had presumed to take over the drugs trade and protection. The mourners, as so often on these occasions, yearned for the return of a world lost for ever.

England in the 1960s never quite knew what to make of its two most famous criminals. The homely and banal world of television commentary or the softly spoken interview came nowhere near defining them. At the same time, abhorrent though they might be, the great public audience could not bear to leave them alone, least of all in the obscurity of their long imprisonment. They were the subject of books, documentaries and a major film. Those who had little interest in crime knew at once who 'The Krays' had been. Yet despite their reputation as icons of that morally versatile decade, they almost seemed to belong to another age.

Perhaps a remoter historian might have seen them for what they were better than the commentators and interviewers of the moment. Suetonius, who wrote biographies of twelve emperors but also *Lives of Famous Whores*, would have recognized their dangerous amalgam of personal power with cruelty, perversion, sentimentality, superstition, family affection, soldierly ambition, the courage of the arena if only at the Albert Hall. A terrifying unpredictability and emotional fragility marked their most violent crimes. Suetonius' subjects displayed such qualities in abundance. Nero's emasculation of Sporus as a 'wife' curiously anticipated the story of Ronnie Kray's plan to have a boy brought to him to castrate. In another context, the gang's rivals or victims, called to a final account by the twins, might have found a grim similarity in Edward Gibbon's portrait of the Emperor Commodus.

> Suspicion was equivalent to proof; trial to condemnation. The execution of a considerable senator was attended with the death of all those who might lament or revenge his fate; and when Commodus had once tasted blood, he became incapable of pity or remorse.[19]

Those who witnessed the butchering of Jack 'The Hat' said afterwards that a madness followed the drawing of the first blood in that drab basement flat at Stoke Newington.

The trials of the Krays had revealed contemporary crime at its most brutal and corrupting. With their departure, governments and political parties flexed their muscles at the hustings and promised to 'tighten up' or 'crack down' on professional villainy. This seldom prevented the annual crime statistics from moving implacably upwards. Sometimes there was rejoicing that the rate of increase had dropped, as if that somehow equated to a decline. By 1970, however, it was not statistics alone that made the fight against crime such a gloomy business. The public, as represented by the press, now became less interested in what the underworld was doing than in what the police were up to. Some of the best crime-fighters had joined the other side in the worst of all worlds. In 1972, Sir Robert Mark became Commissioner of the Metropolitan Police. He gave his definition of a good police force, wryly but poignantly, as one that catches more crooks than it employs.

18

Spare a Copper

To SEE A quarter of the detective strength of Scotland Yard standing in the dock of the Central Criminal Court might have been thought impossible, until it happened. The men who were ultimately convicted had taken money from career criminals and surrendered their principles so entirely that they burnt on their office fires the orders for the arrest of their paymasters. To protect those who corrupted them, they sent telegrams ordering other police forces to release suspects who were arrested, on the pretext of mistaken identity.

This scandal had nothing whatever to do with the fall of the Drug Squad or the Obscene Publications Squad and the trials of Scotland Yard officers between 1972 and 1977. It occurred a century earlier, in October 1877, and led to a shake-up in the Metropolitan Police which made twentieth-century restructuring seem almost timid. As a result of it, the 'detective police' of the 1870s was scrapped and the new CID instituted.

The knowledge that corruption was as old as the police force might be reassuring or alarming. The first Bow Street runners, raised by Henry Fielding as Metropolitan Magistrate in 1754 and maintained by his half-brother Sir John Fielding, were recruited on the principle of setting a thief to catch a thief. When a virtuous householder brought news of a robbery, who more likely to know where to run or whom to look for than one who had been a thief himself? While this early force was not corrupt to a man, its members moved ambiguously between light and shade. Two centuries later, police regulations forbade officers from consorting with criminals. Yet many convictions still came from 'information received'. Had the CID not cultivated its informants it could hardly have remained in business.

To public perception in the earlier twentieth century a few policemen had been scoundrels and some had been martyrs. In 1928 Sergeant George Goddard was sent to prison for eighteen months for taking a fortune in bribes from those who ran nightclubs or brothels in the West End, principally from the ill-famed Kate Meyrick, owner of the Forty-Three Club in Gerrard Street. Yet in the previous September the nation had paid tribute to one of its most gallant defenders, Constable George William Gutteridge, shot dead without warning on a lonely Essex road by two professional criminals, Frederick Browne and William Kennedy, *alias* 'Two-Gun Pat', who were hanged for his murder.

In the years just after the Second World War, there were martyrs enough. PC Nathaniel Edgar, shot by the thief and deserter Donald George Thomas in 1948, and Sidney Miles shot dead by Christopher Craig became the best known. In neither case was the gunman executed because Craig was too young and Thomas committed his crime in the period of automatic reprieves while Parliament discussed the abolition of hanging.

Other cases, no less dramatic, slipped into obscurity. On 4 June 1951, a police sergeant and two constables answered a 999 call from a farm near Chatham. On the way a boy stopped them to report that he and three friends had been fired on near woodland by a man wearing a scarf as a mask. This suspect was with two women. The search was uneventful until Sergeant Sydney Langford saw the silhouette of a man and two women in a shed. The man opened fire with a Sten gun hitting the police driver, Constable Alan Baxter. When Langford reached him, Baxter had only time to say, 'He has got me in the guts, sarge. I have had it. I am going to die.' The killer was identified as yet another army deserter, twenty-year-old Alan Poole.

Poole made for his father's council house in Chatham. When William Poole urged his son to give himself up, Poole shot at him and the father ran for safety. The fugitive was well armed and barricaded the windows with furniture. In a few hours, the house was surrounded by 200 police in a drama resembling the Siege of Sidney Street forty years earlier. Police marksmen were reinforced by troops in steel helmets carrying rifles, automatic weapons and gas masks.

Most of the soldiers were National Servicemen, concealed in gardens, behind fences and crawling along the gutters of the houses. Poole held hostage his mother and two younger children. Gunfire was exchanged for five hours, until two policemen worked their way to the ground-floor windows and lobbed in tear-gas bombs. The firing from the house stopped. When firemen and armed police broke in with axes, Poole was dying. He had been hit in the back by a bullet from the besiegers and with only two rounds left turned his gun on himself.[1]

Hardly less impressive, as the nation's defenders, were those officers who took on gunmen with only a truncheon and formidable courage. Detective Constable John Bailey tackled another deserter, John Allen, in July 1954, while the fugitive was being taken to a police car in a Mitcham street. Allen broke away, drew a gun and fired several times. A final shot at close range would certainly have been fatal, had not Bailey managed to hit him with his truncheon first. In August the following year, a uniformed constable, Keith Burdett, was saved by the thickness of his police helmet as he climbed a wall on a blitz site in South Lambeth, chasing Francis Gellatly who fired a dozen shots, shouting, 'If you come over that wall, I will blow your fucking head off.' Burdett and two companions braved the bullets to get their man.

The most telling tribute was Gellatly's own, before he went to prison for seven years. 'I shot at him to try and get away. He was a game one, I can tell you.' Gellatly might have counted himself fortunate to appear before Mr Justice Glyn-Jones. A man who robbed a jewellers' in Earl's Court and fired at police during a car chase, because 'I panicked and did my nut', came up before Lord Chief Justice Goddard, who was made of sterner stuff. In December he sent Johnnie Cohen down for twenty years, two accomplices for ten and twelve years each.[2]

In parallel with the heroes, there were inevitable cases of police criminality. These were instances of individual dishonesty rather than corruption. Some involved stealing while on the night beat. In 1950, gloves, tie and scarf from the showcase of a shop earned three months in prison, with four months for ties, raincoat, sports jacket and trousers. Three and four years was the tariff for breaking into a butcher's shop and robbing a chemist in 1951. It was simple to force the door of a lock-up shop at night, when men on the beat were expected to test door handles. Other forms of dishonesty involved consorting with criminals, as when a sergeant went to prison for three years in 1952 for passing on to burglars the details of houses temporarily unoccupied in the Hendon area, in exchange for a share in the proceeds of the robberies. In passing sentence, Mr Justice Croom-Johnson remarked that 'In a large force like the Metropolitan Police now and again black sheep come up.' It was not the occasion for moral panic.[3]

There was little suggestion of systematic police corruption for some ten years after the war, though morale was not enhanced by the feeling that the force was undermanned and underpaid. This grievance persisted and much publicity was given as late as 1970 to policemen who resigned and took a better paid job on the corporation dustcart. In 1955, it was already hard to attract sufficient recruits. London, the worst affected force, was 4,000 under strength.[4]

The first major scandal of the post-war years began in 1954 with a case which seemed routine and relatively trivial. About a quarter of the pimps and ponces in the West End were Maltese. It was argued that this was not their fault. They had been corrupted by the Royal Navy for whom Malta was a principal base. Prostitution grew up round the dockyard and someone had to take responsibility for organizing it. A large number of these ponces, who automatically held British passports, then migrated to London where the prospects seemed better.

Like many of them, Joseph Grech was a thief as well as a ponce and brothel-keeper. His business partner was better known, Tony Micallef, brother-in-law of the Messinas and a contender for control of vice in the West End. In 1954, Grech was charged with breaking and entering at a flat in Barry House, Lancaster Gate, and stealing property worth £1,100. After his trial, he admitted it. He had persuaded the maid to lend him the keys for Tony Micallef to copy. When he was arrested, his home at Queen's Gardens, Bayswater, was searched and a key was found which fitted the front-door lock in Barry House. There was no sign of forcible entry and Detective Sergeant Robert Robertson had assumed a duplicate key was used.

At his trial in October 1954, Grech first claimed that the police had planted the key on him. He also produced an alibi for the time of the break-in, according to which he had been with several friends. He then told the jury that the key which fitted the door in Barry House was his. It also fitted his own front door in Bayswater. Sergeant Robertson was recalled to the witness box and confirmed this. It was a powerful coincidence but not impossible. Few locks and keys were unique. The makers had a number of variations but any key would open a number of doors if its owner knew which ones to try.

At his trial, the jury had seen and heard Grech and his friends. They found him guilty and he went to prison for three years. From Maidstone prison he petitioned the Home Secretary. He admitted the burglary but described how Sergeant Robertson had the idea of a duplicate key. In exchange for payment to Robertson of £150 at once and £150 later, the lock on Grech's door would be changed to fit the duplicate key, Robertson would then be recalled to confirm to the jury that it fitted. Grech said he would agree to the deal if his solicitor, Ben Canter, who had one of the largest criminal practices in London and numbered the Messinas among his clients, advised him to. 'It's a walkover,' Canter told him, 'there is no evidence against you except the key.' A lock, made to match the key, had been fitted to the door of Grech's flat.

In November 1955, Canter, Robertson and Canter's 'runner' Morris Page appeared at the Old Bailey before Lord Chief Justice Goddard. Grech was now a principal prosecution witness. What he had revealed so far was a mere beginning. Inspector Charles Jacobs of Scotland Yard, an officer with twenty-two commendations, had been a party to this perversion of public justice. 'Well, Joe,' he had said, according to Grech, 'you have got two charges. It's up to you. Will you pay up, or will you not?' Grech reminded him of £100 already paid and Jacobs asked, 'Do you think I'm a pauper? Your case is breaking and entering, and the charge depends on me.' Grech complained that Jacobs and Robertson had been blackmailing him for years: 'I am not the only Maltese who has paid this money for the last nine years.' Lord Goddard asked, 'What station was this?' 'West End Central, Savile Row . . . For months and years I was a victim of blackmail by Roberston and Inspector Jacobs.'

In the housebreaking case, Robertson not only agreed to bail but accepted as surety Tony Micallef, whom he knew as a convicted brothel-keeper with criminal records in England and Malta. Robertson told the Lord Chief Justice airily that such men 'are accepted every day'. 'Are they?' Goddard exclaimed.

Grech went back to prison. Canter and Robertson were jailed for two years each, while Morris Page went down for eighteen months. The worst of it was that Robertson had seemed a first-rate CID officer with twenty-six commendations to his credit. He had also been in the post-war 'Ghost Squad' at Scotland Yard. Inspector Jacobs, though not prosecuted, was shortly afterwards dismissed from the police force.[5]

That was still only the beginning. On 17 November 1955, the first day of the trial, the *Daily Mail* revealed that Superintendent Herbert Hannam was leading an internal Scotland Yard inquiry into allegations of police corruption in dealing with owners of clubs and gaming houses, prostitutes, brothel-keepers and pimps. In exchange for money, officers had allegedly tipped off clubs and brothels about impending raids. In the case of brothels, they had 'adjusted' the evidence to make conduct seem innocuous so that, for example, naked women were described as being clothed. Prostitutes were also allowed to arrange a rota system for prosecution and could obtain postponements of a court appearance by paying the arresting officer. The *Mail* claimed that Hannam's report included evidence from forty men serving sentences as pimps or ponces and that it showed 'the huge scale upon which bribery was conducted'.

This was worse than anything in the Old Bailey trial. Lord Goddard was handed a copy of the *Daily Mail* by Christopher Shawcross QC, defending Canter, presumably with a view to a writ of attachment for contempt of court. 'It does not refer to this case,' Goddard told him. On the same day Sir John Nott-Bower, Commissioner of the Metropolitan Police, attacked the article as 'grossly unfair'. He was followed next day by Sir Hugh Lucas-Tooth, Under-Secretary at the Home Office, who deplored in the House of Commons the 'irresponsible charges' in the press.

By now other papers had come to the support of the *Mail*. In opposition to these, the Chief Metropolitan Magistrate, Sir Laurence

Dunne, appeared at Bow Street with his fellow justices. Five senior officers from West End Central were in attendance at a special court, where Sir Laurence denounced the 'sensational and misleading' article. James Callaghan MP, as spokesman for the Police Federation, told its meeting that 'We want to see any situation which might exist cleared up for the sake of the 99.9 per cent of the men who are straight, honest and above board.' He added that where an 'aura of this kind' hung over a force, those who were best qualified became reluctant to join. The nation might be left with a police force of second-rate recruits.[6]

Already a further scandal was in the news. A woman reported to Scotland Yard that in another woman's flat she had seen confidential files from the Criminal Record Office. A check was made and the files were indeed missing. Detective Sergeant Robertson admitted at his trial that he had failed to keep track of certain files, last seen at Willesden police station, but this was a separate case. Superintendent Wilfred Daws, in charge of yet another inquiry, went to the woman's flat to retrieve the missing documents. This mystery would run into the following year but there was temporary relief for Nott-Bower on 1 December. Herbert Hannam presented his report on eight officers under suspicion. Six were cleared. The seventh, Robertson, was now in prison.

An eighth man, Inspector Jacobs, was still under investigation. On 13 February 1956, Nott-Bower rejected his appeal against a disciplinary board which recommended his dismissal. The board found him guilty of assisting a convicted prostitute to find premises for prostitution, failing to disclose in court previous convictions of a man found guilty of living on immoral earnings, and failing to account for property taken from another man arrested as a ponce. His dismissal was confirmed by the Home Secretary and upheld in the High Court on 13 April. Despite Grech's claims of wholesale corruption, it seemed that the black sheep had been reduced to two.

The case of the missing files continued. In early December, there had been a drama in Scotland Yard itself. Detective Sergeant John Bruce, assisting Detective Superintendent Stephen Glander over allegations of corruption made by a man in prison, found his private locker smashed open. It was next to his desk in his third-floor office.

There was no evidence as to who had done it. Nothing had been stolen but someone had gone through the papers.

At least the missing files case proved to be the crime of only one man, Detective Sergeant Thomas Mills, who had worked for sixteen years in the Criminal Record Office and was sent to prison for four years in March 1956. He had taken ten files, some to assist a woman in the abortion trade. In a prefab on a housing estate at Beddington in Surrey, he hoarded other acquisitions, including a secret Fraud Squad report on a well-known financier, a message relating to an army officer acquitted of murder, and prison or criminal records of a dozen other people. Among his souvenirs were engraving blocks of wanted men from *Police Gazette* files. Other records were missing with which he had no connection. A check at the time of his arrest revealed that more than seventy files were missing or displaced and that it might take twenty years to put matters right.[7]

The novelty of such cases, which the *Daily Mail* claimed were the worst since the conviction of Sergeant Goddard in 1928, brought them more easily to public attention than accusations which proved false. While Inspector Jacobs left the force in disgrace and Sergeant Mills went to prison, a London detective sergeant and his constable were arrested for 'corruptly accepting money for showing favour' to three men subsequently sent to prison. One prisoner, Alfred Abbott, complained, 'At present I am serving a term of imprisonment – eight years' preventive detention – for nothing.' When he was charged, the detective constable had said outside Marylebone magistrates court, 'You have been in trouble before and due to your previous "cons" you probably will not get bail, but if you want bail it will cost you a score' – meaning £20.

Abbott said he gave £19 to a detective sergeant outside the police station next day. The sergeant then said, 'If you give me three hundred quid, which I shall put in the right place, you will not even stand trial.' Abbott laughed at him and refused. He had only brought the present charge against the two policemen because one had been to the woman Abbott lived with, 'directly before her baby was expected, and took her last £15 off her'. The case against the officers was as bad, in its way, as anything immediately preceding it. In the light of the evidence, however, the charges proved false and both CID men were acquitted. It was a reminder of the caution needed when the only evidence against the police came from criminals themselves.[8]

2

When a Royal Commission on the Police reported in 1962, it made the point that provincial police forces might be harder to control than their Metropolitan counterpart. It recommended a transfer of power from local police authorities to the Home Secretary. Chief constables should be answerable directly to the Home Office and to a panel presided over by the Lord Chief Justice. The recommendations languished but they were not at all unexpected. Whatever the truth of Scotland Yard's dealings with the West End underworld in the 1950s, the attention of the public and the press had soon been directed elsewhere.

On the morning of 18 October 1957, Commander George Hatherill, Detective Superintendent Forbes-Leith, Detective Inspector Tommy Butler of the Flying Squad and several senior colleagues from Scotland Yard were driven to Brighton and called on the Chief Constable, Charles Ridge, just after ten o'clock. They told him that they had come to arrest Detective Sergeant Trevor Heath, under the Prevention of Corruption Act. He was charged with attempting to obtain £50 from a known criminal, Alan Roy Bennett, as a reward for showing favour. Heath had an excellent record since joining the Brighton force fourteen years earlier. He had also served as a Royal Navy sub-lieutenant in the war and commanded a landing craft at D-Day. As a detective constable in 1955 he held the record for more arrests than anyone else of his rank and altogether had earned eleven commendations.

It must have occurred to Chief Constable Ridge, as it might to those reading of the arrest in the evening paper, that his visitors were an extremely high-powered Scotland Yard posse to bring to justice a single detective sergeant for taking a £50 bribe. Heath had just returned to the CID headquarters after investigating a shop-breaking in Gloucester Road, Brighton. He was summoned to the

Chief Constable's office and charged. He was then driven to his bungalow, which he agreed should be searched without a warrant, and remanded in custody – all within two hours. Three days later, Yard officers began to comb through books and records in the local police filing office.

A week to the day after Heath's arrest the posse was back, this time led by Commander Hatherill and Sir William Johnson, Senior Inspector of Constabulary for England and Wales. They arrested Tony Lyons, owner of Sherry's Bar in West Street, Brighton, and two more policemen. The first was Detective Inspector John Hammersley, deputy commander of the CID, one of only two detective inspectors in Brighton. The other was the Chief Constable himself. Charles Ridge bounced back with the aplomb of a rubber ball. 'Well, gentlemen, you have certainly come to the point. I can only say I emphatically deny the allegations.' A Welshman born in Portmadoc and a freeman of the City of London, he had spent almost all his career in the Brighton force, becoming chief constable in 1956. He had risen from detective sergeant to chief constable in eight years. The offences now alleged had occurred when he was still a detective superintendent.

The three men were taken to court and with Sergeant Heath were remanded in custody to Lewes prison. The town's Watch Committee which, three weeks earlier, had announced its 'complete confidence' in its policemen, now communicated urgently with the Home Office to find someone to run its police force. The Chief Constable of Exeter was dispatched at short notice to control law and order in Brighton.

There was a lull in proceedings for just over a fortnight until 12 November when Samuel Bellson, a Brighton bookmaker, was arrested and accused of conspiring with the other defendants to obtain rewards for the three policemen 'for showing or promising favours contrary to their duties as police officers and thereby obstructing the course of public justice'.

Those still not sure what had gone on in Brighton were left in no doubt after the opening of the prosecution case at the magistrates court on 25 November. The government regarded the proceedings as of such importance, even at this preliminary hearing, as to warrant sending the Solicitor-General, Sir Harry Hylton-Foster QC, to present the charges. He began by warning all who heard him that the case depended largely on 'tainted evidence' from those who had broken the law. Yet the case would be powerful and corruption would be exposed. Constable Frank Knight now reported that Heath had asked him if he would be 'interested in earning a tenner a week' for tipping off 'Sammy' Bellson when his Lonsdale Club was about to be raided. Constable Knight was an honest man but Heath shrugged off his refusal and replied, 'I was to get a fiver out of it for fixing it up . . . It won't break me – I have my other fiddles.'

Constable Raymond Hovey now revealed that he had heard Heath ask a man on trial as a housebreaker for a 'pony', or £25, to keep a previous conviction out of the evidence. Hovey said he was disgusted but did not report it at the time. 'Firstly I owe Sergeant Heath some loyalty as my sergeant, and secondly, I thought that if I reported this matter it would obviously come to the attention of the Chief Constable, and I knew Mr Ridge held Sergeant Heath in very high esteem as a CID officer.' It might also have jeopardized the young man's career, if it was true that the chief constable was involved in the conspiracy. Raymond Hovey, who was promoted to Detective Sergeant, Frank Knight and Constable Tullett were later praised for their courage and integrity by Mr Justice Donovan.

The broader story of the conspiracy was that Tony Lyons and Alan Roy Bennett, successive owners of the Astor Club near Brighton's West Pier, and Samuel Bellson the bookmaker had bought the chief constable and his two CID officers. Bellson had taken over the Burlesque Club in West Street and was now running a book-making business there as 'The Lonsdale Club'. In exchange for bribes, the three police officers looked after their clients. In 1953, when a solicitor asked a private inquiry agent to serve a writ on Bellson, the agent was followed by a CID car and cornered in a bar by Detective Inspector Hammersley and another officer. Hammersley told him, 'We have got to look after Sammy Bellson. You had better keep your mouth shut or we will fix you.'

Next door to Bellson's bookmaking business was a fish shop run by John Leach and his father. In 1954, Leach lent money to a customer, Micky Roberts, on a number of rings and three watches, which proved to be stolen. While waiting to hear if he would face charges, Leach alleged he was visited by Bellson who said, 'This case can be straightened out, you know. Shall I do it for you?' Leach's father, Harry Leach, gave Bellson £50 for the policemen. Half an hour later the bookmaker returned, put the money on the table and said, 'That is not enough.' Harry Leach gave him another £50 for Inspector Hammersley. This time the bookmaker came back and said, 'I put it on his desk and he laughed at it.' Harry Leach lost his temper and said, 'Tell them they can do their worst.'

Soon afterwards Charles Ridge arrived, still a detective superintendent. He told Harry Leach he was 'sorry to see your son in trouble'. The old man pleaded, 'Surely we all make mistakes. No doubt you make some yourself. I can only ask you to do the best you can.' Next came Inspector Hammersley and Sergeant Heath together. They told Harry Leach that Micky Roberts was calling John Leach 'the biggest receiver in Brighton'. Hammersley added that if the case went to court, the cost of a solicitor and a barrister would be £300 or £400. The father asked, 'What can I do?' Hammersley told him, 'For £250 the evidence can be taken down and slung in the sea.'

John Leach stood trial but his conviction was quashed on appeal with costs against the police. Charles Ridge invited him to the police station and said, 'I don't want you to have any feelings about this because one day you might be on the Watch Committee.' Ridge then destroyed fingerprint evidence and other papers in Leach's presence. These would have been destroyed anyway. The remarkable thing was that Leach was there to see it done.

Another allegation came from Roy John Mitchell, a convicted thief who now offered further evidence against Hammersley. Mitchell recalled Hammersley saying when he arrested him, 'You can help yourself, Mitch,' in an overt allusion to bribery. Asked why he had not reported this at the time, Mitchell said, 'You do not bite the hand that feeds you. You do not inform on the "bent" law. They are a help to us not to the law . . . I have known for years that certain members of the Brighton police force were what we call "bents".'

This allegation was echoed by a motor dealer and an accomplice, charged with the theft of a car and a safe containing £679 in cash, who stood trial in January 1958. The motor dealer alleged that after his arrest on 17 September 1957, he was interviewed by Hammersley in the cell corridor of Brighton police station. According to the prisoner, Hammersley said:

> This chat is off the record, Arthur. You are in a spot of bother and you have been upsetting the mobile squad for some time. However, I have nothing against you personally and I may be able to help you . . . There is a carve up over this money and there is some £400 missing. Paolella hasn't got it. You must have it . . . You can do quite a lot of things with £400 . . . You can buy things . . . Freedom, for instance . . . In this case, I cannot promise you freedom as there are other factors and officers involved, but I could drop this charge or reduce it for a consideration . . . £250 would be reasonable.

The dealer protested that he had not got £250. Hammersley said, 'Think it over. I will give you an hour.'

This might have seemed to corroborate indirectly the demands made by Hammersley in the Leach case, though in truth it showed how treacherous such evidence might be. The motor dealer also claimed that Hammersley had sprinkled safe-ballast sawdust over his clothing and in his holdall before sending them to the forensic laboratory at Scotland Yard. Yet records showed that these were sent before the alleged conversation in the cell corridor. As the Recorder of Brighton put it, Hammersley would have 'cooked his goose' by contaminating the evidence to ensure a conviction and then offering to get the charge dropped for £250. It was another lesson in the caution needed when sifting allegations by criminals.

In parallel with these allegations by men facing trial ran the story of Alan Roy Bennett, a man with fourteen convictions, who had been released from prison in 1949. In 1954 he had bought the Astor Hotel near the West Pier from Tony Lyons. The basement was turned into the Astor Club, known locally as 'The Bucket of Blood' in tribute to the amount of violence inflicted there. Lyons' wife later described this as very bad. 'People got very drunk because they were drunk before they got there and there were lots of fights.' She saw people carried out drunk and with their noses bleeding.

The Astor was licensed to open during club hours and should have closed at 10.30 p.m. At first business was not good. Then Bennett, *alias* Brown, was visited by Tony Lyons. He told Bennett that if he was not greedy, he could make 'a lot of money'. On Lyons' next visit Bennett alleged that he brought Detective Superintendent Charles Ridge. There was a discussion as to how much Ridge should be paid for turning a blind eye to what went on at the club and how long it stayed open. The sum agreed was 'a score a week – £20'. They went up to the ground floor and Ridge saw Bennett's Mark VII Jaguar parked outside. According to Bennett, he said, 'That's a nice motor car. I can't afford one like that. I don't know how you do it.' Later on he added, 'My wife likes nice things.' 'So does mine,' said Bennett, 'but don't worry. It will be taken care of.' Under their agreement, 10.30 p.m. was when the club opened rather than when it closed. 'It was no use opening before 10.30. That was the time I started taking money.'

For the first few weeks, according to Bennett, Ridge came to the club between five and six in the evening when nobody was about and the owner was 'getting the bar ready'. Bennett handed over four £5 notes. Once he passed the money to Ridge in Sherry's Bar, folded in a newspaper. When Ridge went on holiday to Spain, Detective Sergeant Heath arrived and said, 'From now on I will be calling for the presents.' Bennett asked, 'Has Ridge sent you?' 'Yes,' said Heath, 'from now on, I will be calling.' During the summer of 1954 he called regularly. If Bennett had to leave the hotel, he gave an envelope containing the money to his wife and she kept it under a shelf in the bar, ready for collection. One day, Bennett asked Heath, 'Do you get your whack out of this £20?' Heath replied, 'Occasionally.' After that, Bennett claimed that he used to give Heath £5 whenever he came to collect Ridge's envelope.

One afternoon, according to Bennett, Heath arrived and said, 'We are rather surprised.' Bennett asked, 'Who's we?' 'The governor and I.' Heath produced a police photograph, relating to Bennett's previous convictions. Bennett looked at the photo and said, 'I haven't changed much.' 'We are rather surprised,' Heath went on. 'We didn't expect this.' There were a few more exchanges and then Bennett said, 'This is blackmail. Go and tell your governor to jump off Brighton pier. Not another penny. I have a good mind to report you to the commissioner.'

By now the club was staying open until 3.30 a.m., five hours after closing time. When a receptionist from the Astor Hotel on the floor above, Blanche Cherryman, went to the police to complain about drunkenness, fighting, trouble over women and late hours, she insisted on seeing Charles Ridge because 'I don't know who to trust at the CID'. The only response was a warning call from the chief constable to the reception desk, for transmission to Bennett: 'Tell Alan to close the club tonight. It's Charlie.'

A further allegation was made that the police were trying to take their cut of stolen money. A man wanted for questioning over a theft in East Anglia was staying at the Astor. He complained that £1,000 had been stolen from his room. According to Bennett, Detective Sergeant Heath arrived and accused him of taking the money from the man's hotel room. Bennett pointed out that he had been at Ascot all day. Heath also 'kept on and on and on about this "grand" and his "whack of the grand" but he got no whack of the grand because there was no grand to have a whack out of'.

In 1955, Bennett himself was in trouble over a worthless cheque passed in Leeds. Heath told him, 'The Leeds people want to see you and you will have to go.' Bennett said that he gave Heath £15 or £20 and heard no more of the matter. In the following month, he also gave Heath £70 towards the cost of buying a car and a ring worth £40.

Bennett left Brighton in 1955 but in 1956 Heath had seen him driving round the town in a £7,000 Rolls-Royce. Bennett was then informed that he was wanted for questioning over a £6,000 jewel robbery at Stewarts the Jewellers in Bournemouth on 30 April. He had a complete alibi, having been in Brussels at the time, and told Heath that he must be 'completely mad'. Heath had taken him to Inspector Hammersley's office and told the inspector, 'He has got a cake of notes in his back pocket.' After the alibi was checked and Bennett was about to leave, Heath reminded him 'not to forget John'. Bennett said that he took two £5 notes from his pocket, screwed them up and threw them on the floor by Hammersley's chair.

Subsequently, the Brighton CID received a phone call from their colleagues in Folkestone who told Hammersley that there had been an attempted shopbreaking on 20 May. A man had been identified from a photograph in their 'rogues' gallery', and that man was Bennett. Hammersley replied, 'Oh, he's a bad boy but he hasn't done anything for about ten years.' Bennett then received a telephone message in London. 'Mr Trevor Heath or Hammersley urgently want to talk to Mr Bennett. Do not come to Brighton by car.' When Bennett telephoned, Heath told him to use another number. The line he was using went through the police station switchboard and might be overheard; the second one went direct to the CID office and was secure. When they spoke, Heath warned Bennett that he had been identified as the suspect shopbreaker in Folkestone. He was not to come to Brighton in his car, as the Folkestone CID had the registration number.

In this case too, Bennett was innocent of the crime and could prove it. He was also weary of paying money to the Brighton CID. On 22 June he phoned Heath again and apologized for not having come to Brighton yet. He did not reveal that he had been to Scotland Yard but said that he had found out that everything would be all right. Heath urged him to come down so that matters could be straightened out. It was far too late by then.

In the summer of 1955, Bennett had closed the club, gone on holiday to the South of France and never reopened it. In January 1956, the Astor was taken over by Mary Mason, who had no intention of paying any kind of protection. She generally kept to the licensing hours, though she occasionally served non-members. Tony Lyons suggested that if she paid £5 a week each to two officers at Brighton police station, a system could be arranged whereby she might stay open as late as she liked and on Sunday afternoons. She would be phoned in advance if ever there had to be a raid. She refused. The club was raided soon afterwards at 2.20 a.m. and struck off.

Even had Bennett not gone to Scotland Yard, the conspirators' run of luck would not have lasted much longer. Ernest Waite, greengrocer of Preston Road, Brighton, had criminal convictions going back to 1934, principally as a wholesale receiver of stolen goods but then as a wartime black marketeer. Since 1954 he had also been a police informer reporting to Inspector Hammersley. In 1957, at the time of the corruption scandal, this second career became public knowledge and anonymous voices breathed threats down his telephone line.

As a receiver and Hammersley's informant, Waite had done a deal with the inspector and Sergeant Heath. 'I only had stolen goods from London all the time because they wanted to keep themselves clear of any complications in Brighton. They said that I could get anything stolen in any town except Brighton.' According to Waite, the two officers did not merely allow him to trade in stolen goods, they encouraged it. 'Both put it to me that I could dispose of them, knowing that I had the facilities to shift large commodities. I was more or less an agent and there was nobody else that knew about these stolen goods in the town.' He dealt mainly in consignments of stolen food and disposed of what was unappetizingly called 'illegal meat' through a cat-and-dog meat shop in Marine Gardens, though for human consumption.

When asked if he was a receiver of stolen goods for a major organization of thieves, Mr Waite said modestly, 'Actually, a friend of Mr Hammersley was the contact and I was made their golliwog to dispose of goods.' The quantities brought to the relatively spacious house in Preston Road were sometimes daunting. At Whitsun 1956, a large lorry had arrived in the driveway with sides of bacon, cases of butter and other items, a quantity which filled the house, outhouse and garage. While the stolen food was there, Waite was visited by Hammersley, whose only comment was, 'I see you've got the goods all right.' It was not surprising that it should be all right because the man who drove the lorry from London was a good friend of Hammersley's. Waite added, 'After all the goods were sold the gang, which was six-handed, came down for the money. Hammersley had £50.' Just before Christmas, another lorry parked in the suburban drive at 11 p.m. and there was a 'terrific noise' as it dumped its load, covering the lawn with tins of stolen peaches. The noise was so loud that it attracted a uniformed policeman patrolling the area. As the constable came up the drive, Waite fled, returning half an hour later to find that the lorry and the policeman had gone. At 2 a.m. he began shifting the tins indoors. Whatever report the beat-officer made had no effect. Waite thought proceedings might be taken against two men questioned over the robbery. 'I think Scotland Yard came into it.' If so, they were soon eased out of it again.

Waite held an unofficial licence to trade as a receiver.

> The money I paid the police was a form of blackmail. Nobody else would have had the cheek to ask me for it . . . Hammersley says he's coming down on such-and-such a date at such-and-such a time for his Christmas turkey and his presents. So I has it all ready for him. A tenner with the turkey. Sergeant Heath wants a new suit and will have to rake the money together somehow. So I give him a fiver . . .

From time to time one or other of the officers would come to the shop in New England Road to collect 'presents' of groceries. 'Heath had the pick of the turkeys. Chose them himself. He wouldn't rely on me to send to him 'cos I wouldn't have given him the best.' At other times, the officers stood in a queue to buy £2 or £3 of groceries, then handed over a ten shilling note and expected change. To add insult to injury, Charles Ridge came to the shop every week when meat was still rationed. There was not a single occasion when the future chief constable paid for his black market purchases.

While Scotland Yard began to look into Bennett's allegations, 1,500,000 cigarettes and 40lb of tobacco, valued at £15,000, were stolen in London from the railway goods yard in Bishopsgate, near Liverpool Street station. Their destination was Brighton. The man who brought them was Fred Richardson, a rag and scrap metal dealer with convictions for receiving and loitering with intent to commit a felony. At Easter that year, according to Hammersley, the inspector and his wife had been to Paris on holiday with the Richardsons, in Richardson's car. 'We shared expenses. We were given separate bills at the hotel.' He protested he did not know Richardson had criminal convictions. However, when Waite confided that Richardson had handled the cigarettes and tobacco, the inspector was dismayed. 'Oh, my God. Ricky mustn't drop in it. I must go and see him and tell him to burn the lot.' It was too late. They were delivered in sacks to Waite's shop and hidden in vegetable crates.

Waite claimed to have sold some of the cigarettes at a Brighton hotel. They would be hard to trace if mixed up in the rest of the hotel's stock. Hammersley appeared to reconcile himself to Richardson's involvement, saying to Waite, 'I think we are on to a good thing. We might get £1,500 from an insurance company.' But the goods were already being sold. Unfortunately, 1,500,000 cigarettes were a lot to dispose of without attracting attention, even in a major town. Hammersley phoned the railway police, laying false clues from a non-existent informant, which caused considerable waste of time in searching garages in the Elephant and Castle area, as well as an entire disused British Road Services depot. A man named Ackerman was invented as a hare for the hounds to chase.

At length Nemesis, in the shape of Detective Superintendent Edwin Moody of the British Transport Police, appeared in Brighton. He met Sergeant Heath in the Caxton public house and was taken aback by 'the company Heath was keeping and the drinks that were bought'. When it was Moody's turn, the round cost fifteen shillings. Six rounds at that price would wipe out a weekly wage. 'I thought that money could not be afforded out of a detective sergeant's pay.' Heath made matters worse by telling an unbelievable story of taking in foreign students at £8 a week each. A more probable figure would have been £2 or £3. Moody thought it 'an extraordinary amount to charge', and assumed it was a lie.

He found Hammersley was deliberately 'stalling' on the cigarette robbery. In all his experience he had never known a case where progress was so slow. 'For God's sake, Hammersley,' he said, 'let's have a bit of faith in one another.' It did no good. Moody went to the chief constable to voice his fears, including his misgivings over Heath's drinking bills and his companions. Charles Ridge was reassuring. 'You know from your experience when you are dealing with thieves you have got to think their way, and to think their way you have got to know their ways, and to know their ways you have got to mix with them.' He confirmed that this included standing drinks at fifteen shillings a round.

Moody sent undercover officers of his force secretly to Brighton. 'I no longer trusted the Brighton CID.' He had been told by Hammersley that the CID had a 'contact', as Waite was described, but Moody was not allowed to know who he was. When he complained to Heath, the sergeant advised Moody to arrest the informant. Moody reminded him that he did not know who the man was. Heath said, 'You can soon find out. Tail up Hammersley.' By setting Moody to follow Hammersley it would be easy to take him round and round the town on endless fool's errands. Heath was not to know that Moody's undercover men were already 'tailing' Hammersley but without Hammersley or Heath knowing.

Superintendent Williamson, not directly involved in the inquiry, now received a letter from a Brighton tobacconist. This revealed that Waite was offering large quantities of cigarettes for sale, a fact that seemed to be known to half of Brighton. Already one of Moody's undercover officers had watched Waite and Richardson delivering a load to a local tobacconist. It was the railway police, not the CID, who obtained a warrant to search Waite's premises.

The house in Preston Road and the shop in New England Road were both searched, with Detective Sergeant Heath in charge. 'Don't you worry about it,' he told Waite reassuringly. He also suggested to Waite's common law wife that she should own up to receiving. Waite was an old lag and might go down for a long time. She had no criminal record and would get off with a light sentence. When she told Hammersley, he said, 'No, no, no, don't do that. You sit tight until I tell you what to do.' Meanwhile Waite was about to make a statement at the police station and Heath was advising him, 'Don't make much of your statement. Keep it down.' Waite made so much of it that his prosecutors allowed him to turn Queen's evidence in the corruption case.

Criminal complainants began to emerge on all sides. Some who had been arrested by Heath or Hammersley had been allowed to purchase bail or even to buy their way out of trouble. Others had paid and got nothing. Sheila Swaby reported that her husband, Jim, had been arrested. In May 1957 he had been brought from Paddington Green police station, where he was held after breaking into public houses in Brighton, by the scrupulously honest Detective

Constable Hovey. While he was on remand in Lewes prison, his wife asked Heath to 'do his best for Jim'. She said Heath replied, 'How are you fixed for £50?' In the cells of Brighton police station, at the magistrates' hearing, Swaby asked whether he should request that other offences be taken into consideration. 'That is up to you,' Heath said. Swaby was particularly anxious that a conviction for living on immoral earnings should not be mentioned in court. Heath said that 'for a pony', or £50, he would see what he could do.

Swaby then gave Heath two £5 notes, which he had sewn in the hem of his mackintosh and which were not found when he was searched at Paddington, or at Brighton, or in Lewes prison. Neither he nor his wife had any more money. Heath asked about the money Swaby had stolen but the thief no longer had it. When Swaby was tried at Brighton Quarter Sessions on 20 June, Heath told Constable Hovey to find the man's wife and see if she had 'brought me anything'. She had not. Swaby went to prison for five years and when his character was read out it contained the conviction for living on immoral earnings. When he next saw Mrs Swaby, Heath said, 'You see what has happened? You did not look after me, so I did not look after you.' From his prison cell, Jim Swaby petitioned the Home Secretary.

To what extent the conspiracy involved the hard men of the underworld was not clear. Another complaint was now made by Alice Brabner, serving a sentence for carrying out an abortion in the home of Elizabeth Lawrence. While awaiting trial, Mrs Brabner met Heath in Sherry's Bar and asked if he could not take a few pounds to forget the matter. She paid him £68 in all but was sent to prison for fifteen months at Lewes Assizes in April 1957. Mrs Lawrence said that Tony Lyons had advised her about her own case when she visited Sherry's. 'I think you are in for it but you could get out of it for a ton.' She only had £20 and Lyons said, 'They won't stand for that.' She alleged that she gave Heath £50 rather than the £100 Lyons suggested and escaped imprisonment.

On the second evening of the magistrates court hearing of the corruption case in Brighton, as Mrs Lawrence walked home in the dark, a car drew up and four men got out. One grabbed her, the others stood round her. They had a message from Billy Howard, the South London protection racketeer. It was reinforced by a man who held the open blade of a cut-throat razor against her face. If she gave evidence against Howard's friends in court, Howard would come down to Brighton himself, cut her tongue out and carve her face. She went to the police and the matter was brought up in court next morning by Gerald Howarth QC for the Crown. It was not clear who, among the defendants, was a friend of Billy Howard. Perhaps no one. The four men in the car might have been local thugs using the name of a criminal as they might have used those of Billy Hill or Jack Spot. When the story was told in court, it could well have prejudiced potential jurors against the defendants rather than in their favour.

At the Old Bailey trial in February, Heath did not dispute that there had been attempts to bribe him. When asked by Mr Justice Donovan why he had not charged such people with bribery or at any rate reported the incident, he said, 'Most of them were in trouble already and it would be a bit hard to put them into further trouble.' It sounded a lame excuse. None the less, much of the evidence against the three policemen, the owner of Sherry's Bar and Bellson the bookmaker came from tainted sources. In his summing up, Mr Justice Donovan remarked to the jurors, 'I dare say, having seen Bellson in the witness box, you would not hang a cat on his evidence – let alone a chief constable.'

On the other hand, the jurors heard the honest policemen and Superintendent Moody. These had no reason to lie. Even among men with criminal records Alan Roy Bennett of the Astor Club laid himself open to charges when he went to Scotland Yard and admitted bribing police officers. The unsupported evidence of the Leaches, father and son, might be open to question but there was no dispute that, for example, Sergeant Heath and Tony Lyons had gone to the Astor Club long after the legal hour for closing. Would they have done that if there was a real danger of it being raided? And if there was no danger of a raid, though it was in full swing night after night until 3.00 a.m. on Brighton seafront, did that not suggest that the police had been paid to leave it well alone?

The jury at the Old Bailey in February 1958 had no apparent difficulty in convicting Heath and Hammersley, who went to prison for five years each, or in acquitting the older man Lyons, who according to the evidence was an *éminence grise* behind the conspiracy. After further deliberation, they also convicted Bellson, who went to prison for three years. To the surprise of most observers, they acquitted Chief Constable Charles Ridge. By the rules of procedure, no one would ever know why. At the trial he had sought to prove his innocence, in part by producing tables and graphs prepared from official figures. They related to the years 1948 to 1956, during which he commanded the Brighton CID.

For a century and a half Brighton had not been the most law-abiding town in the land but the number of its crimes had decreased during the eight years of Ridge's command of the CID from 2,183 annually to 1,674, a better result than most forces could boast. The rate of detection rose from 43.8 to 61.3 per cent, which would have been the envy of many other towns and cities. The annual arrest rate went up from 453 to 638. In the spring of 1957 there had also been action against illegal gaming. On 29 March, to coincide with the Grand National meeting, Superintendent Hill, commanding the CID and never accused of corruption, raided a bookmaker's rooms in Duke Street, arresting the staff and thirty-eight punters. On 22 November the Chez-Moi club was struck off after thirty members had been caught drinking after hours.

Perhaps the jurors found the evidence against him unconvincing. It was not supported by the honest witnesses, 'a credit to any force', as Mr Justice Donovan described the young Brighton policemen. Perhaps the figures showed him doing a first-rate job, apparently incompatible with corruption on system.

But given the morass of dishonesty over which he had presided, his career was at an end. Mr Justice Donovan remarked that within a day or so of the cigarette robbery, Waite was offering the goods for sale. It was thanks to a private citizen that this became known and it was then 'studiously concealed' from Superintendent Moody and the railway police. Yet Moody caught Waite within three days. A week later, another Brightonian reported that Waite was selling stolen tins of fruit. The culprit later admitted this but the only immediate result was that someone in the CID warned him a few hours later that he had been found out and had better stop. Before allowing

Charles Ridge to leave the dock, the judge remarked that the conspiracy might be used in Brighton to discredit police officers and their evidence. The force must have a leader 'who will be a new influence and who will set a different example from that which has lately obtained'. It was a damning acquittal. The former Chief Constable of Exeter was confirmed as head of the Brighton force.[9]

Ridge demanded to be reinstated after his acquittal but was dismissed as chief constable, though the courts upheld his right to keep his pension. There had been evidence against him of conspiracy and corruption rather than mere dishonesty. While it was true that the Chief Constable of Worcester, who had been suspended on 20 December 1957, was to be sent to prison next year, and the Chief Constable of Southend would follow him in 1965, both cases were of straightforward embezzlement. Charles Ridge went free, believed guilty of far worse crimes than those for which his peers were sentenced.

The new broom at Brighton swept quickly. Among its targets was William Page, known to Ridge as 'Pagey' and to the town as 'Bookie Page'. He had a substantial criminal record for gaming offences and had organized one of the most notorious greyhound-doping plots ever, for which he went to prison in 1944. He remained an affront to probity in an age when most off-course betting was still illegal and he made his living by organizing it. In a farcical interview, he had confronted Ridge in the chief constable's office, as the scandal broke in 1957, and asked to be allowed to 'clean up' Brighton. Now the righteous had 'Pagey' in their sights, a reminder of the chief constable's legacy.

Even before Mr Justice Donovan had finished with Charles Ridge, the new Brighton CID raided Page's Castle Club in Castle Street on 4 March with a warrant under the Betting Act. The premises were equipped with a blackboard on which the runners were chalked, a 'blower' was connected directly to the racecourses, and a television screen relayed coverage. Ten men and two women were taken to police headquarters. On 27 March, Page was fined £25 for allowing the premises to be used for betting. Six days earlier, two other Brighton men were fined and twenty-eight punters bound over after a raid on illegal betting premises in Russell Square.

On 28 May, Page's club was raided again and he was arrested with twenty-nine customers. He was fined £100, claiming that he had known half an hour before that the police were gathering at the end of the street for a raid but he had gone on betting as a protest against 'a ridiculous law'. It seemed inevitable that he would be sent to prison, as he was on 30 July after another raid on the club. About forty punters were in the ground-floor room, the black-board listing runners at Goodwood, Redcar and Birmingham. Page was organizing the gambling from his office, sitting with eighty-eight slips relating to 152 bets. Protesting that there were seventeen other bookmakers in the town running the same service and that they were never raided or prosecuted, he was jailed for three months, reduced on appeal to one month and a fine of £50.[10]

Two days later, while Page was free on bail pending his appeal, the club was raided again by Inspector Flack and his men who had been keeping watch. But Page had gone straight there from the magistrates court and handed it over to another man, saying, 'Any so-and-so can have this place. It is nothing to do with me any more. I have finished with it.' On 1 August, the police had arrived just as the new owner, two assistants and twenty-two punters were getting ready for the second race at Goodwood. They appeared in court next morning. On the same afternoon, another club had been raided in Bristol Road, Brighton. Solomon Mercado had been sitting at his desk with 262 betting slips from 1,255 bets. Another twenty-eight punters were arrested. More than ninety defendants from the illegal clubs appeared before Brighton magistrates that week, a tribute either to the efficiency of the reformed police force or to the easy-going manners of those who had been removed from it.

3

Apart from the major corruption case of the decade, the police had fared much better. In November 1957, a Scotland Yard detective inspector was cleared at the Old Bailey of conspiracy to defeat the course of justice by concealing the theft of 163 cases of whisky, stolen from a lorry at Friday Hill, Chingford, and of receiving the stolen whisky. The charges were supported by two witnesses, one a police informer. Both had been involved in stealing the consignment. They were not believed. In the same month, two Mitcham policemen were acquitted of taking bribes from men trafficking in obscene pictures. In a third case that month a detective sergeant at Lavender Hill, with twenty-eight years in the Metropolitan Police, was acquitted of accepting money, concealing money, and soliciting a man to commit an assault. In all three cases, the evidence came from men engaged in underworld activities. The jurors had the advantage of seeing and hearing them, and chose not to believe them.[11]

At the Old Bailey on 4 March 1958, a detective sergeant with twenty-three years' service was accused of accepting £20 from one of two men accused of stealing lead. One man was a police informer, run by Inspector Vibart of Scotland Yard. There was no doubt that he had given the detective sergeant £20 in £1 notes. It proved to be money which the detective sergeant had unwisely but sympathetically lent the informer to pay for legal representation on the lead-stealing charge. The jury stopped the trial at the end of the prosecution case, once again having had the chance to see and hear the complainant.

Perhaps the worst that had been said of the Metropolitan Police during these months was a denunciation of its extravagance by Sir Laurence Dunne at Bow Street, who stopped a case against the Stork Club for serving drink after hours. An undercover police inspector and a companion had gone on surveillance. The charge was that the policeman had been served with a bottle of champagne after 2.30 a.m. No corroborative evidence was offered. The only corroborated fact was that total expenses for police entertainment at the club had come to £86, about two months' wages for the average working man.[12]

As yet, allegations of misconduct or corruption on the part of police officers had too often required a jury or a disciplinary board to judge one party's word against the other. That was about to change. In August 1958, in a little-noticed case, a Manchester furniture dealer was interviewed by a detective constable. Shortly afterwards, the constable was suspended from duty and an inquiry was set up. Whatever the outcome, it seemed that it was not to be a case of one man's word against another. Before the interview, in the sitting room of his home, the furniture dealer had hidden a microphone in a drawer. A wire ran down to a tape recorder in the basement. Shortly after the interview, the dealer forwarded to Manchester City Police eight hundred feet of audio tape. The domestic tape recorder had made its appearance in 1955 and at first had been little more than a novelty. From now on, it was to play a major part in allegations of police corruption by a new breed of 'investigative' journalists.

19

A Matter of Confidence

I

WHATEVER ACCUSATIONS WERE brought against the police in the years which followed the Brighton scandal, they could not eclipse the honour of a growing number of heroes and martyrs. There was little glamour in this because their deaths seldom followed any high-profile 'crime fighting'. Too often they were victims of the deranged or the maladjusted, or criminals whose previous offences had been trivial. Few people could have believed that a man surrendering at West Ham police station on a Saturday morning, 3 June 1961, after a domestic quarrel in which he attacked his wife, mother-in-law and sister-in-law, would cause mourners to line three miles of London streets a few days later. He had telephoned to say that he was coming in to give himself up.

John Hall, thirty years old, was received kindly by Detective Inspector George Jones and told, 'It's in your favour that you have come here of your own accord.' Hall apologized for the attack. He had been 'on his knee' to beg forgiveness from the women, whom he attacked with a chair. In the CID office, he was told he would be detained. He became distressed and insisted he could not face being locked up. 'I knew they wanted to put me away,' he said later. He was made to turn out his pockets. From one trouser pocket he produced six bullets. From the other he took an automatic pistol and began to wave it about. Still waving it, he dashed from the police station, pushing shoppers aside as he ran across to a park. Several men from the station followed him and shots were heard. Inspector Jones hurried to Tennyson Road and saw Constable Cox on the pavement. Sergeant Frederick Hutchins was lying on his back with his head on Cox. Hutchins was fatally wounded and Cox badly injured. Nearby was the body of Inspector Philip Pawson. Hall had escaped in a red saloon car.

The manhunt was brief. That evening, Hall telephoned the news-desk of the *Sunday Express* from a kiosk at Wanstead Heath and spoke to the paper's crime reporter, Nelson Sullivan. His first words were, 'I am the killer.' He was distressed, weeping at times, and said he had been trying to find the courage to shoot himself. Despite Sullivan's assurances, he did so as the police closed round the kiosk. He died in the casualty department of Whipps Cross Hospital, gripping Inspector Jones's hand and pleading, 'Say you forgive me. I am sorry. I want to die.' By any customary use of the word, it was a tragedy and the reputation of the police seldom stood higher than in its aftermath. The three-mile route of the cortège was lined by thousands, men bowing their heads, drivers of buses and taxis getting out of their vehicles and standing to attention as the coffins of the two policemen passed. The crowd in Manor Park cemetery was so great that the service was relayed to many more outside.[1]

In the comparative tranquillity of Westmorland, four years later, police near a small village stopped a Morris 1100 car, reported stolen from a car park in Kendal the day before. They faced a man with a gun who promised to 'shoot the first one of you who makes a move', and then ran off. He was found later in a station waiting room. Constable George Russell had time to say, 'Put that gun down, lad, and come out with your hands up,' before he was shot dead and his companion wounded. John Middleton, the gunman, was hunted by armed police and captured after being shot in the leg. Before they could get to him, he also tried to commit suicide by shooting himself in the head. He succeeded only in doing himself severe brain damage and was judged unfit to stand trial.[2]

The headline case of its kind was the Shepherd's Bush police murders of August 1966, when a sergeant and two constables in plain clothes noticed a suspect car in Braybrook Street, near the wall of Wormwood Scrubs prison. The tax disc on the windscreen of the Standard Vanguard had expired and the exhaust pipe was held on by string. It seemed unlikely that the car had passed an MOT test. The police car, 'Foxtrot Eleven', contained Detective Sergeant Christopher Tippett Head, Detective Constable David Wombwell and the driver, Constable Geoffrey Fox. The three men in the suspect car, John Witney, John Duddy and Harry Roberts, were petty criminals who had never made much by their thefts. They were planning the armed robbery of a rent collector. With Roberts as leader they also had an appetite for violence. Proof of this was that the car contained three guns, as well as false number plates and a stocking mask, the tools of their trade. They belonged to a generation of criminals who now spoke of policemen as 'the filth'.

Foxtrot Eleven overtook the Vanguard and Head flagged it down. He mentioned the out-of-date tax disc and Witney, the driver and owner, asked Head to give him a break. Head walked round to the rear of the car and Wombwell stooped to the driver's window to take details from Witney. Roberts produced a gun and shot the young constable through the left eye. As Wombwell fell, Head ran back to the police car. Roberts got out, fired at him, and missed. He fired again and hit him in the back. Head, who had been trying to take cover behind the police car, now lay dying in its path. Duddy fired at the driver, Geoffrey Fox, and missed. Then he drew level and shot him through the open passenger window. As Fox lay dead over the steering wheel, his foot pressed the accelerator and the car bumped forward over Head's body. The three killers jumped into their car with Roberts screaming at Witney, 'Drive, you cunt, unless you want some of the same!'

The Vanguard reversed erratically from the wrecked patrol car and the two bodies in the road, narrowly missing a security supervisor who turned the corner, driving home from work. He saw the carnage and got the car's number. That evening, Witney was arrested in his Paddington flat. Four days later Duddy was arrested in Glasgow and admitted shooting Geoffrey Fox. At the end of August, there was a public funeral for the three murdered policemen. Six days later, Harold Wilson as prime minister and Edward Heath as leader of the opposition led the mourners at a memorial service in Westminster Abbey.

It might have seemed a time for reflection and restraint. Yet police hunting for Roberts had already been under fire from another gang of armed robbers who had used shotguns and automatic weapons in a car chase through Deptford, Rotherhithe and Bermondsey. The four masked gunmen had at first tried to hold up the three unarmed policemen and take their car. Instead the policemen chased and tackled the armed men, capturing three of them. The driver under arrest apologized for the attempted murder of the policemen, 'But what can you do when you have four mad bastards in the motor with you?'[3]

The hunt for Harry Roberts continued. Before leaving London, he had bought army surplus camping equipment, as well as combat jacket and khaki trousers. He was able to live rough in Epping Forest for three months, camouflaging his tent with brown and green paint, behind a barricade of fallen branches. At his trial he pleaded guilty to the murders of Sergeant Head and Constable Wombwell; his accomplices were also convicted of murder. All were sentenced to life imprisonment with a minimum of thirty years. It was what Mr Justice Glyn-Jones described as 'perhaps the most heinous crime to have been committed in this country for a generation or more'.[4]

Mr Justice Glyn-Jones's condemnation of the crime as the most heinous for a generation certainly appeared to be the view of the crowds who gathered outside police stations and courts at the arrival of the accused men, shouting, 'Bring back the rope!' After the Homicide Act of 1957 had divided capital from non-capital murder, its application in practice had been to murders committed with firearms, or in the furtherance of robbery, and any murder of a police officer. With the election of a Labour government in 1964, capital punishment was suspended for a period of five years and its abolition confirmed in 1969. Whether or not it would have saved the lives of Head, Wombwell and Fox at the hands of such men as Roberts was at least questionable.

The three young policemen, like their colleagues on other occasions, were seen to represent the police force at its best. Whatever praise or gratitude they received was amply earned. In a few years, many of those no longer quite sure what the Brighton scandal had been about remembered clearly the dreadful events of a Friday afternoon in a drab street at Shepherd's Bush during August 1966.

In the light of this sacrifice, 'the worst public disturbance in Oxford for many years' a week later was depressing. Drunken violence and drug taking among the young had marked the night of 19 August at the Coconut Grove discotheque. Police who tried to restore order outside in Hythe Bridge Street were dragged to the ground and kicked to the accompaniment of shouts, including, 'It's a pity they didn't shoot more of you bastards!' On 24 September, a Liverpool man, charged with attempted murder after stabbing a policeman, told his captors, 'All police should die. They harass me.'[5]

2

Repellent though the shouts in Oxford may have been, such hostility was not unprecedented. In July 1959 there had been a late-night encounter between police and students outside a coffee bar in the King's Road, Chelsea. When arrested for obstruction, the middle-class young jeered at the police, shouting, 'Do we get the Podola treatment?' It was not a good omen and recalled a comment in the annual report of the Commissioner of Metropolitan Police, quoted by the press in connection with the Podola case, that the public appeared to have lost its respect for the police and its willingness to assist them.[6]

Guenther Fritz Podola was a thirty-year-old Berliner who arrived in England in May 1959. As a boy he had been a member of the Hitler Youth and had survived the battle for Berlin. A fugitive from the Soviet Zone, he made his way to Canada and then to England. He was a small-time criminal and his Soho masquerade as Mike Colato, professional gangster, was a mere pose. On 3 July he broke into the South Kensington flat of a model, Verne Schiffman. He stole jewels, a mink coat and three passports, her own, her daughter's and a friend's. She then received a letter from Podola as 'Levine', an American detective who had compromising letters, as well as pictures and tape recordings of her. She could have them for £500. Verne Schiffman knew that this was nonsense and told the police. It was arranged for 'Levine's' calls to be monitored.

On 13 July, a call was traced to a public phone in South Kensington tube station. Detective Sergeants Raymond Purdy and John Sandford arrived while Podola was still in the kiosk. He was arrested, broke away and after a chase was caught in the hallway of a block of flats. Purdy told him to sit on a windowsill and behave. Then Purdy turned to Sandford and heard too late the other sergeant's shout, 'Look out! He's got a gun!' Podola shot Purdy through the heart and fled.

He was not hard to find. A strange guest was reported by the manager of the Claremont House hotel in Queen's Gate, Kensington. Podola was identified from photographs sent by the Royal Canadian Mounted Police. On 16 July, Detective Chief Inspector Basil Acott, Detective Inspector Peter Vibart, Detective Sergeant Albert Chambers, and a dog-handler with an alsatian went to the hotel room. Vibart tried to force the door. When this failed, he called, 'Police! Open the door!' Podola went to the door but before he could open it the officers outside heard a click, like the cocking of a gun. As it happened, Podola had hidden his gun in the hotel attic. Sergeant Chambers, at sixteen stone, charged the door and burst it open. As he hurtled into the room, he saw the door hit Podola, who fell with Chambers on top of him, bleeding from a small cut above his left eye. A moment later, Podola fainted.

Even ten days after his arrest, press photographs of Podola in a police car suggested a loser who had just stepped from a boxing ring. The injury to his eye was still there at his Old Bailey trial. It seemed likely that this and his loss of consciousness had been caused by the force of the door hitting him. Other stories spread of Podola having been beaten up in the hotel room and bitten by the police dog, in revenge for the death of Sergeant Purdy. His counsel, Frederick Lawton QC, pointed out that two pillowcases were 'deeply stained with blood'. A coverlet was also stained and blood had spattered his trousers. All this could hardly have come from a small cut above his eye. Yet it was not proof that he had been beaten up by the police rather than hit by the door.

Neither Podola nor his counsel claimed that the police had assaulted him. It was not something that went well in court. Podola's defence was that when he was knocked unconscious he lost all memory of recent events. He did not know whether he had been attacked or not, any more than he could recall the alleged murder of Sergeant Purdy. This did not prevent many people from suspecting that the police had beaten him, or had given him 'the Podola treatment'. He was examined at the police station by Dr John Shanahan who judged him dazed, frightened and exhausted. Then he was transferred to St Stephen's Hospital, where the consultant physician found him unaware of his surroundings. These two doctors and two more colleagues believed that his story of amnesia was probably true. He had not the knowledge to fake the symptoms. Podola remembered little of his personal life before his arrest, though retaining such acquired skills as playing pontoon or chess, which was consistent with amnesia.

It was necessary to hold a preliminary hearing to decide whether he was fit to stand trial for murder. Four doctors gave evidence in his favour and two testified that he was faking. The jury decided that his amnesia was a fake. He then had no defence beyond insisting that the first jury had been mistaken and that his amnesia was genuine. A second jury convicted him of murder and he became the last defendant to be hanged for killing a policeman. The verdict did not dispose of the allegation that the police had beaten him up.[7]

In the aftermath of the trial, the press became vigilant for police brutality. Even as the case against Podola was being prepared, on 4 August 1959, three youths were arrested by three young constables, acting as CID 'aides', outside the Manor House pub in Finsbury Park an hour after midnight. At the police station a constable, in the manner of a stage conjuror, put his hand into the empty pocket of one youth and produced a cut-throat razor. When the youth denied it was his, he was punched. A second youth had a cosh 'found' in his jacket. When he protested he was asked, 'How would you like a bash over the head with this?' A third suspect had a razor produced from his pocket and said, 'That's not mine.' He was shown a truncheon and told, 'If you don't tell me the truth, I will hit you on the head with this in a minute.' The three were convicted at the magistrates court; their appeals were rejected at Middlesex Quarter Sessions.[8]

The Home Office refused an inquiry. A police inquiry whitewashed its own officers. The case festered until February 1964, when the Member of Parliament for Islington East, Eric Fletcher, raised it during a debate on the Police Bill. He did so in conjunction with other cases, involving Sergeant Challenor and a further abuse of police power in which two of his own constituents had been 'bundled off to a police station and brutally ill-treated'. Though Challenor had been judged unfit to stand trial, three of his colleagues were convicted in June 1964, in the case of the planted bricks, two going to prison for four years and one for three. The evidence included an account of Challenor behaving at his most grotesque, repeatedly cuffing a political demonstrator and saying, 'There you are, my old darling, have that with me,' or summoning a suspect from his cell with, 'Come out, you black bastard, I want your fingerprints,' punching him when the man asked that his solicitor should be present. The public inquiry heard that when the prisoner complained, the jailer told him, 'This is a tough place and that sergeant is tough.'[9]

In the Finsbury Park case of the planted weapons, after the Home Office had evaded the issue for five years, a committee under William Mars-Jones QC reported on 3 December 1964. It exonerated the three youths, who were given free pardons, announced in the House of Commons on the same day. Sir Richard Jackson, Assistant Commissioner at Scotland Yard, was criticized for failing to put an independent officer in charge of the original police inquiry and for refusing to get a transcript of the appeal proceedings in the case of the three men. Mars-Jones added that he had never known so many irregularities committed by so few police officers in so short a space of time.[10]

By the time of the report, other cases had gone far towards destroying public confidence in the police. In 1963, BBC television's satirical Saturday night show *That Was The Week That Was* presented Lance Percival offering an alternative to the Beatles and 'The Mersey Sound'. It was 'The Sheffield Sound', produced by the actor in police uniform beating a rhino whip on a police station counter.

On 9 March 1963, a special Crime Squad of Sheffield CID had been formed to reverse the decline in arrests. On 14 March, there was a 'pep talk', emphasizing that officers must work long hours, devote themselves to their tasks and get results as a matter of urgency. Two constables arrested three suspected burglars, including two brothers who admitted previous offences. At the magistrates court, however, one of the brothers stripped off his shirt and displayed the marks of a systematic beating. The other had been similarly maltreated.

The beatings had taken place in an interview room with its blinds pulled down so that the assaults should not be seen from the windows of neighbouring flats. Both defendants claimed that their confessions had been beaten from them by the two constables with a truncheon and rhino-tail whip. In reply, the policemen insisted that the brothers were known sadomasochists who had got their injuries elsewhere and, in any case, they had been involved in a fight in the police station lavatory. Little by little, however, the officers were obliged to walk the plank of self-contradiction. They were convicted and fined, after a private prosecution, and dismissed from the police force.[11]

That was not the end of the matter. Sheffield's scandal was national news. The Home Office instituted an inquiry, led by Graham Swanwick QC and Commander W. J. A. Willis, one of Her Majesty's Inspectors of Constabulary. Its report was published on 6 November 1963 as a white paper. It concluded that the two detective constables would not have carried out such assaults 'without the prior authority or the presence and consent of their senior officer'. The Chief Constable, Eric Staines, 'lived somewhat in an ivory tower, barely able to accept that men under his command could be guilty of truly infamous conduct'. On the other hand, apart from the chief constable, 'no one truly wanted to investigate the truth'.

The inquiry was satisfied that Detective Inspector F. J. Rowley, in charge of the Sheffield Crime Squad, who prudently resigned from the police in May 1963, 'was present at and sanctioned the assaults . . . that the assaults were preceded by and interlarded with threats by him of violence'. The chief constable had been 'over-obsessed with the bogey of publicity'. Detective Chief Superintendent George Carnill, commander of Sheffield CID, had at first been put in charge of investigations. Five or six days passed without a search, during which time the rhino-tail whip and a cosh disappeared, while the culprits in the Crime Squad were left 'concocting versions' of what had happened. Both Carnill and the chief constable were suspended. Before matters went further, both men announced their retirements, as did Chief Inspector Ivor Wells. The Sheffield Watch Committee ended their suspensions, allowing them to retire. There would be no further internal investigation and their pensions were secure.[12]

Following the Sheffield inquiry, the Home Secretary, Henry Brooke, spent an hour with 500 representatives of London's Metropolitan Police Federation on 11 November 1963. The chairman, Reg Webb, a police constable, made a plea for support against unfair attacks, malicious and frivolous complaints, and fairness shown to the public at the expense of the police. Henry Brooke promised to 'stand squarely behind the police'. None the less, on the weekend of 16–17 November, the federation issued a newsletter to all branches, attacking the Home Secretary's 'peculiar decision' to hold a public inquiry into the Sheffield case. Only a handful of the 800 policemen in Sheffield had been involved but all were 'besmirched' by the publicity and only criminals had cause to celebrate. The inquiry had allowed interrogations of police officers by those who were 'obviously hostile'. 'We would urge the Secretary of State not to underestimate the bitterness and resentment we have found among the Sheffield force during the hearing.'

What potential recruit of high calibre and ideals would choose to join the police force now? Worse still, what would their substitutes be like? How many jurors would any longer believe police evidence at a trial? Until 1967 it required only one dissenting voice to frustrate the verdict of a jury. The earlier 1960s showed a shift in the opinions of jurors, as surely as in those of the general public. Against the background of the Sheffield case or the Challenor accusations, the question of whether an engaged couple in a car were kissing or behaving in a grossly indecent manner might seem trivial. Yet there were two such cases in 1961–2, which involved a significant question and answer. The circumstances of the alleged offences required the issue to be decided on the basis of one party's word against the other. In the past, juries had been reluctant to disbelieve the police.

In both trials, the jurors were told that if they acquitted the accused couple, the implication would be that police witnesses had committed perjury. Yet in each case the juries acquitted the couple and left the world to draw its conclusion. Worse than this, at the end of the first case, the Chairman of London Sessions unwisely commented that people who are acquitted are not necessarily innocent. He would have done better to keep that view to himself. The result was that the freed couple sued the policemen in the case before another jury in the High Court. Once more the judge asked if the police had committed perjury. The jury could not agree. There was a retrial and, to the accompaniment of national publicity, the couple were awarded £5,200 against the policemen in May 1961. In December, a second couple were acquitted on similar charges at West Kent Quarter Sessions. The chairman told the jury, 'The case boils down to a simple issue. Did the constable see what he has told you he saw?' The jury decided that he did not and the couple thereupon sued him for false imprisonment and malicious prosecution.[13]

As a matter of history, the police of the 1960s were getting the worst press since the Bow Street Runners two centuries before. Those who had reason to resent them had only to portray them as thugs and liars in order to have a better chance than usual of being believed. The Kray twins, of all people, complained of police persecution on the grounds that when they were arrested, the police impounded the pension books of their grandparents. They also alleged, but never substantiated, that a policeman had demanded money from them. Even the strident and self-confident middle class, when caught with drugs, claimed that they had been planted during the police search, which might or might not have been true. After the Challenor case and the Mars-Jones inquiry, 'planting' no longer sounded like a villain's last resort.

One of the most widely publicized cases of the kind, in January 1970, involved Mick Jagger of the Rolling Stones and Marianne Faithfull, who was to be acquitted. Their home in Cheyne Walk, Chelsea, had been raided by the Drug Squad on 28 May 1969. In evidence, Jagger described an acting detective sergeant asking him, 'Where's all your LSD, then?' He replied, 'I have not got any LSD.' The policeman picked up a box, tipped its contents on to white paper and announced that he had found heroin. Jagger said, 'You bastard – you've planted me with heroin.' The sergeant allegedly took him to the end of the room and said, 'Don't worry about it, we can sort something out.' Jagger told him, 'There is nothing you can possibly do.'

According to Jagger, the sergeant then explained, 'If Marianne were to plead guilty and you were to plead not guilty – in that way you'll get off. How much is it worth to you?' He suggested £1,000, adding, 'Don't mention it to anyone,' and 'Don't worry, you can have your money back if it doesn't work.' This bizarre conversation ended when the sergeant, having failed to make progress in the negotiations, produced a piece of cannabis the size of a toecap and said, 'What's this then?' Jagger said, 'Oh, come on now,' adding in court, 'The whole thing was absurd until that, then it became really absurd.'[14]

Though Jagger denied that there was cannabis in the house, he was fined £200 for possessing it. The sergeant was investigated by Scotland Yard and the Director of Public Prosecutions. Jagger's solicitor was told that there was no evidence to support the accusations. It was one more unsatisfactory case in which the truth would never be established. Remarks made in court were privileged and unless repeated outside could not be the subject of an action for libel or slander. The Sheffield case and the Mars-Jones report, as well as the Challenor inquiry, had shown that an unusual number of complaints against the police were justified. On the other hand, there had rarely been as many stories of police brutality and corruption as emanated from the Podola case. According to one of these, some of his injuries were sustained when officers had thrown the suspect down a flight of stairs at the police station. As it happened, the police station was on a single floor reached by a lift.

3

The paradox of the 1960s was that it had also been an age of reform and restructuring. There had been a Royal Commission on the Police in 1961–2 and a Police Act of 1964. The royal commission did not dispute 'the serious and growing problem of organized crime', while warning that 'a police force in which dishonesty is connived at cannot hope for long to retain the confidence of the public.' It also deplored the practice of linking an officer's prospects of promotion to the number of convictions obtained. The provisions of the Police Act were seen as relatively timid developments but were based on the premise that the vast majority of the public trusted the vast majority of the police. In more practical terms, the power of the Home Secretary over provincial police forces was extended and chief constables were encouraged to invite senior officers from other forces to investigate complaints within their own.

More important, in terms of morale and public confidence, the police force of the 1960s now began to place less emphasis on responding to crime and more on finding and arresting those who were about to commit it. The evidence of this appeared in the creation of new branches within the CID, Criminal Intelligence (C.11) and the Stolen Vehicles Inspectorate (C.10), as well as Regional Crime Squads in 1964 and the Special Patrol Groups in 1965. The Regional Crime Squads were intended to match the mobility and organization of modern criminals. Nine squads would cover nine police regions in England and Wales, based on Manchester, Durham, Wakefield, Birmingham, Hatfield, Brighton, Bristol, Cardiff and London. When Detective Chief Superintendent Ian Forbes was appointed as Coordinator of No. 9 (London) Regional Crime Squad in 1969, a good deal of the work was undercover and members of the squad were encouraged to look as little like police officers as possible. At the end of the year Forbes became National Coordinator of Regional Crime Squads as Deputy Assistant Commissioner, describing himself as a spider in the centre of a police web.

Forbes marched his men towards the sound of battle with the intention of hitting the criminals before they hit anyone else. During the night of 27 August 1970, Regional Crime Squads raided eighty homes across the country simultaneously and came away with the five men they had been looking for. On the night of 16 September, No. 7 (Bristol) Regional Crime Squad coordinated raids in an area extending from East Anglia to Monmouthshire, including Newbury,

Welwyn Garden City, Brighton and Cardiff. Four men were arrested on charges of conspiracy to commit a major robbery.

The assaults of the squads on the underworld seemed overwhelming compared with anything that smaller police forces had been able to mount. Until 1969, lorry thefts had increased year by year and those who organized them now became targets. Many of these robberies had always involved inside help and the organizers were currently approaching lorry drivers with an offer of 10 per cent of the proceeds. One self-confident driver who had allowed himself to be hijacked and tied up had even applied to the Criminal Compensation Board and been awarded £184 for his 'ordeal'. From now on the driver was the first suspect. Drivers and owners who protested at this approach were told that anyone attempting to obstruct an inquiry would be charged with conspiracy to commit the crime, which was still a common law offence carrying a maximum sentence of life imprisonment. At the same time, some drivers had received nothing from the thieves who had hired them. It was from these men that the first information flowed into Regional Crime Squad intelligence.

On the night of 1 October 1970, eighty officers from 2 and 9 Squads raided houses in North and East London, and the Home Counties. Fifteen wanted men were seized, on charges relating to £342,000 of goods. Further raids brought the number arrested to thirty-eight. The kingpin, Anthony 'Tubby' Turner, escaped for some months but was caught and went to prison for thirteen years at Hertfordshire Assizes in December 1971. His chief accomplice was jailed for nine years. Twenty-seven of the thirty-six other defendants were convicted. Lorry theft, for a while at least, became unfashionable.

In appearance, undercover police and criminals came to resemble one another. This was true in a range of operations informed by improved criminal intelligence. By 1969, the Flying Squad was anticipating robberies and lying in wait. Information relating to a planned £18,000 robbery of a Securicor van in an alleyway behind the British Home Stores in Wood Green led to armed officers under Detective Inspectors Frank Lovejoy and Michael Miller setting a trap. Three men in a blue van, two with revolvers and one carrying a shotgun, pulled up behind the Securicor truck as two guards went into the store to collect weekend takings on Monday 24 February.

As the Flying Squad men attacked, one smashed the windscreen of the blue van with his truncheon. The rest took on the occupants of the van who had no opportunity to use their weapons. In a running fight, one suspect was reported wounded by a bullet and an ambulance was called to take all three to hospital. In October, the Flying Squad used decoy ambulances to conceal men in ambush before a hold-up at St Thomas's Hospital. Armed officers were crowded into the backs of the vehicles. Even the white-coated doctors and hospital porters on the scene were plain-clothes detectives. As a Security Express van delivered its £30,000 payroll a suspect in the hospital corridor was grabbed before he could make a move; two more were chased and caught in the yard by Flying Squad men who had leapt from the decoy ambulances.

Elsewhere, individual CID officers risked their lives when they penetrated drug gangs, on the pretence of being wholesale buyers for narcotics. Sergeant Leonard Hopkins of Hackney CID masqueraded as a purchaser in negotiations with a gang in Whitechapel. He was told the price would be £15,000 and replied, 'Fair enough, you are in business. But I am coming down with a lot of money and I don't want any funny business or somebody is going to get killed.' He went to the final rendezvous at a Whitechapel café, unarmed and with a briefcase containing only £3 and a stack of waste paper. His safety and his life depended on convincing the gang that there were police about and that there must be a last-minute change of rendezvous. This led them into the police trap. Asked if he realized that he might have been killed or grievously injured had the gang suspected a trap or looked inside the briefcase, he said, 'I volunteered for the job and I was far more concerned with discovering the offences.'[15]

In some cases the police set up fake deals themselves, as in a £1,000,000 forgery plot in 1969. The forgeries were Swiss banknotes printed in England. The counterfeits were so good that they passed the scrutiny of two banks in England and were found in the possession of customers who had acquired them innocently. It was a French bank which first noticed what was described as 'a minute flaw'. The conspiracy was penetrated by two Scotland Yard officers, a detective sergeant and a detective constable, posing as Continental buyers of the currency. The leaders of the plot, whose principal was jailed for five years, were convicted in February 1970.[16]

In a new decade, the post of Commissioner of Metropolitan Police was to be occupied from 1972 to 1977 by Sir Robert Mark, a trenchant and effective reformer with a taste for honesty and integrity. He was the most combative of his kind. When critics pointed out crooked policemen, he was apt to cite crooked lawyers. Among his examples was that of the officer in the witness box who is asked whether he is a member of the Flying Squad. When he agrees, he will be asked whether four or more members of that squad are currently suspended on charges of corruption. The judge will intervene but the jury has already heard the allegation. The impact of the new commissioner's policies in the deployment of units like the Robbery Squad and the Serious Crime Squad was evident in the figures. Bank robberies which had totalled seventy in London during 1972, when Mark took office, dropped to twenty-six in 1973 and seventeen in 1974. The theft of high-value lorryloads, of which there were almost 400 cases in 1972, fell to a third of that after the Regional Crime Squad assaults and to a quarter by the time Mark left office.

Even so, the 1970s became the worst decade that Scotland Yard had ever known. By the autumn of 1969, journalists working for *The Times* had tape-recorded evidence that three Scotland Yard officers, two detective sergeants, John Symonds and Gordon Harris, as well as Detective Inspector Bernard Robson, were 'running' a South London thief, Michael Perry, *alias* Michael Smith. They would assist him with information and protection, he would pay them a commission from his robberies. After Perry took his story to *The Times* he was 'wired' for his next meeting with the officers so that the conversations could be monitored and recorded.

From that moment investigations began, bringing down the Drug Squad, the Obscene Publications Squad and many individual policemen. In the decade before Robert Mark's arrival an average of sixteen officers a year had left Scotland Yard 'in anticipation of criminal proceedings'. During his five years of office, the number reached 477. It was both a warning and a tribute.

During the years that followed, it seemed that Scotland Yard never won a battle, but never quite lost the war. The case of the three bent coppers, as the species was now generally known, and the thief wired to his tape recorder was followed by much worse. The Drug Squad, confiscating drugs from addicts in London and then paying them out to addicts at Oxford in exchange for information, was sympathetically investigated by Commander Wally Virgo of the Obscene Publications Squad. That squad itself was corrupt almost to a man and had for years been taking a fortune from booksellers and others in Soho, in exchange for allowing them free trade. When it was necessary to confiscate obscene material, the traders were given an opportunity to visit the police station where it was held and buy it back. When James Humphreys, pre-eminent in the trade, was asked how he could tell when one of the officers was corrupt, he replied, 'I never knew one who wasn't.'

The truly remarkable aspect of this is that anyone could ever have imagined that such organizations as the Obscene Publications Squad were doing their job. Most people who lived in such areas as Soho or Paddington could have told them precisely which bookshops sold pornography. It had also been common knowledge since the Victorian period that the innocent display in the window and the front of the shop bore no relation to what was available privately in a back room. How could the police possibly not know? If they knew, why did they not simply raid each shop daily until it closed down? It was inconceivable that they were too busy, since they were certainly not doing it anywhere else. If they knew and yet did nothing, what was the reason?

Though it was no defence in morals or in law, some officers who were to be convicted probably felt that they had been set to do a job that no one wanted done. Drug Squad officers were to stamp out a pleasure which more and more of the educated and articulate middle-class young believed, eloquently and stridently, that they had a right to indulge in. Such drugs as cannabis were not hard to come by and if there were those who had no wish to use them, that was their choice. It was a seductive libertarian argument and when many who used soft drugs found that they did not turn into slavering addicts it became plausible. Perhaps it was never more plausible than to officers who might be sworn at, denounced, spat at and accused of 'planting' or 'fitting up'.

In the realm of obscene publications, it proved almost impossible to get a conviction for obscenity in the courts after 1970. Expert witnesses swore that such publications as *Inside Linda Lovelace* were not merely innocuous but benign. Jurors were asked whether they were now depraved or corrupt because they had read Miss Lovelace's account of her sexual eccentricities. As defence counsel put it in addressing the jury:

> Judges and others read this book. If it has a depraving effect, as the Crown claims, we should expect orgies in the Garrick Club, the Central Criminal Court chugging at the hum from vibrators and daisy chains in the lunch hour while eating cheese-and-pickle sand-wiches. If you do not like a book you should not read it, if you do not like a television programme you should switch it off. What is being defended at this trial is the right of the public to make up its own mind. If the book is a bit rude and a bit silly, at times fantastic and at times shocking, should we make up our minds about it or do we need Big Brother to decide?[17]

What role did that leave for the Obscene Publications Squad? Of twelve major prosecutions brought under obscene publications legis-lation at the Central Criminal Court in 1972–6, seven ended in acquittals, in three more the jury could not agree. In only two were the defendants convicted, on six of thirteen counts in the first case and on only one of six counts in the second. Perhaps it seemed to those members of the squad who collected their pay-off from the squad office on Friday evenings that they too had been deputed to do a job which few people in the country wanted done.

On the shores of this moral quicksand, the fight against crime continued. Its victories passed almost unnoticed by comparison with the television documentaries of police corruption and the headlines that announced further revelations. Yet during this period the convic-tions of criminal contenders in the East End ensured that there would be no successors to the Krays or the Richardsons. The Regional Crime Squads dealt not only with lorry theft and bank robbers but with gang warfare itself. Supergrasses, however repulsive to their accomplices, opened the way to the capture of bank robbers and security van hijackers. To curb corruption, a new department had been created under the title of A.10, staffed by uniformed and CID officers, directly responsible to the Deputy Commissioner.

The simple faith in police officers which had been held by many of those they served until after the Second World War would never be restored. Worse still, there were to be accusations of such moral crimes as racism. If 99.9 per cent of the Metropolitan Police wished nothing but good to all races, that left sixteen others to make the headlines, more than it had needed in the Brighton police scandal or the Challenor case. Before the century was over, the crime of 'institutional racism' would be alleged against the force. To be a policeman, it seemed, was to be a racist, a curious doctrine which appeared as the Calvinism of 'political correctness'.

In the meantime and more to the point, men like Robert Mark and successes like those of the Regional Crime Squads had bought time but not redemption. The next thirty years were to determine whether that time could be used to preserve the long English tradition of 'policing by consent' or whether events would yet make it necessary to shift the balance from policing as a means of guarding personal liberty to policing as a form of social control, to which all would be answerable whether they saw good reason for it or not.

20

No One Does That Any More

IN JUNE 1998, an unemployed man entered Barclays Bank in Stockport and patiently joined the queue. At the cashier's guichet, he pushed through a note. It read, 'This is a robbery, give us your money. I've got a gun.' As if to make sure that he was taken seriously, the robber had signed it. Moreover, the note was written on the back of a letter addressed to him by his local council. The bank clerk, no doubt suspecting a hoax, said, 'Will you take a seat, sir? We will deal with you in a moment.' The robber obediently sat down. After a while, he went back to the clerk and said irritably, 'Will you hurry up! I haven't got all day.' He was told to be patient and sat down again.

It might still have been a hoax. Who, after all, would any longer rob a bank face to face in this manner? This time, however, the clerk pressed the alarm button and armed police were on their way. They searched the bank and at first thought that the robber must have left because it had not occurred to them that the man sitting quietly in the waiting area was 'armed and dangerous'. He was identified, arrested and brought to trial. He had a previous conviction for unauthorized possession of a firearm. A penal code that had been revised to equip it for the twenty-first century, and which seemed to owe significant passages of its drafting to Lewis Carroll's Queen of Hearts, imposed a mandatory sentence of imprisonment for life, at Minshull Street Crown Court on 2 March 1999. Bank robbery was no longer either easy or even attractive.

In the penultimate month of the century, November 2000, a small gang of armed robbers smashed its way into the Millennium Dome with a JCB digger, in search of diamonds to the value of £3,500,000. Though they were professionals, in the sense that their lives were devoted to such crimes, some were not in their first youth and they had a dismal record in attempted security van hijacks. On this occasion, though they had a speedboat waiting at a nearby pier for their getaway down the Thames, the Flying Squad had had them under surveillance for months and was lying in wait. These heirs of the smash-and-grabbers never had a chance. Even the diamonds were fakes.

The survivors of the mid-century underworld were moved to nostalgia by the failed robbery. As historians of their craft, they held a universal opinion: 'No one does that kind of thing any longer.' It seemed not so much a crime as the rerun of an episode from the 1970s Flying Squad drama, *The Sweeney*. Even so, it served a purpose in showing how much the underworld had changed.

2

Whatever sleight of hand might be applied to the figures, either by suggesting that much crime in the distant past was not reported or that interviews with researchers were more productive than totalling those offences recorded by the police, the increase since the war remains substantial and almost unremitting. Between 1945 and 1970 the nation's recorded crime had more than tripled, though the rate of detection had fallen by only 2 per cent. In the period from 1971 to 2001 it more than tripled again, while the detection rate collapsed to half of what it had been. There had been warnings from senior police officers that constant allegations of police corruption would undermine collective morale and lead to a shortage of the best recruits. Perhaps that was reflected in this fall in the 'clear up' rate. It was certainly a development of the 1970s. Despite the *Evening Standard*'s headline of 28 June 1962, proclaiming 'An Everybody's Doing It Crime-Wave', reported crime was only 15 per cent of what it would be at the century's end, while the police were still catching almost half of those who committed it.

In many areas – police corruption, professional robbery, drug dealing and prostitution – the pattern of the future was well established by

1970. Even what was referred to later and rather coyly as 'people smuggling' was no novelty. The 1960s fare on the so-called 'pipeline' from the Indian subcontinent was £500–£600 per person. As the law stood, once an illegal immigrant reached English soil, deportation had to take place within twenty-four hours. Failing that there was a right of residence, which extended to dependants who had not yet arrived.

By January 1968, CID officers were being sent to France to pick up the trail of a gang smuggling Pakistanis into Britain. It was reported that twenty-five of the newcomers had left Dunkirk earlier in the month on the Ramsgate motor cruiser *Cedefore*. Detective Inspector Harry Cowan, Deputy Chief of Kent CID, and Detective Chief Inspector Doogan, Thanet CID, had also gone to interview an Englishman sent to prison for eighteen months by a court in Boulogne for stealing the motor cruiser *Phare* and using it to transport a cargo of Pakistanis who were arrested at Sandwich Bay in August 1967.

By 13 July 1970, the trade was sufficiently well established for Leerdert Van der Staag to describe to the Rotterdam newspaper *Algemeen Dagblad* how he had used a small coaster to carry hundreds of Indians and Pakistanis from the city's docks to small ports in England. He had made fifty trips in two years, delivering clients to an address in North London. Like most of those in the trade he was never caught. In November that year, it was a rarity when five Englishmen and an Asian were jailed at Leeds Assizes after they had been caught smuggling forty Indians.[1]

In another sphere, drug taking and drug addiction among the young had been a feature of society since the mid-1950s. As in the age of 'temperance sermons', describing the physical and moral dissolution consequent on drink in any quantity, those who were preached at found that the harm promised them did not occur so easily. For the future, it proved that the best the authorities could hope for was to limit the amount of drug taking, while issuing helpful advice to those who might have their drinks spiked without their knowledge. As time went by, it was evident that drug taking was no passing fashion of the mid-century. Of course, it was good for morale that Customs and Excise or the police should be able to announce 'massive seizures' of drugs from Asia or South America from time to time but this seemed to have no real effect on their easy availability.

If drugs occupied the police and their allies increasingly after 1970, the more traditional 'social evil' of prostitution and sexual vice caused relatively little alarm. So long as all parties were willing participants and the public was not caused annoyance, whose concern was it? If there was a milestone in this progression, it was probably the trials of Mrs Cynthia Payne in 1980 and 1986. These were replete with stories of a homely brothel in a suburban house, catering for its 'regulars', organizing payment by luncheon vouchers, and giving preferential rates to old age pensioners. There were queues on the stairs, said to include a peer of the realm and Members of Parliament. Friendly greetings from passing members of staff included, 'Having fun, mate? It's like bleeding Piccadilly Circus in the rush hour.'

Once they were in the house, undercover policemen struggled desperately to find reasons for 'just wanting to talk' and not accepting the sexual offers pressed upon them by ladies who seemed hardly distinguishable from social workers in their zeal for doing good. In the end, the Vice Squad was driven to such expedients as suggesting erectile difficulties and sending one stalwart constable ambiguously dressed as a bisexual wearing green eyeshadow. The second prosecution collapsed in absurdity, its proceedings accompanied by unsuppressed outbursts of laughter. The public gallery had controlled its hilarity admirably until an account of the police raiders, 'like a rugby team', kicking in the locked bathroom door, a girl who had been kneeling behind it in front of a client leaping to her feet, knocking the client into the bath from which, hampered by his trousers round his ankles, he had to be rescued by the constabulary.

If Cynthia Payne's world was beyond the grasp of the law, its garden of delights for pensioners and top people was also beyond the mental grasp of Bernie Silver and his Maltese henchmen in 'The Syndicate'. The true social evil, to keep the Victorian terminology, was now seen in the growing trade of prostitution by the very young, most of whom had run away from home and were surviving by this means. That they needed money to buy drugs was frequently the case. A graphic illustration of this, at Cardiff in 1991, was the so-called 'Body in the Carpet' trial. The body was that of a fifteen-year-old runaway, Karen Price, who had been murdered ten years earlier. The proceedings revealed the grotesque inadequacy of residential care. Karen Price and her companions had only to walk out of the gates of their institution and catch a bus to dockland where, by fourteen, she was a prostitute whose place of business was either the street or the backs of her clients' cars.

The only roof over her head was that of her fifteen-year-old pimp, who smuggled her in and out of his mother's house without causing suspicion. Glue sniffing or smoking 'a spliff of ganja', perhaps a visit to the Coney Island fairground at Porthcawl or Barry, was their relaxation until a heavyweight thug of twenty-one moved in to take control. In a riverside basement flat, in the summer of 1981, there was a row between the man and the youth. It was a well-known house for Saturday night blue movie shows where the projector was operated, curiously, by a soldier of the SAS. In the course of the argument between the two men, Karen Price was strangled while the sole witness, a girl of thirteen, cowered in the corner. The life and death of this teenager seemed bleak beyond description. No one looked for her or inquired after her, until a decade later workmen digging a drain at the back of the house came across a roll of carpet tied with electric cable.[2]

At the end of the Second World War, fear of the underworld was, for most people, restricted to apprehension of street robbery, usually when carrying wages, or of the intruder by night. For a few it might be the threat of a knife fight on a racecourse train or at a dog track. That something with a screen like a television set might empty their bank accounts or steal their identities would have been the stuff of comedy. Drugs, to most people, were still something prescribed by the doctor. They included new and life-saving wonders like penicillin. The chances of their loved ones ever being in contact with those who resorted to 'Indian hemp' or cocaine were remote to the point of insignificance, unless they moved in the nightclub set or the circles of artistic bohemia.

They had no inordinate fear for their children. Those as young as five or six might walk a short distance to school alone or in small groups. They did not fear the white slaver, as some late Victorians like C. L. Dodgson had done. The greatest danger was that a child might get knocked down by a motor vehicle, and that seemed borne out by events. Children were certainly 'sent out to play' unsupervised. By the time of the three 'little victims' in the separate Cannock Chase murders of 1966–7, let alone the Moors Murders which preceded and overshadowed them, the consequences of allowing young children such freedom seemed plain. Yet most of those who grew up at that time would often reflect in later life that they had seldom or never felt under threat from adults who were strangers to them, or from those who were not.

By the end of the century, the categories of fear had changed. It was natural that the greatest criminal threat should be to life and property. That had always been so. Yet as property was increasingly protected by alarms, as it seldom had been before 1970, the new fear was of an internet which had the power to rob or impersonate its victims, even to seduce them or their children by its sexual and violent imagery. This generation feared so greatly for its children that those who taught or cared for them had first to prove to the authorities that they were not paedophiles – a pedantic and unfamiliar word in the post-war years, now common enough for the tabloid press. They feared perhaps that their children would be made use of in an obscene film and even murdered. It was hard to imagine anyone outside a lunatic asylum being foolish enough to provide conclusive evidence of murder by being filmed in the act, but no one could be sure of that. It was naturally to be hoped that the panic over child abuse was rumour, phobia or witch-hunt because the alternative was to accept that a terrible hatred of children had come about in thousands of people. The last refuge of the opposing argument was that things had always been as bad but they had been 'hushed up'. In the nature of the argument it rested on less than overwhelming evidence.

A contingent fear was over drugs, whose species and availability had proliferated since the 1960s. This too was a fear for one's children, though it seemed that there was little parents could do but bow their heads and wait for the danger to pass. In many cases, people believed that the evil consequences of 'recreational use' had been overstated or were 'scaremongering'. They devoutly wanted to believe so.

One of the worst dilemmas for ordinary people was that fear drew round itself a cloak of mystery or, at least, incomprehension. Was cannabis truly a drug that increased the risks of cancer even more than tobacco because the smoke was held in the lungs for longer – or did it lie in wait, like a beast in the jungle, to punish youthful indulgence by psychiatric illness in later life? Or was it no more harmful than a glass of whisky? There was no comforting certainty for most people.

New crimes boosted the annual statistics as old ones fell away. Some acts that had been criminal before 1970 were no longer so. Homosexuality, some forms of abortion, almost all literature which before 1959 might have been regarded as obscene no longer gave rise to prosecutions. Racial incitement and, more controversially, the expression of extreme opinions on racial or religious matters became criminal. Film censorship withered in the 1970s but censorship blandly masquerading as 'certification' of films and videos in the 1980s made Britain one of the most closely controlled of the liberal democracies in that respect. These were, as much as anything, cultural changes.

3

Confronted by crime and the statistics of crime, governments and political parties flexed their muscles at the hustings and promised again to 'tighten up' or 'crack down' on professional criminals and antisocial 'yobs'. This seldom affected the annual crime figures which still moved implacably upwards. Because it was in the interests of governments to assure the electorate that it lived in the best of times, as Orwell had demonstrated, it was sometimes said that things had been worse in the past than anyone supposed. The voices of the past which made nonsense of this were not much quoted. Television programmes which hoped to persuade their audiences that they were fortunate enough to be alive and watching now, investigated that past and produced selective examples of its secret bigotry or scandals, most of which had been perfectly well known all along.

The final irony was that the underworld, in varying guises, accomplished something by proxy which even in 1970 it would never have thought possible. For some years before that, it had sought to undermine the common law by bribing or threatening witnesses and jurors. The law had found it difficult to meet that challenge. The underworld's brightest stars had defeated police interrogations by exercising or manipulating the right to silence. Given this and the presumption of innocence, murderers like the Krays had appeared in the dock as suited 'company directors' who had never seen the inside of a court of law before and must surely be the victims of some dreadful misunderstanding. 'Harry Boy' Jenkins had tricked his way out of police custody by a hot-off-the-press edition of the evening paper protruding from his pocket at an identity parade.

The law was their enemy and their purpose was to defeat it, except insofar as it protected them. Yet as the crime figures rose and the greater immunity of the criminal appeared in a falling detection rate, governments decided that the English common law in some of its more important aspects might be as much their enemy as it was the enemy of the villain. Traditional forms of liberty became redundant in such circumstances. Ten rather than twelve jurors might convict the accused from 1967. The right to silence under police questioning was removed and a proposal made to restrict the right to trial by jury. Trial by judge alone was mooted. By 2004, the Blair government proposed the abolition of the presumption of innocence to the extent of permitting jurors in important cases to be presented with a list of the defendant's previous convictions before considering their verdict. The government and the judiciary remained at odds as to whether a detainee might be held indefinitely without trial, contrary to the provisions of the Habeas Corpus Act 1679, which required a prisoner to be either charged or released.

These legislative measures had not been undertaken wilfully but in response to the advance of modern crime, which certainly included acts of terrorism, usually indistinguishable from the behaviour of common criminals. These were measures which removed what had been regarded for centuries as safeguards for the protection of the subject, with which the underworld might not be much concerned. Yet by a final irony, the powers of government proposed to complete an overthrow of constitutional freedoms, as if bowing to Billy Hill and his successors.

Notes

Chapter 1. After the War

1. *Evening Standard*, 25 September 1950.
2. *East London Advertiser*, 13 June 1947.
3. Peta Fordham, *The Robbers' Tale*, London: Hodder & Stoughton, 1965, p.61.
4. Captain W. E. Johns, *King of the Commandos: A Story of Combined Operations*, Bickley, Kent: University of London Press, 1943, pp.17–18.

Chapter 2. The Shadow of a Gunman

1. Marlborough Street Magistrates Court, 3 June 1947; 10 June 1947.
2. Marlborough Street Magistrates Court, 3 June 1947; 6 June 1947; Old Bailey, 22 July 1947.
3. Old Bailey, 22 July 1947.
4. Robert Fabian, *Fabian of the Yard*, London: The Naldrett Press, 1950, p.80.
5. Macdonald Hastings, *The Other Mr Churchill*, London: George G. Harrap, 1963, pp.291–2.
6. Fabian, *Fabian of the Yard*, p.81.
7. Marlborough Street Magistrates Court, 3 June 1947; 10 June 1947.
8. Marlborough Street Magistrates Court, 27 May 1947; Old Bailey, 23 July 1947.
9. Old Bailey, 23 July 1947.
10. Marlborough Street Magistrates Court, 27 May 1947.
11. Marlborough Street Magistrates Court, 27 May 1947.
12. Fabian, *Fabian of the Yard*, p.85.
13. Old Bailey, 23 July 1947; PRO/CRIM/1749/16.
14. *The Times*, 16 May 1947.

15. Marlborough Street Magistrates Court, 14 June 1947; Hastings, *The Other Mr Churchill*, p.292.
16. Marlborough Street Magistrates Court, 20 May 1947.
17. Marlborough Street Magistrates Court, 20 June 1947.
18. Old Bailey, 22 July 1947.
19. Old Bailey, 25 July 1947; PRO/CRIM/1749/14–15.
20. Old Bailey, 28 July 1947.

Chapter 3. Welcome Home

1. W. K. Hancock and M. M. Gowing, *British War Economy*, London: HMSO, 1949, p.546.
2. Clerkenwell Magistrates Court, 17 November 1949.
3. *Daily Telegraph*, 24 March 2004.
4. Bow Street Magistrates Court, 23 April 1945; General Court Martial, RAF Halton, 29 January 1946.
5. Bow Street Magistrates Court, 7 December 1944.
6. *Daily Telegraph*, 24 March 2004.
7. *Evening Standard*, 8 May 1946.
8. Simon Garfield, *Our Hidden Lives: The Everyday Diaries of a Forgotten Britain*, London: Ebury Press, 2004.
9. House of Lords, 20 February 1946.
10. George 'Jack' Frost, *Flying Squad*, London: Rockliff, 1948, p.72.
11. *The Times*, 13 August 1946.
12. Ibid., 14 August 1946.
13. Ibid., 19 August 1946.
14. Vacation Court, 24 September 1946.
15. Old Bailey, 31 October 1946.
16. Hartley Witney Rural District Council, 22 August 1950.
17. General Court Martial, Chilwell, Notts, 30 October 1951; General Court Martial, Chelsea Barracks, 12–13 December 1951; Ian Bisset, *Trial at Arms*, London: McGibbon & Kee, 1957, pp.47–56.
18. Charles Vanstone, *A Man in Plain Clothes*, London: John Long, 1961, pp.172–80.
19. Berkshire Quarter Sessions, 6 October 1947.
20. *R. v. Newland and Others*, Court of Criminal Appeal, 5 October 1953.
21. Honeybourne Magistrates Court, 8–13 October 1947; Worcester Assizes, 12 and 15 December 1947.
22. Aylesbury Magistrates Court, 12 March 1946; General Court Martial,

RAF St Athan, 13 December 1949; General Court Martial, RAF Moreton-in-Marsh, 18 December 1951.
23. Chelmsford Assizes, 3 December 1951.

Chapter 4. The Land of the Well-Greased Palm

1. John Nevill Maskelyne, *Sharps and Flats: A Complete Revelation of the Secrets of Cheating*, London: Longmans Green, 1894, pp.15–17.
2. Clerkenwell Magistrates Court, 21 September 1946.
3. Clerkenwell Magistrates Court, 4 April 1947; Tower Bridge Magistrates Court, 14 February 1950.
4. National Federation of Meat Traders, Nottingham, 27 August 1951.
5. Old Street Magistrates Court, 26 July 1946; Court of Criminal Appeal, 14 April 1965.
6. Clerkenwell Magistrates Court, 20 April 1950; Bow Street Magistrates Court, 9 November 1959.
7. Old Bailey, 5 September 1945.
8. Ian Forbes, *Squad Man*, London: W. H. Allen, 1973, pp.177–9.
9. South West London Magistrates Court, 26 January 1946.
10. *Police Review*, 1947, pp.311–17.
11. Slough Magistrates Court, 28 April 1945.
12. Old Bailey, 14 March 1952.
13. Southampton Magistrates Court, 19 October 1951; Winchester Assizes, 16 July 1952.
14. Frank Fraser and James Morton, *Mad Frank and Friends*, London: Little, Brown, 1998, p.41.
15. Old Bailey, 21 June 1945.
16. Leonard Read, *Nipper*, London: Macdonald, 1991, p.14.
17. Old Bailey, 5 April 1946.
18. House of Commons, 3 December 1947.
19. South London Magistrates Court, 12 September 1951.
20. Tower Bridge Magistrates Court, 5 September 1951; 7 September 1951; 14 September 1951; Old Bailey, 30 October 1951; Old Street Magistrates Court, 8 January 1952.

Chapter 5. 'My Victim's Body Had Followed Me Home'

1. *Proceedings of the Tribunal Appointed to Inquire into Allegations reflecting on Ministers of the Crown and other Public Servants* [The Lynskey Tribunal], London: HMSO, 1949, p.5.
2. Mansion House Court, 12 December 1952.
3. *Proceedings of the Tribunal*, pp.595–6.
4. Ibid., p.423.
5. Old Bailey, 22 October 1945; 30 October 1945; Middlesex Sessions, 6 March 1946.
6. Court of Criminal Appeal, 8 December 1953; Old Bailey, 24 June 1954.
7. Old Bailey, 18–26 January 1950.
8. Bow Street Magistrates Court, 17 February 1950; Old Bailey, 26 February 1950.

Chapter 6. 'Real Butter on the Scones'

1. Chelmsford Assizes, 8 November 1950.
2. Old Bailey, 16 July 1957.
3. Conrad Phillips, *Murderer's Moon*, London: Arthur Barker, 1956, p.32.
4. Ibid., p.32; Gerald Byrne, *John George Haigh*, London: Headline Publications, [1949], p.19.
5. Francis Selwyn, *Rotten to the Core? The Life and Death of Neville Heath*, London: Routledge, 1988, p.23.
6. Phillips, *Murderer's Moon*, p.66.
7. *George Orwell: Essays*, London: Penguin Books, 2000, p.348.
8. Selwyn, *Rotten to the Core*, p.64.
9. Old Bailey, 12 July 1938.
10. Paul Hill, *Portrait of a Sadist*, London: Neville Spearman, 1960, p.132.
11. Old Bailey, 24 September 1946.
12. J. D. Casswell, *A Lance for Liberty*, London: George G. Harrap, 1961, p.248.
13. *R. v. Kopsch* (1925).
14. Casswell, *A Lance for Liberty*, p.251.
15. P. Hill, *Portrait of a Sadist*, p.195.
16. Old Bailey, 18 July 1949.
17. Old Bailey, 19 July 1949.

18. Old Bailey, 24 June 1953.
19. Old Bailey, 12 January 1950.
20. *Rillington Place 1949: Report of an Inquiry by the Hon. Mr Justice Brabin into the Case of Timothy John Evans*, London: The Stationery Office, 1999, p.275.
21. *Trials of Timothy John Evans and John Reginald Halliday Christie* [Notable British Trials], Edinburgh: William Hodge & Company, 1957, p.xli.
22. Old Bailey, 24 June 1953.
23. Patrick Hamilton, *Hangover Square: A Story of Darkest Earl's Court*, London: Constable, 1941, p.345.
24. *Report of an Inquiry into Certain Matters Arising out of the Deaths of Mrs Beryl Evans and of Geraldine Evans and out of the Conviction of Timothy John Evans of the Murder of Geraldine Evans*, London: HMSO, 1953, Cmd. 8896 [The Scott Henderson Report].
25. Phillips, *Murderer's Moon*, p.119.
26. *Guardian*, 2 February 1993.
27. James Hadley Chase, *No Orchids for Miss Blandish*, London: Jarrolds, 1939, p.52.
28. Mickey Spillane, *I, the Jury*, London: Transworld Publishers, 1963, p.126.

Chapter 7. Professionals and Amateurs

1. Marylebone Magistrates Court, 31 December 1963.
2. Old Bailey, 22 September 1961.
3. Bow Street Magistrates Court, 6 October 1961.
4. Bow Street Magistrates Court, 21 July 1965.
5. Balham Magistrates Court, 5 January 1967.
6. Old Bailey, 29 June 1964.
7. Old Bailey, 23 July 1957.
8. John Capstick, *Given in Evidence*, London: John Long, 1960, p.93.
9. Thames Magistrates Court, 21 July 1936.
10. Uxbridge Magistrates Court, 12 August 1948.
11. Uxbridge Magistrates Court, 5 August 1948; 12 August 1948; 17 August 1948; Old Bailey, 16 September 1948; 17 September 1948.
12. Bow Street Magistrates Court, 13 August 1952.
13. Hendon Magistrates Court, 20 September 1948.
14. Highgate Magistrates Court, 22 February 1947; 13 March 1947; Old Bailey, 27 March 1947.

15. Donald McKenzie, *Gentlemen at Crime*, London: Elek Books, 1955, p.149.
16. Havant Magistrates Court, 19 December 1950; Winchester Assizes, 12 April 1951; 13 April 1951; 18 April 1951; 19 April 1951; 20 April 1951; 23 April 1951; 24 April 1951.

Chapter 8. Young Thugs

1. East London Juvenile Court, 25 November 1940; 23 December 1940; 13 January 1941; Romford Juvenile Court, 15 April 1942; Lambeth Juvenile Court, 30 January 1942.
2. Brighton Juvenile Court, 2 June 1943; Croydon Juvenile Court, 5 March 1942; Brentford Juvenile Court, 21 December 1942; Clapton Juvenile Court, 23 February 1943; Windsor Juvenile Court, 29 December 1944.
3. Glasgow Central Police Court, 11 January 1944; Old Bailey, 2 April 1943.
4. East London Juvenile Court, 16 July 1945; North London Juvenile Court, 8 January 1946.
5. Edgware Magistrates Court, 28 January 1946.
6. *Evening Standard*, 3 June 1946.
7. Glasgow Southern Juvenile Court, 5 December 1949.
8. Old Street Magistrates Court, 12 September 1949.
9. Chatham Magistrates Court, 15 February 1950; East Ham Juvenile Court, 15 February 1950; Reading Juvenile Court, 16 February 1950.
10. Tower Bridge Magistrates Court, 16 February 1950.
11. Clerkenwell Magistrates Court, 23 February 1950; 2 March 1950.
12. East London Juvenile Court, 5 June 1950.
13. Old Bailey, 30 March 1950; 31 March 1950; Birmingham Juvenile Court, 5 June 1950.
14. Tower Bridge Juvenile Court, 23 March 1948.
15. Reading Juvenile Court, 11 May 1950; 1 June 1950.
16. Court of Criminal Appeal, 18 February 1946.
17. Court of Criminal Appeal, 19 March 1951; 6 July 1953.
18. East Ham Juvenile Court, 15 February 1950; Bedford Quarter Sessions, 28 August 1952.
19. Willesden Magistrates Court, 17 April 1950.
20. Richmond Juvenile Court, 9 May 1951.
21. Southend Juvenile Court, 1 March 1952.

22. Old Bailey, 20 April 1948.
23. Tower Bridge Juvenile Court, 20 April 1948.
24. West Ham Magistrates Court, 20 May 1948; Old Bailey, 16 June 1948.
25. Chingford Magistrates Court, 8 April 1952.
26. Old Bailey, 28–30 October 1952.

Chapter 9. No End of a Lesson

1. Hull Magistrates Court, 11 August 1952.
2. Tottenham Magistrates Court, 21 January 1949.
3. Southampton Juvenile Court, 28 March 1960.
4. Old Bailey, 11 December 1952.
5. Old Bailey, 9 December 1952.
6. John Parris, *Scapegoat*, London: Duckworth, 1991, p.64.
7. Old Bailey, 3 December 1952.
8. Old Bailey, 9–11 December 1952; Court of Criminal Appeal, 13 January 1953.
9. Parris, *Scapegoat*, p.137.
10. Uxbridge Juvenile Court, 6 February 1953; Conservative Political Centre Conference, 28 February 1953.
11. Old Bailey, 11 December 1952.
12. North London Magistrates Court, 23 February 1953; Old Bailey, 30 March 1953.
13. Tony Parker, *The Plough Boy*, London: Hutchinson, 1965.
14. Magistrates Association Annual General Meeting, 22 October 1959.

Chapter 10. 'Who Are You Looking At?'

1. Brentford Magistrates Court, 24 May 1954.
2. Southampton Magistrates Court, 28 June 1954; Acton Magistrates Court, 21 July 1954.
3. Bromley Magistrates Court, 5 March 1956.
4. Old Bailey, 21 April 1955; 22 April 1955; 25 April 1955; 19 May 1955; 25 May 1955; Clerkenwell Magistrates Court, 23 May 1955; 7 June 1955.
5. Samuel Johnson, *The History of Rasselas, Prince of Abyssinia*, Chapter 17.

6. Thames Magistrates Court, 29 August 1956; John Pearson, *The Profession of Violence: The Rise and Fall of the Kray Twins*, London: Weidenfeld & Nicolson, 1972, p.10.
7. Tower Bridge Magistrates Court, 15 May 1959.
8. Wimbledon Magistrates Court, 19 September 1959.
9. Old Street Magistrates Court, 18 January 1965.
10. Highgate Magistrates Court, 5 April 1962; 26 April 1962; 3 May 1962; Old Bailey, 25 June 1962; 9 July 1962; 10 July 1962; Harold Macmillan at Bedford, 20 July 1957.
11. Acton Magistrates Court, 27 July 1954; Kingston-on-Thames Juvenile Court, 19 August 1954.
12. Old Bailey, 14 April 1965.
13. BBC 'Special Inquiry', 20 October 1955; Scouts Chief Commissioner for Lancashire, 15 May 1959.
14. High Wycombe Magistrates Court, 24 September 1956.
15. Stratford East Magistrates Court, 25 September 1957.
16. Southwark Coroner's Court, 8 August 1962.
17. Court of Criminal Appeal, 25 November 1958; Wood Green Magistrates Court, 7 November 1958.
18. These incidents occurred at: Walthamstow, 9 December 1957 (Stratford East Magistrates Court, 11 December 1957); Brighton, 9 January 1958; Godalming, 28 January 1958.
19. Stratford East Magistrates Court, 9 February 1966; London Sessions, 21 February 1966; House of Commons, 4 March 1966; Camden Juvenile Court, 20 April 1965.
20. Old Bailey, 23 September 1960; Court of Criminal Appeal, 24 October 1960.
21. Fredric Wertham, *The Seduction of the Innocent*, London: Museum Press, 1955, p.95.
22. Old Bailey, 9 December 1952.

Chapter 11. 'If the Coke Don't Get You . . .'

1. Lewes Assizes, 21–28 March 1961.
2. Croydon Magistrates Court, 17 August 1966.
3. Marlborough Street Magistrates Court, 25 February 1954.
4. West London Magistrates Court, 16 February 1955.
5. Great Yarmouth Magistrates Court, 30 August 1965.
6. Grays Magistrates Court, 22 July 1964.

7. Margate Magistrates Court, 18 May 1964; Brighton Magistrates Court, 19 May 1964.
8. Brighton Magistrates Court, 12 June 1964.
9. Lambeth Juvenile Court, 28 April 1965.
10. Brighton Magistrates Court, 14 December 1966; 2 January 1967.
11. Brighton Magistrates Court, 24 April 1967.
12. Eastbourne Magistrates Court, 10 May 1965.
13. Middlesex Sessions, 11 July 1967.
14. Southend Magistrates Court, 1 April 1967; 15 April 1967.
15. Westminster Coroner's Court, 18 December 1967.
16. St Pancras Coroner's Court, 18 January 1967.
17. Old Bailey, 8 October 1968; 10 October 1968.
18. Bow Street Magistrates Court, 13 November 1967.
19. Old Bailey, 6 February 1969.
20. Westminster Coroner's Court, 19 September 1969.
21. Westminster Coroner's Court, 8 September 1969.
22. Dunstable Juvenile Court, 9 January 1970.
23. Croydon Juvenile Court, 19 March 1970.
24. Malden and Surbiton Magistrates Court, 5 June 1967.
25. Brighton Magistrates Court, 14 August 1967.
26. House of Commons, 28 July 1967.
27. House of Commons, 24 January 1969.

Chapter 12. Immoral Earnings

1. Billy Hill, *Boss of Britain's Underworld*, London: The Naldrett Press, 1955, p.76.
2. *Shaw v. DPP* (1962).
3. 'Walter', *My Secret Life*, Vols. 1–4, London: Arrow Books, 1994, p.396.
4. Donald Thomas, *An Underworld at War: Spivs, Deserters, Racketeers and Civilians in the Second World War*, London: John Murray, 2003, pp.3 and 269; Duncan Webb, *Crime is my Business*, London: Frederick Muller, 1953, pp.153–4.
5. Sheila Cousins, *To Beg I Am Ashamed: The Autobiography of a London Prostitute*, Paris: The Obelisk Press, 1938, p.264.
6. Neville Cardus, *Autobiography*, London: Collins, 1947, pp.26–30.
7. Old Bailey, 22 April 1947; 24 April 1947.
8. West London Magistrates Court, 25 April 1947; 30 April 1947; 16 May 1947; Old Bailey, 25 June 1947.

9. Marthe Watts, *The Men In My Life,* London: Christopher Johnson, 1960, p.210.

10. Old Bailey, 2–9 May 1951.

11. Marlborough Street Magistrates Court, 13 September 1955.

12. Marlborough Street Magistrates Court, 27 February 1959; 4–10 March 1959; Old Bailey, 9 April 1959.

13. Duncan Webb, *Deadline for Crime*, London: Panther, 1958, p.77.

14. Willesden Magistrates Court, 28 June 1956; 7 July 1956; Old Bailey, 18 September 1956; 19 September 1956; 21 September 1956.

15. Marlborough Street Magistrates Court, 3 August 1960; Old Bailey, 12 September 1960; 16 September 1960; 21 September 1960; *Shaw v. DPP* (1962).

16. Marlborough Street Magistrates Court, 28 October 1960.

17. Bow Street Magistrates Court, 6 January 1960.

18. Birmingham Magistrates Court, 3 August 1966; *Evening Standard*, 10 July 1968.

19. *Daily Sketch*, 30 September 1936.

20. Old Bailey, 23 June 1964; West London Coroner's Court, 24 February 1965.

21. Chelsea Juvenile Court, 23 July 1958; Tower Bridge Magistrates Court, 3 December 1958.

22. Old Bailey, 31 October 1960; 21 November 1960.

23. Marlborough Street Magistrates Court, 29 December 1960; Old Bailey, 14 April 1961.

24. Old Bailey, 5 January 1962.

25. Old Bailey, 14 March 1963; 15 March 1963; Court of Criminal Appeal, 27 May 1963.

26. Old Bailey, 22 July 1963; 25 July 1963; 26 July 1963.

Chapter 13. Robbing the Mail

1. Old Bailey, 20 March 1963; 26 March 1963; 11 June 1963.

2. Bruce Reynolds, *The Autobiography of a Thief*, London: Bantam Press, 1995, p.239.

3. Ibid., p.296.

4. Aylesbury Assizes, 16 April 1964.

5. Lambeth Magistrates Court, 11 July 1942.

6. Chingford Magistrates Court, 10 January 1961; Chelmsford Assizes, 16 February 1961.

7. Clerkenwell Magistrates Court, 2 December 1960; Old Bailey, 19 January 1961; 20 January 1961.
8. Leeds Assizes, 3 December 1954.
9. Marlborough Street Magistrates Court, 5 February 1954; 19 February 1954; Old Bailey, 18 March 1954; Old Bailey, 16 July 1954.

Chapter 14. Cosh and Carry

1. Old Bailey, 15 July 1957; House of Commons, 23 May 1958.
2. Ealing Magistrates Court, 1 April 1950.
3. Brentford Magistrates Court, 27 July 1957; 30 August 1957; Old Bailey, 20 September 1957.
4. Old Bailey, 22 January 1965; 21 January 1966.
5. Sarah Underwood, *Securicor: The People Business*, Oxford: CPL Books, 1997, p.17.
6. Ealing Magistrates Court, 29 July 1969; 4 September 1969.
7. Old Bailey, 5 November 1970.
8. Leeds Assizes, 11 May 1970.

Chapter 15. All the Way to the Bank

1. *Walker v. Milner and another*, Court of Queen's Bench, 14 February 1866.
2. Old Bailey, 13 May 1955; Old Bailey, 5 March 1957.
3. High Court, 18 July 1957.
4. Stratford East Magistrates Court, 23 November 1950.
5. Old Bailey, 15 March 1955; Tottenham Magistrates Court, 19 March 1955.
6. Lambeth Magistrates Court, 3 October 1955; Old Bailey, 7 December 1955.
7. Old Bailey, 25 February 1958.
8. Chingford Magistrates Court, 8 December 1959; Chelmsford Assizes, 15 and 28 March 1960.
9. Old Bailey, 13 March 1958.
10. North London Magistrates Court, 8 November 1958; 10 November 1958; 17 November 1958; Old Bailey, 19 December 1958; 22 December 1958; 23 December 1958.
11. Bow Street Magistrates Court, 5 February 1959; 20 February 1959; Old Bailey, 12 March 1959.

12. Court of Criminal Appeal, 27 June 1966.
13. Old Bailey, 17 November 1956; 19 November 1956.
14. Surrey Quarter Sessions, 12 March 1952.
15. Old Bailey, 23 June 1952; Bristol Magistrates Court, 25 August 1952.
16. Peter Scott, *Gentleman Thief: Recollections of a Cat Burglar*, London: HarperCollins, 1995, pp.171–3.
17. Bath Magistrates Court, 18 September 1953.
18. Old Bailey, 17 March 1954.

Chapter 16. Safety in Numbers

1. Peter Cheyney, *Making Crime Pay*, London: Faber & Faber, 1941, pp.63–6.
2. Percy Sillitoe, *Cloak Without Dagger*, London: Constable, 1955, p.131.
3. G. W. Cornish, *Cornish of Scotland Yard*, New York: Macmillan, 1935, pp.7–8.
4. Hill, *Boss of Britain's Underworld*, pp.8–14.
5. Old Bailey, 17 February 1954.
6. Thames Magistrates Court, 31 May 1955.
7. Old Bailey, 19–26 September 1955.
8. Old Bailey, 28–29 November 1955; 5–7 December 1955.
9. Bow Street Magistrates Court, 22 June 1956; 29 June 1956; Old Bailey, 18 July 1956.
10. Old Bailey, 16 October 1956.
11. Old Bailey, 20 June 1956.
12. Old Bailey, 23 May 1957.
13. Old Bailey, 21 April–9 May 1960.
14. Marlborough Street Magistrates Court, 18 September 1957.
15. Old Bailey, 18 December 1962.
16. Court of Criminal Appeal, 30 March 1965.
17. Marylebone Magistrates Court, 1 July 1963; Read, *Nipper*, pp.67–9.
18. Clerkenwell Magistrates Court, 25 April 1967.
19. St Pancras Coroner's Court, 19 September 1966.

Chapter 17. The Crazy Gang

1. Old Bailey, 24 June 1966; 26 September 1966.
2. Norman Lucas, *Britain's Gangland*, London: Pan Books, 1969, pp.160–63.
3. Old Bailey, 6 April 1967; 7 April 1967; 10 April 1967.
4. Old Bailey, 20 June 1967.
5. Old Bailey, 13 December 1966; 20–21 March 1967.
6. Old Bailey, 27 September 1967; Old Bailey, 2 March 1964; 29 April 1968.
7. Old Bailey, 11 December 1967.
8. Old Bailey, 11 February 1969.
9. Michael Connor, *The Soho Don*, Mainstream Publishing, n.d., pp.95–7.
10. Old Bailey, 23 January 1965; 5 April 1965.
11. Old Bailey, 21 January 1969.
12. Old Bailey, 9 January 1969.
13. Bow Street Magistrates Court, 28 June 1968.
14. Bow Street Magistrates Court, 15 October 1968; 16 October 1968.
15. Bow Street Magistrates Court, 16 October 1968.
16. Old Bailey, 9 January 1969; 10 January 1969.
17. Old Bailey, 6 February 1969.
18. Old Bailey, 22 April 1969.
19. Edward Gibbon, *Decline and Fall of the Roman Empire*, ed. H. H. Milman, London: John Murray, 1846, I, 95.

Chapter 18. Spare a Copper

1. Rochester Coroner's Court, 14 June 1951.
2. Old Bailey, 14 July 1954; 28 August 1955; 29 August 1955; 8 December 1955.
3. North London Magistrates Court, 25 January 1950; Old Bailey, 27 September 1951; 17 June 1952.
4. House of Commons, 24 July 1970.
5. Old Bailey, 17–29 November 1955.
6. Bow Street Magistrates Court, 17 November 1955.
7. Old Bailey, 16 March 1956.
8. Marylebone Magistrates Court, 22 August 1956; 23 August 1956.

9. Brighton Magistrates Court, 25 November–6 December 1957; Brighton Quarter Sessions, 8 January 1958; Old Bailey, 3–28 February 1958; Connor, *The Soho Don*, pp.13–14.
10. Brighton Magistrates Court, 30 July 1958; Brighton Quarter Sessions, 24 September 1958.
11. Old Bailey, 1 November 1957; 8 November 1957; 27 November 1957.
12. Bow Street Magistrates Court, 26 September 1958.

Chapter 19. A Matter of Confidence

1. West Ham Coroner's Court, 22 June 1961.
2. Kendal Magistrates Court, 21 April 1965.
3. Marylebone Magistrates Court, 22 September 1966.
4. Old Bailey, 12 December 1966.
5. Oxford Magistrates Court, 20 August 1966; Liverpool Stipendiary Magistrates Court, 24 September 1966.
6. Marlborough Street Magistrates Court, 23 July 1959; *Empire News*, 26 July 1959.
7. West London Magistrates Court, 14 August 1959; Old Bailey, 10–24 September 1959.
8. Tottenham Magistrates Court, 13 August 1959.
9. House of Commons, 13 February 1964.
10. *The Times*, 4 December 1964.
11. Sheffield Magistrates Court, 24 September 1963.
12. *Sheffield Police Appeal Inquiry*, London: HMSO, 1963, Cmd. 2176.
13. High Court, 30 January 1961; 1–3 February 1961; 6 February 1961; 25 April 1961; 8 May 1961; Maidstone Quarter Sessions, 16 December 1961.
14. Marlborough Street Magistrates Court, 26 January 1970.
15. Old Bailey, 6 February 1964.
16. Old Bailey, 20 January 1970; 16 February 1970.
17. Old Bailey, 27 January 1976.

Chapter 20. No One Does That Any More

1. Leeds Assizes, 17 November 1970.
2. Cardiff Crown Court, 21 January–26 February 1991.

Index